THE REVELS PLAYS COMPANION LIBRARY

Three seventeenth-century plays on women and performance

The Wild-Goose Chase by John Fletcher (1621)
The Bird in a Cage by James Shirley (1633)
The Convent of Pleasure by Margaret Cavendish (1668)

edited by Hero Chalmers
Julie Sanders
Sophie Tomlinson

Manchester University Press
Manchester and New York

distributed exclusively in the USA by Palgrave

Published by Manchester University Press
Oxford Road, Manchester M13 9NR, UK
and Room 400, 175 Fifth Avenue, New York, NY 10010, USA
www.manchesteruniversitypress.co.uk

Distributed in the United States exclusively by
Palgrave Macmillan, 175 Fifth Avenue,
New York, NY 10010, USA

Distributed in Canada exclusively by
UBC Press, University of British Columbia, 2029 West Mall,
Vancouver, BC, Canada V6T 1Z2

British Library Cataloguing-in-Publication Data is available

Library of Congress Cataloging-in-Publication Data is available

ISBN 978 0 7190 6339 8 paperback

First published by Manchester University Press in hardback 2006

This paperback edition first published 2012

Printed by Lightning Source

In memory of Kim Walker

CONTENTS

GENERAL EDITORS' PREFACE   ix

ACKNOWLEDGEMENTS   xi

ABBREVIATIONS AND REFERENCES   xiii

INTRODUCTION   1

   The historical context   1
   The plays   11
   The texts   42
   Stage histories   45

THE PLAYS

   John Fletcher, *The Wild-Goose Chase* (ed. Sophie Tomlinson)   61
   James Shirley, *The Bird in a Cage* (ed. Julie Sanders)   177
   Margaret Cavendish, *The Convent of Pleasure*
      (ed. Hero Chalmers)   267

APPENDICES

   Appendix A: Press variants   309

   Appendix B: Commendatory verses to *The Wild-Goose
      Chase* (1652)   320

INDEX   326

GENERAL EDITORS' PREFACE

Since the late 1950s the series known as The Revels Plays has provided for students of the English Renaissance drama carefully edited texts of the major Elizabethan and Jacobean plays. The series includes some of the best-known drama of the period and has continued to expand, both within its original field and, to a lesser extent, beyond it, to include some important plays from the earlier Tudor and from the Restoration periods. The Revels Plays Companion Library is intended to further this expansion and to allow for new developments.

The aim of the Companion Library is to provide students of the Elizabethan and Jacobean drama with a fuller sense of its background and context. The series includes volumes of a variety of kinds. Small collections of plays, by a single author or concerned with a single theme and edited in accordance with the principles of textual modernisation of The Revels Plays, offer a wider range of drama than the main series can include. Together with editions of masques, pageants and the non-dramatic work of Elizabethan and Jacobean playwrights, these volumes make it possible, within the overall Revels enterprise, to examine the achievements of the major dramatists from a broader perspective. Other volumes provide a fuller context for the plays of the period by offering new collections of documentary evidence on Elizabethan theatrical conditions and on the performance of plays during that period and later. A third aim of the series is to offer modern critical interpretation, in the form of collections of essays or of monographs, of the dramatic achievement of the English Renaissance.

So wide a range of material necessarily precludes the standard format and uniform general editorial control which is possible in the original series of Revels Plays. To a considerable extent, therefore, treatment and approach are determined by the needs and intentions of individual volume editors. Within this rather ampler area, however, we hope that the Companion Library maintains the standards of scholarship that have for so long characterised The Revels Plays, and that it offers a useful enlargement of the work of the series in preserving, illuminating and celebrating the drama of Elizabethan and Jacobean England.

J. R. MULRYNE
SUSAN BROCK
SUSAN CERASANO

ACKNOWLEDGEMENTS

The editors would like to thank the staff of the following libraries: Alexander Turnbull; Auckland City; University of Auckland; Bodleian, Oxford; Boston Public; British Library; University of Canterbury; Christ's, Corpus Christi, Gonville and Caius, King's, and St John's Colleges, Cambridge; University Library, Cambridge; Richard J. Kuhta and the staff of the Folger Shakespeare Library; Hallward Library, University of Nottingham; Houghton Library, Harvard; Huntington, Pasadena; Firestone Library, Princeton University; the Harry Ransom Centre for the Humanities, Austin, Texas; Keele University; Newberry Library, Chicago; All Souls', St John's and Worcester Colleges, Oxford; State Library of Victoria, Melbourne; and the Library of Congress, Washington DC.

We owe a great deal of thanks to Robert Smallwood, the general editor for this volume, who read and commented on the edition in manuscript form with huge diligence and insight. We are grateful for his support and advice. Thanks also to Matthew Frost and Manchester University Press. Brief sections of the introduction to *The Convent of Pleasure* appeared in an earlier form in Hero Chalmers, 'The Politics of Feminine Retreat in Margaret Cavendish's *The Female Academy* and *The Convent of Pleasure*', *Women's Writing*, 6 (1999): 81–94, and we are grateful to the publishers of that journal for permission to re-use aspects of that article.

Hero Chalmers would like to thank Laura Gowing, William Hale, Jonathan Harrison, Ann Keith, Paulina Kewes, Wai Kirkpatrick, Gerard Passannante, Joad Raymond, Nigel Smith, Mark Statham, and Sophie Tomlinson for help with checking press variants and discussion of the texts. Jim Fitzmaurice and Nicole Pohl generously made their (published and unpublished) work readily available.

Julie Sanders is grateful to the British Academy for a research grant that enabled her to undertake collation work in US libraries. For additional support and advice, she would like to thank Jonathan Bate, Karen Britland, Richard Dutton, James McLaverty, and the Shakespeare Association of America panel on 'Caroline Drama' in New Orleans, 2004. She and Hero Chalmers would both like to note a special thanks to Ann Hughes who, beyond the call of duty, checked press variants in the Huntington.

Sophie Tomlinson is grateful to the Royal Society of New Zealand for a Marsden Award, which funded her research for the edition, and the University of Auckland for a period of leave during which she was able to work on it. She wishes to pay a special tribute to Sally Hoare for her expert research assistance. For checking press variants she is grateful to Hero Chalmers, David Gunby, Pam Pryde, Bill Sherman, and Janet Wilson. For invaluable help and advice, warm thanks to Mac Jackson, and to Rosemary Arnoux, Janine Barchas, Bernard Brown, Michael Graves, Peter Haynes, Lorna Hutson, Robert Leek, Gordon McMullan, and Stuart Young.

ABBREVIATIONS AND REFERENCES

EDITIONS AND EDITORIAL

The Wild-Goose Chase

F1	*The Wild-Goose Chase. A Comedie. As it hath been Acted with singular Applause at the Black-Friers*, London, 1652.
F2	Francis Beaumont and John Fletcher, *Fifty Comedies and Tragedies*, London, 1679.
Bowers, *DW*	Bowers, Fredson (gen. ed.), *The Dramatic Works in the Beaumont and Fletcher Canon*, 10 vols, Cambridge University Press, 1966–96.
Colman	Colman, George, *The Dramatick Works of Beaumont and Fletcher*, 10 vols, London: T. Sherlock, 1778.
Dyce	Dyce, Alexander (ed.), *The Works of Beaumont and Fletcher*, 11 vols, London: Edward Moxon, 1843–46.
Fraser and Rabkin	Fraser, Russell A. and Norman C. Rabkin (eds), *Drama of the English Renaissance, II: The Stuart Period*, New York: Macmillan, 1976.
Glover and Waller	Glover, Arnold and A.R. Waller (eds), *The Works of Francis Beaumont and John Fletcher*, 10 vols, Cambridge University Press, 1905–12.
Langbaine	Langbaine, Gerard (ed.), *The Works of Mr Francis Beaumont and Mr John Fletcher*, 7 vols, London: J.N. Tonson, 1711.
Lister	Lister, Rota Herzberg (ed.), *A Critical Edition of John Fletcher's Comedy, The Wild-Goose Chase*, New York and London: Garland, 1980.
Sympson	*The Works of Mr Francis Beaumont and Mr John Fletcher. With notes . . . by Mr Theobald, Mr Seward . . . and Mr Sympson*, 10 vols, London: J. and R. Tonson and S. Draper, 1750.
Weber	Weber, Henry (ed.), *The Works of Beaumont and Fletcher*, 14 vols, Edinburgh: James Ballantyne, 1812.

The Bird in a Cage

Qc	Corrected states of James Shirley, *The Bird in a Cage*, London, 1633.
Qu	Uncorrected states of James Shirley, *The Bird in a Cage*, London, 1633. [Where no variants exist Q stands for all states of the 1633 quarto.]
G	James Shirley, *The Dramatic Works and Poems*, ed. William Gifford and Alexander Dyce, 6 vols, London: John Murray, 1833.
Senescu	Senescu, Frances Frazier (ed.), *A Critical Edition of James Shirley's The Bird in a Cage*, New York and London: Garland, 1980 [1948].

The Convent of Pleasure

F	Margaret Cavendish, *Plays, Never Before Printed*, London, 1668.
Ch	Cambridge, Christ's College Library copy of *F*.
H2	Pasadena, Huntington Library copy of *F*: Huntington 120158.
PFL	Princeton, New Jersey, Firestone Library copy of *F*.
Rowsell	Rowsell, Jennifer (ed.), *The Convent of Pleasure. A Comedy*, Oxford: Seventeenth Century Press, 1995.
Shaver	Shaver, Anne (ed.), *The Convent of Pleasure and Other Plays*, Baltimore and London: Johns Hopkins University Press, 1999.

GENERAL

Abbott	Abbott, E.A., *A Shakespearian Grammar*, New York: Dover Publications, 1966. References are to paragraph numbers.
Baldwin	Baldwin, T.W., *The Organization and Personnel of the Shakespearean Company*, New York: Russell and Russell, 1961 [1927].
Bawcutt	Bawcutt, N.W. (ed.), *The Control and Censorship of Caroline Drama: The Records of Sir Henry Herbert, Master of the Revels 1623–73*, Oxford: Clarendon Press, 1996.
Brewer	Brewer, E. Cobham, *A Dictionary of Phrase and Fable*, new and enlarged edition, Ware: Wordsworth Editions, 1993.
Cotgrave	Cotgrave, Randle, *A Dictionarie of the French and English Tongues*, 1611; facsimile rpt Amsterdam: Theatrum Orbis Terrarum; New York: Da Capo Press, 1971.
Dent	Dent, R.W., *Proverbial Language in English Drama Exclusive of Shakespeare, 1495–1616: An Index*, Berkeley: University of California Press, 1984.
Gurr	Gurr, Andrew, *The Shakespearean Stage 1574–1642*, 3rd ed., Cambridge University Press, 1992.
Hindley	Hindley, Alan *et al.*, *Old French–English Dictionary*, Cambridge University Press, 2000.
JCS	Bentley, G.E., *The Jacobean and Caroline Stage*, 7 vols, Oxford: Clarendon Press, 1941–68.
Lewis and Short	Lewis, C.T. and Charles Short (eds), *A Latin Dictionary*, Oxford: Clarendon Press, 1879.
Littré	Littré, Emile, *Dictionnaire de la langue française*, 7 vols, Paris: Pauvert, 1956–58.
McMullan	McMullan, Gordon, *The Politics of Unease in the Plays of John Fletcher*, Amherst: University of Massachusetts Press, 1994.
Met.	Ovid, *Metamorphoses*, trans. A.D. Melville, ed. by E.J. Kenney, Oxford: Oxford University Press, 1987.
Moryson	Moryson, Fynes, *An Itinerary written by Fynes Moryson Gent. First in the Latine tongue, and then translated by him into English*, London: 1617; rpt Amsterdam: Theatrum Orbis Terrarum; New York: Da Capo Press, 1971.

Nungezer	Nungezer, Edwin, *A Dictionary of Actors and of Other Persons Associated with the Public Representation of Plays in England before 1642*, New York: AMS Press, 1971 [1929].
Onions	Onions, C.T., *A Shakespeare Glossary*, enl. and revised by Robert D. Eagleson, Oxford: Clarendon Press, 1986.
Pollard and Redgrave	Pollard, A.W. and G.R. Redgrave (eds), *A Short-Title Catalogue of Books Printed in England, Scotland, & Ireland . . . 1475–1640*, 2nd ed., London: Bibliographical Society, 1986, begun by W.A. Jackson and F.S. Ferguson, completed by Katharine F. Pantzer.
Shakespeare's England	*Shakespeare's England: An Account of the Life and Manners of His Age*, 2 vols, Oxford: Clarendon Press, 1916.
Tilley	Tilley, M.P., *A Dictionary of the Proverbs in England in the Sixteenth and Seventeenth Centuries*, Ann Arbor: University of Michigan Press, 1950.
Williams	Williams, Gordon, *A Dictionary of Sexual Language and Imagery in Shakespearean and Stuart Literature*, 3 vols, London: Athlone Press, 1994.

PERIODICALS

ELR	*English Literary Renaissance*
EMLS	*Early Modern Literary Studies*
MLR	*Modern Language Review*
RD	*Renaissance Drama*
SQ	*Shakespeare Quarterly*
SEL	*Studies in English Literature 1500–1900*
TLS	*Times Literary Supplement*

References to Shakespeare's plays are to the one-volume *Oxford Shakespeare*, gen. eds Stanley Wells and Gary Taylor, Oxford: Clarendon Press, 1986. References to plays by other writers are to the Revels Plays series; otherwise first editions or Complete Works have been used. The King James Bible has been used throughout the edition.

INTRODUCTION

THE HISTORICAL CONTEXT

There is a recognised history of women and performance in England in the seventeenth century. It suggests that, although at the outset of the century women were prohibited from performing on the commercial stages of London, theatrically engaged court cultures under two successive continental queens consort – Anna of Denmark, wife of James I (1603–25), and Henrietta Maria, the French wife of Charles I (1625–42) – facilitated a growing awareness and acceptance of female theatricals, amateur and professional. A temporary hiatus was caused by the English civil wars and puritan anti-theatrical legislation in the 1640s and 1650s, but this period of interregnum nevertheless saw royalist sympathisers living in exile on the continent where they were witnesses to a well-established tradition of professional female performance.[1] Exposure to this alternative performance tradition, it is suggested generally, smoothed the way for professional women performers to be countenanced and even encouraged on the English stage by the Restoration government of Charles II after 1660.

This particular telling of the story of the 'first English actresses', as one critic has called them,[2] carries considerable intellectual weight – no history of Restoration theatre is complete without due acknowledgement of the seismic shift in theatrical conditions and writing styles that took place in order to accommodate the spectacle of female bodies on the public stages.[3] As a developmental history this version also credits in important ways the influence of elite female culture in the early Stuart period, as well as specific interactions between different spheres of performance in London and the provinces.[4] To a certain extent it is a version of history to which this collection pays homage; the three playtexts we have chosen as our means of exploring the complex topic of women and performance in the seventeenth century – John Fletcher's *The Wild-Goose Chase* (1621), James Shirley's *The Bird in a Cage* (1633), and Margaret Cavendish's *The Convent of Pleasure* (1668) – derive from the Jacobean, Caroline, and Restoration periods respectively, and therefore span the evolutionary moment identified. Our own previous research acknowledged lines of influence and development similar to those described above.[5] And yet as editors we also recognise that a neat, linear account of the 'rise' of the female performer in the seventeenth century represents a dangerous teleology. This narrative assumes an increasingly self-referential and court-driven version of seventeenth-century theatre history from the Caroline period onwards, which has been persuasively challenged of late. Furthermore, it underestimates the persistence of theatrical modes during the interregnum in England.[6] It is a version of development that insists that a shift from amateur to professional status constitutes progress. This in turn both underestimates the diversity of amateur female participation in theatre prior to the Restoration, as well as assuming a one-way traffic between the personal and the commercial that is far from accurate. As the detailed discussion of *The Convent of Pleasure* later in this introduction indicates, complementary theatrical forms such as closet drama, court and provincial masque, and household entertainment or interlude all serve to complicate what we understand as the spaces and opportunities for performance, and intellectual engagement with the concept of theatre, that existed for women, and men, in the seventeenth century.[7]

One means of redrawing the lines of the discussion is to think in terms of moments or episodes of specific import – such as, for example, the arrival of the first professional actresses on the London stages. This event undoubtedly altered the theatrical landscape in terms of performance conventions and writing for the stage. We might also look earlier in the century to the participation of Henrietta Maria and her court ladies in the staging and performance of plays and masques in the late 1620s and 1630s. This social phenomenon created considerable cultural shockwaves, contributing to, if not directly provoking, the puritan lawyer William Prynne's infamous outburst against theatre in his thousand-page pamphlet outpouring *Histriomastix: The Player's Scourge; Or, The Actor's Tragedy* (published by Michael Sparke in November 1632 and discussed in more detail in the section on *The Bird in a Cage*). It is equally important to acknowledge the pioneering effects of Henrietta Maria's decision to speak in her court performances (hitherto, women had remained silent) and to countenance cross-dressing on the part of her fellow female actors.[8] But we need to think in terms not just of radical breaks in practice but of continuities of tradition. From this perspective a more gradual sense of the evolution of female agency in a theatrical context emerges. A revised history of women and performance in the seventeenth century proves consequently to be a narrative not solely of prohibition, or the prosthetic of the boy actor, but one which acknowledges that certain cultural contexts, and even literary genres, were more available to, and sympathetic towards, female performance in the period. In this respect, the dramatic genres of masque and pastoral prove especially significant.

Studies of the seventeenth-century masque, in its courtly and provincial household manifestations, now acknowledge a distinctly female line of influence and sponsorship. Anna of Denmark's commission of Ben Jonson in 1605 to write the text for the *Masque of Blackness*, with Inigo Jones providing the linking designs, represents a watershed. The masques for Anna mark a crucial point of female intervention in English court theatre.[9] Henrietta Maria's subsequent sponsorship of specific masques at the Caroline court, some of them again co-creations by Jonson and Jones, continued this tradition, offering its own innovations, not least the female singing voices of Aurelian Townshend's 1632 *Tempe Restored*.[10] Furthermore, in the polyvalent masquing culture so persuasively identified in the regions and provinces of England and Scotland in recent studies by Martin Butler and James Knowles, the participation of women has come to seem central, inevitable, and almost unsurprising. London household entertainments under the auspices of Lady Rich or the Countess of Carlisle in the late Jacobean and early Caroline years, the masque entertainments composed by the teenage Rachel Fane at the family home in Apethorpe, Northamptonshire, in the late 1620s, the performance of Alice Egerton as the Lady in Milton's *Maske Presented at Ludlow Castle* commissioned for the inauguration of the Earl of Bridgewater as Lord President of Wales and the Marches in 1634, and the decision by the Duke of Newcastle's two eldest daughters, Jane Cavendish and Elizabeth Brackley (Margaret Cavendish's stepdaughters following her recent Paris marriage to their father William), to write a pastoral masque as well as a play at their Nottinghamshire estates in the 1640s are all crucial episodes in this ongoing tradition. A detailed consideration of masquing history, then, renders the Restoration's professional women actors more predictable in the sense that Jacobean and Caroline England, as well as interregnum and exiled communities in the 1640s and 1650s, had been innovating in this area for some time (although not without attendant controversy and debate, as we shall see).

If the masque genre in its plural manifestations provided an obvious sphere for female performance throughout the seventeenth century, the even older literary tradition of pastoral drama further facilitated this activity. It is no coincidence that Henrietta Maria's first full theatrical performance at the Caroline court was a French pastoral, Racan's *Artenice*, in 1626. In 1632 she would follow this with an approximately eight-hour performance of Walter Montagu's specifically commissioned pastoral *The Shepherds' Paradise*. The rehearsals for the latter were presumed by some to have provoked Prynne's outraged insertion in his index to *Histriomastix*, just as it was going to print late in 1632, of the entry 'Women actors – Notorious whores'. The Cavendish sisters' choice of pastoral as the mode for their family masque in the Midlands in the mid-1640s was informed by Caroline culture, reflecting not only what Terry Gifford has described as 'the range of pastoral influences available to a Stuart play-wright'[11] but a developed understanding of the specifically female possibilities made available by the genre.[12] Ian Maclean has detailed the centrality of the pastoral and chivalric genres to salon culture and the wider development of the *femme forte* tradition in seventeenth-century France. He suggests that the escapist templates offered by both provided considerable opportunities and models of agency for women: 'the preoccupation with the relationship between the sexes in an Arcadian setting in which the male-dominated pursuits of politics and war are out of place leads to a concentration on aspects of thought and behaviour – sensibility, spirituality, peace – in which women are the equals or the superiors of men'.[13] Links between Henrietta Maria's theatricals and the salon culture of her native France have been discussed by several critics, but we need to inflect the argument further at the level of genre.[14] None of the three plays included here is specifically a pastoral but each bears traces of influence from the genre. *The Wild-Goose Chase* draws on the language of country games in more than its title, while both *The Bird in a Cage* and *The Convent of Pleasure* play with pastoral motifs of retreat in their tower and convent settings respectively.

The topic of women and performance is refracted in all our plays through their treatment of the wider theme of festive sports and pastimes. The publication of what became known as the 'Book of Sports' by James I in 1618 and its reissue by Charles I in 1633 provides an overarching political framework for the plays' engagement with motifs of revelry appropriate to seasonal periods such as springtime and Christmas. Fletcher's play carries traces of puritan resistance to King James's promotion of May Day celebrations in one character's denunciation of the hero, 'Modesty and good manners are his May games' (3.1.18), where 'May games' functions as a byword for frivolous behaviour. Elsewhere the spirit of playful excess and topsy-turvydom characteristic of festive revelry is embraced by characters who enact gender reversals through cross-dressing, such as *The Bird in a Cage*'s foppish Morello, or role-playing more generally, such as the initiates of Lady Happy in *The Convent of Pleasure*.

If Charles I 'had banished misrule from his own comportment', he gave it licence in the sportiveness of his play-loving wife.[15] In the dedication to *The Bird in a Cage* Shirley entered the political fray by yoking his play's representation of women actors to an attack on Prynne, who was in prison awaiting trial following the publication of *Histriomastix*. As Leah Marcus writes, in his anti-theatrical tract 'Prynne had lumped drama, ecclesiastical ritual and old festival pastimes into one inglorious category and condemned their essential nature' (p. 170). Shirley's gesture of support for the Crown involved an element of opportunism, for, as we will see, his portrayal of female revels in *The Bird in a Cage* is by no means unequivocal. In *The Convent of Pleasure* Margaret Cavendish's espousal of the theme of pastoral retreat and her portrayal of 'rural sports' enacted within the convent carries a specifically royalist valence; yet, although the female lovers distinguish their wooing from 'amorous pastoral verse', the sobriety of their recreations is jeopardised by the suggestion that Lady Happy and her 'Princess' have 'sported too much' (4.1.180). While Cavendish's play derives considerable impetus from the celebration of chastity characteristic of the pastoral dramas sponsored by Henrietta Maria, it reveals a certain 'fragmented purpose and structure' as the seemingly inviolate feminine sanctuary submits to masculine invasion.[16]

As Ben Jonson is an important bridging figure between some of the theatrical modes and moments being discussed here, so too is John Fletcher, who early in his career experimented with the continental form of pastoral tragicomedy in his play *The Faithful Shepherdess* (1608). Fletcher's play failed dismally on the Jacobean public stage; it found favour, however, at the court of Charles and Henrietta Maria where it was performed successfully by the King's Men in 1634. At that historical juncture, as one critic observes, Fletcher's stylised drama, with its focus on chastity, 'must have seemed like an astonishing anticipation of the reigning taste for stylish high-mindedness'.[17] The revival of *The Faithful Shepherdess* was given an enhanced aura of courtliness by the recycling of the costumes worn by the noblewomen who performed in Montagu's *The Shepherds' Paradise*: 'On Monday night the sixth of January and the Twelfe Night was presented at Denmark-house, before the King and Queen, Fletcher's pastorall called The Faithfull Shepheardesse, in the clothes the Queene had given Taylor the year before of her owne pastorall.'[18] In a poem addressed to the leading actor, Joseph Taylor, printed with the third quarto edition, Shakerly Marmion presents the play's progress from the professional stage to the court theatre as a rags to riches story: 'For having cur'd her from her courser rents, / And deckt her new with fresh habiliments, / Thou brought'st her to the Court, and made her be / A fitting spectacle for Majestie.'[19] In Marmion's view, Taylor has performed a 'worthy' rescue of Fletcher's prostituted muse to its more appropriate sphere. This aristocratic disdain for the commercially tainted public theatre influenced Margaret Cavendish's drama. She began her court career as part of the queen's entourage, and therefore Caroline masques and pastoral drama were in effect her artistic heritage, and a strong influence on her dramatic writing later in life.

The rehabilitation of Fletcher's *The Faithful Shepherdess* at court in the 1630s went hand in hand with revivals of his comedies: *The Wild-Goose Chase* in 1632, probably performed at the Blackfriars theatre; *The Woman's Prize, or, the Tamer Tamed* (1611), presented back to back with Shakespeare's *The Taming of the Shrew* at court in 1633; and *The Woman Hater* (1606, revived *c.*1638), the latter written by Francis Beaumont, with some revision by Fletcher.[20] Fletcher had long been a favourite with women at court; in 1624 his *Rule a Wife and Have a Wife* was acted 'at court for the ladies', an occasion which John Astington comments 'demonstrates the influence of female taste and patronage on court culture, even before the arrival of the new queen'.[21] In a pre-emptive placatory move, the courtier-dramatist William Davenant assured women that '[Fletcher's] Muse beleev'd not, what she then did write' in his prologue written for the revival of *The Woman Hater*.[22] The importance of women in the audience is equally apparent in plays staged at the professional theatres such as Shirley's *The Coronation* (1635), whose prologue addresses the 'noble Gentlewomen' as 'free, and high Commissioners of wit'.[23]

Like the comedies of Fletcher and Shakespeare revived in the 1630s, our plays draw energy from, and in turn re-energise, the Renaissance *querelle des femmes* or the controversy about women.[24] Each of them employs the figure of the stage misogynist: *The Wild-Goose Chase*'s hero, Mirabell, combines extreme contempt for women with an avowed libertinism; in *The Bird in a Cage* Philenzo, disguised as Rolliardo, assumes the misogynist's mantle as a strategy to test his beloved, while in *The Convent of Pleasure* the tritely misogynist Monsieurs Facil and Adviser cavil at the 'heretical opinions' of Lady Happy, who has forsworn marriage and sequestered herself from men. The plays engage in different ways with the figure of the 'woman on top'.[25] Fletcher pushes female assertiveness to a drastic extreme in *The Wild-Goose Chase* where a group of women menace the tyrannising Belleur with 'chopping-knives', while in *The Bird in a Cage* the avid thespian Donella proves that women are capable of playing male roles when she enacts the arch seducer Jupiter with compelling suavity and forcefulness. More often than physical violence, the women in our plays use language as their instrument of self-assertion or defence; indeed women's rhetorical prowess is a pronounced facet of Caroline drama and became in turn a key preoccupation of Cavendish's writing, fuelling plays such as *The Female Academy* (1662) and a volume of *Orations of Divers Sorts* (1662).

The Fletcher revival more generally in the 1630s ushers in a further genre central to our discussions: tragicomedy. The year 1634 saw the fourth quarto edition of Beaumont and Fletcher's highly popular romantic tragicomedy *Philaster, or, Love Lies a-Bleeding* (1609) which, like Shakespeare's contemporaneous tragicomedy *Cymbeline*, 'adapt[ed] the romance tradition to the commercial stage in a self-conscious style'.[26] Shirley was strongly influenced by Fletcher in his own experiments in the domains of tragicomedy and romance. *The Bird in a Cage* involves extensive reworking of Fletcher's earlier play of wagers and incarceration, *Women Pleased* (c.1620). In turn, Shirley's work shaped the dramatic writing of others. Like Jonson, he was part of William Cavendish's extensive circle of patronage and influence in the 1630s and 1640s, and his influence, along with that of Jonson and Shakespeare, on Margaret Cavendish's work, not least *The Convent of Pleasure*, has been observed.[27] *The Convent of Pleasure* further reveals the traces in the writings of Margaret Cavendish of all the major contributing factors to the history of women and performance in the seventeenth century that we have been outlining here, from masque to pastoral to tragicomedy.

In the same way that the Fletcher revivals of the 1630s found a new audience and cultural context, the onset of the English civil wars and the associated closure of the theatres in 1642 altered conditions of dramatic performance and reception in ways which impacted both on women's role in the theatre and on the perceived import of the three plays under consideration here. The parliamentary order closing the playhouses in September 1642 radically curtailed public performances, but theatrical modes persisted in diverse ways throughout the period up to the restoration of the monarchy and the official reopening of the theatres in 1660.[28] One strand of the 'para-dramatic' pamphlet dialogues and playlets which flourished at this time drew heavily on the *querelle des femmes*, mobilising its satirical conventions for contemporary political comment from both sides.[29] Here again we witness the persistent suggestiveness of the interface between the *querelle* tradition and the fascination with female performance which characterises our three plays. In *An Exact Diurnal of the Parliament of Ladies* (1647) and *Newes from the New Exchange* (1650), for example, republican Henry Neville belittles the military shortcomings of royalist men by portraying a parliament of their womenfolk whose insatiable sexual appetites lead them to bemoan the underperformance of their men and seek satisfaction in the arms of noted puritans.[30] Such pamphlets demonstrate the continued visibility and appeal of the image of women as theatrical performers as well as its contentiousness – Neville's portrayal of over-sexed, histrionic female royalists exploits the political capital to be gained from their association with the 'notorious whores' of Stuart court theatricals, but has also been read as acknowledging 'women's participation in politics and their grievances, particularly their subordinate position within marriage'.[31]

The importance of printed literature in sustaining drama between 1642 and 1660 is more directly apparent in the increased drive to make plays available to the reader through publication. Although recent criticism has rightly warned against a simplistic vision of parliamentarians as uniformly anti-theatrical during this period, Parliament's closure of the theatres undoubtedly rendered gestures of continued support for theatrical culture – such as play-reading – significant markers of royalist affiliation.[32] The printing of Beaumont and Fletcher's *Comedies and Tragedies* (1647) in prestigious folio format by royalist publisher Humphrey Moseley constitutes an important landmark in this consciously politicised enterprise. While *The Wild-Goose Chase* remained absent from the 1647 folio, it soon appeared in its own folio edition of 1652 with lines from the well-known royalist colonel and poet Richard Lovelace opening a series of commendatory verses welcoming the rediscovery of the play's manuscript.[33] As the discussion below of the textual history of Fletcher's play notes, the particular nature of *The Wild-Goose Chase*'s engagement with female performers enhances its appeal for interregnum royalist readers. The partisan character of its intended reception is underscored by the final commendatory poem, which ends by implying an analogy between the loss and rediscovery of Fletcher's play and the execution of the king and the longed-for restoration of the Stuart monarchy:

> For saints by persecution thrive; and none
> Is martyred, but's oppressed into a throne.
> There reign he to time's end! While we from this
> Do calculate his apotheosis.[34]

The Wild-Goose Chase followed hot on the heels of another high-profile royalist folio from Moseley, William Cartwright's *Comedies, Tragicomedies, With Other Poems* (1651), which commemorates even more markedly certain feminocentric aspects of court culture under Henrietta Maria. The volume features plays such as *The Siege, or Love's Convert* and *The Royal Slave* which celebrated the kind of female heroism embraced in the regal self-fashioning of the queen consort's court theatricals and that was pivotal to Margaret Cavendish's authorial image and dramatic characterisation.[35] While Cavendish's play *Bell in Campo* revisits the motif of the female army from *The Royal Slave*, the description of the 'Princess' in *The Convent of Pleasure* as 'a princely brave woman truly, of a masculine presence' (2.3.9–10) suggests the manner in which the play's cross-dressing allows Cavendish a further exploration of the *femme forte* image.

Apart from any specific correspondences which exist between Cavendish's drama and the printed plays of the 1640s and 1650s, the sheer physical presentation of her two folio collections of *Playes* (1662) and *Plays, Never Before Printed* (1668) 'speaks resonantly in the folio tradition'.[36] A sense of Cavendish's place in this tradition, and of the serious weight allotted to play-reading in the period during which she began her dramatic compositions, acts as a counterweight to the reluctance displayed by some in applying the label 'closet drama' to her work (see p. 48). This designation of 'compositions intended for reading or private recitation' rather than for 'theatrical performance' need not be pejorative.[37] Rather than being regarded as a poor relation to theatre-going, play-reading emerged as a legitimate activity in its own right and one which acted as 'a form of political resistance' for embattled royalists, challenging their marginalisation from public life by situating 'both author and reader simultaneously in the closet and at the theatre, thus guarding privacy while enabling public engagement'.[38] Given the fact that women's access to public office and action was so limited at this time, the enforced 'closet' status of so much drama during the 1640s and 1650s may be seen as an opportunity for them, 'inaugurating a new . . . equality in the status of plays by men and women since neither sex was likely to have plays staged'.[39] It also made it easier to conceptualise the paradox of ostensibly 'private' play-reading or the composition of plays not intended for the theatre as a 'public' intervention for men and women alike.[40]

Even after the Restoration, Cavendish mines the imaginative possibilities of closet plays staged in the 'brain' of author and reader, yet 'read as if . . . spoke or acted',[41] but she also draws on a tradition of actual female performance in the household theatricals which helped to keep theatre alive between 1642 and 1660.[42] The staging of dramatic entertainments in the quasi-monastic country-house setting of *The Convent of Pleasure* draws most immediately on theatrical writings and events associated with Welbeck Abbey and Bolsover Castle, the family seats of Cavendish's husband, William, Duke of Newcastle. Long before his marriage to Margaret he had commissioned Ben Jonson to compose two pieces for the diversion of Charles I and Henrietta Maria on their visits to his estates: *The King's Entertainment at Welbeck* (1633) and *Love's Welcome at Bolsover* (1634). A poet and playwright himself, Newcastle also encouraged his daughters by his first marriage, Jane and Elizabeth, to write.[43] As already noted, their surviving manuscripts feature 'a Pastorall' and a play, *The Concealed Fancies*, which, though probably not performed, was clearly written for performance at Welbeck.[44] The play manifests a strong consciousness of the processes involved in women's staging themselves which echoes the female wooing performances of *The Wild-Goose Chase* and anticipates the ladies' theatricals in *The Convent of Pleasure*.[45] Although the play has been recognised as uncovering and subverting some of the limitations exposed by contemporary expectations of women's domestic duties within the aristocratic household, it serves as an important example of the dramatic freedoms which the household could offer as an arena for women's dramatic composition and performance – not least the reassuring containments of exposure before a solely coterie audience.[46]

The dramatic compositions of the Cavendish sisters – apparently written when they were under siege by parliamentary troops at Welbeck in 1645[47] – serve as a reminder of the way in which the reiteration of theatrical modes associated with the displaced Stuart court could act as a badge of royalist loyalty during this period. In particular their pastoral masque calls on resources which this introduction has already identified as deeply embedded in Jacobean and Caroline court cultures and closely allied with female performance. More famously, Richard Fanshawe's *The Faithfull Shepherd* (1647, 1648) – a translation of Guarini's *Il pastor fido* – makes a political statement not only by redeploying the literary materials of 'the Caroline Arcadia' but by using the pastoral mode for a topically royalist articulation of the notion that true 'authority' can exist apart from material 'power'.[48] Even after the Restoration this remains a highly suggestive dimension of earlier royalist pastoral for Cavendish, whose *The Convent of Pleasure* appears to view this as an empowering concept not simply politically but also in terms of gender. More specifically her play draws on Walter Montagu's *The Shepherds' Paradise* as a model of female theatricals in the pastoral mode. The first-time printing of Montagu's playtext in 1659 indicates the political plangency of such a recollection of the queen's pastoral theatricals, offering 'a statement on the potentially imminent return of the royal family with whom the work was so inalterably associated'.[49]

Like the redeployment of pastoral in the 1640s and 1650s, recollections of court masque helped contribute to a dramatic aesthetics of Stuart loyalism while also registering changed theatrical and historical conditions in the transmutation of the masque form. This even extended to the reworking of the genre for performance at the 'republican court' in Shirley's masque *Cupid and Death* (1653).[50] Less surprisingly, perhaps, the Cavendish sisters' 'Pastorall' features an antimasque of witches reminiscent of Jonson's *Masque of Queens* (1609) in which the eponymous main masque portrayed by Queen Anna's ladies banishes a disruptive crowd of witches.[51] Whilst *The Convent of Pleasure* clearly attests to Cavendish's continuing sense of the dramatic potency of Jacobean and Caroline court masque, it is worth noting that, during the 1650s, the masquing tradition was being appropriated into the newer dramatic form of the opera. The exiled royalist James Howell's *The Nuptials of Peleus and Thetis*, performed in Paris in 1654, casts Henrietta Maria's daughter in the speaking part of the muse, Erato, while William Davenant's operas, sanctioned by the Protectorate, exploit – among other masquing conventions – the dramatic potential of female singers, a feature echoed in Act 4 of *The Convent of Pleasure*.[52]

Margaret Cavendish's evidently strong investment – despite being at least partly a Restoration playwright – in Jacobean and Caroline theatrical conventions, and in the new forms and meanings they acquired during the 1640s and 1650s, reprises our opening caveats against the imposition of too linear a conception of theatrical history as it touches either our three plays or the question of female performance across this period. While the aristocratic Cavendish is nothing if not ambivalent in the welcome she affords professional actors, her prominent near-contemporary Aphra Behn gains vital reinforcement for her role as professional playwright by becoming identified with the highly eroticised and public figure of the Restoration woman actor.[53] The persistent instabilities surrounding the female performer are eloquently suggested by the palpable anxieties that surge beneath Thomas Jordan's attempt to defend the arrival of professional women actors on the Restoration stage:

> 'Tis possible a virtuous woman may
> Abhor all sorts of looseness, and yet play;
> Play on the Stage, where all eyes are upon her;
> Shall we count that a crime *France* calls an honour?[54]

What emerges here, rather than a neat, self-explanatory linear history, is a complicated matrix of influence and interaction: between professional and amateur playwrights and performers, long-established theatrical tradition and radical departures, court and coterie, city and province, Catholic and Protestant, and male and female. There is no one line of argument that dominates: each defined period in the seventeenth century – Jacobean, Caroline, Interregnum, or Restoration – witnesses the coexistence of competing, sometimes contradictory, opinions of women and theatre, and that is as true of our three chosen playtexts as of the wider cultural debate. We have not selected our three plays because they endorse a party line in favour of women actors but rather because they discuss the phenomenon of women (and men) and performance in subtle and nuanced ways, intervening, sometimes by offering up further ambiguities, in an existent set of practices and an emergent debate.

THE PLAYS

The Wild-Goose Chase
John Fletcher was a younger son born to Elizabeth and Richard Fletcher in December 1579 at Rye, Sussex, where his father officiated as a

Protestant minister. Richard Fletcher held a series of clerical positions culminating in his appointment as the Bishop of London in 1595. As a consequence of his second marriage to the widow Lady Mary Baker, Richard Fletcher fell from favour with Queen Elizabeth and appears never to have regained her goodwill before his death in 1596. He left a debt-encumbered estate.

In 1591, at the age of eleven, John Fletcher is believed to have attended Bene't College (now Corpus Christi), Cambridge. There is a gap in records of his movements until the production of *The Woman Hater* in 1606, which marked the beginning of a close personal and productive literary relationship with Oxford-educated Francis Beaumont. The patronage of Henry Hastings, fifth Earl of Huntingdon, and his wife, the Countess Elizabeth, immersed Fletcher in the firmly Protestant tradition of the incumbents of the Huntingdon seat of Ashby-de-la-Zouche in Leicestershire. While Henry and Elizabeth eschewed the 'glittering misery'[55] of court life, their cultural tastes were wide-reaching, and they demonstrated a strong sense of *noblesse oblige* in local matters. Fletcher enjoyed a warm personal association with Lady Elizabeth, a noblewoman of intellectual interests, proudly described by her husband as having 'a judicious conceit and masculine understandinge'.[56]

Fletcher continued work as Shakespeare's successor in the role of chief dramatist for the King's Men, writing with Beaumont, and, after the latter's retirement, with others including Nathan Field, Philip Massinger, Ben Jonson, William Rowley, and George Chapman. No manuscript appears to have survived of a collaborative work by Shakespeare and Fletcher based on Thomas Shelton's translation of *Don Quixote*, and, until recently, critical interest in two other joint works, *The Two Noble Kinsmen* (1613) and *All Is True (Henry VIII)* (1613) has focused primarily on questions of attribution to the respective dramatists.[57] Beaumont retired from the stage in about 1613 but Fletcher continued writing, either alone or with others, until his death in 1625 after contracting the plague.

Prior to the publication of Rota Lister's 1980 edition of *The Wild-Goose Chase*, critics and editors commonly stated that the play had no known source. Rather than identifying one single source, Lister amasses a range of literary materials from which Fletcher may have drawn hints for his main plot: these include chivalric romance, Italian drama, earlier English drama, and the contemporary literature of travel.[58] The relationship between these materials and the events and characters of *The Wild-Goose Chase* is typically one of 'ironic and paradoxical inversion' (p. lii). For instance, the name and plight of Fletcher's heroine, Oriana, may derive from the tremendously popular Spanish romance *Amadis de Gaul*, which tells of the constant love of the British princess, Oriana, for Amadis, the knight to whom she is secretly betrothed. While Amadis overcomes great obstacles to be united with Oriana, in Fletcher's comedy the 'wild goose', Mirabell, is at once the object of Oriana's romantic quest and the chief obstacle to her achieving it, since he refuses to honour the contract he made with Oriana before leaving Paris. The name 'Oriana' gained currency in the Elizabethan and Jacobean periods in musical and theatrical works praising the virtues of Elizabeth I and Anna of Denmark.[59] The name also features in *The Woman Hater* and *The Knight of Malta* (1618), a tragicomedy by Fletcher, Massinger, and Field. Like the Oriana of *The Wild-Goose Chase*, the identically named heroines of these plays are resolute, chaste young women who display a self-assurance which borders on naivety. Each of the three Orianas is willing to run the gauntlet of calumny or humiliation in the process of defending her reputation, and this persistence ultimately pays off.

In Mirabell, Fletcher reworks his wild gallant figure, the prototype of whom is the character of Young Loveless in his city comedy *The Scornful Lady* (1613), written with some assistance from Beaumont. Mirabell's dramatic cousins include stage misogynists such as Benedick and Bosola, and the trickster and libertine Don Juan Tenorio, the hero of the Spanish play *El burlador de Sevilla* (*c.*1616–25?), by Tirso de Molina.[60] Oriana's determination to reform a committed cavalier may bring to mind Helena's dogged pursuit of Bertram in Shakespeare's *All's Well that Ends Well* (1603–4). An important difference between the women's situations is that Oriana has a marriage portion, which at her request her brother, De Gard, has left with Mirabell's father before departing on his travels. Her independent means should make Oriana a more attractive marital prospect to Mirabell than the humble, moneyless Helena is for Bertram. The fact that it does not, and that it takes Oriana's impersonation of a rich Italian lady to arouse Mirabell's interest, indicates the divergent comic emphases of Shakespeare and his successor at the Blackfriars. The thematic concerns of *The Wild-Goose Chase* are secular and satiric, highlighting the connections between sex, money, and power, and the relationship between disguise and desire.[61] Despite some resemblances between the two plots, there is a considerable aesthetic distance between the cynical gaiety of Fletcher's play and Shakespeare's concern with 'spiritual redemption', focused in 'the most overtly religious of [his] heroines'.[62]

The sub-plot of *The Wild-Goose Chase* provides Mirabell with two foils in his travelling companions Pinac and Belleur, who are taken with the 'airy' sisters, Lillia-Bianca and Rosalura, one of whom Mirabell's father hopes to match with his son. When Mirabell 'give[s] up [his] interest' to the less impudent gallants and offers to assist their courtship ventures, he instigates the Fletcherian 'dance of wit'[63] in which young women and men proffer and parry plots and disguises aimed at testing and securing the object of their desire. This combat of the sexes both recalls and revises its Shakespearian antecedents in comedies such as *Love's Labour's Lost*, *Much Ado about Nothing*, and *The Taming of the Shrew*. In common with *The Taming of the Shrew*, *The Wild-Goose Chase* juxtaposes two temperamentally opposed sisters whose education forms a talking-point, and whose fiery relationship with their tutor, Lugier, contributes to their innovative portrayal as 'new women'.[64] Fletcher's Jacobean comedy renders explicit what some feminist critics have argued is merely implied in Shakespeare's satirical farce, namely the performative aspect of femininity.[65] The play's saturation with theatrical imagery and its portrayal of maids with a mania for dancing may reflect the heyday of the Jacobean court, in particular the lively cultural atmosphere generated by Queen Anna as an artistic patron and a performer in her own masques.[66]

The relationship between *The Wild-Goose Chase* and the world of the Jacobean court is strengthened by the play's first recorded staging during the court's Christmas revels of 1621–22.[67] As Paul Salzman suggests, the performance occasion allows us to see Fletcher's play 'as appealing to a court spirit of bravado and witty/rakish comedy, as well as offering a critique of such values'.[68] As we have already suggested, *The Wild-Goose Chase* is supremely a play about playing. Its performance and publishing history span the period covered by this collection, from its Jacobean premiere, its revival at the elite Blackfriars theatre in 1632, its delayed publication in a lavish folio edition in 1652, through to its performance in the first decade of the Restoration theatre.[69] There is a logic in placing this play at the start of a volume whose aims include drawing attention to the shifting status of female theatrical performance in seventeenth-century England, from a haphazardly glimpsed but vividly imagined phenomenon to a firm reality with the advent of the Restoration actress. The ongoing textual-theatrical life of *The Wild-Goose Chase*, with its dynamic emphasis on women as actors and doers, may be seen as contributing to the cultural change from an all-male stage to a commercial theatre newly featuring male and female players. The play's vigorous engagement with the 'woman debate' and its vision of gender as performance render it freshly relevant to current literary studies. Joined with Fletcher's unique strain of 'bravura absurdity', captured in the comedy's title and mirrored in its formal design, these factors make *The Wild-Goose Chase* compellingly stageable.[70]

The particular interest of *The Wild-Goose Chase* in the present context derives in part from its acute perception of women as performers in the

arenas of courtship and marriage. As Lister shows, the play not only contains 'frequent allusions to masques and disguisings' (p. lxxv), but the
structure of many episodes resembles theatrical forms such as the masque
and the mumming (pp. lxxv–lxxvii). These forms are paralleled and con-
trasted within and across acts. In the third act, characters in both sub-
plot and main plot feign noble status by assuming elaborate costume: first
Pinac parades past Lillia-Bianca with an English courtesan masquerading
as his noble mistress; this wedding progress is echoed by Oriana and De
Gard, who appear before Mirabell with De Gard impersonating a nephew
of the Duke of Savoy, intent upon marrying Oriana. In Act 4 all three
heroines adopt pathetic feminine postures: on Lugier's advice, Lillia-
Bianca stands at Pinac's door with a willow garland in hand; in the next
scene Rosalura counterfeits meek acquiescence to Belleur's woman-
taming stance; and in an 'informal play-within-the-play' which she herself
devises, Oriana performs as a young woman driven to madness through
frustrated love (p. lxxv; this section of the play is depicted in the illustration from the 1711 edition of *The Works of Beaumont and Fletcher*
reproduced as the frontispiece to this volume). The fifth act builds
towards Oriana's climactic impersonation of a glorious Italian noblewoman and combines this with Rosalura's and Lillia-Bianca's cheeky
pretence of 'stepping out' with their gallants on their travels. The self-
conscious formalism of *The Wild-Goose Chase* forms a strong link with
The Bird in a Cage and *The Convent of Pleasure*, both of which feature
inset plays and masques performed by women.

Fletcher's comic *œuvre* manifests the immense theatrical potential of
women's conflicted, combative relationships with men. Like his earlier
farce *The Woman's Prize* (1611), *The Wild-Goose Chase* revises and
updates themes shared with Shakespeare's *The Taming of the Shrew* in
that, in this play, the women actively tame and mould the men of their
choice. The wooing process begins in 1.3 where Rosalura and Lillia-
Bianca perform versions of saucy and sober femininity in an effort to whet
the interest of Mirabell, the male prize whom their wealthy father, Nantolet, has in hopeful sight. While the captivation of the onlooking Pinac
and Belleur with the two girls ensures the plot's forward momentum, the
representation of the young women as exotic commodities, 'sweet birds'
bred up in 'the court elements' (1.3.3, 24), highlights two interlinked
themes of the play: women's status as objects in a sexual market, and the
artful, strategic fashioning of feminine identities. While extolling his
daughters' breeding to Mirabell's father, La Castre, Nantolet invokes the
notion of women as merchandise only to reject it. He says that their training has rendered them 'fit for the heirs of that state I shall leave 'em; / To
say more is to sell 'em' (10–11). Despite his disclaimer, Nantolet goes on

to detail Rosalura's and Lillia-Bianca's attractions, presenting them respectively as models of mirth, and 'manners and . . . modesty' (21).

Fletcher does not rest with the image of women as choice commodities; he also represents them as the controllers of goods. In her third ruse to catch Mirabell, Oriana counterfeits the sister of a Genoese merchant whom Mirabell once saved from assault, who has come to Paris to convey Mirabell the bequest left him by her brother. The success of the stratagem rests on the spectacular impact Oriana makes upon Mirabell as a glamorous woman of business. She is first sighted by him on the upper stage buying jewels from a merchant and settling a debt for £10,000 (5.4). Upon their formal meeting Mirabell kisses Oriana and finds 'she has a spring dwells on her lips' (5.6.10); he is then presented with the casket of jewels notionally bequeathed him by her brother. When Mirabell, enthralled by this 'noblest of women', attempts to give back the casket as a testimony of his regard, Oriana claims she must have him too, lest she violate her brother's stipulation that the jewels stay with Mirabell. Oriana thus successfully orchestrates her marriage as a form of reciprocal purchase; she ensnares Mirabell through the counterfeit bequest, while he is endowed with her marriage portion. The concluding intrigue bears out Kathleen McLuskie's characterisation of Fletcherian comedy as 'a world of competitive individualism which was liberating for those women with the wit and the resources to survive within it'.[71] Mirabell is pleased to have been deceived by the witty Oriana and promises 'to turn a new leaf over' (5.6.87). His simultaneous requirement of Oriana that 'these fine clothes you shall wear still' (5.6.88) marks the transition from girlhood to fashionable Parisian wife as entailing a perpetual feminine performance. Oriana must continue to 'show another woman' (5.4.23).

The scenes featuring the courtesan, Mariana, provide a robust counterpoint to the main plot's elegant enactment of the intersection between theatre, money, and sex. Mariana's masquerade as a travelled English lady whom Pinac intends to wed is undone when Lillia, tipped off by a servant, triumphantly exposes Pinac's betrothed as 'Jumping Joan, an ancient sinweaver' (4.1.142), a woman who 'slipped' from the position of lady's chambermaid to London prostitute, withstanding 'the fierce conflicts / Of many a furious term' before being '[at] last shipped over hither' (143, 145–7). The mock-heroic colouring in this account of Joan/Mariana's career transmutes into Lillia-Bianca's description of her rival as 'a stink none can endure' (149), an image which virulently demarcates the social and cultural distance between the French gentlewoman and the English whore. The scene ends with a further feminine victory when Joan refuses to return to Pinac and Mirabell the hired clothes and jewels she wore to impersonate a 'well-bred woman' (3.1.226), asserting, ''Tis not our

English use to be degraded' (4.1.160). Her parting thrust – that if Pinac will visit her and take his venture, he shall have 'pleasure for [his] properties' (162) – highlights the position of women as equal traders in the sexual traffic which the play juxtaposes with the early modern discourses of merchant venturing and travel.

The Wild-Goose Chase suggests the complex mixture of women's subjection to and empowerment by the Jacobean social and cultural codes governing the formation of female selfhood. Fletcher proves elusive on the question of whether femininity is a matter of social engineering or whether women are temperamentally inclined to enact their identities as a series of roles. The language of show and appearance in early modern drama can operate to subordinate or to exalt the feminine self; thus Corvino curtly orders Celia in *Volpone*, 'Go to, show yourself / Obedient, and a wife' (3.7.30–1), while Shakespeare's Cleopatra, preparing for death, implores her maidservants, 'Show me, my women, like a queen' (5.2.223). Self-display unites the spheres of women's education and theatrical performance, and the two spheres converge in the sexual pun on 'parts' in Lugier's boast that Rosalura and Lillia-Bianca 'have handsome parts too, / Pretty becoming parts . . . and handsome education they have had too, / Had it abundantly . . . I have put it to 'em, that's my part' (1.3.29–32, 43). The play's discourse of the bodily humours affords Lillia-Bianca an alternative rationale for her singularity: accounting to Pinac for her unexpectedly lively demeanour in 2.2 she explains, 'we are compounded of free parts, and sometimes too / Our lighter, airy, and our fiery mettles / Break out and show themselves' (110–12). Her lines echo the description of the young women in the dramatis personae as 'the *airy* daughters of Nantolet' (22, emphasis added), implying that Lillia-Bianca and Rosalura are naturally volatile, and therefore, as Lillia-Bianca elaborates, their free dispositions involuntarily disclose themselves. Such exuberant qualities were more likely to find expression in 'free-born maids' (4.1.78), who were distinguished from the vast majority of seventeenth-century Englishwomen by the visible markers of leisure and, in some cases, a private education.

Much of the appeal of the female characters in *The Wild-Goose Chase* resides in their frank and forthright speech. Deflecting De Gard's concern that her love for Mirabell is public knowledge, Oriana pinpoints the source of popular gossip in the rumourmongers' appetite for drink and their susceptibility to romantic fiction. The deftness with which Oriana wields the figures of Portia and Lucretia as ironic *exempla* hints at her classical education, as does Lillia-Bianca's declaration to Pinac, 'I have changed my copy' (2.2.141), where her metaphor is borrowed from humanist pedagogy. The ambiguous status of women's learning in the early Stuart period is registered in Nantolet's qualified commendation of Lillia-Bianca to La Castre, 'if a woman, / With the decency of her sex, may be a scholar, / I can assure ye . . . she understands' (1.3.25–7). Fletcher creates comedy from the spectre of 'Lady Learning' (3.1.179), using it as a springboard for one of Mirabell's satirical cadenzas and for a cameo by a witty servant, who alarms Pinac with his account of Lillia-Bianca as a woman who speaks Greek and discourses of 'stars and firmaments . . . [and] the beginning o' th' world' (2.2.20–3). The schooling of Nantolet's daughters is oriented firmly towards attracting husbands: when Lillia-Bianca questions Lugier, 'to what use serves my reading?' (3.1.56), she speaks not as a frustrated Latinist but as a randy virgin eager for sexual encounter. Fletcher enfranchises his female characters to speak of sex, thus Rosalura proclaims to Lillia-Bianca, 'Give me the puissant pike, take you the small shot' (3.1.129). The dialogue in which the sisters compare their lovers conveys a vivid sense of sexual excitement, and their belief in their ability to handle the men, not just physically, but to 'mould' and 'form' their characters.

Fletcher's jesting portrayal of women scholars perhaps owes something to the changed cultural climate at the Stuart court, and to King James's 'dislike of learned women'.[72] Yet arguably *The Wild-Goose Chase* shows the benefits of women's literacy in the considerable rhetorical power exerted by all three heroines. When a pushy Mirabell becomes sexually aggressive and defamatory towards Rosalura, he is reduced to a stunned silence by the force of her moral indignation. A critical awareness of the injustice of the double standard drives Oriana's questioning reply to Rosalura's speculation that Mirabell is repelled by her 'free behaviour': 'Why should not ye? Are *our* minds only measured?' (2.3.15, emphasis added). Such arguments in favour of women's equality with men were mounted in *A Mouzell for Melastomus* (1617), written by Rachel Speght in answer to Joseph Swetnam's popular *Arraignment of Lewde, Idle, Froward and Unconstant Women* (1615). At times both Mirabell's misogyny and the women's counter-attacks echo the language of the printed controversy about women: when Rosalura accuses Mirabell of being 'a monster, / A blatant beast' (4.3.42–3) for causing Oriana's madness, her description resonates with Speght's contemporaneous imaging of Swetnam as 'a full fed Beast, / Which roared like some monster, or a Devill, / And on *Eves* sex . . . foamed filthie froth'.[73] In the work containing these lines, 'The Dreame', prefixed to *Mortalities Memorandum* (1621), the middle-class, well-educated Speght makes the case for women's equal right to knowledge, an argument grounded in her religious inheritance as the daughter of a Calvinist minister. The language of this poem resonates with the self-articulation of Fletcher's heroines, for whom terms such as 'mind', 'will', and 'conscience' are instrumental in establishing their separate identities.

In accounting for the sustained popularity of *The Wild-Goose Chase* into and beyond the Caroline period we must address the ambivalent comic charisma of Mirabell as part of the panorama of masculinities depicted within the play. De Gard, whose name evokes his role in upholding patriarchal values, describes Mirabell as 'a loose and strong defier of all order' (1.1.143), a phrase which locates Mirabell's libertinism within a broad spectrum of social and sexual transgression. Historians have stressed the contrast between the 'bawdy decadence' of James's reign and the 'image of virtue' presented by Charles I's tightly regulated court.[74] The influence of a Catholic queen consort whose ideals of beauty and love were derived from Christian neoplatonism is apparent in the Caroline vogue for pastoral dramas focused on questions of sexual ethics; it was within this context that Fletcher's *The Faithful Shepherdess* was successfully revived at court some twenty years after its failure on the Jacobean stage. If the Caroline court aspired to an ideal of sexual decorum, the titles of plays such as Shirley's *The Gamester* and *The Lady of Pleasure* signal a parallel interest in behaviour which disrupted this ideal. As an embryonic comedy of manners, *The Wild-Goose Chase* explores the polarities of 'wildness' and 'civility', prompting reconsideration of the social values inherent in epithets such as 'free' and 'liberal'. While Mirabell concedes to Pinac and Belleur that marriage may concern him 'hereafter in [his] gravity', he stakes his claim to 'the freedom of a traveller', declaring 'a new strong lusty bark cannot ride at one anchor' (1.2.70–2). This disdain for marriage anticipates the challenge to social convention posed by later 'wanderers' such as Killigrew's Thomaso, and Restoration rake-heroes such as Etherege's Dorimant and Behn's Willmore.[75]

The tragicomic turn precipitated by Oriana's feigned madness in 4.3 offers a glimpse of a Mirabell stripped of his swagger. Indicted by Oriana's friends as a wronger of women, Mirabell protests, 'when I see cause I can both do and suffer / Freely, and feelingly, as a true gentleman' (30–1). The answering stage image of the distracted Oriana '*on a bed*', heightened by her prettily disordered language, unmasks the wild goose as a man of feeling: 'Oh, fair tears, how ye take me!' (76). Mirabell's real compunction is evident both in his aside, 'is't possible my nature / Should be so damnable to let her suffer?' (67–8) and his tears, emphasised by Oriana's question, 'do you weep too?' (77). The sentimental tableau of the penitent rake at the bedside of the woman he has injured is subverted by the entrance of Belleur, still reeling from his trouncing at the hands of Rosalura and her neighbours. Belleur's discordant ranting about 'a world of madwomen' and his disregard for Oriana's suffering prompt an ironic reversal of roles, as Mirabell berates his friend as a 'wild fool'. The tone shifts again when Oriana, emboldened by Mirabell's new tenderness, discovers her pretence to him *sotto voce*, asking 'will ye be mine?' (130).

The scene shows Fletcher's theatrical virtuosity, switching between ensemble action and the precarious intimacy of a tête-à-tête, and moving from pathos to tragicomic farce to comic élan as Mirabell exults in Oriana's fatal mistake, deriding her to the onstage audience as a woman 'stark mad to be stoned to death' (135). Mirabell's language and demeanour make an audience's response to him here, as throughout the play, radically divided: his reaction to Oriana's feigned distress betokens traits of what Rosalura terms 'a true noble gentleman' (4.2.108), yet his callous shaming of Oriana as sex-starved displays the wild goose's preening as masculinity regains the upper hand. Oriana's humiliation after proposing to Mirabell points up the contradiction inherent in the title 'free-born maid': however privileged by her social status, a maid's conduct remained constrained by the edict of feminine modesty.

Several factors make the *The Wild-Goose Chase* seem proleptic of the social milieu of Caroline England, and account for the comedy's appeal to this audience, as well as the English and émigré royalist culture of the 1650s. The play's Gallic setting, with its hint of Parisian salon culture, and its precocious, histrionic women, could hardly fail to appeal to a court and town set ablaze by a vogue for women actors led by the young French queen. Oriana's climactic impersonation of an Italian grandee whose dress and demeanour stun her onlookers into rapt admiration speaks eloquently to the cosmopolitan, woman-oriented Stuart elite. In the context of its Jacobean performance, the play's catering to the English fascination with foreigners may have accrued topical bite. Referring to the play's performance at court in 1622, Sally Hoare suggests that 'public anxiety surrounding the proposed match between the heir to the English throne [Prince Charles] and the Spanish Infanta may have added extra piquancy to the play's twin scenes (3.1 and 5.6) in which potential exotic marriage partners materialise but are subsequently revealed to be imposters'.[76] Inigo Jones's costume designs for *The Shepherds' Paradise* include a drawing for the character of Fidamira which is clearly modelled upon a portrait of the Infanta thought to have been acquired by James I during negotiations for the Spanish match. Whether or not this, and one other drawing, were intended as 'visual reference[s] to the Spanish court'[77] and to King Charles's first disastrous courtship, the drawings indicate the sophistication with which contemporary audiences might interpret the language of clothes. The possibility that Mirabell's love for Oriana is clinched by her daring assumption of breeches beneath her gown is testimony to the sexually provocative nature of social and theatrical transvestism during this period.

As a comic playwright, Fletcher's investment lay not with the delineation of individual character, nor with the unmasking of patriarchal ideology, but with what one early twentieth-century critic describes as 'the interplay of two humorously conceived groups on the principle of action and re-action'.[78] The doubling of the two groups in the criss-crossing plots of *The Wild-Goose Chase* bears upon one meaning of the title: in the seventeenth century a 'wild-goose chase' was a cross-country horse-race in which whoever took the lead had to be followed by the others, like a flight of wild geese (*OED* 1). Shoichiro Kawai sees this as the key meaning of the phrase in Fletcher's comedy, and the image of a contrived competition is certainly apposite to the play's highly patterned plot with its seemingly random changes of direction.[79] Yet Kawai downplays the degree to which the comedy showcases Mirabell, the wild goose, as a preposterous young man whose ego is sorely in need of deflating. If the meaning of a 'wild-goose chase' as a foolish, hopeless quest did not take definite form until the mid-eighteenth century, we might speculate that a literary work such as Fletcher's was instrumental in bringing this meaning into currency.[80] A usage by the eighteenth-century artist Thomas Gainsborough shows the ease with which the phrase 'wild-goose chase' lends itself to the subjects of courtship and marriage. Communicating to a friend his plan to teach his two daughters landscape painting so that in the event of 'an Accident' they could earn their own livings, Gainsborough wrote, 'I think . . . I had better do this than make fine trumpery of them, & let them be led away with Vanity, & ever subject to disapointment in the wild Goose chace [*sic*]'.[81] Gainsborough's remark offers a glimpse of an uncertain world in which fathers worry about their daughters' success in the lottery of the marriage market.[82] His use of the phrase to signify women's unrealistic hopes of marriage perhaps indicates the prescience of Fletcher's early comedy of manners. Nevertheless, it is the business of comedy chiefly to delight, and Fletcher executes an optimistically sunny ending, in which 'this wild-goose chase is . . . won o' both sides' (5.6.107).

The Bird in a Cage

James Shirley (1596–1666), a Londoner born and bred whose father had been a member of the Drapers' Company, was for much of his dramatic career prior to the English civil wars part of an Inns of Court coterie of writers and courtiers linked specifically to Gray's Inn. Shirley had entered Gray's after studying at the Merchant Taylors' School (1608–12) and at St Catharine's Hall, Cambridge, from which he graduated with a BA in 1617. The Gray's Inn circle in the 1620s and 1630s constituted what Sandra Burner has called a 'literary workshop' and included, among others, William Habington and Endymion Porter; both men had links to the Caroline court and specifically to crypto-Catholic groupings around Henrietta Maria.[83] These courtly and Catholic associations were to become increasingly important in Shirley's career during the Caroline period, although the claims of his first biographer Anthony à Wood that the dramatist converted to Roman Catholicism at this time have never been corroborated.[84] A galvanising force within this group, aside from religious and political sympathies, appears to have been their association with the publisher William Cooke, whose shop was in the Holborn area of London.[85]

In the years of the Personal Rule (1625–40) and the subsequent years of conflict, Shirley was also closely allied to the patronage circles of William Cavendish, then Earl of Newcastle, a connection that would undoubtedly have brought him into contact with fellow Caroline dramatists, including Ben Jonson, John Ford, Richard Brome, and Jasper Mayne. Shirley moved to Ireland in 1636, remaining there until 1640, a move possibly encouraged by a lengthy outbreak of plague in London that caused the extended closure of the public theatres. While in Dublin, Shirley wrote and directed plays for the Werburgh Street Theatre sponsored by the Lord Deputy of Ireland, Thomas Wentworth, Earl of Strafford. On his return to London, he replaced the late Philip Massinger as chief dramatist for the King's Men at the Blackfriars theatre. At the outbreak of the civil wars Shirley joined Newcastle's forces in Nottinghamshire.[86] Several of his poems from this time refer to Nottinghamshire gentry and themes and it seems reasonable to speculate that he might have had contact with Cavendish's daughters, Jane, Elizabeth, and Frances, ensconced as they were in the early 1640s at the family's Welbeck estate. The influence of mainstream Caroline drama on the sisters' own dramatic experimentations has already been highlighted, and this possibility of direct contact with one of the period's major professional playwrights lends credence to the inferences taken from works such as *The Concealed Fancies* and *A Pastorall*. The family's connections with Shirley (he is also believed to have contributed revisions to some of Cavendish's own plays, such as *The Country Captain*, which was staged in the London public theatres in the early 1640s) encourages further speculation about possible influence on the dramatic writings of Margaret, Cavendish's second wife, connections which are explored in more detail in the section on *The Convent of Pleasure*.

As things fared increasingly ill for the royalist forces in the civil wars, and William Cavendish went into voluntary exile in France and the Low Countries, Shirley appears to have retreated into the life of a professional schoolmaster in London. He did not cease his dramatic writing, however, composing several experimentations in the masque form, one of which, *The Contention of Ajax and Ulysses for the Armour of Achilles*, includes poignant references to the recent turmoil in England, and may have been designed for performance by his Whitefriars schoolboys.[87] He was investigated for his role in the civil wars by the Committee for Compounding with Delinquents in January 1651, but, admitting his actions, he sued successfully for clemency. Shirley and his second wife died in the days immediately following the Great Fire of London, possibly from resulting injuries or the shock endured. They were buried together in a single grave in the parish of St Giles in Middlesex on 29 October 1666.

In the Caroline period, Shirley was for the most part linked to a single theatre and theatre company: Queen Henrietta Maria's Men, under the aegis of Christopher Beeston, at the Cockpit theatre in Drury Lane (also known as the Phoenix).[88] John Ford was also working for Beeston and the Cockpit at this time.[89] Shirley wrote for Beeston from 1625 until 1636 and his departure for Dublin. *The Bird in a Cage* is a product of this cultural moment. Written for the Queen's Men and performed at the Cockpit in 1633, it was published the same year in quarto form. *The Bird in a Cage* appears not, however, to have been the playtext's original working title. On 21 January 1633, a play called *The Bewties* was licensed.[90] At some point prior to publication (and possibly performance), Shirley altered the title to *The Bird in a Cage*. The specific motive for this change is suggested by the sardonic dedication attached to the play in print: 'To Master William Prynne, Utter-Barrister of Lincoln's Inn'. When Shirley's play was released in its published form, Prynne, the radical puritan pamphleteer, was a bird in a cage himself, languishing in the Tower of London awaiting trial for libellous material in *Histriomastix*, which had been released in late 1632. That text's infamous index reference equating female actors with 'notorious whores' has already been mentioned.

Prynne's text had been going through the press at the same time as the much reported rehearsals for Montagu's *The Shepherds' Paradise* were taking place at court.[91] This lengthy pastoral had been commissioned by Henrietta Maria to celebrate the king's birthday in November 1632, although such was the difficulty for her and her ladies of learning their parts that the actual first performance at Denmark House was delayed on several occasions, only finally taking place on 9 January 1633, with a repeat performance at Candlemas (2 February). *The Shepherds' Paradise* has been much discussed in recent scholarship as indicative of the increasing participation by elite women in acting at the Caroline court under the aegis of a French queen whose upbringing meant that she was at ease with women actors speaking and even cross-dressing (in the 1626 performance of *Artenice* her ladies-in-waiting wore beards to play the male parts).[92] The newly supportive audiences for Fletcher's revived pastorals in the 1630s, discussed earlier, and for new public theatre plays with a rich concentration on empathetic female protagonists – for example,

Ford's tragedies *'Tis Pity She's a Whore* and *The Broken Heart*, both *c.*1630 – can be firmly located in this increasingly receptive atmosphere for feminocentric theatricals.[93]

Prynne's obsession in his text with the idea of transvestism, and his virulent anti-Catholic diatribes, made connections with the queen consort's court theatricals almost inevitable, although he denied any specific references to Henrietta Maria or the Montagu rehearsals. In an exchange of letters prior to his trial, Prynne asserted that *Histriomastix* had been in preparation since the early 1620s and that it could not therefore have intended any direct reference to the queen.[94] The pamphlet was partially licensed on 16 October 1630, in part confirming Prynne's claims of earlier composition. Nevertheless, it was common practice for much of the prefatory material for published works to be added once the text was in press (Shirley's addition of the sarcastic dedication to *The Bird in a Cage* is a case in point) and it remains likely that Prynne added the index and its polemical reference to women actors in late 1632 when *The Shepherds' Paradise* rehearsals were a *cause célèbre* in London. Prynne may have claimed that his text could not possibly refer to Henrietta Maria, but the truth is that she was already actively engaged in court theatre by 1626, when she acted in *Artenice*.

Shirley's dedicatory poem to the contemporaneous publication of Ford's *Love's Sacrifice* (also performed at the Cockpit) confirms that Prynne's fierce objections to the dramatic genre, let alone the vexed question of female theatricals, were much on the playwright's mind in 1633:[95]

> Look here, thou that hast malice to the stage,
> And impudence enough for the whole age:
> Voluminously ignorant! Be vexed
> To read this tragedy, and thy own be next. (ll. 5–8)[96]

That final reference to Prynne's forthcoming tragedy suggests, as does the dedication to *The Bird in a Cage*, that Prynne was still awaiting trial in early 1633. Harsh punishment was clearly predicted for him, and those suppositions were borne out: Prynne was eventually sentenced to public ear-cropping, the burning of his text, and life imprisonment in the Tower.[97]

Shirley explicitly locates his 'dedication' in this feverish context of claim and counter-claim, praising Prynne with heavy irony for his love of 'the stage and scene' (4), congratulating him on his 'happy retirement' (6), and referring to Prynne's recent authorship of a 'tragedy' (5), adding 'how aptly may I present you, at this time, with *The Bird in a Cage*'. One pertinent question to ask is why Shirley felt compelled to enter the Prynne debate so decisively in 1633. *The Bird in a Cage* positions itself in opposition to Prynne's anti-theatricalism not only in its prefatory material but also by means of the internal representation of female participation in the theatre in the 'interlude' section of 4.2. This is a play that directly involves itself with themes of performance and pretence, seriousness and sports, liberation and constraint, and which at its heart compares and contrasts male and female participation in all these arenas.

The Bird in a Cage centres on the Duke of Mantua's daughter, Eugenia, who is incarcerated in a guarded tower by her father to ensure that she marries the Prince of Florence. The play makes comic capital of various attempts to penetrate the tower by male courtiers, including Philenzo in his guise as Rolliardo the cynic, who has agreed a wager with the duke that he will penetrate the tower within a month. He eventually succeeds by means of an elaborate gift of caged birds, in which he conceals himself. After a lengthy scene in which he tests Eugenia's chastity and resolve, Philenzo eventually reveals himself to be her lover in disguise. Eugenia is accompanied in her imprisonment by several ladies-in-waiting, and to pass the time they decide (3.3) to indulge in the performance of a playlet or 'interlude' based on the story of Jupiter and Danae. This particular mythological tale of a woman incarcerated in a brazen tower which is then penetrated by Jupiter in the form of a shower of gold has obvious parallels with Eugenia's situation, and Shirley's play as a whole maintains an intertextual relationship with Fletcher's *Women Pleased*, in which Blaunchflore is incarcerated in a tower and the subject of a wager.[98]

Shirley's handling of female theatricals in The Bird in a Cage is full of ambivalences and contradictions, and cannot as a result be read as a straightforward defence of women and performance. Nevertheless, by the time he was admitted to Gray's Inn as an honorary member a year after this play was performed and published he was described in the register entry as 'one of the Valets of the Chamber of Queen Henrietta Maria'.[99] This might suggest that Shirley was seeking to identify his work with the court in the 1630s, and more specifically with the queen's circle and its theatrical activities, possibly with promotion and preferment in mind. Shirley's relationship with the Cockpit and its specific connection to the queen's patronage strengthens this possibility. Certainly, in 1634 he won the lucrative commission to write the masque to be staged by, and on behalf of, the Inns of Court as a public apology to the monarch for any offence caused by Prynne's *Histriomastix* (he was one of their members). The resulting masque, *The Triumph of Peace*, clearly satisfied its aims and objectives since it was staged twice at vast expense.[100]

Some critics speculate that the entire sequence of the women's theatrical interlude might be a later addition to The Bird in a Cage, intended, along with the revised title, to make pragmatic cultural capital out of the

Prynne scandal.[101] There is little justification for this claim. The interlude is integral to the play. Both its occurrence and its narrative theme – the mythological resonance of Jupiter's penetration of Danae's brazen tower will be considered later – are clearly prefigured and alluded to at several significant points in the playtext: Philenzo articulates his intention to penetrate the women's 'prison' in terms of the myth: 'I will fall upon her, as Jupiter on Danae. Let me have a shower of gold, Acrisius' brazen tower shall melt again' (1.1.275–6), and Morello envisions his cross-dressing attempt to penetrate the women's guarded confines in parallel terms: 'Great Jupiter, the patron of scapes, assist my petticoat' (3.1.8).[102]

Neither is the revised title of *The Bird in a Cage* or the image of a bird in a cage simply a bolt-on retrospective notion. As well as being the practical means by which Philenzo ultimately gains access to Eugenia – he hides in the pillar of the extravagant wheeled cage of birds that Bonamico designs as thanks for clearing his debts – and therefore a dominant stage property in any production of the play (as Dondolo declares at 5.1.221, 'This was a bird in a cage, indeed!'), the phrase had age-old proverbial resonance.[103] The script of *The Bird in a Cage* is pervaded by ideas of caging and confinement: Eugenia talks of being 'caged up' by her father at 1.1.51, as well as referring to the birds in the wheeled cage as 'fellow prisoners' (4.2.192), resolving to set them free, which action enables Philenzo to reveal himself; in similar terms, Dondolo and Grutti revel in Bonamico's imprisonment for debts following his deception of them with false claims of powers to achieve invisibility: 'Now our invisible merchant is caged, we may redeem our opinion' (3.4.1–2); and, later in the same scene, Bonamico echoes their phraseology when he is released by Philenzo's settlement of his debts: 'The bird is flown again!' (39). This commonplace had a specific female relevance too: Margaret Cavendish talks of women being 'kept like birds in cages to hop up and down in our houses, not suffered to fly abroad.'[104] Of course, Shirley is not averse to comparing the women's incarceration not only to birds in cages and deer in royal parks (1.1.55–7) but also to nuns in convents: at 3.3.13–14, Donella declares: 'I shall never endure to live an anchorite thus' and the duke confirms the analogy at 5.1.156–7 when he doubts Philenzo's claim of having reached his daughter: 'An anchorite lives not prisoned in a wall / With more security.'[105] This has its own resonance for *The Convent of Pleasure*, which has been persuasively linked by several critics with Shirley's play. It seems unlikely that either the bird and cage references or the interlude are later additions to the playtext, although it is clear that Shirley found in them a new currency in the wake of Prynne's arrest.

Valerie Traub has observed the strange tension that exists in *The Bird in a Cage* between the deliberately distancing effects of Shirley's romance setting in Mantua (far from the realism of place in his other 1630s plays, such as *Hyde Park* and *The Lady of Pleasure*) and the mythological content of the playlet as compared with the cultural and contemporary specificity of the Prynne allusions.[106] She suggests that Shirley is deliberately defusing the possibility of any direct allusion to the Caroline court, thereby evacuating the homoerotic content of the playlet's performance of any genuine social or cultural threat. There are certainly several hints in the text that Donella is deploying her performance as Jupiter to enact latent desires for her mistress: as well as her own 'Beshrew the bell-man! And you had not waked as you did, madam, I should ha' forgot myself and played Jupiter indeed with you' (4.2.169–71), there is Cassiana's wish for Donella, 'would she were a man for her sake' (138), and Mardona's suggestive, 'Then your play is interrupted, Jove –' (168), with its pun on 'play' as meaning both the literal performance of the interlude and sexual dalliance.[107] Traub notes the irony, however, that having contained these references within the distancing frame of the women's interlude, Shirley then reinvigorates them by connecting the themes of female theatricality and sexuality to the contemporary debate initiated by *Histriomastix*.

What may well have been a later revision is the specific allusion to Prynne's pamphleteering with which the playtext as published opens. In one of many exchanges in this play about the vanity of courtiers, Orpiano mocks Morello for having his 'amorous lock' of hair out of place (1.1.23). Morello heads straight back to his barber to have the problem rectified, only returning belatedly to be informed of the duke's decision to incarcerate his daughter. It can be no coincidence that at this time Prynne was best known for a pamphlet which railed against the frivolous fashions and vanities of Caroline courtiers, *The Unlovelinesse of Love-locks* (1628 – Shirley makes direct reference to this text in the dedication at l. 10). Although Kim Walker was surely correct in her assertion that *The Bird in a Cage* was not written as a specific refutation of Prynne, by opening the play with this reference Shirley ensures that the play's treatment of women and theatre is seen in the context of contemporary debates around female theatricals.

Where exactly Shirley positions himself in those debates is, however, a matter for ongoing critical debate. For Walker, 'the apparent liberalism of the play's representation of women acting is carefully contained, and a variety of strategies are at work recuperating such deviancy for patriarchy'.[108] Suggesting that there was anxiety even at the Caroline court about the implications of Henrietta Maria's performances, Walker attests that 'The play within the play offers a representation of women actors that, despite its humor and its affirmation of the female characters involved, shows similar anxieties at work in relation to female sexuality and subjectivity'.[109] Sophie Tomlinson previously identified the 'riotous burlesque' of the performance as a less than sympathetic portrayal of women actors, adding that this underscores 'an open contradiction between the text and the playwright's use of the text in the act of publication'.[110] While both arguments are clearly justified in highlighting the comic manner in which the women's performances are handled in *The Bird in a Cage* – much humour is derived from the women's inability to improvise satisfactory rhymes (for example, at 4.2.61–3, 121–2) as well as from the sexual undertow to the performance – the use of comedy in this context need not be assumed to be tantamount solely to critique. At several points during their private performance, the women assert the skill of female actors; at 3.3, Donella declares: 'Do not distrust your own performance. I ha' known men ha' been insufficient, but women can play their parts' (36–7). On the surface, this line asserts women performers' right to assume male roles – a direct refutation of Prynne's objection to female transvestism in *Histriomastix* and an implicit defence of Henrietta Maria's court theatricals – and there is also inescapable sexual double entendre at play. But a further line of interpretation might hear a claim to women's right to play themselves in the professional theatre and not to have their parts ventriloquised by boy actors.

In his recent edition of Jonson's *Epicene*, Richard Dutton has argued for a form of 'sanctioned playfulness' in Jonson's satirical treatment of female social agency, and something similar might be ascribed to Shirley's careful handling of the theme of women and performance in *The Bird in a Cage*.[111] Walker notes the trouble taken by the dramatist to protect his elite female protagonist from charges of impropriety: it is not Eugenia, for example, who initiates the performance, but Donella, and Eugenia's casting as Danae is entirely suitable to her social standing. Nor does Eugenia participate in the verbal clowning engaged in by Mardona and Cassiana: indeed she converses in formal tetrameter during the performance, while they banter in more lowbrow balladic metrics.[112] As Traub reflects (pp. 162–3), the homoerotics of the performance are knowingly displaced on to the outspoken Donella as are the most overt statements in favour of women actors.

Rather than reading these facts as indices of Shirley's nervousness about his subject of women actors, we might opt to see them as careful attempts to maintain an air of decorum around the notion of the performing Queen, while nevertheless making comic opportunity from the interlude scene in a public theatre context. There is great stress laid on the fact that this is a private performance, with no audience other than the people depicted in the tapestries that hang on the walls of the apartments. Nor is there any of the visible cross-dressing in 4.2 that so surprised the audiences for

Artenice and *The Shepherds' Paradise* and so appalled Prynne: Donella, assigning to Mardona the role of Danae's father Acrisius, observes: 'No matter for properties – we'll imagine, madam, you have a beard' (4.2.17–18).[113] The notable care to maintain the decorum of the performances can be viewed either as a conscious recontainment of the possibility of female performance (Walker's interpretation) or alternatively – bearing in mind the Caroline context – as a careful delineation of female performance as a countenanced activity for elite women. Donella describes their performance as an 'interlude', stressing that they do not have enough performers to mount a full-blown play; this might also serve to reinscribe acceptable female performance in the 1630s within the context of household entertainment, rather than as matter for the public or professional stages. Tellingly, the performance is never described as a 'masque', but, as the discussion of closet drama in our introduction indicates, it is inaccurate to read this solely in terms of a negative containment. The writing, reading, and performing of closet drama in the mid seventeenth century became a genuine outlet for elite female cultural agency and, from that angle at least, Shirley's playtext appears more empathetic to the notion of women and performance than has sometimes been assumed.

Of course, layers of doubleness and contradiction remain in the fact that *The Bird in a Cage* is a public theatre playtext and therefore the roles of Eugenia and her ladies would have been performed by boy actors at the Cockpit. The possibility remains that contemporary audiences would simply have recognised a guying of female performance by boy actors in this public context, but this interpretation ignores the diverse approach to notions of gender and performance exhibited elsewhere in the play. We need to move away from an 'either/or' approach that places Caroline dramatists either wholly in support of or necessarily ranged against female performance and recognise the range of contexts for female performance at this time, and the complexity of response these encouraged.

In some respects, Donella's claim that women can play men's parts as well as, possibly better than, male actors can impersonate the female is validated in *The Bird in a Cage*, not least by Morello's hopeless attempts at cross-dressing in order to gain access to the women's 'prison' (a scene which is remembered and intriguingly reinterpreted by Margaret Cavendish in *The Convent of Pleasure*). Not only does Morello inadvertently reveal the breeches beneath his petticoat when trying to find money with which to bribe the guards (3.1.24–5) but he has failed to think through his performance in any detail: he does not even have a name for the female character he has created, hastily improvising the title of Mistress Thorn (17–19). When his failed disguise is revealed to the duke, he is sentenced to remain in his petticoat for a further month. Admirably, on this second occasion, Morello seizes the performative opportunity wholesale, asking that he may serve as the duke's jester for that period. With this role-play, Morello brings onstage the additional semiotics of the fool's motley wardrobe. As a jester Morello is privileged to speak the truth without fear of punishment – he is 'fool-free' as the play memorably terms it (4.1.40). In this way he becomes a happy counterpart to Philenzo's self-assigned role as Rolliardo, the social misanthrope and cynic.

The role of social performance extends, then, far beyond the confines of Eugenia's apartment and the parameters of the Jupiter–Danae playlet in *The Bird in a Cage*, since Philenzo is Eugenia's true love in disguise. As well as performing the part of Rolliardo, Philenzo plays the further role of Prince of Florence in order to test Eugenia even when he finally gains access to her apartment via the cage of birds. His earlier claim that he will 'play Jupiter' in penetrating her prison proves worryingly accurate as he threatens Eugenia with rape as a test of her constancy, only finally revealing himself when she passes her test with dignity and forbearance. The rape scene is comically prefigured in the feigned attempt to 'rape' the cross-dressed Morello by the all-knowing guards in 3.1. We might interpret this, alongside the Jupiter–Danae storyline, as a further defusing of the complicated realities of the threat of rape, but by choosing not to place his audience in a state of privileged knowledge about Philenzo's identity, Shirley seems conversely to darken and deepen our responses to a possibility we have only laughed at previously.

A complicated final act ensues in which Philenzo reveals his true identity for a second time – this time in open court – only to be sentenced to death (also for the second time). Offstage happenings involving a vial of poison – which, in a reworking of *Romeo and Juliet*, is really a sleeping draught – contribute to Philenzo being declared dead, only to revive onstage. It becomes increasingly difficult to determine the difference between illusion and reality in Mantuan society by the close of the play and this aspect of the plot is underscored by a sub-plot involving the indebted Bonamico and his deception of the gullible courtiers, Dondolo and Grutti. In his performance as the mountebank Altomaro, Bonamico claims to be able to go 'invisible, all but – my hand' (2.1.416). Bonamico's financial needs parallel him with Philenzo's persistent pursuit of finance – 'Let me have money enough' is a phrase reiterated on several occasions in 1.1 (see, for example, 201, 224, 237, 241, 269, and 356) – and the trick with the letter that follows links in turn to a host of other letters which serve as significant properties and advancers of plot in this play. As with the multiple playlets of *The Wild-Goose Chase*, acting, disguise, social agency, and counterfeit are all invoked in *The Bird in a Cage* in a sustained rumination on performance.

The Jupiter–Danae plotline may constitute a mythological distancing in Traub's account of *The Bird in a Cage*, but the fact remains that the subject of the interlude echoes many of the play's themes. The wider relevance of *topoi* of incarceration and rape has been noted, and is acknowledged by the women performers: accepting the role of Danae, Eugenia reflects: "twill suit with my present fortune' (4.2.12). Several critics have observed that the Danae storyline was popular in early modern poetry and drama not least because of the issues of female sexual agency it raised. The myth was also open to reinterpretation in a materialist mode; in many reworkings, Jupiter's penetration of the lock on Danae's brazen tower in the form of a golden shower was reduced to a literal bribing of her guards with gold. *The Bird in a Cage*, in its obsession with money, debts, and the possibility of bribes, is clearly alert to this means of appropriating the myth of Danae. The mythological subject matter effects its own connections with the early Stuart court masque, and yet, in the 1630s, there was a parallel set of referents that connected the impregnation of the incarcerated Danae to the story of the Virgin Mary. In an era when the iconography surrounding Henrietta Maria was making conscious capital of the Englishing of her name as Mary and her Catholic faith, these associations cannot have escaped Shirley's attention.[114] The interlude once again proves to be multivalent in its referents and allusions, making possible readings that both endorse and condemn female agency.[115]

It is perhaps an indicator of the plurality of Shirley's approach that many of the recurrent phrases in this play, in which, as we have already seen, there is a dramaturgic awareness of the revisionary impulse implicit in repetition, have conflicting meanings according to point of use. We have already considered the alternative literal and figurative senses of penetration in the context of the attempts, failed and successful, to gain access to Eugenia and her incarcerated ladies. Other refrains in the play relate to themes of festivity and sports. 'Sport' and 'game' are used and re-used in the dialogue of *The Bird in a Cage* with differing effects. For example, when the duke sentences Morello to his month in a petticoat, it is for his personal amusement or 'sport' (4.1.18); whereas when Morello is invited to 'wrestle' with the guards at 3.1.57–60, the notion of 'sport' troublingly slips into connotations of rape and enforced violence despite the term's provenance in the notion of combative masculine sports (see, for example, 3.1.73). That Morello previously uses the term 'wrestle' in the context of a mock-chivalric allusion to freeing Eugenia from her enchanted castle (see 1.1.368–9) merely adds to the progressive darkening of tone we have identified elsewhere. As the general introduction has already outlined, the notion of 'sports' had a festive but also a political context in the seventeenth century, not least in 1633 when Charles I reissued his father's 1618 'Book of Sports'. The language of holiday in which Philenzo confronts the duke at 5.1.50–5 has a serious subtext.

The semantic pliability of vocabulary in Shirley's play hints at the slippage of clearly identifiable politics in the representation of his central themes, not least that of women and performance. We might wish to ask whether he is in 'earnest' when he chooses to treat this theme in the context of a dramatic comedy. This is another term with multiple resonances in *The Bird in a Cage*. In the context of chivalric romance – a mode and genre that *The Bird in a Cage* (like *The Wild-Goose Chase* before it) both invokes and parodies – to be 'in earnest' was to show ardour in battle. In a sense that survives today it could also indicate seriousness of intent; this is Eugenia's meaning, for example, at 4.2.186 when she dismisses her female companions, and one which informs Morello's song lyrics at 5.1.30. But, as in his adaptation of the Jupiter–Danae storyline, Shirley is equally aware of the financial undertow to the term: 'earnest' could mean a sum of money paid in instalments, what we might now call a 'deposit'. It is in this sense that Philenzo deploys the word at 1.1.355, having agreed his month's wager with the duke; and we cannot ignore monetary implications in a play replete with bribes, wagers, and financial contracts of all kinds.

Finally, it is worth noting that, for all the material signifiers that abound in this play, it is ultimately the female characters who remain in 'earnest'. At 4.2.290, Eugenia wholeheartedly rejects the fiscal terminology that has dominated so many of the play's exchanges: 'I am not bought and sold I hope?' The women's 'sports', the decision to perform a play to pass the time during their period of imprisonment, prove to be communal, joyous activities that stand in stark contrast to the manipulative, often self-serving deployments of art and disguise performed elsewhere in the play by their male counterparts.[116] If, as Morello's final costume of fool's motley appears to indicate, truth can rest most securely in the forms of comedy and performance, perhaps we can argue that Shirley provided the subject of women's theatricals with the most sympathetic context possible in *The Bird in a Cage*.

The Convent of Pleasure

Margaret Cavendish was born in 1623, the daughter of Thomas Lucas – one of the wealthiest landed gentlemen in Essex – and his wife, Elizabeth, at St John's Abbey just outside Colchester. The youngest of eight children to survive until adulthood, Margaret – like her four sisters – was tutored in the arts of singing, dancing, music, reading, writing, and needlework, whilst her brothers pursued the more masculine accomplishments of 'fencing, wrestling, shooting', and the like.[117] Nevertheless, she was to glean elements of a wider, more academic education by associating with her university-trained brothers, in particular the scholarly John, a keen student of the natural philosophy which was to become a lifelong fascination for Margaret.[118] At the outbreak of the civil wars in 1642, parliamentary forces drove the Lucases from their home. By the summer of the following year Margaret was travelling to Oxford from London to join the displaced court and fulfil the ambition she had conceived to become one of Henrietta Maria's ladies-in-waiting. She accompanied the queen to Paris in 1644 and it was here that she met her future husband, William Cavendish, Marquess – later Duke – of Newcastle, a wealthy widower, thirty years her senior, and now widely discredited owing to his summary flight after defeat at the battle of Marston Moor as the commander of the king's forces in the north of England.

The couple married in 1645 and began their life of exile, first in Paris and ultimately in the equally vibrant atmosphere of Antwerp. During this time, Margaret began to forge many of the connections that would shape her concerns as an author. Both William and his brother, Charles, showed a keen interest in natural philosophy and gathered around them a circle of pioneering thinkers in the field including Thomas Hobbes and René Descartes. As we have seen, Newcastle was an equally keen patron of the arts, exposing Margaret to the theatrical endeavours of men such as Jonson and Shirley as well as to the literary pursuits of himself and his daughters by his first marriage. Crucially for his wife, he also became a supporter of her own authorial activities.

Although she had begun to write some years earlier, Margaret's first published effort, *Poems and Fancies* (1653), appeared in London towards the end of her visit there with her brother-in-law from 1651 to 1653 in an unsuccessful attempt to petition Parliament for her husband's sequestered estates. From then on Margaret – who never had any children of her own despite much anguish and grim medical interventions – embarked upon a prolific and varied publishing career. Her works cover the genres not only of poetry, drama, and natural philosophy but also essays, orations, romance, biography, and letters.

She began writing her first volume of *Playes* (1662) while still in Antwerp, but publication was delayed by the loss of the manuscript at sea en route for England. *The Convent of Pleasure* was printed in her second and final volume of dramatic works, *Plays, Never Before Printed* (1668). Nevertheless, it strongly registers the theatrical, literary, and philosophical interests of her formative years during the civil war and interregnum as well as the conditions of life after 1660. For, despite the restoration of their Stuart masters to the throne, Margaret and William found themselves largely ignored by the new regime under Charles II and devoted their lives to rebuilding their shattered country estates. Whilst William was to live well into old age, Margaret predeceased him by three years, dying in 1673 at the age of fifty after a sudden illness.[119]

Cavendish's plays evidence an enduring preoccupation with women performers of all kinds. *Youth's Glory and Death's Banquet* (1662) and *The Sociable Companions* (1668), for example, present courtship as explicit role-play in a manner akin to *The Wild-Goose Chase*. Yet, in *The Female Academy* (1662) and *The Convent of Pleasure*, the concept of female performance is largely uncoupled from the goal of wooing potential husbands, becoming instead a means of self-realisation and recreation as well a tool with which to explore and challenge the bounds of conventional feminine social identities. This is made possible in *The Convent of Pleasure* by a plot in which Lady Happy and her band of women decide to 'incloister' (1.2.15) themselves simply in order to 'enjoy pleasure' (1.2.95) free from the restraints of marriage and male company. The motif of the separatist female community clearly echoes *The Female Academy* which presents an educational institution that excludes men and teaches women the skills of public speaking and rhetorical disputation, but *The Convent of Pleasure* goes even further in severing its female characters' experiments with performance from either educational or matrimonial ambitions.

Both plays draw on a common Shakespearean source in *Love's Labour's Lost* with the monastic pretensions of its all-male 'academe' (2.1.13), ostensibly sealed off from the incursions of the opposite sex.[120] Much of the comic impetus and dramatic tension in all three pieces turns on the efforts of the invading group of women or men to win over those who have sworn to reject them, with a foreign princess as the pivotal visitor from the outside in both *Love's Labour's Lost* and *The Convent of Pleasure*. Yet, despite Shakespeare's famous last-minute deferral of the anticipated nuptial conclusion, his male courtiers succumb to female charm relatively early on in that play and devote their energies overwhelmingly to wooing. In contrast, the women of *The Female Academy* and *The Convent of Pleasure* appear unconcerned with the activities of the men until the final scenes reveal somewhat perfunctory comic closures in marriage. Such a closure is interestingly catalysed in *The Convent of Pleasure* by the fifth-act arrival of an 'ambassador' from a potentially hostile neighbour state (who reveals the visiting 'princess' as his prince), thereby echoing the unexpected appearance of a French messenger in the court of Navarre who conversely disrupts the comic structure of *Love's Labour's Lost* by announcing the death of his princess's father.

The action of both comedies turns importantly on the device of the play-within-a-play, albeit with significantly different emphases in each case. Where the pageant of the worthies staged by Holofernes, the pedant, in the final scene of *Love's Labour's Lost* serves as a burlesque to console the courtiers that there is 'one show worse than the King's and his company' (5.2.509–10), Cavendish's Act 3 interlude – with its series of short scenes gravely depicting the miseries of marriage and childbearing for women – elicits sympathy for the plight of characters across the social spectrum, including the 'mean women' (3.2) and 'citizen's wife' (3.6) who might be expected to be a traditional butt of 'low' comedy. In the (failed) stratagems of Shakespeare's male courtiers to woo the women by dressing up as 'Muscovites or Russians' (5.2.121), as in the women's cunning rebuttal by means of trickery and mask-wearing, *Love's Labour's Lost* foregrounds courtship as the motivating force behind such acting games. Although Lady Happy (unlike Shakespeare's women) is duped by male disguise when she finds that the interloping princess is actually a cross-dressing prince, the fact that she remains ignorant of his sex until the very end distances their lavishly masque-like enactments of wooing in Act 4 from the more pragmatic approach to heterosexual courtship goals in *Love's Labour's Lost*. Indeed 'act[ing] lovers' parts' (3.1.14–15) is simply one element of the ladies' dramatic activities in the convent, with their all-female theatricals serving variously as a medium of instruction, display of authority, and sheer recreation, releasing the characters to enjoy fantasy worlds and allowing Cavendish – through her protagonists – to expound her recurrent intellectual concerns with natural philosophy and theories of good government.

Like *Love's Labour's Lost*, *The Convent of Pleasure* provides a platform for another of Cavendish's preoccupations: namely, the pros and cons of marriage. While Shakespeare initially focuses on male resistance to matrimony, Cavendish takes a more unusual line in expounding the case against marriage for women. If we read *The Convent of Pleasure* in the context of the entire volume of her *Plays* (1668) we can see the nuptial theme continued from her previous play, *The Bridals*. The groomsmen of the earlier play, Take-Pleasure, Facil, Adviser, and Courtly, reappear as thwarted would-be wooers, excluded from the convent. Similarly, Lady Amorous and Lady Virtue from *The Bridals* resurface in 2.3 of *The Convent of Pleasure* to continue the former play's illustration of differing approaches to marriage as well as fleshing out the theoretical debates on marriage in 1.2 of *The Convent of Pleasure* and anticipating its Act 3 series of playlets on the woes of matrimony for women. True to her name, Lady Virtue has made a contented marriage, but Lady Amorous (née Lady Coy) is 'not so well as I wish I were' (2.3.3) having lurched from excessive prudery to its extreme opposite in marrying Sir John Amorous. This may imply a moral criticism of Lady Amorous's conduct in marriage, but the main thrust of the discussion of women and marriage in *The Convent of Pleasure* is to outline the manifold disadvantages it can bring to them through no fault of their own. As Lady Happy trenchantly puts it, 'women, where fortune, nature, and the gods are joined to make them happy, were mad to live with men, who make the female sex their slaves' (1.2.106–9). The fact that Lady Happy succumbs to marriage in Act 5 seems too generically predictable to efface the play's earlier critique of matrimony. Some critics have pointed out that the presence of printed slips in many copies of *The Convent of Pleasure* alerting us to the fact that some, at least, of the final two scenes were 'Written by my Lord Duke', may suggest that Cavendish herself was not directly responsible for writing the marital closure.[121] Nevertheless, she must have been aware of the generic impetus towards marital closure and the proleptic ironies which underlie Lady Happy's apparent ignorance of her wooer's true sex.

Some of Cavendish's reflections on marriage in her other writings appear simply to reiterate conventional advice on the need for women to strive to please their husbands once married,[122] but we also have other evidence of her exploring the more polemical approach to the subject taken by Lady Happy. In her *Orations of Divers Sorts* (1662), for example, *A Young New-Married Wif's Funeral Oration* states that 'Death is far the Happier Condition than Marriage' (168) while *A Child-Bed Womans Funeral Oration* considers 'those Women . . . most Happy that Never Marry', concluding that the dead woman 'Lives not to Indure more Pain or Slavery' (183).[123] The *querelle des femmes* had intermittently recognised the potential hardships women might suffer in marriage but tended to counsel patience or heavenly reward as the solution.[124] Yet, the marital perils catalogued in the Act 3 playlets of *The Convent of Pleasure* do resonate with some of the pre-existing pamphlet literature of the times. For example, William Heale, in *An Apology for Women* (1609), offers 'a sober and reasoned argument against wife beating' while Edward Gosynhill, in *Mulierum paean* (1542?), considers the sufferings of women in labour.[125] However, even by the mid to late seventeenth century, Cavendish was relatively unusual in having her characters put forward so unequivocally the view that a single life was to be preferred for women, despite the fact that this period saw a peak in the numbers of unmarried women and thus it might appear an apt moment positively to celebrate the virtues of their state.[126]

This demographic feature may have had its impact on contemporary Roman Catholic arguments encouraging girls to eschew marriage and adopt the cloister instead. Literary considerations of marriage in the post-Reformation period were necessarily often influenced by the desire to valorise a Christian 'ideal of conjugal affection' in opposition to 'the medieval Catholic ideal of chastity, as a legal obligation for priests, monks and nuns and as an ideal for all members of the Christian community'.[127] Yet, the backlash against Protestant attempts to raise the religious stakes of marriage opens the way for a critique of matrimony from the woman's point of view and offers Cavendish a precedent for Lady Happy's quasi-monastic withdrawal and rejection of men, claiming, 'marriage to those that are virtuous is a greater restraint than a monastery' (1.2.21–2). The title page of Lawrence Anderton's *The English Nunne* (1642), for example, states that he 'endeavoureth to draw young and unmarried Catholike Gentlewomen to imbrace a Votary, and Religious Life'. He goes on to try to persuade them by showing 'the accustomed miseries of a married lyfe, and of having issue' with accounts of childbirth, husbandly infidelity, or dissipation of 'Estate and Patrimony' which smack of the scenes in Act 3 of *The Convent of Pleasure*.[128]

Yet, if pro-monastic arguments against marriage offer Cavendish a partial template for Lady Happy's opinions and conduct, she is never-theless ultimately highly critical of religious monasticism, presenting the convent of pleasure as an alternative to either married life or the religious cloister for women. Like the topic of marriage, monasticism becomes the subject of a set-piece debate between Lady Happy and her waiting-woman, Madam Mediator, in the early stages of the play, with the former representing religious asceticism merely as an affectation 'for opinion's sake' (1.2.40–41) and at 'variance' with 'nature' (54), not because it is natural for humans to marry but because no 'rational creature' (41) can possibly 'think or believe the gods take delight in the creature's uneasy life' (41–2). Cavendish's other writings show that she was clearly attracted by elements of the life of monastic withdrawal, as in her story 'The She Anchoret' in which a woman rejects marriage and lives 'incloistred by her selfe alone; vowing chastity, and a single life'.[129] Even here, however, a preface tells readers that the main aim of this mise-en-scène is to allow the author to use the 'anchoret' as a mouthpiece to expound ideas about natural philosophy that she wishes she had added to her last scientific work (p. 393). Lady Happy's trenchant critique of monastic asceticism is, finally, consistent with the views put forward by Cavendish in her most thoroughgoing treatment of the subject, the essay on 'A Monastical Life' in her *Worlds Olio* (1655, pp. 30–1). The degree to which such a topic might function as a ready fulcrum for religious disagreement in her period is demonstrated by the fact that the views she expressed in her essay drew the fire of an earnest Roman Catholic critic, Du Verger, who denounced Cavendish's opinions as morally corrupt.[130]

Nevertheless, the notion of the architectural space of the convent as a site of liberation does have some suggestive contemporary corollaries, not least the order of nuns founded by Henrietta Maria at the Chaillot estate, near Paris, in 1651, which sought to eschew austerity in favour of comfort. Cavendish had, of course, been nurtured in the abbey of St John's as a child, and her husband's country home at Welbeck Abbey had a history of staging aristocratic theatricals within a one-time convent setting.[131] *The Convent of Pleasure* may also draw on a tradition of female recreation in convent theatricals.[132]

Positing an alternative both to religious monasticism and marriage for women, then, the play embraces the virtues of retreat as a means to enjoy pleasure in a secular sense. Yet, for Lady Happy, the word 'pleasure' tends to diverge from the more salacious or morally dubious overtones which might otherwise accompany it in this context, as she eschews the frivolous or sexualised inflections epitomised in Shirley's representation of female pleasure-seeking in *The Lady of Pleasure* (1635), a play to which Cavendish evidently pays titular homage. Hence, although the play may be read as poking gentle fun at Lady Happy for her unwitting infatuation with the disguised prince, despite having forsworn male company, Cavendish presents an ostensibly non-phallocentric fantasy of collective female self-indulgence in a manner clearly distinct from the satirical vein which characterises a number of precursor depictions of separatist female communities in Jacobean and Caroline drama such as the female commonwealths of Fletcher's *The Sea Voyage* (1622) and Cartwright's *The Lady Errant* (1637).

Whilst obliquely related to these, *The Convent of Pleasure* offers a more direct reworking of Shirley's handling of a single-sex retreat in *The Bird in a Cage*, challenging some of the satirical containments which sometimes appear to hedge his exploration of all-female community and performance. Drawing on the thespian pursuits of Henrietta Maria and her ladies at court, Lady Happy and her companions 'accoutre themselves in masculine habits and act lovers' parts' (3.1.14–15), heightening the connection with court drama in Act 4 by the assumption of the pastoral mode which invariably characterised the queen's theatricals. As already seen, Shirley's account of courtly female acting oscillates teasingly between the loyal defence mandated by his office and an approach which seems to respond to contemporary suspicions. From the outset his play depicts the women's sexual desire for men chafing at their enforced all-female seclusion, with their playacting presented as an extension of such frustrated desire. On one level, the decision to act the story of Jupiter and Danae wryly reflects their barely disguised hopes that a male lover will penetrate their confinement. The link between sexuality and acting culminates in the near-lesbian encounter between Donella and Eugenia (playing Jupiter and Danae). Where *The Bird in a Cage* insinuates that exclusively female groupings may be underpinned or subverted by women's heterosexual desire, *The Convent of Pleasure* goes much further towards offering the model of an all-female society as self-sufficient. The voluntary seclusion of Lady Happy and her women is untroubled by the overt longing for men which plagues Eugenia's companions. Unlike the suggestive interlude about Jupiter and Danae, the histrionic pursuits of the convent allow some credence to the Platonic love theme so central to Henrietta Maria's all-female dramas, with Lady Happy and the princess playing out the roles of 'mistress' and 'loving servant' (3.1.9, 16). The withheld disclosure that Lady Happy's female lover is a man allows a more serious exploration of love between women despite the ironic hints which emerge with the benefit of hindsight. Although the dénouement reveals the princess to be an interloping prince, the withholding of the dramatis personae until the end of the play in print may reinforce the first-time reader's acceptance of him as a woman until the last moment, since the play was not performed.

Lady Happy's rhetorical question, 'But why may not I love a woman with the same affection I could a man?' (4.1.3–4), epitomises the play's interest in the acceptable boundaries of female same-sex relations.[133] The deliberations of Lady Happy and the princess on this matter appear to reflect the ambivalent attitude identified by recent commentators who argue that, while such relations were far from invisible in early modern literature, during the seventeenth century even representations of avowedly chaste affection between women might come to be regarded as potentially suspicious.[134] The clearest analogue for Cavendish's ostensible depiction of a courtly love relationship between women lies in the poems of her contemporary Katherine Philips.[135] The princess's suggestion that she and Lady Happy should 'mingle souls together' (4.1.19–20) echoes the Platonic construct so central to Philips's depiction of loving relationships between women.[136] Similarly, in Cavendish's own fantasy voyage, *The Description of a New World Called the Blazing-World* (1666), the soul of her namesake, the Duchess of Newcastle, combines with that of the Empress of the Blazing World to 'produce such an intimate friendship between them, that they became *Platonick* Lovers, although they were both *Females*' (92). Yet *Blazing World* also reminds us that Cavendish was capable of a satirical approach to the possible pretensions of Platonic love and its potential abuse as a cover for illicit sexual activity as evidenced in the ironic fervency of the princess and Lady Happy's supposedly innocent kiss (4.1.24SD).[137]

The Convent of Pleasure's relationship to courtly female performance, and to the model of female community it provided, is further elucidated by comparison with Montagu's *The Shepherds' Paradise*. Cavendish may have seen one of the manuscript versions or read the first printed edition, which appeared in 1659.[138] Both *The Convent of Pleasure* and *The Shepherds' Paradise* centre on eponymous female-governed, quasi-monastic retreats for those of noble birth, with the sanctuary being infiltrated in each case by a disguised prince. While the 'Brothers' and 'Sisters' entering the 'Order' of the shepherds' paradise 'vow chastity and single life', the women inhabitants of the convent of pleasure 'live a single life and vow virginity' (1.2.113).[139] Yet, where Cavendish presents a more self-sufficient female community that attempts to exclude men altogether, the shepherds' paradise functions as a haven for unrequited lovers of both sexes driven there by thwarted matrimonial aspirations rather than personal preference. Once a year the queen of Montagu's retreat licenses male and female inhabitants to marry one another and leave if they so wish. Miranda's refusal of the king's offer of marriage provides some precedent for the rejection of marriage championed throughout the greater part of *The Convent of Pleasure*. Yet, on the whole, *The Shepherds' Paradise* depicts a negatively motivated withdrawal from the world which may, with luck, be alleviated by marriage which differs markedly from the eager espousal of retreat in Cavendish's play.

The self-sufficiency of the female community in *The Convent of Pleasure* – with 'women for every office and employment' (2.1.65) – extends to their refusal to allow the male gaze to sanction their activities or constitute their identity. Lady Happy refuses to have any 'grates about the cloister' (2.1.56), much to the frustration of the excluded men who even consider trying to take bricks out of the wall so they can 'peek' in (2.4.29). This contrasts sharply with Montagu's play where, although the shepherds' paradise is governed by a female monarch elected by the votes of women only, the stipulation that 'beauty' must be the chief criterion in the election reminds us that female power here is entirely dependent on an approving external gaze. The arch suggestion that men are excluded from the voting because they might be too partial to one woman underlines the all-important evaluating gaze of male members of the audience (p. 27). After all, one of its central purposes was to provide an idealised display of Henrietta Maria in her role as Queen Bellesa, the *apogée* of beauty. As others have pointed out, certain plays by Cavendish explore this link between feminine control and women's manipulation of 'erotic spectacle'.[140] Yet, *The Convent of Pleasure* appears to challenge rather than restate the gender dynamics of female display associated with the Caroline court and its drama. The assured authority of Lady Happy and her women is not dependent on manipulating male onlookers through visual display (even if withholding it gives them a perverse power over the men). Instead Cavendish suggests that it is the male characters whose stability relies on being able to look rather than the women who need to be looked upon. The panicky disarray of the men when they cannot see the women may be seen to expose the manner in which men in the Platonic culture of the Caroline court reinforce their sense of identity through chivalrous admiration of female beauty.

In the impressive scene shifting of Act 4 Cavendish draws not only on Henrietta Maria's pastoral drama but on the staging conventions of court masques in the Jacobean and Caroline period – in particular the sliding shutters of Inigo Jones's stage designs and the masques of Ben Jonson.[141] Tanya Wood points out that the description of a masque in Cavendish's story 'The Contract', where 'lords and ladies come down in a scene', suggests her familiarity with such technical developments.[142] The much greater specificity (compared to the Act 3 playlets) of the pastoral and marine settings described in Act 4, along with the seamless visual transformations implied by the way in which they 'vanish' (4.1.159SD, 290SD), suggest that Cavendish may have been imagining the use of sliding shutters here. The iconic presentation of Lady Happy and the Princess as pastoral figures or as Neptune and a sea-goddess is also highly redolent of the mythical roles taken by royalty and the aristocracy in court masques and entertainments.[143] Like Henrietta Maria's Platonic pastoral dramas, the masque provides Cavendish with another enabling version of female performance. In placing her series of playlets on the woes of womanhood, with their inclusion of sub-aristocratic characters and glances at low comedy, before the masque-like scenes of Act 4, Cavendish may be gesturing towards the use of a so-called antimasque in Jonsonian masquing convention.[144] Here the main masque is preceded by an antimasque in which low or disruptive forces are represented only to be banished by the governing forces of order played by king, queen, or courtiers. Yet, the sense of inclusive sympathy and serious engagement which *The Convent of Pleasure* generates towards all the women in the playlets (irrespective of social rank) also suggests a reworking of the structural logic usually associated with the antimasque.

The Convent of Pleasure evidently owes a great deal to the dramatic traditions of the Jacobean and Caroline courts in a manner inextricably connected to the vicissitudes of Cavendish's fortunes as a Stuart loyalist. Her recollections of pre-civil-war theatrical culture pick up on the spirit of interregnum royalist nostalgia for the disbanded court that prevailed during the 1650s when she first began writing plays. While the play appeared after the Restoration when Cavendish was no longer exiled abroad, the political marginalisation experienced by the Newcastles after 1660 functioned as a form of internal exile. Julie Crawford reads the play's detailed concern with lavish arrangements for household comfort and security as a reaction not only to Cavendish's experiences of the degradation of the Lucas and Newcastle country estates in the civil war but also to the post-Restoration royalist sense that the new regime was taking insufficient care to help its supporters rebuild their property.[145] The embracing of pastoralised retreat recalls other royalist literary responses to the period of exile and decisive defeat. The play's depiction of rural sports and games suggests the pastoral activities of Shakespeare's *As You Like It* and *The Winter's Tale*. The conventional pastoral *topos* of the wooing competition – imaged here in the first and second shepherds' competition for the hand of Lady Happy, figured as the 'daughter' of Madam Mediator (4.1.43) – is suggestive of Sir Philip Sidney's entertainment *The Lady of May*, performed for Elizabeth I at Wanstead Manor in Essex in 1578 or 1579 in which two shepherds vie for the daughter of a country woman.[146] *The King's Entertainment at Welbeck* also features a May-Lady and rustic 'maids', while three shepherds woo three shepherdesses in the Cavendish sisters' *Pastorall*.[147] Hence *The Convent of Pleasure* draws on the rustic festivities which became a topic of controversy between royalists and disapproving puritans from the 1620s onwards, and which we have identified in this edition as an active theme in *The Wild-Goose Chase* and *The Bird in a Cage*.[148]

THE TEXTS

The Wild-Goose Chase
The Wild-Goose Chase was omitted from the Beaumont and Fletcher First Folio of 1647 because, according to the stationer Humphrey Moseley, it had been borrowed from the actors by 'a *person of quality*' and '(by the negligence of a Servant) it was never return'd'.[149] Whether or not the manuscript that was subsequently discovered was the one that was lost, Moseley's appeal for the text's restoration was answered, and the play was published in a lavish folio edition in 1652 (*F1*). *F1* is the copy-text for this edition.

In his critical old-spelling edition of *The Wild-Goose Chase*, Fredson Bowers deduces that the text was printed in two sections, probably in two different printing-shops, and he finds evidence of three compositors at work, one on the first section and two on the second section.[150] Both Lister and Bowers surmise that the copy-text for the 1652 edition is likely to have been a playhouse prompt book, adducing as evidence the placement of stage directions in the right-hand margin and the completeness of the dramatis personae.[151] Two stage directions in *F1* indicate entries in the prompt book for the 1632 revival: sig. I2v of *F1* reads, in the right-hand margin, '*Enter Lever- / duce, des Lugier, / Mr Illiard.*' (this edition,

3.1.311SD). A copy of *F1* in the University Library, Cambridge, contains
the stage direction, on sig. K2v, '*Enter, Mirabell, Pinac, Mariana, Priest,
R. Baxt. Attendants*' (this edition, 4.1.22SD). Eyllaerdt Swanston joined
the King's Men *c.*1624 and Richard Baxter is recorded as playing parts
for the company from 1628.

Critics have remarked on the attention paid to women as audience and
readers of Beaumont and Fletcher's plays, both by the dramatists in pro-
logues and epilogues and in the prefatory matter to the 1647 folio.[152] The
collation for this edition revealed material evidence of female readership.
One copy of the 1647 folio is marked 'Florence Baber Her Booke', while
a copy of the 1652 folio of *The Wild-Goose Chase* bears the inscription,
'Dorothy Wind hers'. A third inscription reads: 'Edward Proger / his
Booke / Catherine Proger' (see Appendix A for details of these inscribed
copies). A sceptic might supply a fourth line reading 'his Wife', but the
optimistic interpreter may find in this joint signature evidence of a
couple's mutual pleasure in play-reading.

For the purposes of this edition sixteen copies of *F1* have been collated
and the press variants checked against those recorded by Bowers and
Lister. A number of new variants and states were found in both sections
of the text.

The Bird in a Cage

The first edition of *The Bird in a Cage* was the 1633 quarto (henceforth
Q) printed by Bernard Alsop and Thomas Fawcett for William Cooke, a
Holborn publisher with whom Shirley had an ongoing relationship (see
p. 22). It was published soon after the play's initial performance at the
Cockpit theatre in Drury Lane, also known as the Phoenix, which is the
name by which it is referred to on the title page. The title page also carries
a unique reference to Shirley as a 'Servant to Her Majesty'. The final corrected version of this has been deployed as the copy-text for this edition.
In all seventeen copies were collated. The collation process has involved
rechecking some of the US-held copies seen by Senescu for her 1948
edition of the play and adding extensive evidence from UK-held copies
for the first time.

Though it was not uncommon for plays to be published soon after
their first performance, the speed with which *The Bird in a Cage* appears
to have travelled through the press may be explained in part by the publishers' understanding that it was a timely publication in view of its contribution to the debate over female theatricals stirred up by Prynne's
Histriomastix. The existence of at least four stages of correction in extant
copies of Q strengthens this suggestion, first put forward by Senescu
(p. iii). The four states indicate a compositor trying to make sense of

difficult formes while the printing job was in progress, undertaking multiple stop-press corrections in some instances until he had got the sense
right. The inclusion of an Errata page at K4r is a further indicator that
Q had been printed at some speed, causing various slips. The best example
of this can be seen in the three variant states of B4v. While Gifford offered
an emendation at ll. 2–6 in his 1833 edition that to him made better sense
than the quarto reading, Senescu was able to prove that this was a genuine
textual variant, available in her personal copy of Q. She suggested that
it indicated a third attempt by the compositor to make sense of a confused section in the manuscript from which he was working. The problem
for the modern reader of her edition is that Senescu offered no indication
of the provenance of her copy, nor do we know where this copy is now.
In checking her claims against copies of Q held in British libraries,
however, we have been able to confirm this third state in at least three
copies (one in the British Library, another at St John's College, Oxford,
and the third at King's College, Cambridge). Gifford's hunch turns out to
have substantial textual endorsement. The Bridgewater Library copy of
Q now in the Huntington Library is another interesting case: on C1r and
C4r there appear to be unique variants (at least among copies so far
viewed). The Huntington copy seems to derive from somewhere in the
early to middle period of the print run, since it corrects some variants
while retaining others. Copies in the Folger Shakespeare Library and that
at St John's College, Oxford, appear to be versions from late in the run
(for full details see Appendix A).

There have been only three editions of *The Bird in a Cage* following
Q. In 1745 Robert Dodsley included the play, along with another by
Shirley, *The Gamester*, in his *Select Collection of Old Plays*. This modernised spelling and punctuation but did not involve any collation work.
In 1833, William Gifford edited *The Bird in a Cage* for the second volume
of his edition of Shirley's complete works, co-produced with Alexander
Dyce. Gifford also modernised spelling and punctuation, reduced the
number of capitals, and smoothed out metrical irregularities. He added
considerable editorial material in the form of stage directions, asides, and
indications of location. In this edition, many of his stage directions and
asides have been preserved, but the indications of location, in accordance
with Revels editorial practice, have been omitted. As is typical of Gifford's
editorial practice, he undertook only limited collation and therefore
certain variants are wrongly identified as misprints in Dodsley. Nevertheless many of his emendations are sound and have since been found to
have textual provenance.

In 1948 Frances Frazier Senescu produced her edition of *The Bird in
a Cage* as a doctoral thesis at the University of Chicago. This was pub-

lished in 1980 as part of the Garland series. Readers of this edition are directed to her detailed analysis of the compositorial history of *Q* in that edition. We have merely updated the material provided there in terms of press variants and included this in Appendix A; no substantial departures from her interpretation of the evidence have emerged. Her edition of the text was, however, a reconstruction of *Q*, whereas we have modernised spelling and punctuation for our edition.

The Convent of Pleasure

Margaret Cavendish's two folio volumes of dramatic writings, *Playes* (1662) and *Plays, Never Before Printed* (1668), which contains *The Convent of Pleasure*, did not appear in any subsequent editions. The version of *The Convent of Pleasure* that appears in *Plays, Never Before Printed* (henceforth *F*) is the copy-text for this edition. Comparisons between nineteen copies of *F* yielded evidence of only two printed variants in *The Convent of Pleasure*. There are also a small number of manuscript adaptations in a seventeenth-century hand which have been collated where significant spelling modernisations are involved. Printed slips pasted into the text to indicate contributions made to the play by Cavendish's husband, William, have been recorded in Appendix A.[153] *The Convent of Pleasure* exists in two other minimally edited editions: Rowsell (1995) and Shaver (1999). Rowsell, who takes Oxford's Bodleian Library, Vet. A3. c. 113, as her copy-text, defines her edition as 'almost a facsimile' but with discretionary modernisation of spelling. Meanwhile, Shaver – using the Newberry Library copy – retains the original spelling and punctuation 'with a few noted exceptions'. Significant departures from *F*'s spelling and punctuation in these editions have been recorded in the collations.

STAGE HISTORIES

The Wild-Goose Chase

The success of *The Wild-Goose Chase* on the stage is attested by the title page to the 1652 folio, which states that it was 'acted with singular applause at the Blackfriars'. Although the first recorded performance was at the court of King James on 24 January 1622, it is likely that Fletcher's comedy was performed publicly earlier that season.[154] It was revived by the King's Men in 1632 and it is this performance which is recorded and celebrated in the descriptive cast-list printed with the first edition.[155] The play's popularity in Fletcher's lifetime is invoked in the dedication to the folio by the two leading players of the King's Men, John Lowin and Joseph Taylor, who acted Belleur and Mirabell:

The play was of so general a received acceptance that, he himself a spectator, we have known him unconcerned, and to have wished it had been
none of his; he, as well as the thronged theatre (in despite of his innate
modesty) applauding this rare issue of his brain. ('The Dedication',
ll. 8–12)

This exquisite cameo of a diffident Fletcher moved to applaud his own
play captures the urbane tone of the private playhouses before the closure
of the theatres. That *The Wild-Goose Chase* was lucrative is shown by
the fact that Sir Henry Herbert, the Master of the Revels, chose it as his
winter's benefit play in 1632, earning the large sum of £15 as his share
of the receipts.[156] Parliament's ban on stage plays and the straying of the
King's Men's playbook put *The Wild-Goose Chase* out of theatrical and
printed circulation (see above, 'The Texts'); however, the publication of
the play in 1652, with its elaborate cast-list, encouraged readers to visu-
alise the stellar performances of the Caroline era. The descriptions praising the acting of select members of the King's Men suggest that theatrical
performance formed part of the literary connoisseurship that was an out-
growth of the private theatre culture.[157]

When public playing recommenced prior to the Restoration, Fletcher's
comedy featured in the repertory of John Rhodes's company acting at the
Cockpit and it was staged by the newly formed King's company in
February 1662.[158] On 11 January 1668 Samuel Pepys recorded having
seen *The Wild-Goose Chase* at 'the King's House' (i.e. the Theatre Royal),
which he had 'long longed to see, it being a famous play', but he was dis-
appointed, finding 'nothing extraordinary at all, but very dull inventions
and designs'.[159]

Pepys's dissatisfaction with Fletcher's play was undoubtedly influenced
by the fact that dramatists such as John Dryden and George Etherege
were writing contemporary comedies of sexual intrigue against which *The
Wild-Goose Chase* may have seemed dated and tired. The play went
unperformed for the next three decades, until at the turn of the century
it was supplanted by George Farquhar's adaptation, *The Inconstant; or,
The Way to Win Him*, which was performed at Drury Lane in February
1702. *The Inconstant* was a new vehicle for the leading actor Robert
Wilks, after his success as the hero of Farquhar's *Sir Harry Wildair*, produced in April of the previous season.[160] In his dedication, Farquhar
instances his Young Mirabel and Wildair as examples of his generally
credited skill 'in drawing a gay, splendid, generous, easie, fine young
Gentleman'.[161] His cast streamlines Fletcher's original: Mirabell's two
companions become 'Captain Duretete', while the airy sisters are con-
densed into '*Bisarre. A whimsical Lady*'. Farquhar's genial prose comedy
replaces the outrageous brilliance of Fletcher's Jacobean play with a lev-

elling sentimentality and didacticism.[162] Instead of appearing as a great
Italian lady, Oriana's last disguise is as a pretty boy, a gender switch which
was injected with a new realism by the professional actress but by 1702
had become a theatrical cliché. Hired by Young Mirabel as his page,
Oriana saves him from murder at the hands of the bravoes attending
Lamorce, a fleecing whore whom he has taken for a rich beauty at the
playhouse. The multilateral victory and sprightly repartee of Fletcher's
final scene is narrowed in Farquhar's recension to a demonstration of how
a man may tell a good woman from a bad. But for Young Mirabel's and
Oriana's trading the threats of divorce and alimony, we might almost be
back at the outset of Elizabethan drama.

Shoichiro Kawai observes that 'actors' virtuosity always comprises a
vital aspect of Fletcher's drama'.[163] As he points out, the climax of *The
Wild-Goose Chase* hinges upon the boy actor's ability convincingly to
portray Oriana's new voluptuousness in her Italian guise.[164] The theatrical effectiveness of both Fletcher's and Farquhar's plays is indicated by
the latter's becoming a 'perennial repertory piece'[165] on the English stage
in the eighteenth and nineteenth centuries, featuring celebrated actors
such as David Garrick in the role of Durete, Charles Kemble as Young
Mirabel, and Peg Woffington, famed for her breeches parts, as Oriana.
During this time *The Wild-Goose Chase* was staged only once, in 1747,
for the benefit of the actress Kitty Clive, who played Lillia-Bianca.[166]
There were four documented productions of Fletcher's comedy in the
early twentieth century, but none of these met with sufficient acclaim to
give *The Wild-Goose Chase* an enduring life in the theatre.[167] The last
decade has witnessed a revival of interest in Fletcherian drama from both
a critical and a theatrical standpoint; this has issued in successful productions by the Royal Shakespeare Company of *The Island Princess* and
The Tamer Tamed.[168] *The Wild-Goose Chase* was staged in an abridged
version by students of the Royal Academy of Dramatic Art, London, in
2000. Directed by Gregory de Polnay, this performance created an effect
of perpetual motion, the focus of the action constantly shifting between
the male and female leads, but conveying a strong impression of the
women exercising control.[169] One hopes for a full production of Fletcher's
comedy that will do justice to its extraordinary theatrical energy and its
'robust and masterly expression [and] imagination'.[170]

The Bird in a Cage
What little evidence we have for the original staging of *The Bird in a Cage*
derives from the title page of Q, where we are informed that the play was
first performed at the Phoenix theatre in Drury Lane. This is the theatre
better known to current historians of the period as the Cockpit. Shirley

had a close relationship with this playhouse and its resident company, the Queen's Men, further strengthening the links between *The Bird in a Cage* and the theatrical interests and innovations of Henrietta Maria, the company's patron. No further details of the initial performance have been traced. If supposition about the play's title in performance being *The Bewties* is correct, it is likely that this performance took place as early as January 1633 (when the play of that name was entered in the Stationers' Register), prior to the switch of title in advance of publication.

Allardyce Nicoll found evidence for possible Restoration revivals in a document dated 20 August 1668 in the Lord Chamberlain's papers which lists *The Bird in a Cage* among the 'Playes allowed to be acted by his Royal Highnesse ye Duke of Yorkes Comoedians'.[171] There was an eighteenth-century performance at Covent Garden on 24 April 1786, a benefit performance for an actor called Quick, when the play carried the telling subtitle *Money Works Wonders*. Some critics also suggested that Thomas Dibdin's opera *The Cabinet*, which also played at Covent Garden, on 9 February 1802, was influenced in its device of the bird-cage, although Dibdin himself denied this.[172]

The play has not been much revived on the commercial stage since 1633, perhaps because its reputation became so closely bound up with the Prynne scandal – although, as we argue in this introduction, the play's composition and performance predate the furore over Prynne's outburst. It was the preliminary materials such as the dedication, added to the printed edition of the play, which cemented that relationship. We have not been able to trace any recent productions in either a professional or amateur capacity, although the play's extended interest in questions of gender and performance make it ripe for retrieval by a modern theatre company.

The Convent of Pleasure

As the general introduction has already indicated, Margaret Cavendish's attraction towards a pre-Restoration theatrical aesthetic in *The Convent of Pleasure* registers in the play's status as closet drama. Yet some recent commentators have been highly resistant to designating any of her plays with this label, fearing that it somehow diminishes them, treating them as 'unperformable' because 'unperformed'.[173] These sentiments gave rise to what appears to be the first ever performance of the central section of *The Convent of Pleasure* at the University College of Ripon and York St John on 4 March 1995, under the direction of Gweno Williams and Bill Pinner.[174] The convent wall which, as Williams notes, 'simultaneously confines and protects the women', was at various points in the play scaled, albeit unsuccessfully, by drunken men; it became the focal point of the set, 'an important physical presence' (p. 142). The wall self-consciously

recalls Shirley's 'New Prison' in *The Bird in a Cage*, another stage thresh-
old that is breached in the course of performance, and is a further indicator of Cavendish's subtle understandings of theatrical practice and the
'mechanics of stage production' (p. 141). The York production cast 'an
identifiably male' actor in the role of the prince/princess, although a later
performance at the University of Auckland deliberately sought to preserve
the possibilities of gender fluidity by assigning the part to a more androg-
ynous performer.[175]

NOTES

1 Michael Shapiro, 'The Introduction of Actresses in England: Delay or Defensiveness?', in Viviana Comensoli and Anne Russell (eds), *Enacting Gender on the
  Renaissance Stage* (Urbana and Chicago: University of Illinois Press, 1999), pp.
  177–200.
2 Elizabeth Howe, *The First English Actresses: Women and Drama, 1660–1700*
  (Cambridge University Press, 1992).
3 See, e.g., Richard W. Bevis, *English Drama: Restoration and Eighteenth Century,
  1660–1789* (London: Longmans, 1988), p. 35; Sandra Richards, *The Rise of the
  English Actress* (Basingstoke: Macmillan, 1993). Histories influenced by Howe,
  The First English Actresses, who acknowledges the significance of Caroline inno-
  vation in the realm of women and theatre, include Deborah Payne Fisk, 'The
  Restoration Actress', in Susan J. Owen (ed.), *A Companion to Restoration Drama*
  (Oxford: Blackwells, 2001), pp. 69–91; and Ann Thompson, 'Women/"women"
  and the Stage', in Helen Wilcox (ed.), *Women and Literature in Britain,
  1500–1700* (Cambridge University Press, 1996), pp. 100–16.
4 Groundbreaking studies in this area include Clare McManus (ed.), *Women and
  Culture at the Courts of the Stuart Queens* (London: Palgrave, 2003); Karen Brit-
  land, 'Neoplatonic Identities: Literary Representation and the Politics of Queen
  Henrietta Maria's Court Circle' (unpublished PhD dissertation, University of
  Leeds, 2000). Sophie Tomlinson's monograph *Women on Stage in Stuart Drama*
  (Cambridge University Press, forthcoming), will further widen the discussion.
5 See, for example, Hero Chalmers, 'The Politics of Feminine Retreat in Margaret
  Cavendish's *The Female Academy* and *The Convent of Pleasure*', *Women's
  Writing*, 6 (1999), 81–94; Julie Sanders, ' "A Woman Write a Play!": Jonsonian
  Strategies in the Dramatic Writing of Margaret Cavendish; or, Did the Duchess
  Feel the Anxiety of Influence', in S.P. Cerasano and Marion Wynne-Davies (eds),
  Readings in Renaissance Women's Drama (London: Routledge, 1998), pp.
  293–305; Sophie Tomlinson, ' "She that Plays the King": Henrietta Maria and the
  Threat of the Actress in Caroline Culture', in Gordon McMullan and Jonathan
  Hope (eds), *The Politics of Tragicomedy: Shakespeare and After* (London:
  Routledge, 1992), pp. 189–207.
6 S.J. Wiseman, *Drama and Politics in the English Civil War* (Cambridge University
  Press, 1997); Dale B.J. Randall, *Winter Fruit: English Drama 1642–1660*
  (Lexington: University Press of Kentucky, 1995); Hero Chalmers, *Royalist
  Women Writers, 1650–1689* (Oxford: Clarendon Press, 2004); Janet Clare (ed.),
  Drama of the English Republic, 1649–60, Revels Plays Companion Library
  (Manchester University Press, 2002).

 7 Women as playgoers and patrons should also be included in this discussion. See,
    for example, David M. Bergeron, 'Women as Patrons of Renaissance Drama', in
    Guy Fitch Lytle and Stephen Orgel (eds), *Patronage in the Renaissance* (Princeton
    University Press, 1981), pp. 274–90; and Linda Levy Peck, 'The Caroline
    Audience: Evidence from Hatfield House', *SQ*, 51 (2000), 474–7.
 8 On pioneering activities see Tomlinson, ' "She that Plays the King" ' and Britland,
    'Neoplatonic Identities'.
 9 Clare McManus, *Women on the Renaissance Stage: Anna of Denmark and
    Female Masquing in the Stuart Court 1590–1619* (Manchester University Press,
    2002).
10 For a more detailed discussion of this event see Sophie Tomlinson, 'Theatrical
    Vibrancy on the Caroline Court Stage: *Tempe Restored* and *The Shepherds' Par-
    adise*', in McManus (ed.), *Women and Culture*, pp. 186–203; and Roy Booth, 'The
    First Female Professional Singers: Madame Coniack', *N&Q*, 44 (1997), 533. In
    'Memorializing Anna of Denmark's Court: *Cupid's Banishment* at Greenwich
    Palace' (in her *Women and Culture*, pp. 81–99), Clare McManus points out that in
    1619 *Cupid's Banishment* staged the female body and voice in radical ways (p. 90).
    Ongoing research by Karen Britland suggests that the female singers of *Tempe
    Restored* may not have been professionals, although the masque's emphasis on the
    female voice remains crucial.
11 Terry Gifford, *Pastoral* (London: Routledge, 1999), p. 62.
12 Chalmers, *Royalist Women Writers*, traces at length the impact of Caroline culture
    on royalist women's writing in the 1640s and 1650s.
13 Ian McLean, *Woman Triumphant: Feminism in French Literature, 1610–52*
    (Oxford: Clarendon Press, 1977), p. 208.
14 Erica Veevers, *Images of Love and Religion: Queen Henrietta Maria and Court
    Entertainments* (Cambridge University Press, 1989); Julie Sanders, 'Caroline Salon
    Culture and Female Agency: The Countess of Carlisle, Henrietta Maria, and Public
    Theatre', *Theatre Journal*, 52 (2000), 449–64.
15 Leah S. Marcus, *The Politics of Mirth: Jonson, Herrick, Milton, Marvell and the
    Defense of Old Holiday Pastimes* (University of Chicago Press, 1986), p. 14.
16 Gisèle Venet, 'Margaret Cavendish's Drama: An Aesthetic of Fragmentation', in
    Line Cottegnies and Nancy Weitz (eds), *Authorial Conquests: Essays on Genre in
    the Writings of Margaret Cavendish* (London: Associated University Presses,
    2003), pp. 213–28 (219); see also pp. 222–5.
17 Philip J. Finkelpearl, *Court and Country Politics in the Plays of Beaumont and
    Fletcher* (Princeton University Press, 1990), p. 114. See also Annabel Patterson,
    *Censorship and Interpretation: The Conditions of Writing and Reading in Early
    Modern England* (Berkeley: University of California Press, 1987), pp. 171–4.
18 Bawcutt, p. 186 (No. 280). It is likely that the 'Pastorall' performed at the Cockpit-
    in-the-court on 8 April the same year was also *The Faithful Shepherdess* (p. 188,
    No. 283).
19 'Unto his worthy friend Mr. *Joseph Taylor* upon his presentment of the *Faithfull
    Shepherdesse* before the King and Queene, at White-hall, on Twelfth night last.
    1633', Bowers, *DW*, 3.498, ll. 7–10.
20 *JCS*, 3.426; Bawcutt, p. 185 (Nos 274–5); George Walton Williams, Textual Intro-
    duction to *The Woman Hater*, Bowers, *DW*, ll. 148, 150–1.
21 John Astington, *English Court Theatre 1558–1642* (Cambridge University Press,
    1999), p. 180.
22 'The Prologue to the *Woman-hater*, or the *Hungry Courtier*', l. 21, Bowers, *DW*,
    1.236–7. Davenant's prologue was printed in his *Madagascar, with Other Poems*

(1638) with the heading 'Prologue to a reviv'd Play of Mr Fletcher's, call'd *The Woman-hater*', and in a quarto edition of *The Woman Hater* published in 1649.

23 Cited by Richard Levin, 'Women in the Renaissance Theatre Audience', *SQ*, 40 (1989), 165–74 (p. 169).

24 See Linda Woodbridge, *Women and the English Renaissance: Literature and the Nature of Womankind 1540–1620* (Brighton: Harvester Press, 1984), esp. chapters 10–12 on the drama's response to the formal controversy, and Constance Jordan, *Renaissance Feminism: Literary Texts and Political Models* (Ithaca: Cornell University Press, 1990).

25 Natalie Zemon Davis, 'Women on Top: Symbolic Sexual Inversion and Political Disorder in Early Modern Europe', in Barbara Babcock (ed.), *The Reversible World: Symbolic Inversion in Art and Society* (Ithaca: Cornell University Press, 1978), pp. 148–83.

26 Michael Shapiro, *Gender in Play on the Shakespearean Stage: Boy Heroines and Female Pages* (Ann Arbor: University of Michigan Press, 1994), p. 191.

27 Chalmers, 'The Politics of Feminine Retreat'; Sanders, ' "A Woman Write a Play!" '.

28 See Randall, *Winter Fruit*; Wiseman, *Drama and Politics*.

29 The phrase 'paradramatic' is Nigel Smith's in his *Literature and Revolution in England, 1640–1660* (New Haven and London: Yale University Press, 1994), p. 47. On the *querelle* see Randall, *Winter Fruit*, pp. 51–65; Wiseman, *Drama and Politics*, pp. 19–39.

30 See Smith, *Literature and Revolution*, pp. 47–8; Susan Wiseman, ' "Adam, the Father of all Flesh": Porno-Political Rhetoric and Political Theory in and after the English Civil War', in James Holstun (ed.), *Pamphlet Wars: Prose in the English Revolution* (Portland, Oregon: Frank Cass, 1992), pp. 134–57 (146–8).

31 Mihoko Suzuki, *Subordinate Subjects: Gender, the Political Nation, and Literary Form, 1588–1688* (Aldershot: Ashgate, 2003), p. 158. See also p. 155. Suzuki (p. 158) regards such satires as informing Cavendish's articulations of debates over power relations between the sexes.

32 See Wiseman, *Drama and Politics*, p. 7.

33 Richard Lovelace, 'On the best, last, and only remaining comedy of Master Fletcher', Appendix B.

34 James Ramsey, 'On Master Fletcher's *Wild-Goose Chase* recovered', Appendix B, ll. 15–18.

35 See Chalmers, *Royalist Women Writers*, chapter 1; Sophie Tomlinson, ' "My Brain the Stage": Margaret Cavendish and the Fantasy of Female Performance', in Clare Brant and Diane Purkiss (eds), *Women, Texts and Histories, 1575–1760* (London and New York: Routledge, 1992), pp. 134–63 (147–9).

36 Jeffrey Masten, *Textual Intercourse: Collaboration, Authorship, and Sexualities in Renaissance Drama* (Cambridge University Press, 1997), p. 156.

37 Karen Raber, *Dramatic Difference: Gender, Class, and Genre in the Early Modern Closet Drama* (Newark: University of Delaware Press; London: Associated University Presses, 2001), p. 13.

38 Marta Straznicky, 'Reading the Stage: Margaret Cavendish and Commonwealth Closet Drama', *Criticism*, 37:3 (1995), 355–90 (359). See also Raber, *Dramatic Difference*, pp. 188–90.

39 Wiseman, *Drama and Politics*, p. 92.

40 Julie Sanders, ' "The Closet Opened": A Reconstruction of "Private" Space in the Writings of Margaret Cavendish', in Stephen Clucas (ed.), *A Princely Brave Woman: Essays on Margaret Cavendish, Duchess of Newcastle* (Aldershot:

Ashgate, 2003), pp. 127–40 (pp. 128, 135–7). See also Chalmers, *Royalist Women Writers*, chapter 3.

41 Margaret Cavendish, *Playes* (London, 1662), A2r, A6v.

42 See e.g. Randall, *Winter Fruit*, p. 287; Smith, *Literature and Revolution*, p. 85; Wiseman, *Drama and Politics*, p. 94.

43 Alison Findlay, '"She Gave You the Civility of the House": Household Performance in *The Concealed Fancies*', in S.P. Cerasano and Marion Wynne-Davies (eds), *Readings in Renaissance Women's Drama: Criticism, History, and Performance 1594–1998* (London and New York: Routledge, 1998), pp. 259–71 (259).

44 See Lisa Hopkins, 'Play Houses: Drama at Bolsover and Welbeck', *Early Theatre*, 2 (1999), 25–44 (32).

45 Tomlinson, '"My Brain the Stage"', pp. 138, 145; see also Sophie Tomlinson, 'Too Theatrical?: Female Subjectivity in Caroline Interregnum Drama', *Women's Writing*, 6 (1999), 65–79.

46 Findlay, '"She Gave You the Civility of the House"', pp. 265–6.

47 *Ibid.*, p. 263.

48 Wiseman, *Drama and Politics*, p. 195.

49 Randall, *Winter Fruit*, p. 231.

50 Wiseman, *Drama and Politics*, p. 122; Clare, *Drama of the English Republic*.

51 See Randall, *Winter Fruit*, p. 326. Alison Findlay, Gweno Williams, and Stephanie J. Hodgson-Wright, '"The Play is ready to be Acted": Women and Dramatic Production, 1570–1670', *Women's Writing*, 6 (1999), 137, also note a 'masque-like interlude' in *The Concealed Fancies*.

52 For Howell's and Davenant's operas see Wiseman, *Drama and Politics*, pp. 127–9, 141.

53 See e.g. Margaret Cavendish, *Playes* (London, 1662), sig. A4[2]r. On Behn see Chalmers, *Royalist Women Writers*, chapter 4. In putting forward this argument, it is important to avoid the conflation of women actors with prostitutes contested by Derek Hughes in his robust attack on the notion that Behn, as a Restoration woman author, identifies herself with the figure of the prostitute; see Hughes, 'The Masked Woman Revealed; or, the Prostitute and the Playwright in Aphra Behn Criticism', *Women's Writing*, 7 (2000), 149–64 (154).

54 'A Prologue to introduce the first *Woman* that came to Act on the Stage in the Tragedy, Call'd The Moor of Venice', in Thomas Jordan, *A Royal Arbor of Loyal Poesie* (London, 1663), pp. 21–2.

55 Hastings, quoted in Finkelpearl, *Court and Country Politics*, p. 31.

56 Cited in McMullan, p. 27.

57 See, however, Lois Potter's edition of *The Two Noble Kinsmen* (1997), and Gordon McMullan's edition of *King Henry VIII* (2000), both for The Arden Shakespeare.

58 For a full discussion of sources and analogues for *The Wild-Goose Chase* see Lister, pp. xlvii–lxiii.

59 See Roy C. Strong, 'Queen Elizabeth as Oriana', *Studies in the Renaissance*, 6 (1959), 251–60. On the possible political resonances of Fletcher's use of the name Oriana in 1621 see McMullan, pp. 192–3.

60 For the dating and authorship of *El burlador*, see the Introduction to Tirso de Molina, *The Trickster of Seville and the Stone Guest*, transl. Gwynne Edwards (Warminster: Aris and Phillips, 1986), pp. xix–xx.

61 On the satirical dimensions of the play see Kathleen McLuskie, 'The Plays and Playwrights, 1613–42', in Philip Edwards *et al.*, *The Revels History of Drama in English*, vol. 4, 1613–60 (London: Methuen, 1981), pp. 194–6; Sandra Clark, *The Plays of Beaumont and Fletcher: Sexual Themes and Dramatic Representation* (New York and London: Harvester Wheatsheaf, 1994), pp. 144–8.

62 Park Honan, *Shakespeare, a Life* (Oxford University Press, 1998), pp. 309–10.

63 Kathleen McLuskie, *Renaissance Dramatists* (Hemel Hempstead: Harvester Wheatsheaf, 1989), p. 198.

64 The phrase is Theodore Leinwand's, who credits Jacobean city comedy with inventing a 'new woman' who is 'able, witty and self-sufficient'; quoted by Sandra Clark, *Plays of Beaumont and Fletcher*, p. 152. The relationship of the sisters with Lugier in *The Wild-Goose Chase* has elements in common with that between the Princess of France and her ladies, and Boyet in *Love's Labour's Lost*. Notwithstanding the difference in status between Fletcher's scholar and Shakespeare's lord, both men act as protectors who manifest a sexual interest in their young charges; moreover, both characters function as dramatic facilitators of sorts.

65 Ann Thompson traces the origins of this critical approach to the mid twentieth century in her introduction to the New Cambridge edition of *The Taming of the Shrew*, updated edition (Cambridge University Press, 2003), pp. 37–41. In her chapter 'Renaissance Family Politics and Shakespeare's *Taming of the Shrew*' Karen Newman employs Luce Irigaray's notion of 'mimeticism' as a way of explicating Kate's compliance with Petruchio's will: *Fashioning Femininity and English Renaissance Drama* (University of Chicago Press, 1991), pp. 33–50 (42–50). Barbara Freedman uses *Shrew* as a springboard for exploring the relationship between feminism, theatre, and sexual difference in her essay 'Frame-Up: Feminism, Psychoanalysis, Theatre', in Helene Keyssar (ed.), *Feminist Theatre and Theory* (Basingstoke: Macmillan, 1996), pp. 78–108.

66 See Leeds Barroll, *Anna of Denmark, Queen of England: A Cultural Biography* (Philadelphia: University of Pennsylvania Press, 2001); McManus, *Women on the Renaissance Stage*.

67 *JCS*, 3.425.

68 Paul Salzman, *Literary Culture in Jacobean England: Reading 1621* (Basingstoke and New York: Palgrave Macmillan, 2002), p. 96.

69 *JCS*, 3.425–7.

70 Lois Potter, 'Songs of Excess', review of the Royal Shakespeare Company's production of Fletcher's *The Island Princess*, TLS, 12 July 2002, p. 19.

71 McLuskie, *Renaissance Dramatists*, p. 222.

72 Jane Stevenson, 'Women Latin Poets in Britain in the Seventeenth and Eighteenth Centuries', *The Seventeenth Century*, 16 (2001), 1–36 (3). Stevenson's essay revises the long-held view that the level and quality of literate Englishwomen's education declined between the reigns of Queen Elizabeth I and King James I. For further evidence challenging this view see Margaret Ezell, *The Patriarch's Wife: Literary Evidence and the History of the Family* (Chapel Hill and London: University of North Carolina Press, 1987), pp. 9–16.

73 *Mortalities Memorandum, with A Dreame Prefixed, imaginarie in manner; reall in matter*, ll. 241–3 in Barbara Kiefer Lewalski (ed.), *The Polemics and Poems of Rachel Speght* (Oxford University Press, 1996). The phrase 'blatant beast' alludes to Edmund Spenser's representation of Slander in Book Five of *The Faerie Queene*; see note to 4.3.43. On Speght's invocation of Spenser see Suzuki, *Subordinate Subjects*, pp. 123–5.

74 See Kevin Sharpe, 'The Image of Virtue: The Court and Household of Charles I, 1625–1642', in David Starkey (ed.), *The English Court: From the Wars of the Roses to the Civil War* (London and New York: Longman, 1987), pp. 226–60.

75 The heroes, respectively, of Thomas Killigrew's *Thomaso, or, The Wanderer* (1654), George Etherege's *Sir Fopling Flutter, or, The Man of Mode* (1676), and Aphra Behn's *The Rover, or, the Banished Cavaliers* (1677). Behn's play is an adaptation of Killigrew's closet drama.

76 Sally Ann Hoare, 'Annotations for an Edition of John Fletcher's *The Wild-Goose Chase*' (unpublished MA thesis, University of Auckland, 2002), Introduction to Language, p. xix.

77 Veevers, *Images of Love and Religion*, p. 42.

78 Orie Latham Hatcher, *John Fletcher: A Study in Dramatic Method* (Chicago: Scott, Foresman, and Company, 1905), pp. 97–8.

79 'The Taming of the Shrewd Critics Who Talk Wild of *The Wild-Goose Chase*', in Yasunari Takahashi (ed.), *Hot Questrists After the English Renaissance: Essays on Shakespeare and his Contemporaries* (New York: AMS Press, 2000), pp. 53–67 (pp. 54–5).

80 Samuel Johnson's *Dictionary* (1755) defines 'wild goose chase' as 'a pursuit of something as unlikely to be caught as the wild goose' (*OED* 2).

81 Thomas Gainsborough to James Unwin, 1 March 1764, in John Hayes (ed.), *Letters of Thomas Gainsborough* (New Haven: Yale University Press, 2001), p. 26.

82 Gainsborough's pragmatic approach to his daughters' future reflects his mercantile background, which endowed him with a chariness about his family's financial security; this is not an anxiety that affects the wealthy gentlefolk of Fletcher's play.

83 Sandra A. Burner, *James Shirley: A Study of Literary Coteries and Patronage in Seventeenth-Century England* (New York and London: University Press of America, 1988), p. 48.

84 Anthony à Wood, *Athenae Oxoniensis*, 3rd ed. (London, 1817). Burner identifies Habington, a practising Catholic, with links to Catholic coteries such as the Tixall circle in Staffordshire, as a 'pivotal figure' in Shirley's life (*James Shirley*, p. 51).

85 Allan H. Stevenson, 'Shirley's Publishers: The Partnerships of Crooke and Cooke', *The Library*, 25 (1945), 140–61.

86 Shirley's productions at Werburgh Street included the site-specific *St Patrick's for Ireland* (*c.*1639) and a production of Jonson's *The Alchemist* (1637). See also Alan J. Fletcher, *Drama, Performance, and Polity in Pre-Cromwellian Ireland* (University of Toronto Press, 2000); Allan H. Stevenson, 'Shirley's Years in Ireland', *RES*, 20 (1944), 20–8.

87 See Ronald Huebert's Introduction to his edition of Shirley's *The Lady of Pleasure*, Revels Plays (Manchester University Press, 1986), p. 4. For additional ideas on Shirley's interregnum writings see Clare, *Drama of the English Republic*; Wiseman, *Drama and Politics*.

88 For a detailed and illuminating discussion of this company see A.T. Moore's introduction to his edition of John Ford's *Love's Sacrifice*, Revels Plays (Manchester University Press, 2002). All further references to this play are to this edition. On the Cockpit theatre, see Appendix A in Huebert's edition of *The Lady of Pleasure*.

89 Lisa Hopkins reflects on the significance of Ford's coterie groupings in her *John Ford's Political Theatre*, Revels Plays Companion Library (Manchester University Press, 1994).

90 Bawcutt, p. 178 (No. 248).

91 Letter from John Pory to Viscount Scudamore, 3 November 1632 (PRO C115/M35/8416). Cited in Walter Montagu, *The Shepherds' Paradise*, ed. Sarah Poynting, Malone Society Reprints, Vol. 159 (Oxford University Press, 1997), p. viii.

92 See e.g. Tomlinson, ' "She that Plays the King" '; Kim Walker, 'New Prison: Representing the Female Actor in Shirley's *The Bird in a Cage* (1633)', *ELR*, 21 (1991), 385–400; Julie Sanders, *Caroline Drama* (Plymouth: Northcote House, 1999), esp. pp. 30–42. On the identities of the elite women who performed in Montagu's pas-

toral see Sarah Poynting, ' "In the name of all the sisters": Henrietta Maria's Notorious Whores', in McManus, *Women and Culture*, pp. 163–85.

93 For related arguments for shifts in the representation of women characters in
Jonson's Caroline drama see Julie Sanders, ' " 'Twill Fit the Players Yet": Women
and Theatre in Jonson's Late Plays', in Richard Cave, Elizabeth Schafer, and Brian
Woolland (eds), *Ben Jonson and Theatre* (London: Routledge, 1999), pp. 179–90.

94 A letter from Prynne to Archbishop Laud in June 1634 claims that *Histriomastix*
was available 'above four weeks before her Majesty's pastoral'; see S.R. Gardiner
(ed.), *Documents Relating to the Proceedings against William Prynne in 1634 and
1637* (London, 1877). Walker, 'New Prison', includes a detailed discussion of
Prynne's retrospective account of the affair.

95 This allusion was recognised in the nineteenth century; see Octavius Gilchrist, *A
Letter to William Gifford, Esq. on the Late Edition of Ford's Plays* (London:
Murray, 1811).

96 A.T. Moore records in his introduction (p. 5) the critical speculation that Ford's
play itself contains references to the *Shepherds' Paradise* rehearsals, in its 3.2 allusion to a Brussels performance involving female actors in an 'antic' (19), but he
disagrees with this, noting that the reference is hardly flattering, and suggesting
that its stressed continental resonance makes it more likely that the reference is to
visiting French troupes in the London public theatres in the late 1620s and early
1630s. These companies included professional women actors.

97 Although, in truth, the full cropping of his ears did not take place until his sub-
sequent sentence in 1637, along with Bastwick and Burton, for continuing his sedi-
tious writings from prison. On the details of this later trial see Andrew McRae,
'Stigmatizing Prynne: Seditious Libel, Political Satire, and the Construction of
Opposition', in Ian Atherton and Julie Sanders (eds), *The 1630s* (Manchester
University Press, forthcoming).

98 McMullan suggests this play was significantly revised after 1618 in the wake of
'The Book of Sports', which offers a further analogue to the concerns of *The Bird
in a Cage*; p. 126.

99 See Ray Livingstone Armstrong (ed.), *The Poems of James Shirley* (New York,
1941), esp. pp. xiii–xvii (xv).

100 Marvin Morillo, 'The Preferment of James Shirley at the Court of Charles I', *SEL*,
1 (1961), 101–17.

101 This critical history is reviewed by Frances Frazier Senescu in her edition of the
play, produced initially as her doctoral thesis in 1948 and reproduced as *A Critical Edition of James Shirley's 'The Bird in a Cage'* (New York: Garland, 1980).
Senescu rejects the reading of the play by F.G. Fleay and Robert S. Forsythe that
argues for the interlude as a later interpolation (pp. xlviii–xlix), arguing instead
in favour of the play's unity of conception.

102 Interestingly, Morello's choice of phrase here echoes the title of a 1623 play, a production which was a conflation of Heywood's two Jacobean *Ages* plays, *The Silver
Age* and *The Golden Age*, the latter of which features the Jupiter–Danae seduction:
Sir Henry Herbert records: 'An old Playe called the Escapes of Jupiter taken from
the Cockpit upon the remove of some of the sharers' (Bawcutt, p. 87 (No. 50)).

103 See, for example, Dent B384.01 'To be like a bird (birds) in a golden cage' and
B387.1 'To sing like bird(s) in a cage'. Dent also cites John Davies's *Poems* (1608):
'Wives are as birdes in a golden cage kept'.

104 *Philosophical and Physical Opinions* (1655); cited in Kate Aughterson (ed.),
Renaissance Woman: Constructions of Femininity in England, a Sourcebook
(London and New York: Routledge, 1995), p. 288.

105 Intriguingly, Thomas Heywood uses the same analogy for his Danae in *The Golden Age* who declares at 4.1, p. 58, 'Why am I cloyster'd thus, / And kept a prisoner from the sight of man?'

106 Valerie Traub, 'The (In)significance of "Lesbian" Desire in Early Modern England', in Susan Zimmerman (ed.), *Erotic Politics: Desire on the Renaissance Stage* (London: Routledge, 1992), pp. 150–69, and her *The Renaissance of Lesbianism in Early Modern England* (Cambridge University Press, 2002), esp. chapter 4.

107 Cf. *The Winter's Tale*, 1.2.188–9.

108 Walker, 'New Prison', p. 400.

109 *Ibid.*, p. 394. Walker suggests that the Caroline court's anxiety about Henrietta Maria's theatrical innovating is indicated both by the limited audience for the performance of Racan's *Artenice* in 1626 (Stephen Orgel and Roy Strong note the dispatch of the Tuscan Resident on this occasion: 'The performance was conducted as privately as possible, inasmuch as it was an unusual thing in this country to see the Queen upon the stage', *Inigo Jones: The Theatre of the Stuart Court*, 2 vols (London, Berkeley and Los Angeles: Sotheby Parke Bernet and University of California Press, 1973), 1.384), and by Charles I's refusal to allow the publication of the pastoral in the late 1620s, whereas he freely allowed the publication of comparable masque texts. Walker further notes that Montagu's *Shepherds' Paradise* was not entered on the Stationers' Register until 1658 (p. 387). The late 1620s were, however, hiatus years for the court masque so it is difficult to extract any absolute confirmation of anxiety about Henrietta Maria's court theatre from their publishing history. The initial low-scale reaction to *Histriomastix* may imply the opposite, at least by the early 1630s: when first approached about the publication both Charles I and the attorney general saw little cause for prosecution; the fervour whipped up in response to Prynne seems rather to have been the product of Archbishop Laud's interventions.

110 Tomlinson, ' "She that Plays the King" ', p. 196.

111 Ben Jonson, *Epicene, or The Silent Woman*, ed. Richard Dutton, Revels Plays (Manchester University Press, 2003), p. 24.

112 Walker, 'New Prison', pp. 395–6.

113 Will Fisher, 'Staging the Beard: Masculinity in Early Modern English Culture', in Jonathan Gil Harris and Natasha Korda (eds), *Staged Properties in Early Modern English Drama* (Cambridge University Press, 2002), pp. 230–57. Fisher makes the very useful observation that beards were both accepted signifiers of male identity in portraiture of the period and yet endlessly pliable prosthetics in the context of stage performance, adding that early modern drama's 'obsession with facial hair needs to be understood in relation to one of its primary themes: the mutability or transferability of identity' (p. 245). For the salient exposition of these themes in a twentieth-century theoretical context see Judith Butler, *Gender Trouble: Feminism and the Subversion of Identity* (London: Routledge, 1990).

114 Danielle Clarke, 'The Iconography of the Blush: Marian Literature of the 1630s', in Kate Chedgzoy, Melanie Hansen, and Suzanne Trill (eds), *Voicing Women: Gender and Sexuality in Early Modern Women's Writing* (Keele University Press, 1996), pp. 111–28. In an unpublished doctoral dissertation, Martin Benedict Andrew has also made the link to significant folklore and fairytale, in particular the story of Rapunzel, and the classical tale of Hero. Andrew helpfully identifies an enduring interest in these motifs in Shirley's drama, noting the parallel incarceration of another earlier Eugenia in *Love in a Maze*. In both cases Shirley deploys the language of chivalric romance, albeit in a quasi-parodic context, to signify these links. In *Love in a Maze* Eugenia is 'the lady in the enchanted castle' (3.3,

p. 321), and in *The Bird in a Cage* Morello declares at the close of Act 1, 'Like errant knights, our valiant wits must wrestle / To free our ladies from the enchanted castle' (1.1.359–60). Andrew also discusses Fletcher's *Women Pleased*; see 'Women and Enclosure: The Imprisoned Woman in English Renaissance Drama from Kyd to Shirley' (University of Otago, New Zealand, 1991).

115 For a more detailed analysis of the myth of Danae in this play and other early modern literature see Julie Sanders, ' "Powdered with Golden Rain": The Myth of Danae in Early Modern Drama', *EMLS*, 8 (2002), 1–23.

116 It is perhaps significant that it is this theatrical definition of sports that predominates in Ben Jonson's most obvious Caroline intervention into the question of women and theatricals, *The New Inn* (1629): see Julie Sanders, ' "The Day's Sports Devised i' the Inn": Jonson's *The New Inn* and Theatrical Politics', *MLR*, 91 (1996), 545–60.

117 'A True Relation of my Birth, Breeding, and Life', in Margaret Cavendish, *Natures Pictures Drawn by Fancies Pencil to the Life* (London, 1656), pp. 370–1, 372.

118 For Cavendish's natural philosophy see Stephen Clucas, 'The Atomism of the Cavendish Circle: A Reappraisal', *The Seventeenth Century*, 9 (1994), 247–73, and 'Variation, Irregularity and Probabilism: Margaret Cavendish and Natural Philosophy as Rhetoric', in Stephen Clucas (ed.), *A Princely Brave Woman: Essays on Margaret Cavendish, Duchess of Newcastle* (Aldershot: Ashgate, 2003), pp. 199–209; Sarah Hutton, 'In Dialogue with Thomas Hobbes: Margaret Cavendish's Natural Philosophy', *Women's Writing*, 4 (1997), 421–32, and 'Margaret Cavendish's Natural Philosophy', in Clucas (ed.), *A Princely Brave Woman*, pp. 185–98; Susan James, 'The Innovations of Margaret Cavendish', *British Journal for the History of Philosophy*, 7 (1999), 219–44; Lisa Sarasohn, '*Leviathan* and the Lady: Cavendish's Critique of Hobbes in *Philosophical Letters*', in Line Cottegnies and Nancy Weitz (eds), *Authorial Conquests: Essays on Genre in the Writings of Margaret Cavendish* (Madison, Teaneck: Fairleigh Dickinson University Press; London: Associated University Presses, 2003), pp. 40–58; Jay Stevenson, 'The Mechanist-Vitalist Soul of Margaret Cavendish', *SEL*, 36 (1996), 427–43; Jo Wallwork, 'Margaret Cavendish's Response to Hooke's *Micrographia*', in Jo Wallwork and Paul Salzman (eds), *Women Writing 1550–1750*, a special issue of *Meridian*, 18 (2001), 191–200.

119 For the details of Cavendish's biography see Cavendish, 'A True Relation'; Douglas Grant, *Margaret the First: A Biography of Margaret Cavendish Duchess of Newcastle 1623–1673* (London: Rupert Hart Davis, 1957); Katie Whitaker, *Mad Madge: Margaret Cavendish, Duchess of Newcastle, Royalist, Writer and Romantic* (London: Chatto and Windus, 2003).

120 See Irene G. Dash, 'Single-Sex Retreats in Two Early Modern Dramas: *Love's Labor's Lost* and *The Convent of Pleasure*', *SQ*, 47 (1996), 387–95.

121 The most categorical assertion of this argument is Tanya Wood, 'Margaret Cavendish, Duchess of Newcastle, *The Convent of Pleasure* (1668), Ending Revised by her Husband, the Duke of Newcastle', in Helen Ostovich and Elizabeth Sauer (eds), *Reading Early Modern Women: An Anthology of Texts in Manuscript and Print, 1550–1700* (New York and London: Routledge, 2004), pp. 435–7. For a more circumspect approach see Tomlinson, ' "My Brain the Stage" ', p. 157. Meanwhile, Julie Crawford, 'Convents and Pleasures: Margaret Cavendish and the Drama of Property', *RD*, 32 (2003), 177–223, reads the printed slips as evidence of the 'productive partnership' between Margaret Cavendish and her husband. Part of the difficulty in extrapolating any clear interpretation from this textual feature lies in the fact that the text does not indicate where William

Cavendish's contributions end. Shaver's edition assumes too much in concluding that 'since no terminus is given, it seems that he is author of the final two scenes and the epilogue' (p. 238).

122 For a discussion of seventeenth-century conduct books taking this approach see Hilda Smith, *Reason's Disciples: Seventeenth-Century English Feminists* (Urbana: University of Illinois Press, 1982), p. 51.

123 See also Anne Shaver, 'Agency and Marriage in the Fictions of Lady Mary Wroth and Margaret Cavendish, Duchess of Newcastle', in Sigrid King (ed.), *Pilgrimage for Love: Essays in Early Modern Literature in Honor of Josephine A. Roberts* (Tempe, Arizona: Arizona Center for Medieval and Renaissance Studies, 1999), pp. 177–90. For a more conventional approach to marriage in Cavendish's work see e.g. her *Worlds Olio* (London, 1655), p. 80.

124 See Smith, *Reason's Disciples*, p. xiv.

125 See Katherine Usher Henderson and Barbara F. McManus (eds), *Half Humankind: Contexts and Texts of the Controversy about Women in England, 1540–1640* (Urbana: University of Illinois Press, 1985), pp. 15, 160–1. Cf. *The Convent of Pleasure*, 3.2.7–8; 3.3; 3.7; 3.9. See also John Taylor, *A Juniper Lecture* (1639), in Henderson and McManus (eds), *Half Humankind*, pp. 292, 293. Cf. *The Convent of Pleasure*, 3.2; 3.6.

126 See Smith, *Reason's Disciples*, p. 28.

127 Lawrence Stone, *The Family, Sex and Marriage in England 1500–1800* (London: Weidenfeld and Nicolson, 1977), p. 135.

128 [Lawrence Anderton], *The English Nunne* (London, 1642), pp. 7–9.

129 Cavendish, *Natures Pictures*, p. 289.

130 'The Epistle to the ... Marchionesse of Newcastle', in *Du Vergers Humble Reflections Upon Some Passages of the ... Lady Marchionesse of Newcastles Olio* (London, 1657).

131 Crawford, 'Convents and Pleasures', pp. 178, 202–4; Rebecca D'Monté, 'Mirroring Female Power: Separatist Spaces in the Plays of Margaret Cavendish, Duchess of Newcastle', in Rebecca D'Monté and Nicole Pohl (eds), *Female Communities, 1600–1800: Literary Visions and Cultural Realities* (Basingstoke: Macmillan, 2000), pp. 93–110 (99); Hopkins, 'Play Houses', p. 36; Nicole Pohl, *Architectures of Transformation: Women's Utopianism, 1600–1800* (forthcoming), chapter 4.

132 See Elissa Weaver, 'Spiritual Fun: A Study of Sixteenth-Century Tuscan Convent Theater', in Mary Beth Rose (ed.), *Women In the Middle Ages and the Renaissance: Literary and Historical Perspectives* (Syracuse University Press, 1986), pp. 173–205.

133 See 3.1.20–3; 4.1.3–26.

134 See Harriette Andreadis, *Sappho in Early Modern England: Female Same-Sex Literary Erotics, 1550–1714* (University of Chicago Press, 2001); Valerie Traub, *The Renaissance of Lesbianism in Early Modern England* (Cambridge University Press, 2002).

135 Katherine Philips, *The Collected Works of Katherine Philips, the Matchless Orinda: Volume I. The Poems*, ed. Patrick Thomas (Stump Cross: Stump Cross Books, 1990).

136 See for example Philips, 'A retir'd friendship, to Ardelia' where the poet speaks of 'mingling souls' (l. 2): 'Friendship in Emblem, or the Seale, to my dearest Lucasia' (ll. 21–52) which borrows Donne's image of the compasses from 'A Valediction: forbidding Mourning'; 'L'amitié: To Mrs M. Awbrey' (ll. 1–4).

137 See, for example, *Blazing World*, pp. 98, 110; *Worlds Olio*, p. 211.

138 For manuscript versions see *JCS*, 4.920.

139 Walter Montagu, *The Shepheard's Paradise* [*sic*] (London, 1659), p. 22.

140 See Tomlinson, '"My Brain the Stage"', p. 145; Susan Wiseman, 'Gender and Status in Dramatic Discourse: Margaret Cavendish, Duchess of Newcastle', in Isobel Grundy and Susan Wiseman (eds), *Women, Writing, History, 1640–1740* (London: Batsford, 1992), pp. 159–77 (165).

141 See Graham Parry, *The Golden Age Restor'd: The Culture of the Stuart Court, 1603–42* (Manchester University Press, 1981), p. 185.

142 Tanya Wood, 'The Fall and Rise of Absolutism: Margaret Cavendish's Manipulation of Masque Conventions in "The Claspe: *Fantasmes* Masque" and *The Blazing World*', *In-Between: Essays and Studies in Literary Criticism*, 9 (2000), 287–99 (289). Cavendish's implied staging in Act 4 may also provide further evidence of the influence of *The Shepherds' Paradise* since Jones's stage design for Montagu's play included provision for shutters and numerous scene changes. See Montagu, *The Shepherds' Paradise* (ed. Poynting), p. xi.

143 For discussions of the likely sources of Cavendish's knowledge of masquing conventions see Tomlinson, '"My Brain the Stage"', pp. 139, 144; Wood, 'The Rise and Fall of Absolutism', pp. 288–90.

144 See D'Monté, 'Mirroring Female Power', p. 100; Tomlinson, '"My Brain the Stage"', p. 154.

145 Crawford, 'Convents and Pleasures'.

146 See Sir Philip Sidney, *A Critical Edition of the Major Works*, ed. Katherine Duncan-Jones, Oxford Authors (Oxford University Press, 1989), pp. 5–13, 334.

147 Crawford, 'Convents and Pleasures', 185.

148 See especially *The Convent of Pleasure*, 4.1.26SD; 4.1.136SD.

149 *Comedies and Tragedies written by Francis Beaumont and John Fletcher, gentlemen*, 1647, sig. A4r.

150 Bowers, *DW*, vol. 6, Textual Introduction to *The Wild-Goose Chase*, pp. 228–35.

151 Bowers, Textual Introduction, pp. 235, n. 1, 240–1; Lister, pp. xl–xli.

152 See for example McLuskie, *Renaissance Dramatists*, pp. 212–13. For evidence of an avid female reader and collector of Shakespeare and his contemporaries see Paul Morgan, 'Frances Wolfreston and "Hor Bouks": A Seventeenth-Century Woman Book-Collector', *The Library*, 11 (1989), 197–219.

153 James Fitzmaurice, 'Margaret Cavendish on her own Writing: Evidence from Revision and Handmade Correction', *Papers of the Bibliographical Society of America*, 85:3 (1991), 297–308, demonstrates Cavendish's involvement in these kinds of interventions in a range of her texts, suggesting that the *Plays, Never Before Printed* was adapted in this way 'probably at the behest of its author' (305).

154 *JCS*, 3.425–7.

155 *Ibid.*, 428–9; Lister, pp. xxiv–xxv; T.W. Baldwin, *The Organization and Personnel of the Shakespearean Company* (New York: Russell and Russell, 1961 [1927]), p. 193, n. 53. In chapters 7 and 8 of his study Baldwin conjectures at length on the 'types' represented by the actors comprising the 1632 cast of *The Wild-Goose Chase*.

156 Bawcutt, p. 176 (No. 242). Bentley notes, 'this sum was the second largest [Herbert] recorded, exceeded only by the 1628 revival of [Fletcher and Massinger's] *The Custom of the Country*', *JCS*, 3.429.

157 The inclusion of a list of actors assigned to individual roles was uncommon in plays published in the first half of the seventeenth century. However, T.J. King, *Casting Shakespeare's Plays: London Actors and their Roles, 1590–1642* (Cambridge University Press, 1992, chapter 3), examines fifteen cast-lists from manu-

script and printed plays published between 1623 and 1655, which present evidence of a growing change in practice towards naming the actors of principal male and female roles. Only one other play among those King analyses prints evaluative descriptions of actors' performances, Robert Davenport's *King John and Matilda* (1655).

158 *JCS*, 3.426.
159 *The Diary of Samuel Pepys*, eds Robert Latham and William Matthews, 11 vols (London: Bell and Hyman, 1976), 9.19.
160 *The London Stage 1660–1800*, Part 2: 1700–1729, ed. by Emmett L. Avery (Carbondale: Southern Illinois Press, 1950), pp. 18, 10.
161 *The Works of George Farquhar*, ed. Shirley Strum Kenny, 2 vols (Oxford: Clarendon Press, 1998), 1.403, ll. 10–11.
162 For a sustained comparison of the two plays see A.C. Sprague, *Beaumont and Fletcher on the Restoration Stage* (Cambridge, Massachusetts: Harvard University Press, 1926), pp. 248–55.
163 Kawai, 'The Taming of the Shrewd Critics', p. 60.
164 *Ibid.*, pp. 60–1. Kawai states that 'Oriana's glamour is heightened by her singing' (p. 61), but as lines 2–3 of Act 5, scene 6 make clear, the song is sung not by Oriana but by the 'Singing Boy' named in the dramatis personae.
165 Kenny, *Works of George Farquhar*, 1.392.
166 Lister, p. xxvii.
167 For excerpts from reviews of these productions see Lister, pp. xxix–xxxiii.
168 *The Island Princess* opened at the Swan Theatre, Stratford-upon-Avon, on 26 June 2002 and transferred to the Gielgud Theatre, London, in December of that year. *The Tamer Tamed* opened at the Swan on 6 March 2003 and played alongside Shakespeare's *The Taming of the Shrew* in the Royal Shakespeare Theatre. The two latter productions opened at the Queen's Theatre, London, in January 2004.
169 Personal communication from Gordon McMullan.
170 Leigh Hunt, *The Dramatic Works of Wycherley, Congreve, Vanbrugh and Farquhar* (London: Routledge, Warne, and Routledge, 1860), p. lvii.
171 See Appendix B to his *A History of Restoration Drama, 1660–1700* (Cambridge University Press, 1923), p. 315.
172 This is recorded in John Genest, *Some Account of the English Stage*, vol. 6 (Bath: Carrington, 1832), pp. 399–400.
173 Findlay *et al.*, ' "The Play is ready to be Acted" ', p. 129. See also Shaver, p. 8.
174 For an account of this performance see Findlay *et al.*, ' "The Play is ready to be Acted" ', pp. 140–4.
175 Findlay *et al.*, ' "The Play is ready to be Acted" ', p. 143; Sophie Tomlinson, 'Cavendish's *The Convent of Pleasure*, presented by the Diploma in Drama, 1999, University of Auckland, New Zealand. Directed by Murray Edmond, advised and assisted by Sophie Tomlinson', *Margaret Cavendish Society Newsletter*, 5:1 (2000).

The Wild-Goose Chase
John Fletcher

edited by Sophie Tomlinson

The Wild-Goose Chase] The phrase describes a form of sixteenth-century horse-race requiring riders to follow the course of a leader at a definite interval, resembling a flock of wild geese in flight. The phrase may describe an erratic course taken by one person and followed by another, or 'a pursuit of something as unlikely to be caught as the wild goose'; a foolish or hopeless quest (*OED* 2). The proverb 'to run the wild-goose chase' surfaces in *Romeo and Juliet* in Mercutio's witty compliment to Romeo: 'Nay, if our wits run the wild-goose chase, I am done, for thou hast more of the wild goose in one of thy wits than I am sure I have in my whole five' (2.3.66–8).

The title page of the 1652 folio reads as follows: 'The / Wild-Goose Chase. / A / COMEDIE. / As it hath been Acted with singular / Applause at the *Black-Friers*: / Being the Noble, Last, and Onely *Remaines* / of those Incomparable *Drammatists*, / {FRANCIS BEAUMONT, / AND / JOHN FLETCHER,} Gent. / Retriv'd for the publick delight of all the Ingenious; / And private Benefit / Of {JOHN LOWIN, / And / JOSEPH TAYLOR,} Servants to His late MAJESTIE. / By a Person of Honour. / *Ite bonus avibus* – / LONDON, / Printed for *Humpherey Moseley*, and are to be / sold at the *Princes Armes* in St *Pavles* / Church-yard, 1652.'

The epigram is taken from Ovid's valedictory Epilogue at the end of *Met.*, 15. 871–9: 'Yet with my better part I shall soar'.

While the title page attributes the play to both Beaumont and Fletcher, the Dedication to *The Wild-Goose Chase* ascribes the play to Fletcher alone (6–7). Four of the five commendatory verses (see Appendix B) laud Fletcher as sole author of the play. For a discussion of stylistic evidence in favour of Fletcher's sole authorship see Lister, pp. xv–xix.

THE DEDICATION

To the honoured few, lovers of dramatic poesy.

Noble Spirits!
It will seem strange to you that we should beg a pardon from you before
you know a crime committed; but such is our harsh fate that we shall
want as much of your mercy to the forgiving of this sad presumption   5
of offering to your view these few poor sheets, the rich remains of our
too-long-since lost friend, Master Fletcher, as we shall your favourable
acceptance and encouragement in it. The play was of so general a
received acceptance that, he himself a spectator, we have known him
unconcerned, and to have wished it had been none of his; he, as well   10
as the thronged theatre (in despite of his innate modesty) applauding
this rare issue of his brain. His complacency in his own work may be,
perhaps, no argument to you of the goodness of the play, any more
than our confidence of it; and we do not expect our encomium can do
anything with you when the play itself is so near: that will commend   15
itself unto you. And now, farewell our glory! Farewell your choice
delight, most noble gentlemen! Farewell the grand wheel that set us
smaller motions in action! Farewell the pride and life o' th' stage! Nor

---

1. honoured few, lovers] *Dyce (subst.)*; Honour'd, Few, Lovers *F1*; Honored Few
Lovers *Fraser and Rabkin.*   7. Master] *Dyce*; M^r. *F1*.

---

4. *our harsh fate*] (1) the closure of public playhouses in 1642 by parliamentary
order; (2) John Lowin, one of the writers of the dedication, was caught and punished
under the Commonwealth for playing surreptitiously at the Cockpit theatre in 1649
(Phyllis Hartnoll and Peter Found, (eds) *The Concise Oxford Companion to the
Theatre*, second edition (Oxford University Press, 1992), 'Lowin, John'.
   6. *too-long-since . . . Fletcher*] John Fletcher died in 1625.
   8–9. *was of . . . acceptance*] received such widespread approval.
   10. *unconcerned*] detached.
   12. *complacency*] satisfaction.
   16–18. *farewell . . . stage*] Fraser and Rabkin point out that this passage may parody
Oth. 3.3.353–62.
   17–18. *grand wheel . . . action*] (1) Fletcher is figured as the 'Primum Mobile' of a
Ptolemaic theatrical universe. In the medieval version of the Ptolemaic system, the
Primum Mobile was an outermost sphere, supposed to revolve around the Earth in
twenty-four hours, carrying with it the inner spheres; (2) *motion* was used of a puppet
or puppet show; see Jonson, *Bart. Fair*, where Sharkwell refers to Lantern Leatherhead's puppet show of 'Hero and Leander': ''Tis a motion' (5.3.3).

can we, though in our ruin, much repine that we are so little, since he
that gave us being is no more. 20

Generous Souls!
'Tis not unknown to you all how by a cruel destiny we have a long time
been mutes and bound, although our miseries have been sufficiently
clamorous and expanded, yet till this happy opportunity, never durst
vex your open ears and hands: but this we're confident of will be the 25
surest argument for your *noblesses*. What an ingenious person of
quality once spoke of his amours, we apply to our necessities:

> Silence in love betrays more woe
> Than words, though ne'er so witty:
> The beggar that is dumb, you know, 30
> Deserves a double pity.

But be the comedy at your mercy as we are. Only we wish that you
may have the same kind joy in perusing of it as we had in the acting.
So *Exeunt*

Your grateful servants, 35
John Lowin,
Joseph Taylor.

---

19. *repine*] complain.
19–20. *he . . . being*] (1) Fletcher; (2) '*i.e.* King Charles I' (Weber).
26. noblesses] Fr. nobility; a flattering address to the elite audience and market to
whom the dedication of the handsome folio edition is addressed.
26–7. *person of quality*] Sir Walter Ralegh.
27. *necessities*] condition (*OED* 3a). Actors were deprived of a livelihood and
socially marginalised by the two ordinances against theatres of September 1642 and
February 1648.
28–31. *Silence . . . pity*] adapted from 'Sir Walter Ralegh to the Queen', ll. 31–4,
attributed posthumously to Ralegh: Michael Rudick (ed.), *The Poems of Sir Walter
Ralegh: A Historical Edition* (Tempe, Arizona: Arizona Center for Medieval and
Renaissance Studies, in conjunction with Renaissance English Text Society, 1999).
33. *kind*] agreeable, pleasant (*OED* kind a. 7)
36. *John Lowin*] See Dramatis Personae, l. 14n. Lowin and Taylor were among ten
actors from the King's Men who appear as signatories to the dedicatory epistle in the
Beaumont and Fletcher First Folio of 1647.
37. *Joseph Taylor*] See Dramatis Personae, l. 9n.

DRAMATIS PERSONAE

DE GARD, *a noble staid gentleman that, being newly lighted from his travels, assists his sister Oriana in her chase of Mirabell, the wild goose. Acted by Master Robert Benfield.*

LA CASTRE, *the indulgent father to Mirabell. Acted by Master Richard Robinson.* 5

MIRABELL, *the wild goose, a travelled monsieur and great defier of all ladies in the way of marriage, otherwise their much loose servant, at last caught by the despised Oriana. Incomparably acted by Master Joseph Taylor.*

---

3. Master] Dyce; Mr. *F1*. Also at lines 4, 8, 11, 14, 15, 18, 20, 25, 27.

---

1. DE GARD] Deriving from the French 'garde' (m.), 'a guardian, warden, keeper' (Cotgrave), perhaps also evoking the position of defence in fencing, 'en garde', appropriate to one who is ready to use his sword in defending Oriana's honour.

1. staid] dignified and serious in demeanour or conduct (*OED* 2).

1. lighted] arrived.

3. Robert Benfield] Benfield appears to have joined the King's Men in 1615 and specialised in dignified roles, playing kings, senators, and elderly men.

4. LA CASTRE] (1) Latin 'castrum' (n.), 'castle' (Lewis and Short); (2) an aural echo of Latin 'castro', 'to castrate' (Lewis and Short) and its French derivative, 'chastrer', meaning 'to geld' (Cotgrave), foreshadowing the idea of Mirabell as heir assuming his father's potency.

4–5. Richard Robinson] His skills as a female impersonator were highly praised by Ben Jonson in *The Devil Is an Ass* (1616). By 1619 he was playing men's roles, including the Cardinal in Webster's *The Duchess of Malfi*.

6. MIRABELL] (1) suggesting the marvellous; from the Latin 'mirabilis', 'to be wondered at', 'extraordinary' (Lewis and Short), appropriate to a character whose 'admirable imperfections' (1.1.129) are a perpetual source of amazement; (2) 'an admirer of female beauty', from the Latin 'miror', 'to admire', and 'bellus', 'fine, pretty'. This edition retains the spelling used in the 1652 Folio which was adopted by Congreve for the hero of *The Way of the World* (1700).

7. loose servant] promiscuous admirer.

9. Joseph Taylor] Taylor (*c.*1585–1652) was already a well-known actor when he joined the King's Men in 1619. On the death of Richard Burbage in that year, Taylor took on many of Burbage's former roles, including Hamlet, as well as playing Iago, Mosca, and Truewit. In September 1632, when Henrietta Maria and her ladies were rehearsing Montagu's *The Shepherds' Paradise*, John Pory noted that 'Taylour the prime actor at the Globe goes every day to teach them action' (cited in Philip Edwards *et al.*, *Revels History of Drama in English* (London and New York: Methuen, 1981),

64

PINAC, *his fellow traveller, of a lively spirit, and servant to the no less*   10
sprightly Lillia-Bianca. Admirably well acted by Master Thomas
Pollard.
BELLEUR, *companion to both, of a stout blunt humour, in love with*
Rosalura. Most naturally acted by Master John Lowin.
NANTOLET, *father to Rosalura and Lillia-Bianca. Acted by Master*   15
William Penn.
LUGIER, *the rough and confident tutor to the ladies and chief engine*
to entrap the wild goose. Acted by Master Eyllaerdt Swanston.

---

18. Eyllaerdt] *Lister;* Hilliard *F1.*

---

vol. 4, 1613–60, p. 13). Taylor was buried in November 1652, the year *The Wild-Goose Chase* was published for his and John Lowin's 'private benefit' (title page to 1652 folio).

10. PINAC] Pronounced 'Pi'nak', with the stress on the second syllable. The name conveys the sense of fulfilling a supportive function, from its lexical similarity to 'pinnace' (Italian 'pinnacia'), a light sailing craft 'often in attendance on a larger vessel as a tender or scout' (*OED* 1); or from the Latin 'pinna' (n.); (1) a wing; (2) flight; (3) a feathered arrow, or 'pignus' (n.), 'that which one bets, a wager' (Lewis and Short), in keeping with the 'gamester' theme of the drama.

11–12. Thomas Pollard] Pollard probably joined the King's Men in 1616–17 and became a well-known actor of comic roles.

13. BELLEUR] Pronounced with the stress on the second syllable, the name signifies martial qualities; from the French 'bellateur' (m.) meaning 'a warrior, a professed souldier' (Cotgrave). It is not dissimilar to the French 'belier' (m.), 'battering ram' (Littré). Belleur's bulky size may be the inspiration for a homonymic pun on the Latin noun 'belva' (f.), 'a beast distinguished for size or ferocity' (Lewis and Short).

14. John Lowin] Lowin (1576–1653) joined the King's Men in 1603 and remained with the company until the closure of the theatres, often performing roles in which he played 'the blunt foil for the hero, tyrants or soldiers' (Gurr, p. 105). Fletcher plays upon Lowin's corpulence as Belleur, and the actor's size contributed to many of the roles he is recorded as having acted, among them Falstaff, Henry VIII, and Sir Epicure Mammon. See Shoichiro Kawai, 'John Lowin as Iago', *Shakespeare Studies* (Tokyo) 30 (1996), 17–34.

15. NANTOLET] Possibly a play on the French 'nantois', a coin minted in Nantes and used figuratively of an object of little value (Hindley); or 'nantir', 'to monopolise', or 'nanter', 'to pledge' (Hindley).

16. William Penn] Penn began his stage career as a boy and is thought to have joined the King's Men in 1625. He often played the role of a dignified older man.

17. LUGIER] from the Latin 'lugubre', (adv.) meaning 'mournfully' (Lewis and Short). Pedants were commonly portrayed as melancholic by nature or through study.

chief engine] the mastermind, but also draws on another use of *engine* as a 'snare or trap to catch game' (*OED* 5c).

18. Eyllaerdt Swanston] Bentley describes Swanston as 'a leading utility man' for the King's Men. Among his roles were Othello and Bussy D'Ambois. Swanston's Christian name appears as 'Hilliard' in the Folio's cast-list, but he signed himself 'Eyllaerdt' in his only known signatures (*JCS*, 2.584–5).

ORIANA, *the fair betrothed of Mirabell and witty follower of the chase.*
Acted by Master Stephen Hammerton.   20
ROSALURA   [*acted by*] William Trigg.
                } *the airy daughters of Nantolet.*
LILLIA-BIANCA   [*acted by*] Alexander Gough.
PETELLA, *their waiting woman.*
Their Servant, [*acted by*] Master Shank.   25
MARIANA, [*the disguised name of* JOAN], *an English* Courtesan.
A Young [Man *disguised as a*] Factor [*acted*] *by Master John*
Honeyman.

---

20. Stephen] Dyce; Steph. F1.   23. Alexander] Lister; Sander F1.   24–5.] Bowers;
PETELLA, their waiting-woman. Their Servant Mr Shanck. F1.   26.] This ed.;
MARIANA, an English Courtezan. F1.   27–8.] Weber; A young FACTOR. By Mr. John
Hony-man. F1.

---

19. ORIANA] A name which may derive from the Latin 'aurea' (adj.) meaning
'adorned with gold' (Spanish 'oria'), and the Romance suffix '-ana' (Edwin B. Place,
'The Amadis Question', *Speculum* 1:25 (1950), 357–66). 'Oriana' is the heroine of the
Spanish chivalric romance cycle *Amadis de Gaul*, translated into English in the late sixteenth century (see Introduction, pp. 12–13).

20. Stephen Hammerton] Described by the Restoration theatre historian James
Wright as 'a most noted and beautiful Woman Actor', Hammerton went on to become
a popular player of romantic leads (*JCS*, 2.461).

21. ROSALURA] Combining the attributes of a rose-pink complexion and feminine
'allure'.

William Trigg] Trigg's performance in the role of Rosalura is an exception to his customary performance of minor female parts for the King's Men during the 1620s and
1630s. Baldwin notes, 'the actor list of [*The Wild-Goose Chase*] as published in 1652
distinguishes those who had become members [of the company] before publication from
non-members by "Mr" ' (p. 60). Trigg and Gough (below, 23n) are the only non-
members listed.

22. airy] lively, sprightly (*OED* 6C).

23. LILLIA-BIANCA] Lily-white; possibly an evocation of the demure character Bianca
in Shakespeare's *The Taming of the Shrew*.

Alexander Gough] Bentley believes that Gough was apprenticed to the King's Men
at an early age but played minor parts when he became too old for female roles (*JCS*,
2.446).

24. PETELLA] from the Latin 'peto', 'to go to fetch'; or 'patella', 'knee-cap', with reference to a subservient posture (Lewis and Short). Bowers conjectures that the part of
Petella was played by a boy, who probably doubled as Mariana and one of the four
women (*DW*, 6.336.)

25. Master Shank] 'John Shank was a well-known comedian, specializing in clown's
parts, and therefore should be assigned the role of the loose-talking impertinent Servant
to the two daughters' (Bowers, *DW*, 6.336).

26.] The courtesan is introduced to Lillia-Bianca as 'Mariana' by Pinac at 3.1.227.
She is unmasked by Lillia-Bianca as 'Jumping Joan' at 4.1.142.

27. A Young . . . Factor] a mercantile agent (*OED* 4a); calls himself 'Foss' at 5.2.75.
Not a genuine merchant's factor, but, as the context of Act 5 makes clear, one of La
Castre's 'secret friends' (5.1.13) enlisted in the disguise plot to catch Mirabell.

27–8. John Honeyman] Honeyman's death in his mid-twenties in 1636 halted the

Page.
Servants.   30
Singing Boy.
Two Gentlemen.
Two [*men disguised as*] Merchants.
Priest.
Four Women.   35

The scene, Paris.

---

32. *Two* Gentlemen] *Dyce (subst.); not in F1.*   33.] *Dyce (subst.);* TWO MER-
CHANTS. *F1.*

---

career of a player described as 'one of the most important boy actors in the [King's]
company from about 1626 to about 1630' (*JCS*, 2.476).
   29. *Page*] 'i.e. the "Footboy", who appears at the opening of the play' (Dyce).
   32. *Two Gentlemen*] The gentlemen, not listed in *F1*, enter with Belleur at 3.1.270.
   34. *Priest*] It is not clear whether the priest in 4.1 is an accomplice disguised as a
priest, or whether he is a bona-fide priest, who has been deceived into believing that a
wedding between Pinac and Mariana will actually take place. The part was played by
Richard Baxter in the 1632 revival of *The Wild-Goose Chase* (see below, Press
Variants, Notes, sig. K2v, 17.1).

ACT I

Enter DE GARD *and a* Footboy.

De Gard. Sirrah, you know I have rid hard; stir my horse well,
And let him want no litter.
Boy.   I am sure I have run hard,
Would somebody would walk me and see me littered!
For I think my fellow horse cannot in reason
Desire more rest, nor take up his chamber before me: 5
But we are the beasts now, and the beasts are our masters.
De Gard. When you have done, step to the ten-crown ordinary –
Boy. With all my heart, sir, for I have a twenty-crown stomach.
De Gard. And there bespeak a dinner.
Boy. [Going]   Yes, sir, presently.
De Gard. For whom, I beseech you, sir?
Boy.   For myself, I take it, sir.   10
De Gard. In truth, ye shall not take it; 'tis not meant for you;
There's for your provender. [*Gives money.*] Bespeak a dinner
For Monsieur Mirabell and his companions;
They'll be in town within this hour. When you have done, sirrah,
Make ready all things at my lodging for me,   15
And wait me there.

---

oSD] *Weber; Enter* Monsieur De Gard, *and a* Foot-boy *F1.*   7. ordinary –] *Colman;*
Ordinary. *F1.*   8. have a twenty-crown] *F2;* have Twenty Crown *F1.*   9SD] *Colman;
not in F1.*   12SD] *Dyce; not in F1.*

---

1. *Sirrah*] a term of address used to men or boys, sometimes employed less seriously
in addressing children (*OED* 1).
stir] walk the horse to cool it down before it is stabled; not in *OED.*
2. *litter*] straw or rushes used as bedding for animals.
6. *we ... masters*] cf. Beaumont's *The Woman Hater* (with some revision by
Fletcher): ''tis the fashion of our gentry to have their horses wait at dore like men,
while the beasts their maisters, are within at racke and mainger' (4.2.123–5).
7. *ordinary*] an eating-house or tavern serving meals at a fixed price (*OED* 14b); in this
case for ten crowns (£2.50 in modern terms), a lavish amount for a dinner at this time.
9. *presently*] immediately (*OED* 3).
12. *provender*] food, provisions esp. dry food as corn or hay, for horses etc. (*OED*
2).

Boy.   The ten-crown ordinary?
De Gard. Yes, sir, if you have not forgot it.
Boy.   I'll forget my feet first;
    'Tis the best part of a footman's faith.   *Exit* Footboy.
De Gard.   These youths,
    For all they have been in Italy to learn thrift,
    And seem to wonder at men's lavish ways,   20
    Yet they cannot rub off old friends, their French itches.
    They must meet sometimes to disport their bodies
    With good wine and good women, and good store too.
    Let 'em be what they will, they are armed at all points,
    And then hang saving, let the sea grow high!   25
    This ordinary can fit 'em of all sizes,

            Enter LA CASTRE *and* ORIANA.

    They must salute their country with old customs.
Oriana. Brother.
De Gard.   My dearest sister.   [*Oriana and De Gard embrace.*]
Oriana.   Welcome, welcome:
    Indeed ye are welcome home, most welcome!
De Gard.   Thank ye.

---

20. men's lavish] *F2*; menslavish *F1*.   25. saving, let . . . high!] *Colman*; saving. Let
. . . high, *F1*.   28SD] *This ed.*; *not in F1*.

18. *footman's faith*] (1) i.e. to know where the eating-houses are located; (2) 'The
faith alluded to, in the sense of profession or mystery, turns upon the pun on feet (l.17),
"feet" and "faith" being near homophones in the seventeenth century' (Lister).

18–19. *These . . . thrift*] i.e. Mirabell and his travelling companions with whom De
Gard has recently renewed his acquaintance. De Gard views with scepticism the idea
that, for young men, travel outside one's native country is morally and intellectually
beneficial. In early modern England, travel was seen as involving a 'wholesome hardship' which contributed to its function as a rite of passage in the formation of English
upper-class manhood (see Michèle Cohen, 'The Grand Tour: Constructing the English
Gentleman in Eighteenth-Century France', *History of Education* 21 (1992), 241–57
(251)). Fletcher here transposes the English fascination with foreign travel and cultures
on to the differences between France and Italy.

21. *French itches*] implying both sexual desire and syphilis, known as 'the French
disease'.

24. *armed . . . points*] fully prepared for all eventualities; a phrase referring to battlefield armoury. Cf. the ghost of Hamlet's father appearing clad in armour from head
to toe: 'Armed at all points exactly, cap-à-pie' (*Ham.* 1.2.200).

25 *let . . . high*] variation of the proverb, 'Let the sea swell and rise as high as he
will, yet hath God appointed how far he shall go' (Tilley S176).

27. *salute . . . customs*] 'i.e. celebrate their return home in a typical manner' (Lister).

You are grown a handsome woman, Oriana –   30
Blush at your faults – I am wondrous glad to see ye.
Monsieur La Castre, let not my affection
To my fair sister make me be held unmannerly:
I am glad to see ye well, to see ye lusty,
Good health about ye, and in fair company.   35
Believe me, I am proud –
La Castre.   Fair sir, I thank ye.
Monsieur de Gard, you are welcome from your journey;
Good men have still good welcome. Give me your hand, sir.
Once more, you are welcome home! You look still younger.
De Gard. Time has no leisure to look after us;   40
We wander everywhere – age cannot find us.
La Castre. And how does all?
De Gard.   All well, sir, and all lusty.
La Castre. I hope my son be so; I doubt not, sir,
But you have often seen him in your journeys,
And bring me some fair news.
De Gard.   Your son is well, sir,   45
And grown a proper gentleman: he is well and lusty.
Within this eight hours I took leave of him,
And over-eyed him, having some slight business
That forced me out o' th' way: I can assure you,
He will be here tonight.
La Castre.   Ye make me glad, sir,   50
For, o' my faith, I almost long to see him;
Methinks he has been away –
De Gard.   'Tis but your tenderness;

30–1. Oriana – / Blush . . . faults –] *Lister; Oriana, /* (Blush . . . faults) *F1.*   33. me be]
F2; me held *F1.*   41. wander everywhere – age] *This ed.;* wander, everywhere: Age *F1;*
wander everywhere: Age *F2;* wander everywhere, age *Lister.*   48. over-eyed] *This ed.;*
over-eyd *F1;* over-ey'd *F2;* over-rid, over-yed *conj. Sympson;* over-hied *conj. Colman;*
over-hied *Weber.*

---

31. *Blush at your faults*] Proverbially, 'blushing is virtue's colour (is a sign of grace)'
(Dent B480).
34. *lusty*] also at 1.1.42 and 1.1.46: healthy, strong, vigorous (*OED* 5a).
39. *still*] always.
40. *after*] back on.
46. *proper*] (1) of good character or standing; honest, respectable, worthy (*OED*
8b); (2) good-looking and handsome (*OED* 9).
48. *over-eyed*] observed, cast my eye over.
51. *almost*] greatly; used as an intensifier.
52. *tenderness*] weakness (*OED* 1).

What are three years? A lovesick wench will allow it!
His friends that went out with him are come back too,
Belleur and young Pinac. He bid me say little,					55
Because he means to be his own glad messenger.
La Castre. I thank ye for this news, sir. He shall be welcome,
And his friends too: indeed, I thank you heartily.
And how (for I dare say you will not flatter him)
Has Italy wrought on him? Has he mewed yet					60
His wild fantastic toys? They say that climate
Is a great purger of those humorous fluxes.
How is he improved, I pray ye?
De Gard.					No doubt, sir, well;
H'as borne himself a full and noble gentleman.
To speak him farther is beyond my charter.					65
La Castre. I am glad to hear so much good. Come, I see
You long to enjoy your sister; yet I must entreat ye,
Before I go, to sup with me tonight,
And must not be denied.
De Gard.					I am your servant.
La Castre. Where you shall meet fair, merry and noble company –					70
My neighbour Nantolet and his two fair daughters.
De Gard. Your supper's seasoned well, sir; I shall wait upon ye.
La Castre. Till then I'll leave ye, and you're once more welcome.
De Gard. I thank ye, noble sir.					*Exit* [LA CASTRE.]
					Now, Oriana,
How have ye done since I went? Have ye had your health well,					75
And your mind free?
Oriana.					You see I am not bated;

---

53. *allow it*] 'i.e. *agree* that three years' absence are no such great matter' (Colman).

54. *went out*] went abroad. Cf. *Lear* 1.1.32–3 (Quarto); 1.1.31–2 (Folio), 'He hath been out nine years, and away he shall again.'

60–1. *Has he mewed ... toys*] Has he abandoned his extravagant or impulsive ways? 'Mewing' is a term from falconry = to moult, shed, or change feathers.

62. *humorous fluxes*] La Castre has in mind the physiological impact of climate as it related to humoral theory; i.e. the notion derived from the ancient Greek physician Galen, that the body's physical appearance and mental disposition were determined by the relative proportions of four fluids: blood, phlegm, choler and melancholy, or black choler. Cf. *Oth.* 3.4.29–31: 'Is he not jealous? / Who, he? I think the sun where he was born / Drew all such humours from him.'

64. *full*] one whose mind is richly stored (*OED* 2d); cf. Francis Bacon: 'Reading maketh a Full Man; Conference a Ready man; And Writing an Exact Man', *The Essayes or Counsels, Civill and Morall*, ed. Michael Kiernan (Oxford: Clarendon Press, 1985), p. 153.

65. *To speak ... charter*] De Gard tactfully excuses himself from attesting further to Mirabell's character by invoking the limitations of legal contract.

76. *bated*] reduced in weight.

Merry, and eat my meat.
De Gard.   A good preservative.
And how have you been used? You know, Oriana,
Upon my going out, at your request,
I left your portion in La Castre's hands,   80
The main means you must stick to: for that reason,
And 'tis no little one, I ask ye, sister,
With what humanity he entertains ye,
And how you find his courtesy?
Oriana.   Most ready.
I can assure you, sir, I am used most nobly.   85
De Gard. I am glad to hear it. But I prithee tell me,
And tell me true, what end had you, Oriana,
In trusting your money here? He is no kinsman,
Nor any tie upon him of a guardian;
Nor dare I think ye doubt my prodigality.   90
Oriana. No, certain, sir, none of all this provoked me;
Another private reason.
De Gard.   'Tis not private,
Nor carried so; 'tis common, my fair sister,
Your love to Mirabell – your blushes tell it.
'Tis too much known, and spoken of too largely;   95
And with no little shame I wonder at it.
Oriana. Is it a shame to love?
De Gard.   To love undiscreetly:

---

90. dare I think] *F1*; dare, I think *Sympson*.

---

77. *meat*] food.

80. *portion*] dowry; the money or property a wife brings to her husband in marriage.

81. *main . . . to*] 'Your dowry is the most important support you must cling to, because on it depends the kind of marriage and future you will be able to achieve' (Lister).

84. *courtesy*] courteousness, generosity (*OED* 2a); may also convey a sense of benevolence towards a dependant as a favour, rather than prompted by familial or legal duty (*OED* 2b, 3a).

88–9. *He is no kinsman . . . guardian*] De Gard is concerned that Oriana appears too eager in her pursuit of Mirabell, leaving herself open to public censure, but his question also expresses the concern that La Castre has administered her estate fairly.

90. *doubt my prodigality*] (1) fear that I will act improvidently; (2) doubt my generosity.

92. *'Tis not private*] i.e. secret, as distinct from *private* in Oriana's part-line, which carries the sense of 'personal'.

93. *common*] common knowledge.

95. *largely*] widely.

A virgin should be tender of her honour,
Close, and secure.
Oriana.   I am as close as can be,
And stand upon as strong and honest guards too;   100
Unless this warlike age need a portcullis.
Yet, I confess, I love him.
De Gard.   Hear the people.
Oriana. Now I say hang the people! He that dares
Believe what they say dares be mad, and give
His mother, nay, his own wife, up to rumour.   105
All grounds of truth they build on is a tavern,
And their best censure's sack, sack in abundance;
For as they drink they think: they ne'er speak modestly,
Unless the wine be poor, or they want money.
Believe them? Believe *Amadis de Gaul*,   110
The Knight o' th' Sun, or *Palmerin of England*,
For these, to them, are modest and true stories.

---

98. *tender of*] careful to preserve, considerate of (*OED* 9a).

99. *Close, and secure*] Discreet.

101. *warlike age*] At the time of the court performance of *The Wild-Goose Chase*, during the Christmas season of 1621-2, the Catholic government of France was beset with civil unrest and Protestant rebellion. The Twelve Years' Truce between King Philip III of Spain and his rebellious Dutch subjects had just ended and war had resumed. The Thirty Years' War, which began in 1618 with a Bohemian Protestant rebellion against the Holy Roman Emperor, Ferdinand II, was in the process of becoming a general European conflict. In 1613 Elizabeth, daughter of England's King James I, married Frederick V, Elector Palatine, who assumed leadership of the Bohemian Protestant rebels. However, in 1620 an imperial army suppressed the rebellion and in 1621 Spanish forces invaded the Palatinate, driving Frederick and Elizabeth into exile. Although James preferred neutrality, in 1621 he came under great parliamentary pressure to end negotiations for his son, Charles, to marry the Spanish Infanta and instead to relieve the Palatinate.

portcullis] the gateway to a fortress or fortified town (*OED* 1). For the bawdy sense in which *portcullis* is used figuratively in relation to sexual siege see Williams, p. 1073. The dentate structure of the portcullis invoked associations with the genital 'teeth' that women were thought to possess. For a discussion of the political and sexual resonances of this exchange see McMullan, pp. 168-9.

102. *Hear the people*] Pay attention to gossip about you (Lister).

107. *sack*] sweetened wine. Cf. *The Bird in a Cage*, 2.1.267.

110-11. Amadis . . . England] titles of translations of Spanish and Portuguese chivalric romances which enjoyed great popularity with Elizabethan readers but were often invoked satirically by seventeenth-century dramatists, pre-eminently by Beaumont in *The Knight of the Burning Pestle* (1613). The three romances Oriana cites are alluded to in the first chapter of *Don Quixote* (1605, trans. 1616) and in Robert Burton's *The Anatomy of Melancholy* (1621).

Pray understand me; if their tongues be truth,
And if *in vino veritas* be an oracle,
What woman is, or has been ever, honest?   115
Give 'em but ten round cups, they'll swear Lucretia
Died not for want of power to resist Tarquin,
But want of pleasure that he stayed no longer;
And Portia, that was famous for her piety
To her loved lord, they'll face ye out, died o' th' pox.   120
De Gard. Well, there is something, sister.
Oriana.   If there be, brother,
'Tis none of their things; 'tis not yet so monstrous:
My thing is marriage; and at his return
I hope to put their squint eyes right again.
De Gard. Marriage? 'Tis true, his father is a rich man,   125
Rich both in land and money; he his heir,
A young and handsome man, I must confess too;
But of such qualities and such wild flings,
Such admirable imperfections, sister,
(For all his travel and bought experience)   130
I should be loath to own him for my brother.
Methinks a rich mind in a state indifferent
Would prove the better fortune.
Oriana.   If he be wild,

---

114. And if] *F1*; As if *Weber.*

114. in vino veritas] Proverbially, 'in wine there is truth' (Dent W465)
116. *round*] full, generous (*OED* 8b & c).
Lucretia] Lucretia, wife of Tarquinius Collatinus, was raped by Sextus Tarquinius, son of the Etruscan King of Rome, Tarquinius Superbus, whilst Sextus was a guest in her house. After commanding her family to avenge her rape, Lucretia fatally stabbed herself so that other women who committed adultery would not use her case as a precedent to avoid the Roman punishment for adultery, death. Lucretia's rape was used by Lucius Junius Brutus as the trigger for expelling the Tarquins from Rome, leading to the founding of the Roman Republic. Fletcher's *The Tragedy of Valentinian* (1614) is loosely based on this story.
116–18. With the slander against Lucretia compare the boast of the First Daughter of Fletcher's heroine Bonduca, before stabbing herself; *Bonduca* 4.4.115–19.
119. *Portia*] the wife of Marcus Brutus. Portia, like Lucretia, became an emblem of wifely constancy.
120. *face ye out*] brazenly insist; cf. 'this outfacing fellow, Mirabell' at 3.1.9.
pox] syphilis.
124. *squint eyes*] malicious or erroneous judgement.
129. *admirable imperfections*] a pun on Mirabell's name, suggesting the ambivalent reactions of shock and wonder that his transgressive behaviour provokes.
132. *a rich mind . . . indifferent*] i.e. a 'full' man (cf. 1.1.64) with a moderate estate or of lesser rank.

The reclaiming him to good and honest, brother,
Will make much for my honour; which, if I prosper,   135
Shall be the study of my love, and life too.
De Gard. Ye say well; would he thought as well, and loved too!
He marry? He'll be hanged first! He knows no more
What the conditions and the ties of love are,
The honest purposes and grounds of marriage,   140
Nor will know, nor be ever brought t' endeavour,
Than I do how to build a church. He was ever
A loose and strong defier of all order;
His loves are wanderers, they knock at each door
And taste each dish, but are no residents.   145
Or say he may be brought to think of marriage –
As 'twill be no small labour – thy hopes are strangers.
I know there is a laboured match now followed,
Now at this time, for which he was sent for home too.
Be not abused; Nantolet has two fair daughters,   150
And he must take his choice.
Oriana.   Let him take freely.
For all this, I despair not. My mind tells me
That I, and only I, must make him perfect,
And in that hope I rest.
De Gard.   Since y' are so confident,
Prosper your hope! I'll be no adversary: 151
Keep yourself fair and right, he shall not wrong ye.
Oriana. When I forget my virtue, no man know me.   *Exeunt.*

SCENE 2

Enter MIRABELL, PINAC, BELLEUR, *and* Servants.

Mirabell. Welcome to Paris once more, gentlemen!
We have had a merry and a lusty ordinary,

---

150. Nantolet] *Langbaine*; Natolet *F1*.   154. y' are] *F1*; you're *Colman*.

140. *honest purposes ... marriage*] According to the Anglican marriage service, the three ends of marriage are the procreation of children, the avoidance of fornication, and the mutual society and help of the partners.

148. *laboured match*] a marriage to be brought about by others' striving, with a probable pun 'anticipating the woman's labour in childbed, which will be the result of that match' (Lister).

now followed] under negotiation.

150. *Be not abused*] Be under no misapprehension.

157. *no man know me*] i.e. let me be denied the company of civil society.

2. *lusty ordinary*] hearty, abundant meal; cf. 1.1.7.

And wine, and good meat, and a bouncing reckoning.
And let it go for once – 'tis a good physic –
Only the wenches are not for my diet,   5
They are too lean and thin, their embraces brawn-fall'n.
Give me the plump Venetian, fat and lusty,
That meets me soft and supple, smiles upon me
As if a cup of full wine leaped to kiss me –
These slight things I affect not.
Pinac.   They are ill-built,   10
Pin-buttocked, like your dainty Barbaries,
And weak i' th' pasterns; they'll endure no hardness.
Mirabell. There's nothing good or handsome bred amongst us:
Till we are travelled and live abroad we are coxcombs.
Ye talk of France – a slight, unseasoned country,   15
Abundance of gross food, which makes us blockheads!
We are fair set out indeed, and so are fore-horses.
Men say we are great courtiers – men abuse us:
We are wise and valiant too – *non credo, signor!*
Our women the best linguists – they are parrots;   20
O' this side the Alps they are nothing but mere drolleries.

---

3. *bouncing reckoning*] a huge bill.
6. *brawn-fall'n*] lacking passion.
7. *plump Venetian*] Visiting Venice in the late sixteenth century, Fynes Moryson remarked that the women 'weare gownes, leaving all the necke and brest bare, and they are closed before with a lace, so open, as a man may see the linnen which they lap about their bodies, to make them seeme fat, the Italians most loving fat women' (Moryson, *Itinerary*, Part 3, Bk 4, Ch. 1, p. 172).
10. *These*] i.e., Parisian women.
affect not] am not attracted to.
11. *Pin-buttocked*] Having a narrow or sharp-boned buttock; often used to describe horses (*OED* VI 18).
Barbaries] Breed of African horse prized for its swiftness and endurance in war service.
12. *pasterns*] that part of a horse's foot between the fetlock and the hoof (*OED* 2), corresponding to the human ankle. In Fletcher's *The Humorous Lieutenant*, Leucippe, a bawd, recruits girls after a physical inspection: 'Let me see your leg; – she treads but low in the pasternes' (2.3.68–9).
14. *coxcombs*] fools (*OED* 3). Literally, the cap worn by a professional fool (*OED* 1).
15. *unseasoned*] insignificant, boring.
17. *fore-horses*] the leading horses in a team, which were sometimes adorned with plumes and flowers.
19. non credo, signor!] I don't believe it, Sir!
21. *mere drolleries*] absolute puppets (*OED* drollery 2a, citing this line); cf. 'puppies' at l. 28 below.

Ha! *Roma la Santa*, Italy for my money:
  Their policies, their customs, their frugalities,
  Their courtesies so open, yet so reserved too,
  As when ye think y' are known best, ye are a stranger;   25
  Their very pickteeth speak more man than we do,
  And season of more salt.
Pinac.   'Tis a brave country;
  Not pestered with your stubborn precise puppies,
  That turn all useful and allowed contentments
  To scabs and scruples – hang 'em, capon-worshippers!   30
Belleur. I like that freedom well, and like their women too,
  And would fain do as others do; but I am so bashful,
  So naturally an ass: look ye, I can look upon 'em,
  And very willingly I go to see 'em,
  (There's no man willinger), and I can kiss 'em,   35
  And make a shift –
Mirabell.   But if they chance to flout ye,
  Or say, 'ye are too bold! Fie, sir, remember!
  I pray sit farther off –'
Belleur.   'Tis true, I am humbled,
  I am gone, I confess ingenuously I am silenced,
  The spirit of amber cannot force me answer.   40

37–8] *Colman;* Or say ye are . . . / . . . off; – *F1.*   39. ingenuously I] *F1;* ingenuously,
I *Sympson.*

---

22. Roma la Santa] (1) 'Holy Rome' (Fraser and Rabkin); (2) perhaps the
seventeenth-century equivalent of 'Rome the Eternal City', since John Florio's
Italian–English dictionary of 1598 includes a definition of the masculine form, *santo,* as
'of entire life' (Florio, *A Worlde of Wordes,* 1598, rpt Hildesheim: Olms, 1972, p. 343).

22. *Italy for my money*] echoing the title of William Haughton's play *Englishmen
for my Money, or, A Woman Will Have Her Will* (1598), in which the three daughters
of a Portuguese Jew living in London resist their father's attempts to marry them to
foreigners and eventually marry the English suitors of their choice.

26. *pickteeth*] toothpicks, in fashionable use as an accessory to gesticulation. Cf.
Jonson, *Volpone* 4.1.139–41: 'I went and bought two toothpicks, whereof one / I burst
immediately in a discourse / With a Dutch merchant, 'bout *ragion' del stato'.*

27. *brave*] an expression of admiration or praise, meaning 'excellent', 'good', 'fine'.

28. *stubborn . . . puppies*] (1) puritan sticklers for morality; (2) rigidly puritanical
women (Lister).

30. *capon-worshippers*] 'admirers of men who are no more masculine than castrated
cocks' (Lister). Pinac disparages Frenchmen as eunuchs, while identifying with the
reputedly virile Italians.

32. *fain*] gladly (OED 4B).

36. *make a shift*] manage to.

flout] mock (OED 1).

40. *spirit of amber*] a distillation with rousing and reputedly aphrodisiacal qualities.

Pinac. Then would I sing and dance.
Belleur.   You have wherewithal, sir.
Pinac. And charge her up again.
Belleur.   I can be hanged first:
     Yet where I fasten well, I am a tyrant.
Mirabell. Why, thou dar'st fight?
Belleur.   Yes, certainly I dare fight;
     And fight with any man, at any weapon –   45
     Would th' other were no more! But a pox on't,
     When I am sometimes in my height of hope,
     And reasonable-valiant that way, my heart hardened,
     Some scornful jest or other chops between me
     And my desire. What would ye have me to do then, gentlemen?   50
Mirabell. Belleur, ye must be bolder. Travel three years
     And bring home such a baby to betray ye
     As bashfulness? A great fellow, and a soldier?
Belleur. You have the gift of impudence; be thankful,
     Every man has not the like talent. I will study,   55
     And if it may be revealed to me –
Mirabell.   Learn of me,
     And of Pinac. No doubt you'll find employment,
     Ladies will look for courtship.
Pinac.   'Tis but fleshing,
     But standing one good brunt or two. Hast thou any mind to
          marriage?
     We'll provide thee some soft-natured wench, that's dumb too.   60
Mirabell. Or an old woman that cannot refuse thee in charity.
Belleur. A dumb woman, or an old woman that were eager,
     And cared not for discourse, I were excellent at.
Mirabell. You must now put on boldness, there's no avoiding it,

---

51. Belleur] *Sympson*; Belvere *F1*.   55–6. study, / And if] *Sympson*; study / And if *F1*.
56. me –] *Sympson*; me. *F1*.

---

42. *charge her up*] renew the attack.
   43. *where . . . tyrant*] (1) 'when I am resolved on a woman, I am resolute'; (2) 'when I make a strong impression on someone, I am despotically demanding' (Lister).
   46. *Would . . . more*] Belleur wishes that the armaments and tactics of sexual warfare were as uncomplicated as those of military combat.
   48. *reasonable-valiant*] Two adjectives were often hyphenated, cf. *1H4* 5.1.90: 'More active-valiant or more valiant-young'.
   56. *And if*] As punctuated in *F1*, 'if indeed' (Abbott 105). Sympson's punctuation is more likely to make sense onstage.
   58. *fleshing*] initiation in warfare (*OED* flesh v. 2a).
   59. *brunt*] sharp blow; metaphor of courtship as battle.

And stand all hazards; fly at all games bravely;   65
They'll say you went out like an ox, and returned like an ass else.
Belleur. I shall make danger, sure.
Mirabell.   I am sent for home now.
I know it is to marry, but my father shall pardon me:
Although it be a weighty ceremony,
And may concern me hereafter in my gravity,   70
I will not lose the freedom of a traveller;
A new strong lusty bark cannot ride at one anchor.
Shall I make divers suits to show to the same eyes?
'Tis dull and homespun: study several pleasures,
And want employments for 'em? I'll be hanged first!   75
Tie me to one smock? Make my travels fruitless?
I'll none of that; for every fresh behaviour,
By your leave, father, I must have a fresh mistress,
And a fresh favour too.
Belleur.   I like that passingly;
As many as you will, so they be willing;   80
Willing, and gentle, gentle.
Pinac.   There's no reason
A gentleman and a traveller should be clapped up,
(For 'tis a kind of bilboes to be married)
Before he manifest to the world his good parts:
Tug ever like a rascal at one oar?   85

---

67. danger, sure.] *Weber*; danger sure *F1*. 69. weighty] *Sympson*; witty *F1*.
83. bilboes] *Sympson*; Baeboes *F1*. 85. *This ed.*; Tug ever, like a rascal, at one oar?
Colman. 85. like a] *Langbaine*; like at a *F1*.

---

67. *make danger, sure*] certainly risk it (*OED* danger 8).
69. *weighty*] Reed judged *F1*'s 'witty' 'not entirely indefensible' on the grounds that,
in Fletcher's time, 'wit' and 'wisdom' were 'synonomous terms' (Colman). Lister notes
the complementarity of 'weighty' and 'gravity' in l. 70, observing 'a weighty ceremony
is one of great significance and solemnity'.
72. *bark*] sailing vessel (*OED* 1).
ride at one anchor] i.e. be captured by one woman.
73. *make divers suits*] employ different courtship techniques.
76. *smock*] woman's undergarment; here used metonymically for womankind.
79. *favour*] (1) i.e., face. In chivalric literature a 'favour' was a gift of a glove or
ribbon, worn as a token of affection; (2) For the bawdy sense of *favour* = 'sexual benevolence' see Williams, p. 468.
83. *bilboes*] (1) a long iron bar, furnished with sliding shackles to confine the ankles
of prisoners, and a lock by which to fix one end of the bar to the floor or ground (*OED*
bilbo²).

Give me the Italian liberty!
Mirabell.   That I study,
And that I will enjoy. Come, go in, gentlemen;
There mark how I behave myself, and follow.   *Exeunt.*

SCENE 3

Enter LA CASTRE, NANTOLET, LUGIER, ROSALURA,
[*and*] LILLIA-BIANCA.

La Castre. You and your beauteous daughters are most welcome,
Beshrew my blood they are fair ones! – Welcome beauties,
Welcome sweet birds.
Nantolet.   They are bound much to your courtesies.
La Castre. I hope we shall be nearer acquainted.
Nantolet.   That's my hope too.
For certain, sir, I much desire your alliance.   5
You see 'em, they are no gypsies; for their breeding,
It has not been so coarse but they are able
To rank themselves with women of fair fashion;
Indeed, they have been trained well.
Lugier.   Thank me!
Nantolet. Fit for the heirs of that state I shall leave 'em;   10
To say more is to sell 'em. They say your son,
Now he has travelled, must be wondrous curious
And choice in what he takes: these are no coarse ones.
Sir, here's a merry wench, [*Presenting Rosalura*] let him look to
    himself,
(All heart, i' faith) may chance to startle him,   15
For all his care and travelled caution,
May creep into his eye. If he love gravity,
Affect a solemn face, [*Indicating Lillia-Bianca*] there's one will fit
    him.

9. *Nantolet.* Indeed . . . well.] *F1*; *La Castre.* Indeed . . . well. *Sympson.*   14SD] *This
ed.; not in F1;* [*Indicating Rosalura*] *following 'Sir', Lister;* [Rosalure.] *in right margin
opp. l. 14 Bowers.*   18SD] *Lister (subst.); not in F1;* [Lylia-Biancha] *in right margin
opp. l. 18 Bowers.*

86. *Italian liberty*] sexual and moral freedom of the Italians, contrasting with the
shackled slavery imaged in the previous lines.

2. *Beshrew my blood*] 'indeed'.

6. *gypsies*] (1) ill-bred, 'wild'; (2) a contemptuous term for a woman, as being
cunning, deceitful or fickle (*OED* gypsy 2b).

10. *state*] estate (*OED* 2a).

12–13. *wondrous curious . . . choice*] very difficult to satisfy, discerning; *curious*
may imply connoisseurship (*OED* 6a).

La Castre. So young and so demure?
Nantolet.   She is my daughter,
   Else I would tell you, sir, she is a mistress   20
   Both of those manners and that modesty
   You would wonder at. She is no often speaker,
   But when she does, she speaks well; nor no reveller,
   Yet she can dance, and has studied the court elements,
   And sings, as some say, handsomely; if a woman,   25
   With the decency of her sex, may be a scholar,
   I can assure ye, sir, she understands too.
La Castre. These are fit garments, sir.
Lugier.   Thank them that cut 'em:
   Yes, they are handsome women; they have handsome parts too,
   Pretty becoming parts.
La Castre.   'Tis like they have, sir.   30
Lugier. Yes, yes, and handsome education they have had too,
   Had it abundantly. They need not blush at it –
   I taught it, I'll avouch it.
La Castre.   Ye say well, sir.
Lugier. I know what I say, sir, and I say but right, sir:
   I am no trumpet of their commendations   35
   Before their father; else I should say farther.
La Castre. Pray ye, what's this gentleman?
Nantolet.   One that lives with me, sir;
   A man well bred and learned, but blunt and bitter,
   Yet it offends no wise man; I take pleasure in't:
   Many fair gifts he has, in some of which,   40
   That lie most easy to their understandings,
   H'as handsomely bred up my girls, I thank him.

---

42. H'as] *F2*; Has *F1*.

---

24. *court elements*] accomplishments appropriate to life at court; these might include dance, needlework, musical skills, and civil conversation.

25–6. *if a woman ... scholar*] Nantolet's use of the conditional registers the view, widespread in the Renaissance, 'that the virtuous woman should not pursue indecorously advanced studies' (Anthony Grafton and Lisa Jardine, *From Humanism to the Humanities: Education and the Liberal Arts in Fifteenth- and Sixteenth-Century Europe* (Cambridge, Massachusetts: Harvard University Press, 1986), p. 35). For a discussion of the theme of women's education in *The Wild-Goose Chase* see Introduction, pp. 17–18.

27. *understands*] has comprehension or intellectual understanding.

28. *fit garments*] appropriate adornments.

29–30. *parts*] (1) qualities; (2) here and at 1.3.43–4, *part* may carry a secondary bawdy meaning of 'genitals' (Williams, p. 996). Cf. *The Bird in a Cage* 3.3.37.

Lugier. I have put it to 'em, that's my part, I have urged it,
   It seems they are of years now to take hold on't.
Nantolet. He's wondrous blunt.
La Castre.   By my faith, I was afraid of him: 45
   Does he not fall out with the gentlewomen sometimes?
Nantolet. No, no; he's that way moderate and discreet, sir.
Rosalura. If he did, we should be too hard for him.
Lugier.   Well said, sulphur!
   Too hard for thy husband's head, if he wear not armour.
Nantolet. Many of these bickerings, sir.
La Castre.   I am glad they are no oracles: 50
   Sure as I live, he beats them, he's so puissant.

   Enter MIRABELL, PINAC, [BELLEUR,] DE GARD, *and* ORIANA.

Oriana. Well, if ye do forget –
Mirabell.   Prithee hold thy peace!
   I know thou art a pretty wench; I know thou lov'st me;
   Preserve it till we have a fit time to discourse on't,
   And a fit place. I'll ease thy heart, I warrant thee: 55
   Thou see'st I have much to do now.
Oriana.   I am answered, sir:
   With me ye shall have nothing on these conditions.
De Gard. [*To Mirabell*] Your father and your friends.
La Castre.   You are welcome home, sir;
   Bless ye, ye are very welcome. Pray know this gentleman,
   And these fair ladies.
Nantolet.   Monsieur Mirabell,   60
   I am much affected with your fair return, sir:
   You bring a general joy.
Mirabell.   I bring you service,

43–4. *Lugier.* I have . . . hold on't.] *Sympson; speech prefix omitted F1.*   45. *Nantolet.* He's . . . blunt.] *F1; La Castre.* He's . . . blunt. *Sympson.*   51. *Sure as] Colman.*
Sure, as *F1.*   51SD] *Weber; in right margin opp. ll. 50–1 F1.*

44. *to take hold on't*] (1) to capitalize on it; (2) Lugier uses the terminology of
animal husbandry, by which the male bull or horse is *put* to the female and covering
(mating) is encouraged or *urged*. If the animal successfully conceives, the pregnancy is
said to have *taken hold* (OED 15d).
   48. *sulphur*] implying a volatile temperament, a play on the fiery qualities of sulphur,
otherwise known as 'brimstone', 'a virago, a spit-fire' (OED 4).
   49. *Too hard . . . armour*] likely to give a husband the metaphoric 'horns' associated
with a cuckold, unless he is vigilant.
   51. *puissant*] (1) authoritative; (2) sexually potent, cf. 'the puissant pike' at 3.1.129.
   57. *nothing on these conditions*] i.e., no extramarital sexual dalliance.

And these bright beauties, sir.
Nantolet.   Welcome home, gentlemen,
   Welcome with all my heart!
Belleur, Pinac.   We thank ye, sir.
La Castre. Your friends will have their share too.
Belleur.   Sir, we hope   65
   They'll look upon us, though we show like strangers.
Nantolet. Monsieur De Gard, I must salute you also,
   And this fair gentlewoman: you are welcome from your travel too,
   All welcome, all.   [*La Castre and Mirabell speak apart.*]
De Gard.   We render ye our loves, sir,
   The best wealth we bring home – By your favours, beauties! –   70
   [*Aside to Oriana*] One of these two: you know my meaning.
Oriana.   Well, sir;
   They are fair and handsome, I must needs confess it,
   And let it prove the worst, I shall live after it:
   Whilst I have meat and drink, love cannot starve me;
   For if I die o' th' first fit, I am unhappy,   75
   And worthy to be buried with my heels upward.
Mirabell. To marry, sir?
La Castre.   You know I am an old man,
   And every hour declining to my grave,
   One foot already in; more sons I have not,
   Nor more I dare not seek whilst you are worthy;   80
   In you lies all my hope, and all my name,
   The making good or wretched of my memory,
   The safety of my state.
Mirabell.   And you have provided,
   Out of this tenderness, these handsome gentlewomen,
   Daughters to this rich man, to take my choice of?   85
La Castre. I have, dear son.
Mirabell.   'Tis true, ye are old and feebled;
   Would ye were young again, and in full vigour!
   I love a bounteous father's life, a long one.
   I am none of those that, when they shoot to ripeness,
   Do what they can to break the boughs they grew on;   90

69SD] Weber; *not in* F1.   71SD] Bowers; *not in* F1.   84. these . . . gentlewomen]
F2; this . . . Gentlewoman F1.

---

   65. *friends . . . share too*] La Castre includes Belleur and Pinac in the welcome.
   75. *if I die . . . fit*] (1) 'if I perish at the first conflict'; (2) a quibble on *die* as orgasm
(Williams, p. 373) and *fit* as coitus.
   76. *buried . . . heels upward*] (1) the alleged burial position of cowards; (2) alluding
to sexual posture.

I wish ye many years, and many riches,
And pleasures to enjoy 'em. But for marriage,
I neither yet believe in't, nor affect it,
Nor think it fit.
La Castre.   You will render me your reasons?
Mirabell. Yes, sir, both short and pithy, and these they are: 95
You would have me marry a maid?
La Castre.   A maid? What else?
Mirabell. Yes, there be things called widows, dead men's wills;
I never loved to prove those; nor never longed yet
To be buried alive in another man's cold monument.
And there be maids appearing, and maids being: 100
The appearing are fantastic things, mere shadows;
And if you mark 'em well, they want their heads too;
Only the world, to cozen misty eyes,
Has clapped 'em on new faces. The maids being
A man may venture on, if he be so mad to marry,   105
If he have neither fear before his eyes, nor fortune;
And let him take heed how he gather these too;
For look ye, father, they are just like melons,
Musk-melons are the emblems of these maids;
Now they are ripe, now cut 'em, they taste pleasantly,   110
And are a dainty fruit, digested easily.
Neglect this present time, and come tomorrow,
They are so ripe they are rotten, gone, their sweetness
Run into humour, and their taste to surfeit.
La Castre. Why, these are new ripe, son.
Mirabell.   I'll try them presently,   115

---

99. another man's] *F2*; anothers mans *F1*.   113. rotten, gone,] *Lister*; rotten gon, *F1*;
rotten grown, *conj. Sympson*; rotten – gone! *Colman*.   115. new] *Bowers*; now *F1*.

---

97. *dead men's wills*] a depersonalising image describing widows in terms of the
wealth willed to them by their former husbands. Jacobean drama frequently portrays
widows as financially and sexually voracious.
  98. *prove*] try.
  101. *fantastic*] illusory (*OED* A.1a).
  102. *they . . . heads*] they lack their maidenheads.
  109. *Musk-melons*] a highly perishable fruit. Thomas Coryate praised musk-melons
sold in Venice as 'one of the most delectable dishes for a Sommer fruite of all Chris-
tendome', but warns that they may be 'sweete in the palate, but sowre in the stomacke,
if . . . not soberly eaten' (Coryate, *Coryat's Crudities*, 1611, rpt London: Scolar Press,
1978), p. 257.
  114. *humour*] pulp, mush.
  surfeit] cloying.

        And if I like their taste –
La Castre.   Pray ye please yourself, sir.
Mirabell. That liberty is my due, and I'll maintain it –
        Lady, what think you of a handsome man now?
Rosalura. A wholesome too, sir?
Mirabell.   That's as you make your bargain.
        A handsome, wholesome man then, and a kind man,   120
        To cheer your heart up, to rejoice ye, lady?
Rosalura. Yes, sir, I love rejoicing.
Mirabell.   To lie close to ye?
        Close as a cockle? Keep the cold nights from ye?
Rosalura. That will be looked for too, our bodies ask it.
Mirabell. And get two boys at every birth?
Rosalura.   That's nothing;   125
        I have known a cobbler do it, a poor thin cobbler,
        A cobbler out of mouldy cheese perform it,
        Cabbage, and coarse black bread: methinks a gentleman
        Should take foul scorn to have an awl out-name him.
        Two at a birth? Why, every house-dove has it: 130
        That man that feeds well, promises as well too,
        I should expect indeed something of worth from.
        Ye talk of two?
Mirabell. [*Aside*]   She would have me get two dozen,

---

119. sir?] *Colman*; sir. *F1.*   129. an awl] *F2*; a Nawl *F1.*   133SD] *Dyce; not in F1.*

119. *wholesome*] (1) sound in physical and mental condition; (2) 'free from venereal disease' (Fraser and Rabkin).
    120. *kind*] loving, intimate (*OED* kind a. 6).
    123. *Close as a cockle*] a variation of the phrase 'close as a clam', here meaning as
tightly locked together as a clam shell and as safe from intrusion as the clam in its shell
(Brewer, p. 263). 'Close' carries sexual overtones and cockles are erotically symbolic
(Williams, p. 264, quoting this line) (Dent C499).
    124. *looked for*] expected, hoped for (*OED* look v. 15).
    126. *cobbler*] Cobblers and tailors shared a reputation for lasciviousness because of
the opportunities for intimate access to women's bodies afforded by fitting footwear
and clothing.
    127. *out of*] fed on
    127–8. *mouldy cheese . . . bread*] 'A diet illustrating the proverbial poverty of shoe-
makers' (Lister).
    129. *awl*] (1) a small pricking tool used by shoemakers; (2) a metonym for 'cobbler';
(3) a pejorative term for a clumsy workman.
    out-name] surpass. Rosalura claims that the superior diet of a gentleman should
render him more virile than the malnourished cobbler.
    130. *house-dove*] a woman who stays in the house (*OED* 2).

Like buttons, at a birth.
Rosalura.   You love to brag, sir;
If you proclaim these offers at your marriage,   135
(Ye are a pretty-timbered man, take heed!)
They may be taken hold of, and expected,
Yes, if not hoped for at a higher rate too.
Mirabell. I will take heed, and thank ye for your counsel. –
Father, what think ye?
La Castre.   'Tis a merry gentlewoman;   140
Will make, no doubt, a good wife.
Mirabell.   Not for me:
I marry her and, happily, get nothing;
In what a state am I then, father? I shall suffer,
For anything I hear to the contrary, *more majorum*;
I were as sure to be a cuckold, father,   145
A gentleman of antler –
La Castre.   Away, away, fool.
Mirabell. As I am sure to fail her expectation:
I had rather get the pox than get her babies!
La Castre. Ye are much to blame; if this do not affect ye,
Pray try the other; she is of a more demure way.   150
Belleur. [*Aside*] That I had but the audacity to talk thus!
I love that plain-spoken gentlewoman admirably,
And certain I could go as near to please her,
If downright doing – she has a parlous countenance! –
If I could meet one that would believe me,   155
And take my honest meaning without circumstance.
Mirabell. You shall have your will, sir, I will try the other,

135–6.] *Colman (subst)*; If . . . Mariage, / Ye . . . heed, *F1.* 143. then, father?]
Colman; then? Father, *F1.* 146–7. antler – / / . . . expectation:] *Langbaine*; Antler. / /
. . . expectation, *F1.* 151SD] *Weber; not in F1.* 154. parlous] *This ed.*; per'lous *F1*;
perilous *Colman*.

---

136. *a pretty-timbered man*] a good, handsome physical specimen.
142. *happily, get nothing*] perhaps beget nothing, cf. 'two boys at every birth' at
1.3.125.
144. *more majorum*] Latin tag, meaning 'in the manner of our ancestors', 'in the
traditional manner'.
146. *gentleman of antler*] cuckold; the stag's horns symbolised cuckoldry.
149. *affect ye*] 'move your liking' (Dyce).
154. *downright doing*] (1) a straightforward approach; (2) 'activity directed straight
downward, another sexual pun' (Lister).
parlous] forbidding, terrible; a shortened form of 'perilous'.
156. *honest . . . circumstance*] frank intention without fuss or formality.

But 'twill be to small use – I hope, fair lady,
(For methinks in your eyes I see more mercy)
You will enjoin your lover a less penance;　　　　160
And though I'll promise much, as men are liberal,
And vow an ample sacrifice of service,
Yet your discretion and your tenderness,
And thriftiness in love, good housewives' carefulness
To keep the stock entire –
Lillia-Bianca.　　　　Good sir, speak louder,　　　　165
That these may witness too ye talk of nothing;
I should be loath alone to bear the burden
Of so much indiscretion.
Mirabell.　　　　Hark ye, hark ye;
Od's-bobs, you are angry, lady.
Lillia-Bianca.　　　　Angry? No, sir;
I never owned an anger to lose poorly.　　　　170
Mirabell. But you can love, for all this, and delight too,
For all your set austerity, to hear
Of a good husband, lady?
Lillia-Bianca.　　　　You say true, sir;
For by my troth, I have heard of none these ten years,
They are so rare, and there are so many, sir,　　　　175
So many longing women on their knees too,
That pray the dropping down of these good husbands,
The dropping down from heaven – for they are not bred here –
That you may guess at all my hope, but hearing –
Mirabell. Why may not I be one?
Lillia-Bianca.　　　　You were near 'em once, sir,　　　　180
When ye came o'er the Alps; those are near heaven:
But since ye missed that happiness, there's no hope of ye.

---

174. years] *F2*; year *F1*.

---

162. *service*] the devotion of a professed lover, with the additional sense of 'sexual intercourse' (*OED* service n¹, 6c).

164–5. *good housewives' . . . entire*] (1) play on *stock* as a metaphor for 'maidenhead', implying that women, wishing to retain their virginity, are parsimonious in amorous transactions; (2) *stock* = 'familial descent' and women's desire to preserve a pure bloodline; (3) 'to live on the husband's sexual surplus, rather than to make inroads into his sexual capital' (Lister).

169. *Od's-bobs*] a corruption (to avoid blasphemy) of 'God's blood', an expression of exasperation.

170.] 'I would not lose my temper on such trivial grounds'.

172. *set*] (1) fixed; (2) deliberate; (3) contrived to deceive; (4) formal (Lister).

180–1. *You were near . . . heaven*] The high altitude of Mirabell's journey over the Alps is as near as he will ever get to joining the company of 'good' husbands who drop from heaven.

Mirabell. Can ye love a man?
Lillia-Bianca.   Yes, if the man be lovely;
That is, be honest, modest. I would have him valiant,
His anger slow, but certain for his honour;   185
Travelled he should be, but through himself exactly,
For 'tis fairer to know manners well than countries.
He must be no vain talker, nor no lover
To hear himself talk; they are brags of a wanderer,
Of one finds no retreat for fair behaviour.   190
Would ye learn more?
Mirabell.   Yes.
Lillia-Bianca.   Learn to hold your peace then.
Fond girls are got with tongues, women with tempers.
Mirabell. Women, with I know what; but let that vanish:
Go thy way, Goodwife Bias! Sure thy husband
Must have a strong philosophers' stone, he will ne'er please thee
   else.   195
Here's a starched piece of austerity. – Do you hear, father?
Do you hear this moral lecture?
La Castre.   Yes, and like it.
Mirabell. Why, there's your judgement now; there's an old bolt shot!
This thing must have the strangest observation,

---

199. thing] *F2*; Thing *F1*.

---

183. *lovely*] worthy of love (*OED* 2).

185. *certain for his honour*] sufficient to protect his honourable reputation.

186–7.] Knowledge and experience gained abroad is commendable but first a man should know himself thoroughly, cf. Webster, *The Duchess of Malfi* 1.1.435–7: 'If you will know where breathes a complete man – / I speak it without flattery – turn your eyes / And progress through yourself.'

190. *retreat*] return, reward.

192. *Fond*] Foolish.

tempers] judicious self-control.

194. *Goodwife Bias*] Mirabell mocks the didactic strain of Lillia-Bianca's speech by addressing her as *Bias*, one of the Seven Sages of Greece, to each of whom some wise maxim is attributed by ancient writers; cf. 2.2.142. The humour is compounded by the homely term *goodwife*, commonly used by the middling sort of men in addressing their wives.

195. *philosophers' stone*] (1) supposed by alchemists to possess the property of changing other metals into gold or silver (*OED* 1); (2) wordplay on *stone* = 'testicle': 'the mysteries of alchemy were comically identified with those of sex through the figure of the philosophers' stone' (Williams, p. 1322).

198. *old bolt shot*] i.e. La Castre has 'lost it'. A variant of the expression 'to have shot one's bolt' (Tilley B512).

199. *thing*] here used humorously or contemptuously to imply that the learned woman is a monstrous or unnatural object. Cf. the use of 'thing' at 4.2.93 and 5.2.27.

strangest observation] most intense observance.

(Do you mark me, father?) when she is married once,   200
The strangest custom, too, of admiration
On all she does and speaks – 'twill be past sufferance.
I must not lie with her in common language,
Nor cry, 'Have at thee, Kate!' – I shall be hissed then;
Nor eat my meat without the sauce of sentences,   205
Your powdered beef and problems, a rare diet.
My first son, Monsieur Aristotle, I know it,
Great master of the metaphysics, or so;
The second, Solon, and the best law-setter;
And I must look Egyptian godfathers,   210
Which will be no small trouble. My eldest daughter
Sappho, or such a fiddling kind of poetess,
And brought up, *invita Minerva*, at her needle.
My dogs must look their names too, and all Spartan,
Lelaps, Melampus; no more Fox and Bawdyface.   215
I married to a sullen set of sentences,
To one that weighs her words and her behaviours
In the gold weights of discretion? I'll be hanged first!

---

204. '*Have at thee, Kate*'] a preliminary call to sexual encounter, cf. *Shrew*, where
Petruchio goads Katherina into fighting with the Widow: 'To her, Kate!', and encourages Bianca: 'Have at you for a better jest or two' (5.2.35, 47).

205. *sentences*] pithy sayings or opinions.

206. *powdered beef and problems*] beef seasoned with salt or powdered spice for
preserving, 'with a possible allusion to the Latin metaphor of salt representing wit, and
questions of logic. Problems were proposed for academic discussion (*OED* 2)' (Lister).

rare] here used ironically; 'fine'.

209. *Solon*] a sixth-century Athenian, one of the seven wise men of Greece (along
with Bias, cf. 1.3.194n). His legal reforms survived for more than four hundred years.

210. *look*] search out (*OED* look v. 6d).

212. *Sappho*] Greek lyric poet from the island of Lesbos, born *c.*612 BC. Her poems
to other women made 'lesbian' a synonym for female homosexuality. See John Donne's
verse-letter, 'Sappho to Philaenis'.

fiddling] addicted to futile and petty activity (*OED* 2a).

213. invita Minerva] 'in spite of Minerva', the Roman goddess of wisdom, warlike
prowess and skill in the arts of life; without natural aptitude (*OED*).

214. *look*] expect (*OED* look v. 3c)

215. *Lelaps, Melampus*] In Greek mythology Lelaps was a dog that never failed
to seize and conquer whatever animal it was ordered to pursue; Lelaps (Laelaps)
and Melampus were two of Actaeon's dogs that tore their master to pieces after
Actaeon had been turned into a stag by Diana. See J. Lemprière, *Lemprière's Classical
Dictionary of Proper Names Mentioned in the Ancient Authors*, rev. F.A. Wright
(London: Routledge, 1951).

Bawdyface] *Baudiface* = 'Dirty-face' (Dyce).

218. *gold weights*] the finely adjusted scales used for weighing gold. Cf. Fletcher's
Love's Pilgrimage 1.1.47.

La Castre. Prithee reclaim thyself.
Mirabell.   Pray ye, give me time then.
     If they can set me anything to play at   220
     That seems fit for a gamester, have at the fairest!
     Till then, see more and try more.
La Castre.   Take your time then;
     I'll bar ye no fair liberty – Come, gentlemen,
     And ladies, come; to all once more a welcome,
     And now let's in to supper.
                    [*Exeunt* LA CASTRE, NANTOLET, LUGIER,
                         ROSALURA, *and* LILLIA-BIANCA.]
Mirabell.   How dost like 'em?   225
Pinac. They are fair enough, but of so strange behaviours.
Mirabell. Too strange for me: I must have those have mettle,
     And mettle to my mind. Come, let's be merry.
Belleur. Bless me from this woman! I would stand the cannon
     Before ten words of hers.
De Gard.   Do you find him now?   230
     Do you think he will be ever firm?
Oriana.   I fear not.
                                        Exeunt.

221–2. fairest! / Till then,] *Colman (subst.)*; fairest / Till I *F1*   225SD] *Dyce; not in*
F1; Sympson [*Exit*].

   221. *gamester*] one addicted to amorous sport (*OED* 5).
   227. *mettle*] (1) spirited temperament (*OED* 3); (2) sexual vigour (Williams, p. 881).
   231. *firm*] constant, steadfast (*OED* 6a).

ACT 2

> *Enter* MIRABELL, PINAC, [*and*] BELLEUR.

Mirabell. Ne'er tell me of this happiness, 'tis nothing.
The state they bring with being sought to, scurvy!
I had rather make mine own play, and I will do.
My happiness is in mine own content,
And the despising of such glorious trifles,   5
As I have done a thousand more. For my humour,
Give me a good free fellow, that sticks to me,
A jovial fair companion; there's a beauty.
For women, I can have too many of them –
Good women too, as the age reckons 'em,   10
More than I have employment for.
Pinac.   You are happy.
Mirabell. My only fear is that I must be forced,
Against my nature, to conceal myself:
Health and an able body are two jewels.
Pinac. If either of these two women were offered to me now,   15
I would think otherwise, and do accordingly,
Yes, and recant my heresies, I would, sir.
And be more tender of opinion,
And put a little of my travelled liberty
Out of the way, and look upon 'em seriously.   20
Methinks this grave-carried wench –
Belleur.   Methinks the other,
The home-spoken gentlewoman that desires to be fruitful,

---

19. of] *Langbaine; off F1.*

2. *state . . . to*] the pride affected by Lillia-Bianca and Rosalura as prospective wives;
cf. the 'states, and wild stubbornness' of women at 4.1.61 and the 'state' of Oriana in
disguise at 5.6.4.
2. *scurvy*] pitiful.
8. *fair*] reasonable, easy-going.
11. *happy*] lucky.
14.] Evokes by association the biblical proverb of which Mirabell seems oblivious:
'Who can find a virtuous woman? For her price is far above rubies', Proverbs, 31.10.
18. *tender of*] sensitive to.
21. *grave-carried*] behaving seriously (Lister).

That treats of the full manage of the matter –
For there lies all my aim – that wench, methinks,
If I were but well set-on, for she is affable,   25
If I were but hounded right, and one to teach me –
She speaks to th' matter and comes home to th' point:
Now do I know I have such a body to please her
As all the kingdom cannot fit her with, I am sure on't,
If I could but talk myself into her favour.
Mirabell.   That's easily done.   30
Belleur. That's easily said – would 'twere done!
You should see then how I would lay about me.
If I were virtuous it would never grieve me,
Or anything that might justify my modesty;
But when my nature is prone to do a charity,   35
And my calf's tongue will not help me –
Mirabell.   Will you go to 'em?
They cannot but take it courteously.
Pinac.   I'll do my part,
Though I am sure 'twill be the hardest I e'er played yet.
A way I never tried too, which will stagger me,
And if it do not shame me, I am happy.   40

---

25. affable] *conj. Sympson; Dyce;* a fable, *F1.*

23.] That speaks directly and unreservedly about sexual matters.

25. *well set-on*] encouraged in the pursuit; cf. 4.3.128.

affable] Most editors have accepted Sympson's conjecture, which accords with Belleur's sense of Rosalura's pleasant directness of speech. Lister, however, retains *F1*'s 'she is a fable', glossing the phrase as, 'she is as unusual as the persons and events of fabulous stories of love and adventure'. Fletcher uses 'affable' in *The Elder Brother* 3.1.6, *The Scornful Lady* 1.1.247 and *The Spanish Curate* 1.1.49.

26. *hounded right*] (1) urged on, as hounds are incited to attack a prey; (2) from hunting: had the support of well-trained hounds, since Belleur is the pursuer, not the quarry.

27. *to th' matter*] candidly.

comes home . . . point] (1) gets to the central issue of the matter; in hawking terminology 'making a point' describes the action of a hawk hovering over its concealed quarry; (2) Williams cites this line as an example of the bawdy use of *point* for 'penis' (Williams, p. 1067).

32. *lay about me*] do my utmost; a term of combat, 'to strike out in all directions' (*OED* 19).

34. *justify my modesty*] vindicate my bashfulness.

35. *prone . . . charity*] (1) inclined to doing acts of kindness (*OED* 6); (2) with bawdy secondary sense of *prone* = 'lying face downwards' (*OED* 1a) and *charity* = act of sexual benevolence (Williams, p. 230, citing this phrase).

36. *calf's tongue*] embarrassing inarticulacy.

39. *stagger me*] undermine my confidence.

Mirabell. Win 'em and wear 'em, I give up my interest.
Pinac. What say ye, Monsieur Belleur?
Belleur.   Would I could say,
  Or sing, or anything that were but handsome,
  I would be with her presently.
Pinac.   Yours is no venture;
  A merry ready wench.
Belleur.   A vengeance squibber!   45
  She'll fleer me out of faith too.
Mirabell.   I'll be near thee;
  Pluck up thy heart, I'll second thee at all brunts.
  Be angry, if she abuse thee, and beat her a little –
  Some women are won that way.
Belleur.   Pray be quiet,
  And let me think. I am resolved to go on;   50
  But how I shall get off again –
Mirabell.   I am persuaded
  Thou wilt so please her, she will go near to ravish thee.
Belleur. I would 'twere come to that once. Let me pray a little.
Mirabell. Now for thine honour, Pinac; board me this modesty,
  Warm but this frozen snowball, 'twill be a conquest   55
  (Although I know thou art a fortunate wencher,
  And hast done rarely in thy days) above all thy ventures.
Belleur. You will be ever near?
Mirabell.   At all necessities,
  And take thee off, and set thee on again, boy,
  And cherish thee, and stroke thee.
Belleur.   Help me out too?   60

---

41. *Win 'em, and wear 'em*] variant of the proverb 'Win it and wear it' (Dent W408);
for examples of *wear* = 'to draw on in coition like a garment' see Williams, p. 1508.
  44. *presently*] immediately.
  venture] challenge.
  45. *ready*] willing (*OED* 2b).
  vengeance squibber] (1) one who uses witty sarcasm. A 'squib' was both an explo-
sive device used as a means of attack and a witty, satirical composition (*OED* 2a, 3);
(2) powerful squibber; for the use of *vengeance* as an intensifier see *OED* 5a.
  46. *fleer . . . faith*] ridicule me until I am thoroughly humiliated.
  47. *brunts*] attacks.
  50. *go on*] proceed (*OED* 2a); undertake an action (*OED* 61c).
  51. *get off*] escape (*OED* 70a).
  54. *board me*] an incitement to Pinac to broach Lillia-Bianca's austerity. Cf. *TwN*
1.3.53–4: ' "Accost" is front her, board her, woo her, assail her.'
  60. *cherish*] cheer, encourage (*OED* 4).
  stroke] soothe (*OED* 1e).

For I know I shall stick i' th' mire. If ye see us close once,
Be gone, and leave me to my fortune, suddenly,
For I am then determined to do wonders.
Farewell, and fling an old shoe. How my heart throbs!
Would I were drunk! Farewell, Pinac; heaven send us   65
A joyful and a merry meeting, man.
Pinac.   Farewell,
And cheer thy heart up, and remember, Belleur,
They are but women.
Belleur.   I had rather they were lions.
Mirabell. About it; I'll be with you instantly.

                            Exeunt [PINAC *and* BELLEUR].

                    Enter ORIANA.

Shall I ne'er be at rest? No peace of conscience,   70
No quiet for these creatures? Am I ordained
To be devoured quick by these she-cannibals?
Here's another they call handsome; I care not for her,
I ne'er look after her. When I am half tippled
It may be I should turn her, and peruse her,   75
Or in my want of women I might call for her;
But to be haunted when I have no fancy,
No maw to th' matter. – Now, why do you follow me?
Oriana. I hope, sir, 'tis no blemish to my virtue;
Nor need you, out of scruple, ask that question,   80
If you remember ye, before your travel
The contract you tied to me. 'Tis my love, sir,

69SD *Enter* ORIANA.] *F2; in right margin opp. l. 70 F1.*

61. *close*] come together in combat (*OED v.* intr. 13); here of a sexual kind.
62. *suddenly*] immediately (*OED* 2).
64. *fling an old shoe*] proverbial: 'To cast an old shoe after one for luck' (Dent S372).
72. *quick*] alive.
she-cannibals] Women were commonly thought to possess a voracious sexual appetite; cf. John Marston, *The Dutch Courtesan* 1.2.90, in which Freevill assures Malheureux that Franceschina is 'none of your ramping cannibals that devour man's flesh'.
74. *half tippled*] half drunk.
75. *turn her*] turn to her; for *turn* used allusively for coitus here and at 2.1.124 see Williams, p. 1440.
78. *maw*] appetite, inclination.
82. *contract*] Mirabell does not deny that he has entered into what appears to be a *de futuro* marriage contract with Oriana, cf. 2.1.101–2. The *de futuro* spousal was a contract to marry in the future, not a marriage contract in itself. However, Oriana's claim seems difficult to enforce because, according to Martin Ingram, 'a contract *de futuro* did not at once create an irrevocable union, it could be dissolved by the continued absence of one of them, and [relevant here] by fornication with a third party'

That makes me seek ye, to confirm your memory,
And that being fair and good, I cannot suffer.
I come to give ye thanks too.
Mirabell.   For what, prithee?   85
Oriana. For that fair piece of honesty ye showed, sir,
That constant nobleness.
Mirabell.   How? For I am short-headed.
Oriana. I'll tell ye then. For refusing that free offer
Of Monsieur Nantolet's, those handsome beauties,
Those two prime ladies, that might well have pressed ye,   90
If not to have broken, yet to have bowed your promise.
I know it was for my sake, for your faith sake,
You slipped 'em off: your honesty compelled ye;
And let me tell ye, sir, it showed most handsomely.
Mirabell. And let me tell thee, there was no such matter,   95
Nothing intended that way, of that nature.
I have more to do with my honesty than to fool it,
Or venture it in such leak-barks as women.
I put 'em off because I loved 'em not,
Because they are too queasy for my temper,   100
And not for thy sake, nor the contract sake,
Nor vows, nor oaths. I have made a thousand of 'em;
They are things indifferent, whether kept or broken,
Mere venial slips, that grow not near the conscience.
Nothing concerns those tender parts – they are trifles.   105

---

92. faith sake] *F1;* faith's sake *Lister.*

(Ingram, 'Spousals Litigation in the English Ecclesiastical Courts c.1350–c.1640', in R.B. Outhwaite (ed.), *Marriage and Society: Studies in the Social History of Marriage* (London: Europa Publications, 1981), pp. 38–41).
    87. *short-headed*] of weak memory.
    91. *bowed*] bent. Proverbially, 'Better bow than break' (Dent B566).
    93. *slipped 'em off*] evaded them.
    97. *fool it*] trifle with it.
    98. *leak-barks*] leaking, and hence unreliable, boats. A common metaphor expressing the misogynistic view that women lack discretion and are unable to keep a secret. On women's susceptibility to the 'leakage' of bodily fluids (menstrual blood, urine, lactation and tears), which was believed to confirm women's unreliability and lack of self-control, see the essay by Gail Kern Paster, 'Leaky Vessels: The Incontinent Women of City Comedy', *RD*, n.s., 18 (1987), 43–65.
    100. *queasy*] fastidious.
    103. *indifferent*] (1) of no consequence (*OED* 10b); (2) that may equally be observed or neglected (*OED* 10c).
    104. *venial slips*] (1) pardonable errors, as opposed to deadly or mortal sins; (2) followed by 'grow', a pun on 'slip' in the sense of a shoot or cutting.

For, as I think, there was never man yet hoped for
Either constancy or secrecy from a woman,
Unless it were an ass ordained for sufferance;
Nor to contract with such can be a tie-all.
So let them know again; for 'tis a justice   110
And a main point of civil policy,
Whate'er we say or swear, they being reprobates,
Out of the state of faith, we are clear of all sides,
And 'tis a curious blindness to believe us.
Oriana. You do not mean this, sure?
Mirabell.   Yes, sure, and certain;   115
And hold it positively as a principle,
As ye are strange things, and made of strange fires and fluxes,
So we are allowed as strange ways to obtain ye,
But not to hold; we are all created errant.
Oriana. You told me other tales.
Mirabell.   I not deny it;   120
I have tales of all sorts for all sorts of women,
And protestations likewise of all sizes,
As they have vanities to make us coxcombs.
If I obtain a good turn, so it is,
I am thankful for it; if I be made an ass,   125

---

109. tie-all] *conj. Dyce; Fraser and Rabkin;* Tiall *F1.*

108. *an ass . . . sufferance*] a fool destined to suffer the consequences of women's unruly behaviour since 'to wear the ears of the ass' is a metaphor for cuckoldry.

109. *tie-all*] tie, obligation (*OED* tial 2b, citing this line).

110. *let . . . again*] reappraise them.

110–13. *justice . . . sides*] Mirabell mixes legal and theological terminology to argue that women are damned because of Eve's transgression, therefore men have the right to deceive them and are free of fault in so doing.

112. *reprobates*] rejected by God (*OED* 1), abandoned or unprincipled persons (*OED* 2).

117. *fires*] possibly the burning passions which lovers were said to suffer (see Lawrence Babb, *The Elizabethan Malady* (East Lansing: Michigan State College Press, 1951), pp. 13, 132).

fluxes] functions of the female reproductive organs, such as menstruation and expulsion of the afterbirth, cf. 'leak-barks' at 2.1.98. On the effluent female body see Gail Kern Paster, *The Body Embarrassed: Drama and the Disciplines of Shame in Early Modern England* (Ithaca, New York: Cornell University Press, 1993), pp. 192–4.

119. *errant*] sinful; wordplay on 'err' and the concept of original sin; that humankind was created errant.

120. *I not deny*] For the omission of 'do' before 'not' see Abbott 305.

124. *turn*] (1) sexual favour; (2) change of posture (*OED* 8a); cf. *A&C* 2.5.58–9: 'He's bound unto Octavia. / For what good turn? / For the best turn i' th' bed.'

The mends are in mine own hands, or the surgeon's,
And there's an end on't.
Oriana.   Do not you love me then?
Mirabell. As I love others, heartily I love thee;
When I am high and lusty, I love thee cruelly:
After I have made a plenteous meal and satisfied   130
My senses with all delicates, come to me,
And thou shalt see how I love thee.
Oriana.   Will not you marry me?
Mirabell. No, certain, no, for anything I know yet;
I must not lose my liberty, dear lady,
And like a wanton slave cry for more shackles.   135
What should I marry for? Do I want anything?
Am I an inch the farther from my pleasure?
Why should I be at charge to keep a wife of mine own
When other honest married men will ease me,
And thank me too, and be beholding to me?   140
Thou thinkst I am mad for a maidenhead; thou art cozened:
Or, if I were addicted to that diet,
Can you tell me where I should have one? Thou art eighteen now,
And if thou hast thy maidenhead yet extant,
Sure 'tis as big as cod's-head; and those grave dishes   145
I never love to deal withal. Dost thou see this book here?
Look over all these ranks; all these are women,

---

145. as cod's-head] *F1*; as a Cods-head *Langbaine*.

126. *mends*] amends.
surgeon's] who cures the venereal disease that may follow.
129. *high and lusty*] drunk and randy.
cruelly] excessively (OED 4); fiercely and savagely (Lister).
135. *wanton . . . shackles*] i.e. luxuriating in his imprisonment.
136. *want*] lack.
139. *honest*] upright.
143–6. *Thou art eighteen . . . withal*] Mirabell's allegation that, at eighteen, Oriana is no longer a nubile maid is discussed by Kawai, who points out that 'although the average age of marriage for women during 1598–1619 was 20.5 in London . . . it was considerably lower for dramatic characters . . . Thus, when female characters in love are aged eighteen, it means they have every reason to be eager for marriage' (Kawai, 'The Taming of the Shrewd Critics', pp. 58–9).
145. *cod's-head*] Dent C503, quoting this line. Cod is also known as the 'bag-fish' because of its shape. Cf. *codpiece* at 2.1.165; thus (1) a membrane so thick or so stretched that only a fool would want to bother with it; see 'cod's-head', OED 2; (2) a hymen of the size of a scrotum (Lister).
grave] unappetising.
146. *withal*] with (OED B, prep.).
147. *ranks*] (1) lines of women's names; (2) ranks of women, as in a female army.

Maids, and pretenders to maidenheads. These are my conquests –
All these I swore to marry, as I swore to thee,
With the same reservation, and most righteously,   150
Which I need not have done neither; for alas they made no scruple,
And I enjoyed 'em at my will, and left 'em.
Some of 'em are married since, and were as pure maids again,
Nay, o' my conscience, better than they were bred for;
The rest, fine sober women.
Oriana.   Are ye not ashamed, sir?   155
Mirabell. No, by my troth, sir; there's no shame belongs to it:
I hold it as commendable to be wealthy in pleasure
As others do in rotten sheep and pasture.

Enter DE GARD.

Oriana. [*Aside*] Are all my hopes come to this? Is there no faith,
No troth, nor modesty in men?   [*Weeps.*]
De Gard.   How now, sister,   160
Why weeping thus? Did I not prophesy?
Come, tell me why –
Oriana.   I am not well; pray ye pardon me.   *Exit.*
De Gard. Now, Monsieur Mirabell, what ails my sister?
You have been playing the wag with her.
Mirabell.   As I take it,
She is crying for a codpiece. Is she gone?   165
Lord, what an age is this! I was calling for ye,
For as I live, I thought she would have ravished me.
De Gard.   Ye are merry, sir.
Mirabell. Thou knowst this book, De Gard, this inventory?
De Gard. The debt-book of your mistresses; I remember it.
Mirabell. Why, this was it that angered her; she was stark mad   170
She found not her name here, and cried downright
Because I would not pity her immediately,

159SD] *This ed.; not in F1.*   160SD] *Weber; not in F1.*

148. *pretenders to maidenheads*] (1) women who pretend to be virgins; (2) possibly
a quibble on 'pretender' as one who aspires to the throne, hence 'would-be virgins'. Cf.
'Maids appearing' at 1.3.100 and 'pure maids again' at l. 153 below.
    150. *reservation*] tacit limitation (*OED* 4a).
    158. *rotten*] affected by rot, a disease caused by the presence of fluke-worms in the
liver of sheep (*OED* rot n. 2a). Mirabell asserts that sexual greed is no better and no
worse than greed for land or, implicitly, wealth.
    165. *crying for a codpiece*] longing for intercourse (Williams: codpiece 2. penis,
p. 269). A *codpiece* was the bag-shaped appendage worn at the front of men's hose
or breeches, often conspicuous or ornamented (*OED* 1).

And put her in my list.
De Gard.   Sure she had more modesty.
Mirabell. Their modesty is anger to be overdone;
    They'll quarrel sooner for precedence here,   175
    And take it in more dudgeon to be slighted
    Than they will in public meetings; 'tis their natures.
    And, alas, I have so many to dispatch yet,
    And to provide myself for my affairs too,
    That, in good faith –
De Gard.   Be not too glorious foolish;   180
    Sum not your travels up with vanities,
    It ill becomes your expectation.
    Temper your speech, sir. Whether your loose story
    Be true or false (for you are so free, I fear it),
    Name not my sister in't. I must not hear it;   185
    Upon your danger, name her not! I hold her
    A gentlewoman of those happy parts and carriage,
    A good man's tongue may be right proud to speak her.
Mirabell. Your sister, sir? D' ye blench at that, d' ye cavil?
    Do you hold her such a piece she may not be played withal?   190
    I have had an hundred handsomer and nobler
    Have sued to me too for such a courtesy;
    Your sister comes i' th' rear. Since ye are so angry,
    And hold your sister such a strong recusant,
    I tell ye I may do it, and it may be will too;   195
    It may be have too; there's my free confession –
    Work upon that now.
De Gard.   If I thought ye had, I would work,
    And work such stubborn work should make your heart ache;
    But I believe ye, as I ever knew ye,
    A glorious talker and a legend-maker   200

---

192. Have] *Langbaine*; Has *F1*.

---

174. *overdone*] outdone (by other women); assigned a less prominent position in Mirabell's 'debt-book' of mistresses.

176. *take . . . dudgeon*] be more annoyed, resent it more.

177. *public meetings*] social gatherings.

180. *glorious*] boastfully.

181-2.] Don't let boorish behaviour diminish the benefits accruing from your travels.

182. *your expectation*] the expectation others have of you.

187. *happy . . . carriage*] favoured by admirable qualities and behaviour.

190. *piece*] (1) prized specimen; (2) piece of flesh – used contemptuously of a woman (OED 2d); (3) pun on chess piece (OED 12).

194. *recusant*] one who refuses to submit to some authority, here the 'authority' of Mirabell's libido (OED 2, citing this line).

198. *stubborn*] ruthless, fierce (OED 1a).

Of idle tales and trifles; a depraver
Of your own truth: their honours fly about ye.
And so I take my leave, but with this caution,
Your sword be surer than your tongue, you'll smart else.
Mirabell. I laugh at thee, so little I respect thee;   205
And I'll talk louder, and despise thy sister,
Set up a chambermaid that shall outshine her,
And carry her in my coach too, and that will kill her.
Go get thy rents up, go!
De Gard.   Ye are a fine gentleman.   *Exit.*
Mirabell. Now have at my two youths; I'll see how they do,   210
How they behave themselves, and then I'll study
What wench shall love me next, and when I'll loose her.

SCENE 2

Enter PINAC *and a* Servant.

Pinac. Art thou her servant, sayst thou?
Servant.   Her poor creature,
But servant to her horse, sir.
Pinac.   Canst thou show me
The way to her chamber, or where I may conveniently
See her, or come to talk to her?
Servant.   That I can, sir.
But the question is, whether I will or no.
Pinac.   Why, I'll content thee.   5
Servant. Why, I'll content thee then; now ye come to me.
Pinac. There's for your diligence.   [*Gives money.*]
Servant.   There's her chamber, sir,

---

202. about] *F1;* above *conj. Sympson.*   212. loose] *F1;* lose *F2.*

7SD] *Weber; not in F1.*

  202. *their . . . ye*] the maligned women's honour is pitched at a level above Mirabell's power to damage.
  209. *get thy rents up*] collect your rent money; a derisory expression from Mirabell, the urban sophisticate, implying that De Gard's moral values are those of the small-minded country gentry.
  210. *have . . . youths*] I'll seek out my two young friends.
  212. *loose*] cast off; part of the play's hawking imagery.
  5. *content*] remunerate.
  6. *content*] Fletcher's witty servant puns on 'content' (line 5), answering the sense of 'remunerate' with his sense of 'satisfy'.
  now . . . me] 'now you're talking'.

And this way she comes out; stand ye but here, sir,
You have her at your prospect or your pleasure.
Pinac. Is she not very angry?
Servant.   You'll find that quickly.   10
Maybe she'll call ye saucy, scurvy fellow,
Or some such familiar name. Maybe she knows ye,
And will fling a pisspot at ye, or a pantofle,
According as ye are in acquaintance. If she like ye,
Maybe she'll look upon ye, maybe no,   15
And two months hence call for ye.
Pinac.   This is fine.
She is monstrous proud then?
Servant.   She is a little haughty;
Of a small body, she has a mind well mounted.
Can ye speak Greek?
Pinac.   No, certain.
Servant.   Get ye gone then –
And talk of stars and firmaments and firedrakes?   20
Do you remember who was Adam's schoolmaster,
And who taught Eve to spin? She knows all these,
And will run ye over the beginning o' th' world
As familiar as a fiddler. Can ye
Sit seven hours together, and say nothing?   25
Which she will do, and when she speaks, speak oracles,
Speak things that no man understands, nor herself neither.
Pinac. Thou mak'st me wonder.
Servant.   Can ye smile?
Pinac.   Yes, willingly,
For naturally I bear a mirth about me.
Servant. She'll ne'er endure ye then, she is never merry,   30

24–5. fiddler. Can ye] *Colman*; Fidler. / Can ye *F1*.

9. *prospect*] view, vantage point, often with sense of anticipation.

11. *scurvy*] worthless, contemptible (*OED* 2).

13. *pantofle*] type of indoor slipper or loose shoe, especially high-heeled, cork-soled chopin (*OED*).

14. *According . . . acquaintance*] Depending on how well she knows you.

18.] For a physically small person she has an imposing intellect.

20. *firedrakes*] (1) mythical fiery dragons (*OED* 1A); (2) fiery meteors (*OED* 2a).

21–2. *Do you . . . spin*] Cf. the saying 'When Adam delved and Eve span, who was then the gentleman?'

24. *As familiar . . . fiddler*] A variation on the saying 'Drunk as a fiddler' (Brewer, p. 457). The servant is comparing Lillia-Bianca's arcane knowledge to a strolling musician's familiarity with his repertoire.

If she see one laugh, she'll swoon past *aqua vitae*.
Never come near her, sir – if ye chance to venture
And talk not like a doctor, you are damned too.
I have told ye enough for your crown, and so good speed ye!

                                                          Exit.

Pinac. I have a pretty task if she be thus curious,   35
As sure it seems she is. If I fall off now
I shall be laughed at fearfully; if I go forward
I can but be abused, and that I look for,
And yet I may hit right, but 'tis unlikely.
Stay! In what mood and figure shall I attempt her?   40
A careless way? No, no, that will not waken her;
Besides, her gravity will give me line still
And let me lose myself; yet this way often
Has hit, and handsomely. A wanton method?
Ay, if she give it leave to sink into her consideration.   45
But there's the doubt: if it but stir her blood once,
And creep into the crannies of her fancy,
Set her agog – but if she chance to slight it,
And by the power of her modesty fling it back,
I shall appear the arrantest rascal to her,   50
The most licentious knave, for I shall talk lewdly.
To bear myself austerely? Rate my words,

---

31. *swoon past* aqua vitae] suffer a fainting attack so severe that she cannot be revived by spirits such as brandy and whisky.

33. *doctor*] (1) one who is university-educated or qualified; (2) authoritatively, learnedly.

34. *crown*] the coin with which the Servant was bribed at 2.2.5.; perhaps a pun on *crown* as Pinac's skull which, without the servant's warning, may have been a target for a flying pantofle.

good speed ye] an expression of farewell; good luck!

36. *fall off*] retreat.

38. *look for*] expect (OED 6g).

40. *mood and figure*] posture, style.

41. *waken*] an obsolete form of 'weaken'; reduce her resistance.

42–3. *give . . . self*] (1) metaphor based on 'playing' a hooked fish at the end of a line; (2) metaphor from falconry, where the falconer plays out the leash of a hunting bird. In both fishing and falconry the handler of the lure risks losing the attached object, if the retrieval is inexpertly handled. Cf. the saying, 'Give a thief rope enough and he will hang himself' (Dent T104).

44. *wanton*] risqué.

50. *arrantest*] most notorious (OED 3).

51. *lewdly*] lasciviously (OED 4).

52. *Rate*] Weigh (Fraser and Rabkin).

And fling a general gravity about me
As if I meant to give laws? But this I cannot do,
This is a way above my understanding: 55
Or if I could, 'tis odds she'll think I mock her;
For serious and sad things are ever still suspicious.
Well, I'll say something –
But learning I have none, and less good manners,
Especially for ladies. Well, I'll set my best face.   60

    Enter LILLIA[-BIANCA], PETELLA[, *and musicians*].

I hear some coming –
               This is the first woman
I ever feared yet, the first face that shakes me.   [*Stands apart.*]
Lillia-Bianca. Give me my hat, Petella; take this veil off,
This sullen cloud, it darkens my delights.
Come wench, be free, and let the music warble;   65
Play me some lusty measure.   [*Music.* LILLIA-BIANCA *dances.*]
Pinac. [*Aside*]   This is she, sure,
The very same I saw, the very woman,
The gravity I wondered at. Stay, stay;
Let me be sure. Ne'er trust me, but she danceth!
Summer is in her face now, and she skippeth: 70
I'll go a little nearer.
Lillia-Bianca.   Quicker time, fellows!

    Enter MIRABELL.

I cannot find my legs yet. – Now, Petella!
Pinac. [*Aside*] I am amazed; I am foundered in my fancy.

60SD] *Sympson; Enter Lillia, Petella. F1.*   62SD] *Weber; not in F1.*   66SD *Music.*
LILLIA-BIANCA *dances.*] *Lister; not in F1;* [*Music*] *Weber.*   66SD *Aside*] *Fraser and
Rabkin; not in F1;* [*Aside, and then advances a little*] *in right margin opp. l. 71 Dyce.*
73SD] *Dyce; not in F1.*

54. *give laws*] pontificate, prescribe laws.
57. *sad*] sober, cf. *sadder* at l. 109 below.
ever still suspicious] always give rise to doubts.
60SD] In the Jacobean and Caroline theatres the musicians may have played from
a room above the stage (see Gurr, pp. 147–8). While Lillia-Bianca addresses a group
of musicians at ll. 71, 86, and 128, it is clear from ll. 65–6, 72, and 96 that Petella
also plays an instrument such as a lute or recorder. As Petella is a non-speaking part,
it is possible that she was played by a musician.
66. *lusty measure*] (1) a merry tune; (2) 'measure' as in dance rhythm.
72. *find my legs*] dance in time to the rhythm.
73. *foundered . . . fancy*] my assumptions (regarding Lillia-Bianca) are shattered.

Mirabell. [*Aside*] Ha, say ye so? Is this your gravity,
This the austerity ye put upon ye?   75
I'll see more o' this sport.   [*Stands on the other side.*]
Lillia-Bianca.   A song now;
Call in for a merry and a light song,
And sing it with a liberal spirit.

                    Enter a Singing Boy.

Singing Boy.   Yes, madam.
Lillia-Bianca. And be not amazed, sirrah, but take us for your own
          company. –   [Boy *sings and then exits.*]
Let's walk ourselves: come, wench, would we had a man or two!   80
Pinac. Sure she has spied me, and will abuse me dreadfully;
She has put on this for the purpose; yet I will try her. –
                                        [*Advances.*]
Madam, I would be loath my rude intrusion,
Which I must crave a pardon for –
Lillia-Bianca.   O ye are welcome,
Ye are very welcome, sir; we want such a one. –   85
[*To the musicians*] Strike up again. – I dare presume ye dance well:
Quick, quick, sir, quick! The time steals on.
Pinac.   I would talk with ye.
Lillia-Bianca. Talk as ye dance.   [*They dance.*]
Mirabell. [*Aside*]   She'll beat him off his legs first.
This is the finest masque!
Lillia-Bianca.   Now, how do ye, sir?

74SD] *Dyce; not in F1.*   76SD] *Bowers; not in F1.*   78SD] *Weber;* Enter a man. *F1.*
79SD] *Dyce (subst.); not in F1.*   82SD] *This ed.; not in F1;* [*Aside, and then advances*]
Dyce.   86SD] *This ed.; not in F1.*   88SD* They dance.] *Weber; not in F1.*   88SD
Aside.] *Dyce; not in F1.*

74. *say ye so*] 'is this the way it is?' (Fraser and Rabkin).
78SD] Enter a *Singing Boy.*] Weber's emendation of *F1* has been accepted by most
modern editors. The Dramatis Personae names a 'Singing-Boy', but not a 'Man', and
it is a 'Boy' who performs the scripted song at 5.6.12f. Lillia-Bianca's 'be not amazed,
sirrah' (l. 79) suggests a youthful singer.
79. *amazed*] confused.
79SD] There is no information available on this or the following songs.
take . . . company] act as if we were of your own social rank (Lister).
82. *put . . . purpose*] this is a deliberate ruse to humiliate me.
89. *masque*] Mirabell is relishing the high entertainment value of the scene. Suzanne
Gossett argues that Fletcher applies the word 'masque' generically to 'any kind of spectacle or show' ('The Term "Masque" in Shakespeare and Fletcher, and *The Coxcomb*',
SEL, 14 (1974) 285–95 (p. 289)).

Pinac. You have given me a shrewd heat.
Lillia-Bianca.   I'll give ye a hundred.   90
   Come, sing now, sing; for I know ye sing well;
   I see ye have a singing face.
Pinac. [*Aside*]   A fine modesty!
   If I could she'd never give me breath. –
   Madam, would I might sit and recover.
Lillia-Bianca.   Sit here, and sing now;
   Let's do things quickly, sir, and handsomely. –   95
   Sit close, wench, close. Begin, begin!   *Song* [*sung by* PINAC].
Pinac. [*Aside*]   I am lessoned.
Lillia-Bianca. 'Tis very pretty, i' faith. Give me some wine now.
Pinac. I would fain speak to ye.
Lillia-Bianca.   You shall drink first, believe me:
   Here's to ye a lusty health.
Pinac.   I thank ye, lady.
   [*Aside*] Would I were off again; I smell my misery!   100
   I was never put to this rack; I shall be drunk too.
Mirabell. [*Aside*] If thou be'st not a right one, I have lost mine aim
      much:
   I thank heaven that I have 'scaped thee! To her, Pinac,
   For thou art as sure to have her, and to groan for her –
   I'll see how my other youth does; this speeds trimly.   105
   A fine grave gentlewoman, and worth much honour!   *Exit.*
Lillia-Bianca. Now, how do ye like me, sir?
Pinac.   I like ye rarely.
Lillia-Bianca. Ye see, sir, though sometimes we are grave and silent,
   And put on sadder dispositions,

92SD] *Dyce; not in* F1.   96SD *Song* [*by Pinac*]] F1; *in right margin opp. l.* 96 *Dyce.*
96SD *Aside.*] *Lister; not in* F1.   100SD] *Dyce; not in* F1.

   90. *shrewd heat*] intense fever.
   96. *lessoned*] (1) subdued, humbled (*OED* lesson v. 1), perhaps similar to the
modern phrase 'That'll teach me!'; (2) pun on 'lessened'. The question of how Pinac
aquits himself in his song is open to interpretation. His exhausting wooing of Lillia-
Bianca in this scene is ironically juxtaposed with his earlier boast to Belleur, 'Then
would I sing and dance' (1.2.41). By placing l. 96 before the stage direction Dyce inter-
prets it to mean, more simply, 'I am instructed', in response to Lillia-Bianca's 'begin!'.
   100. *I . . . misery*] I sense I am, or about to be, humiliated. After dancing vigorously,
Pinac may suffer body odour and an actor could convey embarrassment by sniffing his
armpit.
   101. *put to this rack*] forced to undergo this painful ordeal.
   102. *right one*] 'real devil' (Fraser and Rabkin).
   104. *groan for her*] (1) with sexual pleasure (Williams, p. 626, citing this phrase);
(2) in misery, as a result of Lillia-Bianca's mischief.
   105. *this speeds trimly*] (1) 'this is looking promising'; (2) 'this youth (i.e. Pinac) is
doing nicely'.

Yet we are compounded of free parts, and sometimes too   110
Our lighter, airy, and our fiery mettles
Break out and show themselves. And what think you of that, sir?
Pinac. Good lady, sit, for I am very weary,
And then I'll tell ye.
Lillia-Bianca.   Fie, a young man idle!
Up and walk; be still in action!   115
The motions of the body are fair beauties;
Besides, 'tis cold. 'Od's-me, sir, let's walk faster.
What think ye now of the Lady Felicia?
And Bellafront, the Duke's fair daughter, ha?
Are they not handsome things? There is Duarta,   120
And brown Olivia –
Pinac.   I know none of 'em.
Lillia-Bianca. But brown must not be cast away, sir; if young Lelia
Had kept herself till this day from a husband,
Why, what a beauty, sir! You know Ismena,
The fair gem of Saint-Germain?
Pinac.   By my troth, I do not.   125
Lillia-Bianca. And then I know you must hear of Brisac,
How unlike a gentleman –
Pinac.   As I live, I have heard nothing.
Lillia-Bianca. [*To the musicians*] Strike me another galliard.
Pinac.   By this light, I cannot;
In truth, I have sprained my leg, madam.
Lillia-Bianca.   Now, sit ye down, sir,
And tell me why ye came hither, why ye chose me out?   130
What is your business, your errand? Dispatch, dispatch!
Maybe ye are some gentleman's man, and I mistook ye,
That have brought me a letter, or a haunch of venison,

---

131. errand] *Langbaine*; errant *F1*.

110-12. *we... Break out*] we are composed of qualities that resist restriction or compulsion, and sometimes the impetuous, frivolous, and spirited aspect of our temperament breaks out.

117. *'Od's-me*] an exclamation; a corrupted form of oath to avoid blasphemy, possibly an abbreviation of 'God save me'.

122. *brown... away*] (1) 'a proverbial expression in its day' (Weber, quoted in Dyce) possibly relating to *brown* = the burnt part of a roast of meat (OED 3a); (2) *brown* = a person of brown complexion, a brunette (OED 3c).

125. *Saint-Germain*] (1) the Faubourg Saint-Germain, on the Left Bank of Paris, the quartier in which, in the early seventeenth century, the Marquise de Rambouillet established her prestigious salon frequented by the social and intellectual elite; (2) Saint-Germain-en-Laye, village near Paris (Fraser and Rabkin).

131. *Dispatch*] Hurry up!

Sent me from some friend of mine.
Pinac.   Do I look like a carrier?
You might allow me what I am, a gentleman.   135
Lillia-Bianca. Cry ye mercy, sir, I saw ye yesterday,
Ye are new come out of travel. I mistook ye.
And how does all our impudent friends in Italy?
Pinac. Madam, I came with duty, and fair courtesy,
Service, and honour to ye.
Lillia-Bianca.   Ye came to jeer me.   140
Ye see I am merry, sir, I have changed my copy:
None of the sages now, and pray ye proclaim it.
Fling on me what aspersion you shall please, sir,
Of wantonness or wildness – I look for it.
And tell the world I am an hypocrite,   145
Mask in a forced and borrowed shape – I expect it;
But not to have you believed. For mark ye, sir,
I have won a nobler estimation,
A stronger tie by my discretion
Upon opinion (howe'er you think I forced it)   150
Than either tongue or art of yours can slubber,
And when I please I will be what I please, sir,
So I exceed not mean; and none shall brand it
Either with scorn or shame, but shall be slighted.
Pinac. Lady, I come to love ye.
Lillia-Bianca.   Love yourself, sir;   155
And when I want observers I'll send for ye.

---

156. I'll] F2; 'll F1.

138. *impudent friends*] i.e. Venetian courtesans.
141. *copy*] behaviour (OED copy n. 11a). The phrase refers to the humanist peda-
gogical practice of using Latin or Greek verse or compositions as literary paradigms
(OED 7a). Cf. Jonson, *Every Man in His Humour*, Quarto text, 2.3.38–9: 'My father
had the proving of your copy some hour before I saw it', J.W. Lever (ed.), *Every Man
in His Humour: A Parallel-Text Edition of the 1601 Quarto and the 1616 Folio*,
Regents Renaissance Drama (London: Edward Arnold, 1972). For the positive connotations of the Latin 'copia' in the sense of an imitation of a text, as distinct from the
pejorative sense of our modern 'copy', see Terence Cave, *The Cornucopian Text: Problems of Writing in the French Renaissance* (Oxford: Clarendon Press, 1979), pp. 1–2.
142. *None . . . now*] Cf. 1.3.194–5.
146. *Mask . . . borrowed shape*] That I pretend to be other than I am.
151. *slubber*] sully (OED 1b).
153. *So . . . mean*] as long as I do not go to extremes (OED mean n² 1b, citing this
phrase). The golden mean constitutes the classical concept of moderation.
156. *want observers*] lack obsequious followers.

Heigh-ho! My fit's almost off; for we do all by fits, sir.
If ye be weary, sit till I come again to ye.
        [*Exeunt* LILLIA-BIANCA, PETELLA, *and* Musicians.]
Pinac. This is a wench of a dainty spirit; but
    Hang me if I know yet either what to think   160
    Or make of her. She had her will of me,
    And baited me abundantly, I thank her.
    And I confess I never was so blurted,
    Nor never so abused. I must bear mine own sins.
    Ye talk of travels; here's a curious country!   165
    Yet I will find her out, or forswear my faculty.   *Exit.*

SCENE 3

            Enter ROSALURA, ORIANA[, *and* PETELLA].

Rosalura. Ne'er vex yourself, nor grieve; ye are a fool then.
Oriana. I am sure I am made so: yet before I suffer
    Thus like a girl, and give him leave to triumph –
Rosalura. You say right; for as long as he perceives ye
    Sink under his proud scornings, he'll laugh at ye.   5
    For me, secure yourself; and for my sister,
    I partly know her mind too: howsoever,
    To obey my father, we have made a tender

158SD] *Lister; Exit. F1; Exit with* Petella. *Weber.*   159–61. but / Hang . . . think / Or
. . . me] *Sympson;* but hang . . . yet / Either . . . me, *F1.*
0.] *A garden belonging to the house of Nantolet, with a summer house in the background. Dyce.* 0SD] *Bowers;* Enter Rosalura, *and* Oriana. *F1;* Enter ROSALURA,
ORIANA [*and Maidservant*] *Lister.*

157. *by fits*] (1) impulsively; (2) mocking reference to 'fits of the mother', the
hysteria that women were thought to suffer as a result of disturbances of the uterus.
    163. *never . . . blurted*] was never treated so contemptuously (*OED* 2b, citing this
phrase).
    165–6. *curious . . . out.*] For the bawdy pun on 'country' and the figuring of woman
as land, land as woman in the discourse of discovery see Louis Montrose, 'The Work
of Gender in the Discourse of Discovery', in Stephen Greenblatt (ed.), *New World
Encounters* (Berkeley: University of California Press, 1993), pp. 1–41 (p. 12).
    166. *forswear my faculty*] disclaim my ability.

    0SD] Petella's presence is required at the start of the scene as she is addressed by
Rosalura at l. 20.
    2–3. *before . . . girl*] The first use of the demonstrative 'thus' in a scene which focuses
upon action and demeanour. On Oriana's last appearance, she exited the stage weeping
(1.3.162).
    6. *For me . . . self*] 'As for me, rest assured'.
    8. *tender*] offer.

Of our poor beauties to the travelled monsieur,
Yet two words to a bargain. He slights us   10
As skittish things, and we shun him as curious.
Maybe my free behaviour turns his stomach,
And makes him seem to doubt a loose opinion:
I must be so sometimes, though all the world saw it.
Oriana. Why should not ye? Are our minds only measured?   15
As long as here ye stand secure –
Rosalura.   Ye say true;
As long as mine own conscience makes no question,
What care I for report? That woman's miserable
That's good or bad for their tongue's sake. Come, let's retire –
And get my veil, wench – by my troth, your sorrow   20
                                          [*Exit* PETELLA.]
And the consideration of men's humorous maddings
Have put me into a serious contemplation.

          Enter BELLEUR, *and after him* MIRABELL.

Oriana. Come, faith, let's sit and think.
Rosalura.   That's all my business.
                                  [*They retire and sit.*]
Mirabell. Why standst thou peeping here? Thou great slug, forward!
Belleur. She is there, peace!
Mirabell.   Why standst thou here then,   25
Sneaking and peeking, as thou wouldst steal linen?
Hast thou not place and time?
Belleur.   I had a rare speech
Studied, and almost ready, and your violence
Has beat it out of my brains.

---

15. our] *F1*; *not Colman, Fraser and Rabkin.*   20SD] *This ed.; not in F1*; [*Exit Maidservant.*] *Lister; Exit Petella*; *brings veil. Bowers.*   22SD] *Bowers*; Enter *Mirabell and
Bellure. F1*; Enter MIRABELL *and* BELLEUR, *and stand apart. Weber.*   23SD] *This ed.; not
in F1*; [*They retire.*] *Fraser and Rabkin*; [*They go into the summer-house, and sit down,*
ROSALURA *having taken her veil from a table, and put it on.*] *Dyce.*

10. *two . . . bargain*] 'there are two sides to the transaction' (Tilley W827), a proverbial expression used in demanding equitable treatment.
11. *skittish*] spirited, frolicsome (*OED* 4, citing this line).
curious] difficult to satisfy (*OED* 2); cf. 1.3.12
13. *doubt a loose opinion*] suspect a tarnished reputation.
15. *Are . . . measured*] (1) Are women the only ones whose minds (and the behaviours our minds dictate) are observed and judged? (2) Must we always behave moderately, in a measured manner?
21. *humorous maddings*] foolish behaviour arising from a disordered state of the
humours.

Mirabell.   Hang your rare speeches!
Go me on like a man.
Belleur.   Let me set my beard up.   30
How has Pinac performed?
Mirabell.   He has won already:
He stands not thrumming of caps thus.
Belleur.   Lord, what should I ail?
What a cold I have over my stomach; would I had some hum!
Certain I have a great mind to be at her,
A mighty mind.
Mirabell.   On, fool!
Belleur.   Good words, I beseech ye;   35
For I will not be abused by both.
Mirabell.   Adieu, then,
I will not trouble you. I see you are valiant,
And work your own way.
Belleur.   Hist, hist, I will be ruled,
I will, i' faith, I will go presently.
Will ye forsake me now and leave me i' th' suds?   40
You know I am false-hearted this way; I beseech ye,
Good sweet Mirabell! I'll cut your throat if ye leave me,
Indeed I will, sweetheart.
Mirabell.   I will be ready,
Still at thine elbow; take a man's heart to thee,
And speak thy mind, the plainer still the better.   45
She is a woman of that free behaviour,
Indeed, that common courtesy, she cannot deny thee;
Go bravely on.
Belleur.   Madam – [*To Mirabell*] keep close about me,
Still at my back – Madam, sweet madam –
Rosalura.   Ha!
What noise is that? What saucy sound to trouble me?   50

48SD] Lister; *not in F1.*

30. *set my beard up*] (1) trim or curl up the beard (*OED* set 154m, citing this line; (2) given Belleur's pugilistic nature, perhaps there is a sense of 'lifting one's chin' in defiance.

32. *thrumming . . . caps*] wasting time with trivial tasks (*OED* thrum v.²). Thrumming involved twisting threads to make a fringe.

33. *hum*] a strong or double ale (*OED* II 3, citing this line).

40. *i' th' suds*] Proverbial, Dent S953, in difficulties, in embarrassment (*OED* 5a). The theatrical image is realised in Marston's *The Dutch Courtesan* 2.3.80–1, where Mulligrub, abandoned by the barber, says 'why / Andrew, Andrew, dost leave me in the suds?'

41. *false-hearted this way*] cowardly in initiating courtship.

Mirabell. What said she?
Belleur.   I am saucy.
             [*Rosalura and Oriana rise and come forward.*]
Mirabell.   'Tis the better.
Belleur. She comes. Must I be saucy still?
Mirabell.   More saucy.
Rosalura. Still troubled with these vanities? Heaven bless us,
   What are we born to? Would ye speak with any of my people?
   Go in, sir, I am busy.
Belleur.   This is not she, sure: 55
   Is this two children at a birth? I'll be hanged then!
   Mine was a merry gentlewoman, talked daintily,
   Talked of those matters that befitted women.
   This is a parcel-prayerbook. I'm served sweetly!
   And now I am to look to; I was prepared for th' other way.   60
Rosalura. Do you know that man?
Oriana.   Sure I have seen him, lady.
Rosalura. Methinks 'tis pity such a lusty fellow
   Should wander up and down, and want employment.
Belleur. [*Aside*] She takes me for a rogue! [*To her*] You may do well,
   madam,
   To stay this wanderer, and set him awork, forsooth;   65
   He can do something that may please your ladyship;
   I have heard of women that desire good breedings,
   Two at a birth, or so.
Rosalura. The fellow's impudent.
Oriana.   Sure he is crazed.
Rosalura. [*To Belleur*] I have heard of men too that have had good
   manners –   70
   [*To Oriana*] Sure, this is want of grace. Indeed, 'tis great pity
   The young man has been bred so ill, but this lewd age
   Is full of such examples.
Belleur. [*Aside*]   I am foundered,

51SD] Dyce; not in F1; [ROSALURA, in a veil, and ORIANA come forward.] *following
l. 52 Fraser and Rabkin.* 64SD Aside] Lister; not in F1. 64SD To her] Lister; not
in F1. 70SD] This ed.; not in F1. 71SD] This ed.; not in F1. 73SD] Lister; not in
F1.

---

54. *What . . . born to*] expression of exasperation, originating from the Renaissance
belief that the position of the planets or constellation at one's birth governed one's
destiny.
   56. *two . . . birth*] Cf. 1.3.125.
   59. *parcel-prayerbook*] a 'walking-' or 'mini-' prayer-book; *parcel* = part, partly;
often hyphenated (OED B1b).
   60. *to look to*] to beware (OED 21e).

And some shall rue the setting of me on.
Mirabell. Ha? So bookish, lady, is it possible?   75
Turned holy at the heart too? I'll be hanged then:
Why, this is such a feat, such an activity,

[*Enter* PETELLA, *with a veil.*]

Such fast and loose – A veil too for your knavery?
O dio, dio!
Rosalura.   What do you take me for, sir?
Mirabell. An hypocrite, a wanton, a dissembler,   80
How e'er ye seem, and thus ye are to be handled –
Mark me, Belleur – [*To Rosalura*] and this you love, I know it.
                        [*Takes hold of her.*]
Rosalura. Stand off, bold sir!
Mirabell.   You wear good clothes to this end,
Jewels; love feasts and masques.
Rosalura.   Ye are monstrous saucy.
Mirabell. All this to draw on fools? And thus, thus lady   85
Ye are to be lulled.
Belleur.   Let her alone, I'll swinge ye else,
I will, i' faith; for though I cannot skill o' this matter
Myself, I will not see another do it before me,
And do it worse.
Rosalura.   Away, ye are a vain thing!
You have travelled far, sir, to return again   90
A windy and poor bladder. You talk of women,

77SD] *This ed.; not in F1; Enter Servant, with a veil. Colman;* [*Enter Maidservant with a veil and exit.*] *Lister.*   82SD *To Rosalura*] *Lister; not in F1.*   82SD *Takes hold of her*] *Weber, following 'lady', l. 85, not in F1;* [*Attempts to remove the veil.*] *Dyce.*

74. setting . . . on] inciting (OED 148c), cf. 2.1.25.
77. activity] nimbleness (OED 2).
78. *fast and loose*] shifty or inconstant behaviour, cf. 3.1.72; the phrase refers to a game played with a stick and a belt or string, relying on the deftness of the operator to cheat the spectator.
79. O dio, dio!] O God, God!, an Italian expression of disapproval.
86. *lulled*] (1) soothed with sounds or caresses (OED 1); (2) pulled about (by the ears) (OED 2). The nature of the (attempted) actions which accompany Mirabell's 'thus ye are to be handled' (l. 81), and 'thus . . . ye are to be lulled' is an intriguing and open question. The responses of both Rosalura and Belleur suggest that Mirabell's action is indecorous and aggressive.
swinge] thrash (OED 1).
87. *cannot skill o'*] am not skilled at.
91. *windy . . . bladder*] verbose, pretentious man, a 'windbag'.

That are not worth the favour of a common one;
The grace of her grew in an hospital.
Against a thousand such blown fooleries
I am able to maintain good women's honours,   95
Their freedoms and their fames, and I will do it.
Mirabell. She has almost struck me dumb too.
Rosalura.   And declaim
Against your base malicious tongues, your noises,
For they are nothing else. You teach behaviours?
Or touch us for our freedoms? Teach yourselves manners,   100
Truth and sobriety, and live so clearly
That our lives may shine in ye; and then task us.
It seems ye are hot – the suburbs will supply ye!
Good women scorn such gamesters; so I'll leave ye.
I am sorry to see this; 'faith, sir, live fairly.   105
                    [*Exeunt* ROSALURA, ORIANA, *and* PETELLA.]
Mirabell. This woman, if she hold on, may be virtuous;
'Tis almost possible: we'll have a new day.
Belleur. Ye brought me on, ye forced me to this foolery;
I am shamed, I am scorned, I am flirted; yes, I am so!
Though I cannot talk to a woman like your worship,   110
And use my phrases and my learnèd figures,
Yet I can fight with any man.
Mirabell.   Fie!
Belleur.   I can, sir,
And I will fight.
Mirabell.   With whom?
Belleur.   With you, with any man;
For all men now will laugh at me.
Mirabell.   Prithee be moderate.

105SD] *This ed.; Exit* F1.

92. *not worth . . . one*] not worth even a prostitute's favour, or kind look.
93. *hospital*] orphanage or workhouse for poor children.
94. *blown fooleries*] inflated nonsense.
98. *noises*] common talk, slander (*OED* noise 2a).
101. *clearly*] cleanly.
102. *task*] censure (*OED* II.5).
103. *suburbs will supply ye*] i.e. with prostitutes. 'Suburb sinner' = prostitute (*OED* suburb 4b). Brothels ('stews') abounded in both Paris and in London, provoking Thomas Nash to protest in 1593: 'London, what are thy Suburbes but licensed Stewes', *Christs Tears over Jerusalem* (Menston: Scolar Press, 1970), p. 77.
104. *gamesters*] Cf. 1.3.221n.
109. *flirted*] sneered at, verbally rapped (*OED* flirt *v.* 4b).
110. *your worship*] Belleur uses the honorific mockingly.

Belleur. And I'll beat all men. Come –
[Challenges Mirabell.]

Mirabell.   I love thee dearly.   115
Belleur. I beat all that love; love has undone me!
   Never tell me, I will not be a history.
Mirabell. Thou art not.
Belleur.   'Sfoot, I will not; give me room,
   And let me see the proudest of ye jeer me,
   And I'll begin with you first.
Mirabell.   Prithee Belleur,   120
   If I do not satisfy thee –
Belleur.   Well, look ye do.
   But now I think on't better, 'tis impossible;
   I must beat somebody; I am mauled myself,
   And I ought in justice –
Mirabell.   No, no, no, ye are cozened;
   But walk, and let me talk to thee.
Belleur.   Talk wisely,   125
   And see that no man laugh, upon no occasion;
   For I shall think then 'tis at me.
Mirabell.   I warrant thee.
Belleur. Nor no more talk of this.
Mirabell.   Dost think I am maddish?
Belleur. I must needs fight yet; for I find it concerns me –
   A pox on't, I must fight.
Mirabell.   I'faith, thou shalt not.   130
Exeunt.

---

115. Come –] *This ed.*; Come. F1; Come! *Colman.*   115SD] *This ed.*; *not in* F1.

117. *history*] i.e. the victim of public ridicule; the subject of a ballad or anecdote.
118. *'Sfoot*] an oath; a contraction of 'God's foot'.
123. *mauled*] battered, as with a mallet (*OED* v¹ 2).
128. *maddish*] somewhat mad (*OED* b).

ACT 3

Enter DE GARD *and* LUGIER.

De Gard. I know ye are a scholar, and can do wonders.
Lugier. There's no great scholarship belongs to this, sir;
　　What I am, I am. I pity your poor sister,
　　And heartily I hate these travellers,
　　These gimcracks, made of mops and motions.　　　　　5
　　There's nothing in their houses here but hummings –
　　A bee has more brains. I grieve and vex too
　　The insolent licentious carriage
　　Of this outfacing fellow, Mirabell,
　　And I am mad to see him prick his plumes up.　　　　10
De Gard. His wrongs you partly know.
Lugier. 　　　　　　　　　　Do not you stir, sir.
　　Since he has begun with wit, let wit revenge it;
　　Keep your sword close – we'll cut his throat a new way.
　　I am ashamed the gentlewoman should suffer
　　Such base lewd wrongs.
De Gard. 　　　　　　I will be ruled; he shall live,　　15
　　And left to your revenge.
Lugier. 　　　　　　　　Ay, ay, I'll fit him.
　　He makes a common scorn of handsome women;

---

oSD *Sympson*; Enter *De Gard*, and *Leverdure*, alias, *Lugier.* F1.

　5. *gimcracks*] affected, showy persons (*OED* 3).
　mops and motions] (1) exaggerated mannerisms; (2) grimaces and antics, especially those of a monkey (*OED* mop n.3 and motion n.3a, citing this line).
　6. *houses*] heads.
　7. *I . . . vex*] I am distressed (*OED* 5).
　9. *outfacing*] arrogant; the phrase draws upon a gaming table expression relating to bluffing at cards: 'to face it out with a card of ten' = to brag, put on a bold front (*OED* card n² 4).
　10. *prick . . . up*] display himself proudly, an image appropriate to a 'wild goose', perhaps also implying 'the ostentatious display of a plumed cavalier hat as a symbol of libertine insolence' (Lister).
　13. *close*] sheathed.
　16. *left*] be left.
　fit] punish (*OED* 12); 'give him his due' (Lister).

Modesty and good manners are his May games;
He takes up maidenheads with a new commission;
The church-warrant's out of date. Follow my counsel,   20
For I am zealous in the cause.
De Gard.   I will, sir,
And will be still directed; for the truth is,
My sword will make my sister seem more monstrous:
Besides, there is no honour won on reprobates.
Lugier. You are i' th' right. The slight he has showed my pupils   25
Sets me a-fire too. Go, I'll prepare your sister,
And as I told ye –
De Gard.   Yes, all shall be fit, sir.
Lugier. And seriously, and handsomely.
De Gard.   I warrant ye.
Lugier. A little counsel more.   [*Whispers.*]
De Gard.   'Tis well.
Lugier.   Most stately.
See that observed, and then –
De Gard.   I have ye every way.   30
Lugier. Away then, and be ready.
De Gard.   With all speed, sir.   *Exit.*

Enter LILLIA[-BIANCA], ROSALURA, [*and*] ORIANA.

Lugier. We'll learn to travel too, maybe beyond him –
Good day, fair beauties.
Lillia-Bianca.   You have beautified us,
We thank ye, sir; ye have set us off most gallantly
With your grave precepts!
Rosalura.   We expected husbands   35
Out of your documents and taught behaviours,
Excellent husbands; thought men would run stark mad on us,
Men of all ages and all states. We expected
An inundation of desires and offers,
A torrent of trim suitors; all we did,   40

29SD] *Colman; not in* F1.

18. *May games*] i.e. a source of amusement and ridicule, cf. Belleur's 'I'll be no May game' at 3.1.277. The first of May was traditionally held to be the first day of spring and associated with pre-Christian fertility rites.
19.] i.e. Mirabell has authorised himself to deprive maidens of their virginity.
20. *church-warrant*] i.e. religiously solemnised marriage.
23.] 'to fight a duel on Oriana's behalf will reflect badly on her reputation'.
24. *reprobates*] See 2.1.112n.
30. *have . . . way*] understand you thoroughly.

Or said, or purposed, to be spells about us,
  Spells to provoke.
Lillia-Bianca.   Ye have provoked us finely!
  We followed your directions, we did rarely,
  We were stately, coy, demure, careless, light, giddy,
  And played at all points: this you swore would carry.   45
Rosalura. We made love and condemned love; now seemed holy,
  With such a reverent put-on reservation
  Which could not miss, according to your principles,
  Now gave more hope again; now close, now public,
  Still up and down we beat it like a billow,   50
  And ever those behaviours you read to us,
  Subtle and new. But all this will not help us.
Lillia-Bianca. They help to hinder us of all acquaintance,
  They have frighted off all friends. What am I better
  For all my learning, if I love a dunce,   55
  A handsome dunce? To what use serves my reading?
  You should have taught me what belongs to horses,
  Dogs, dice, hawks, banquets, masques, free and fair meetings,
  To have studied gowns and dressings.
Lugier.   Ye are not mad, sure?
Rosalura. We shall be if we follow your encouragements;   60
  I'll take mine own way now.
Lillia-Bianca.   And I my fortune;
  We may live maids else till the moon drop millstones.
  I see your modest women are taken for monsters,
  A dowry of good breeding is worth nothing.
Lugier. Since ye take it so to th' heart, pray ye give me leave yet,   65
  And ye shall see how I'll convert this heretic;
  Mark how this Mirabell –
Lillia-Bianca.   Name him no more,
  For, though I long for a husband, I hate him,
  And would be married sooner to a monkey

---

45. *played at all points*] tried a variety of behaviours (*OED* play v. 10c), cf. 'armed at all points', 1.1.24.
  carry] succeed, win us the advantage.
  50.] We fought relentlessly to no avail; *billow* sustains the aquatic imagery of the 'inundation of desires' and 'torrent' of suitors at ll. 39 and 40 above (*OED* beat v.¹ 1c).
  51. *read . . . us*] you taught us; Lugier is a reader in coquetry.
  62. *till . . . millstones*] i.e. for ever. Proverbially said of a hard-hearted person (Dent M967).

Or to a Jack of Straw, than such a juggler.   70
Rosalura.   I am of that mind too: he is too nimble,
And plays at fast and loose too learnedly
For a plain-meaning woman, that's the truth on't.
Here's one too that we love well, would be angry,
                                 [*Indicating Oriana*]
And reason why. No, no, we will not trouble ye   75
Nor him, at this time. May he make you happy.
We'll turn ourselves loose now to our fair fortunes,
And the downright way.
Lillia-Bianca.   The winning way we'll follow,
We'll bait that men may bite fair, and not be frighted.
Yet we'll not be carried so cheap neither, we'll have some sport,   80
Some mad morris or other for our money, tutor.
Lugier. 'Tis like enough. Prosper your own devices;
Ye are old enough to choose. But for this gentlewoman,
So please her give me leave –
Oriana.   I shall be glad, sir,
To find a friend whose pity may direct me.   85
Lugier. I'll do my best, and faithfully deal for ye;
But then ye must be ruled.
Oriana.   In all, I vow to ye.
Rosalura. Do, do. He has a lucky hand sometimes, I'll assure ye,
And hunts the recovery of a lost lover deadly.
Lugier. You must away straight.
Oriana.   Yes.
Lugier.   And I'll instruct ye.   90
Here ye can know no more.
Oriana.   By your leave, sweet ladies,
And all our fortunes arrive at our own wishes!
Lillia-Bianca. Amen, amen.
Lugier.   I must borrow your man.
Lillia-Bianca.   Pray take him;
He is within: to do her good, take anything,

74SD] *Sympson (subst.); not in F1.*   84. her give me leave –] *Sympson;* her, give me
leave. *F1.*

---

70. *Jack of Straw*] man of no substance, worth or consideration (*OED* 1).
  juggler] (1) one who deceives by trickery, or plays fast and loose (*OED* 3), cf. 'fast
and loose', 2.3.78n and l. 72 below; (2) fornicator (Williams, p. 749).
  79. *bait*] (1) furnish (a hook, trap) with a bait; with play on 'bite' in this line; (2)
allure, entice (Lister).
  80. *carried*] won, with perhaps the idea of being military spoils (see *OED* carry 16a).
  81. *morris*] i.e. amusement. The morris dance was performed by persons in fancy
costume on May Day and on other festive occasions, cf. 'May games' at 3.1.18.
  88. *a lucky hand*] Continuing the image of card-playing in 'deal' in l. 86 above.

Take us and all.
Lugier.   No doubt ye may find takers;   95
And so we'll leave ye to your own disposes.
                                   Exeunt [LUGIER *and* ORIANA].
Lillia-Bianca. Now, which way, wench?
Rosalura.   We'll go a brave way, fear not –
A safe and sure way too, and yet a byway.
I must confess I have a great mind to be married.
Lillia-Bianca. So have I too a grudging of good will that way,   100
And would as fain be dispatched. But this Monsieur Quicksilver –
Rosalura. No, no; we'll bar him, by and main. Let him trample;
There is no safety in his surquedry;
An army royal of women are too few for him.
He keeps a journal of his gentleness,   105
And will go near to print his fair dispatches,
And call it his *Triumph over Time and Women.*
Let him pass out of memory. What think ye
Of his two companions?
Lillia-Bianca.   Pinac, methinks, is reasonable;
A little modesty he has brought home with him,   110
And might be taught in time some handsome duty.
Rosalura. They say he is a wencher too.
Lillia-Bianca.   I like him better;
A free light touch or two becomes a gentleman,

96SD] *Sympson; Exit F1.*

100. *grudging*] secret inclination (OED 4).
101. *Quicksilver*] (1) a reference to Mirabell's 'mercurial' nature; (2) a derogatory epithet: quicksilver (meaning the metal mercury) was used in the treatment of syphilis.
102. *we'll bar . . . main*] we'll put him entirely out of our consideration (OED bar v.8, OED by n² 1).
trample] behave contemptuously (OED 3b).
103. *surquedry*] (1) arrogance (OED surquidry, surquedry 1); (2) lust (Williams, p. 1342).
104. *army royal*] an army marching with heavy canon, capable of besieging a strong, well-fortified city (OED royal); cf. Middleton and Rowley, *The Changeling*, 2.2.60–4.
105. *journal . . . gentleness*] (1) Mirabell's book of sexual conquests, see 2.1.146 and 2.1.169; (2) wordplay on the French *gentil*, used here ironically for 'conquests'.
107. Triumph . . . Women] Rosalura puns on the dramatic performance of the 'triumph', and Mirabell's sexual victory. The *Triumph* originates from the celebratory entrance into Rome of a successful commander with his soldiers and their spoils of war. This classical format was adapted during the Renaissance period to mark royal entrances or civic pageants. Fletcher's *Four Plays or Moral Representations, in One* (c.1612–15), written with Nathan Field, concludes with *The Triumph of Time.*
112. *wencher*] one who associates with common women (OED).

And sets him seemly off, so he exceed not,
But keep his compass clear, he may be looked at.   115
I would not marry a man that must be taught,
And conjured up with kisses. The best game
Is played still by the best gamesters.
Rosalura.   Fie upon thee!
What talk hast thou?
Lillia-Bianca.   Are not we alone and merry?
Why should we be ashamed to speak what we think? Thy
    gentleman,   120
The tall fat fellow, he that came to see thee –
Rosalura. Is't not a goodly man?
Lillia-Bianca.   A wondrous goodly!
H'as weight enough, I warrant thee. Mercy upon me,
What a serpent wilt thou seem under such a Saint George!
Rosalura. Thou art a fool. Give me a man brings mettle,   125
Brings substance with him, needs no broths to lard him.
These little fellows show like fleas in boxes,
Hop up and down, and keep a stir to vex us:
Give me the puissant pike, take you the small shot.
Lillia-Bianca. Of a great thing, I have not seen a duller.   130
Therefore methinks, sweet sister –

---

115. compass clear, he] *Langbaine*; Compass, clear he *F1*.   126. lard] *Fraser and
Rabkin*; Lare *F1*.

114. *so*] provided that.
115. *keep . . . clear*] (1) does not exceed the bounds of sexual propriety; (2) stays
free from venereal disease; 'compass' = penis (Frankie Rubinstein, *A Dictionary of
Shakespeare's Sexual Puns and their Significance*, London: Macmillan, 1984, p. 53).
    looked at] considered as a potential suitor, cf. 'look upon' at 2.2.15.
120. *Why . . . think*] Lillia-Bianca's liberal attitude echoes that of Crispinella in
Marston's *The Dutch Courtesan*: 'Let's ne'er be ashamed to speak what we be not
ashamed to think', 3.1.26–7.
124. *Saint George*] dragon-slayer, patron saint of England (Fraser and Rabkin).
126. *broths*] believed to have restorative and aphrodisiacal powers.
    lard] to 'grease' or 'baste'; a play on figurative use of culinary terms and sexual
appetite: to 'baste' Belleur and make him 'hot and juicy'.
129. *puissant pike*] mighty, powerful pike: (1) echoes *H5* 4.1.41, where Pistol asks
the disguised Henry, 'Trail'st thou the puissant pike?' A *pike* was a military weapon
consisting of a long wooden shaft with a metal head; (2) bawdy play on *pike* = 'penis',
supporting the innuendo at l. 124 above, cf. *The Woman's Prize* 1.4.27; (3) a large,
voracious freshwater fish (*OED* n.4).
    small shot] In a military context, shot are lead bullets, thus by extension, *small shot*
= small 'balls' = testicles. An alternative reading is possible, expanding the image of
men as fish in l. 79 above, as a shot is a fish resembling a trout but smaller (*OED*
shoat[1]).
130. *great thing*] imposing form, with bawdy innuendo on 'thing'.

Rosalura.   Peace, he's modest;
A bashfulness, which is a point of grace, wench:
But when these fellows come to moulding, sister,
To heat and handling –

                    Enter MIRABELL.

                    as I live, I like him,
And methinks I could form him.
Lillia-Bianca.   Peace! The firedrake.   135
Mirabell. Bless ye, sweet beauties, sweet incomparable ladies,
    Sweet wits, sweet humours. Bless you, learnèd lady,
    And you, most holy nun; bless your devotions.
Lillia-Bianca. And bless your brains, sir, your most pregnant brains, sir,
    They are in travail; may they be delivered   140
    Of a most hopeful wild goose!
Rosalura.   Bless your manhood.
    They say ye are a gentleman of action,
    A fair accomplished man, and a rare engineer.
    You have a trick to blow up maidenheads,
    A subtle trick, they say abroad.
Mirabell.   I have, lady.   145
Rosalura. And often glory in their ruins.
Mirabell.   Yes, forsooth;
    I have a speedy trick. Please you to try it,
    My engine will dispatch ye instantly.
Rosalura. I would I were a woman, sir, fit for ye,
    As there be such, no doubt, may engine you too,   150
    May with a countermine blow up your valour.
    But in good faith, sir, we are both too honest;

133-5. *moulding . . . form*] The tactile verbs in these lines suggest a reversal of the Pygmalion myth (*Met.*, 10.243–97) whereby Rosalura aims to fashion Belleur to her desired image.

135. *firedrake*] see 2.2.20n.

140. *in travail*] from the French *en travail*; a pun on 'labour', strengthening the imagery of childbirth in 'pregnant' (l. 139) and 'delivered' in this line.

142. *gentleman of action*] setting up the following conceit of seduction as military assault.

143. *engineer*] (1) a plotter; (2) one who designs and constructs military works for attack or defence (*OED* 2b); (3) pun on 'engine' = 'sexual organ' at l. 148 below (see Williams, p. 439).

144. *blow up*] deflower.

146. *forsooth*] in truth.

150. *engine you*] deceive, ensnare you (*OED* v.2).

151. *countermine*] (1) counteraction; (2) possibly implying that a female sexual partner carrying venereal disease would deliver Mirabell a fitting *coup de grâce*.

And the plague is, we cannot be persuaded.
For look ye, if we thought it were a glory
To be the last of all your lovely ladies –   155
Mirabell. Come, come, leave prating; this has spoiled your market.
This pride and puffed-up heart will make ye fast, ladies,
Fast when ye are hungry too.
Rosalura.   The more our pain, sir.
Lillia-Bianca. The more our health, I hope too.
Mirabell.   Your behaviours
Have made men stand amazed – those men that loved ye,   160
Men of fair states and parts. Your strange conversions
Into I know not what, nor how, nor wherefore.
Your scorns of those that came to visit ye,
Your studied whim-whams, and your fine set faces:
What have these got ye? Proud and harsh opinions.   165
A travelled monsieur was the strangest creature,
The wildest monster to be wondered at,
His person made a public scoff, his knowledge
(As if he had been bred 'mongst bears or bandogs)
Shunned and avoided, his conversation snuffed at.   170
What harvest brings all this?
Rosalura.   I pray ye proceed, sir.
Mirabell. Now ye shall see in what esteem a traveller,
An understanding gentleman, and a monsieur,
Is to be held, and to your griefs confess it,
Both to your griefs and galls.
Lillia-Bianca.   In what, I pray ye, sir?   175
We would be glad to understand your Excellence.
Mirabell. Go on, sweet ladies, it becomes ye rarely.
For me, I have blessed me from ye; scoff on, seriously,
And note the man ye mocked. You, Lady Learning,
Note the poor traveller that came to visit ye,   180
That flat unfurnished fellow; note him throughly,

---

161. conversions] *Sympson*; conventions *F1*.

157–8. *fast . . . hungry*] i.e., as a result of your pride, you will be left as unmarried
women craving sexual liaisons.
164. *whim-whams*] odd fancies (*OED* 2, citing this line).
169. *bandogs*] ferocious dogs restrained by a 'band', used to bait bears and bulls as
public entertainment.
170. *snuffed at*] disdained by an expression of contemptuous sniffing (Lister).
178. *blessed . . . from ye*] protected myself from you, sometimes effected by making
the sign of the cross (*OED* 3b).
181. *throughly*] thoroughly.

You may chance to see him anon.
Lillia-Bianca.   'Tis very likely.
Mirabell. And see him courted by a travelled lady,
 Held dear and honoured by a virtuous virgin,
 Maybe a beauty not far short of yours, neither,   185
 It may be, clearer.
Lillia-Bianca.   Not unlikely.
Mirabell.   Younger,
 As killing eyes as yours, a wit as poignant,
 Maybe a state too that may top your fortune.
 Enquire how she thinks of him, how she holds him,
 His good parts, in what precious price already;   190
 Being a stranger to him, how she courts him –
 A stranger to his nation too, how she dotes on him.
 Enquire of this, be sick to know. Curse, lady,
 And keep your chamber; cry and curse! A sweet one,
 A thousand in yearly land, well bred, well friended,   195
 Travelled, and highly followed for her fashions.
Lillia-Bianca. Bless his good fortune, sir.
Mirabell.   This scurvy fellow,
 I think they call his name Pinac, this serving-man
 That brought ye venison, as I take it, madam,
 Note but this scab; 'tis strange that this coarse creature, 200
 That has no more set off but his jugglings,
 His travelled tricks –
Lillia-Bianca.   Good sir, I grieve not at him,
 Nor envy not his fortune. Yet I wonder;
 He's handsome, yet I see no such perfection.
Mirabell. Would I had his fortune, for 'tis a woman   205
 Of that sweet-tempered nature and that judgement,
 Besides her state, that care, clear understanding,
 And such a wife to bless him.
Rosalura.   Pray ye, whence is she?
Mirabell. Of England, and a most accomplished lady,
 So modest that men's eyes are frighted at her,   210

---

184. dear and honoured] *Sympson*; dear, and honour'd *F1*. 188. too] *Sympson*; to
F1.

187. *poignant*] keen or pointed (OED 4).
189. *holds*] esteems.
195. *A thousand . . . land*] £1000 a year from leased land.
197. *scurvy*] contemptible.
200. *scab*] scoundrel.
201. *has no . . . but*] is distinguished by no more attractive qualities than.

Enter a Boy.

And such a noble carriage. How now, sirrah?
Boy. Sir, the great English lady –
Mirabell.   What of her, sir?
Boy. Has newly left her coach, and coming this way,
    Where you may see her plain. Monsieur Pinac
    The only man that leads her.

Enter PINAC, MARIANA, *and* Attendants.

Mirabell.   He is much honoured;   215
    Would I had such a favour – Now vex, ladies,
    Envy, and vex, and rail.
Rosalura.   Ye are short of us, sir.
Mirabell. Bless your fair fortune, sir.
Pinac.   I nobly thank ye.
Mirabell. Is she married, friend?
Pinac.   No, no.
Mirabell.   A goodly lady;
    A sweet and delicate aspect.
    [*To Lillia-Bianca and Rosalura*] Mark, mark and wonder! –   220
    Hast thou any hope of her?
Pinac.   A little.
Mirabell.   Follow close, then,
    Lose not that hope.
Pinac.   To you, sir.   [*Mariana curtsies to Mirabell.*]
Mirabell.   Gentle lady.
Rosalura. She is fair indeed.
Lillia-Bianca.   I have seen a fairer, yet she is well.
Rosalura. Her clothes sit handsome too.
Lillia-Bianca.   She dresses prettily.
Rosalura. And, by my faith, she is rich; she looks still sweeter.   225
    A well-bred woman, I warrant her.
Lillia-Bianca.   Do you hear, sir,
    May I crave this gentlewoman's name?
Pinac.   Mariana, lady.

---

213. and] *F1;* and's *Sympson.*   220SD] *This ed.; not in F1.*   222. Lose] *F2;* loose
F1.   222SD] *Sympson (subst.); not in F1.*

---

216. *vex*] be vexed (see 3.1.7n).
217. *Ye are short of us*] You are mistaken in your estimation of us.
219. *goodly*] attractive, fine.
225. *still sweeter*] sweeter and sweeter.
226. *I warrant her*] I wouldn't mind betting.

Lilllia-Bianca. I will not say I owe ye a quarrel, monsieur,
    For making me your stale: a noble gentleman
    Would have had more courtesy, at least, more faith,   230
    Than to turn off his mistress at first trial.
    You know not what respect I might have showed ye;
    I find ye have worth.
Pinac.   I cannot stay to answer ye –
    Ye see my charge. I am beholding to ye
    For all your merry tricks ye put upon me,   235
    Your bobs and base accounts. I came to love ye,
    To woo ye and to serve ye. I am much indebted to ye
    For dancing me off my legs, and then for walking me;
    For telling me strange tales I never heard of,
    More to abuse me; for mistaking me,   240
    When ye both knew I was a gentleman,
    And one deserved as rich a match as you are.
Lillia-Bianca. Be not so bitter, sir.
Pinac.   You see this lady,
    She is young enough, and fair enough to please me;
    A woman of a loving mind, a quiet,   245
    And one that weighs the worth of him that loves her.
    I am content with this and bless my fortune,
    Your curious wits and beauties.
Lillia-Bianca.   Faith, see me once more.
Pinac. I dare not trouble ye.
Lillia-Bianca.   May I speak to your lady?
Pinac. I pray ye, content yourself. I know ye are bitter,   250
    And in your bitterness ye may abuse her,
    Which if she comes to know (for she understands ye not)
    It may breed such a quarrel to your kindred,
    And such an indiscretion fling on you too,
    For she is nobly friended.
Lillia-Bianca. [*Aside*]   I could eat her!   255

255SD] *Weber; not in F1.*

   229. *stale*] a lover or mistress whose devotion is turned into ridicule for the amusement of a rival or rivals (OED 6).
   236. *bobs . . . accounts*] tricks and degrading treatment.
   245. *quiet*] quiet woman.
   248. *curious*] abstruse, subtle (OED 10b), cf. 1.3.12n.
   250. *content yourself*] be satisfied.
   254. *indiscretion*] stigma, blemish.
   255. *eat*] destroy by devouring (as a beast of prey) (OED 8a).

Pinac. Rest as ye are, a modest noble gentlewoman,
          And afford your honest neighbours some of your prayers.
                    Exeunt [PINAC, MARIANA, *and Attendants*].
Mirabell. What think you now?
Lillia-Bianca.   Faith, she's a pretty whiting;
          She has got a pretty catch too.
Mirabell.   You are angry,
          Monstrous angry now, grievously angry,   260
          And the pretty heart does swell now.
Lillia-Bianca.   No, in truth, sir.
Mirabell. And it will cry anon, 'a pox upon it!'
          And it will curse itself, and eat no meat, lady,
          And it will fight.
Lillia-Bianca.   Indeed you are mistaken;
          It will be very merry.
Rosalura.   Why, sir, do you think   265
          There are no more men living, nor no handsomer
          Than he or you? By this light, there be ten thousand,
          Ten thousand thousand – comfort yourself, dear monsieur –
          Faces and bodies, wits, and all abiliments:
          There are so many we regard 'em not.   270

                    Enter BELLEUR *and two* Gentlemen.

Mirabell. That such a noble lady – I could burst now!
          So far above such trifles –
Belleur.   You did laugh at me,
          And I know why ye laughed.
1 Gentleman.   I pray ye be satisfied.
          If we did laugh, we had some private reason,
          And not at you.
2 Gentleman.   Alas, we know you not, sir.   275
Belleur. I'll make you know me. Set your faces soberly,
          Stand this way, and look sad; I'll be no May game!
          Sadder, demurer yet.
Rosalura. What's the matter? What ails this gentleman?

257SD] *Colman*; Exit. *F1*.   272. trifles –] *Sympson*; triffles? *F1*.

258. *whiting*] (1) a term of endearment (*OED* 2b); (2) small white-fleshed edible fish.
    262. *it . . . cry*] you will cry; 'it' is an infantilising form.
    anon] soon (*OED* 5).
    263. *meat*] See 1.1.77n.
    269. *abiliments*] (1) mental faculties (*OED* 6); (2) garments appropriate to any office or occasion (*OED* 4).
    277. *sad*] solemn, cf. 2.2.57.

Belleur. Go off now backward, that I may behold ye,   280
And not a simper, on your lives!
Lillia-Bianca.   He's mad, sure.
Belleur. Do you observe me too?
Mirabell.   I may look on ye.
Belleur. Why do you grin? I know your mind.
Mirabell.   You do not.
You are strangely humorous. Is there no mirth nor pleasure,
But you must be the object?   285
Belleur. Mark, and observe me: wherever I am named
The very word shall raise a general sadness
For the disgrace this scurvy woman did me;
This proud pert thing; take heed ye laugh not at me;
Provoke me not, take heed.
Rosalura.   I would fain please ye,   290
Do anything to keep ye quiet.
Belleur.   Hear me.
Till I receive a satisfaction
Equal to the disgrace and scorn ye gave me,
Ye are a wretched woman. Till thou woo'st me,
And I scorn thee as much, as seriously   295
Jeer and abuse thee, ask what Jill thou art,
Or any baser name; I will proclaim thee,
I will so sing thy virtue, so bepaint thee –
Rosalura. Nay, good sir, be more modest.
Belleur.   Do you laugh again?
Because ye are a woman, ye are lawless,   300
And out of compass of an honest anger.
Rosalura. Good sir, have a better belief of me.
Lillia-Bianca.   Away, dear sister.
                    Exeunt [ROSALURA *and* LILLIA-BIANCA].
Mirabell. Is not this better now, this seeming madness,
Than falling out with your friends?

295–6. as much, as seriously/ Jeer] *F2*; asmuch, as, seriously, / Gear, *F1*.   302SD
Weber; Exit. *F1*.

296. *Jill*] a familiar or contemptuous term applied to a woman; a wench (*OED* gill,
jill n.[4] 1a).

298. *sing thy virtue*] spoken sarcastically: proclaim aloud your dishonour.

bepaint] slander.

300. *lawless*] (1) uncontrolled by law, unbridled (*OED* 2a), therefore ruled by
passion; (2) licentious (Fraser and Rabkin).

301. *out . . . compass of*] beyond the scope of.

honest anger] possibly the physical beating with which Belleur threatens Rosalura at
4.2.37.

Belleur.   Have I not frighted her?
Mirabell. Into her right wits, I warrant thee. Follow this humour,   305
And thou shalt see how prosperously 'twill guide thee.
Belleur. I am glad I have found a way to woo yet. I was afraid once
I never should have made a civil suitor.
Well, I'll about it still.   *Exit.*
Mirabell.   Do, do, and prosper. –
What sport do I make with these fools! What pleasure   310
Feeds me, and fats my sides at their poor innocence!

                    Enter LUGIER [*disguised*].

Wooing and wiving, hang it! Give me mirth,
Witty and dainty mirth. I shall grow in love sure
With mine own happy head. Who's this? To me, sir?
[*Aside*] What youth is this?
Lugier.   Yes, sir, I would speak with you,   315
If your name be Monsieur Mirabell.
Mirabell.   Ye have hit it.
Your business, I beseech ye?
Lugier.   This it is, sir:
There is a gentlewoman hath long time affected ye,
And loved ye dearly.
Mirabell.   Turn over, and end that story,
'Tis long enough: I have no faith in women, sir.   320
Lugier. It seems so, sir. I do not come to woo for her,
Or sing her praises, though she well deserve 'em;
I come to tell ye, ye have been cruel to her,
Unkind and cruel, false of faith, and careless,

311SD] *Dyce (subst.), following* 'head', *l.* 314; *Enter Lever- / duce, des Lugier, / Mr.
Illiard. F1; Enter* Leverduce, *alias* Lugier, *Mr. Illiard. F2.*   315SD] *Dyce; not in F1.*
324. *false] Sympson; falser F1.*

311SD] *F1*'s 'des' is a printer's misreading of 'alias', as in *F1*'s stage direction at
3.1.0SD, 'Enter . . . *Leverdure*, alias, *Lugier*'. Leverdure is the name of the merchant
supposedly at Orléans at the time of 5.2.78–9, to whom the Young Man pretends to
be a factor (76–7). 'Mr. Illiard' refers to Eyllaerdt Swanston, who acted Lugier in the
1632 revival of *The Wild-Goose Chase* (see Dramatis Personae). However, Lugier is
not in disguise at the start of Act 3, nor does Mirabell show any recognition of him in
the dialogue following 311.1. Both stage directions seem to represent 'a positive error,
or change of plan not rectified' (Bowers, *DW*, 6.236).
    313–14. *I shall . . . head*] Cf. Mosca in Jonson's *Volpone*: 'I fear I shall begin to grow
in love / With my dear self, and my most prosperous parts' (3.1.1–2).
    319. *turn over*] i.e. turn the page.
    324. *false of faith*] alluding to Mirabell reneging on his marriage contract.

Taking more pleasure in abusing her,   325
Wresting her honour to your wild disposes,
Than noble in requiting her affection:
Which, as ye are a man, I must desire ye
(A gentleman of rank) not to persist in,
No more to load her fair name with your injuries.   330
Mirabell. Why, I beseech ye, sir?
Lugier.   Good sir, I'll tell ye,
And I'll be short; I'll tell ye, because I love ye,
Because I would have you shun the shame may follow.
There is a nobleman, new come to town, sir,
A noble and a great man, that affects her,   335
A countryman of mine, a brave Savoyan,
Nephew to th' duke, and so much honours her,
That 'twill be dangerous to pursue your old way,
To touch at anything concerns her honour,
Believe, most dangerous. Her name is Oriana,   340
And this great man will marry her. Take heed, sir;
For howsoe'er her brother, a staid gentleman,
Lets things pass upon better hopes, this lord, sir,
Is of that fiery and that poignant metal,
(Especially provoked on by affection)   345
That 'twill be hard – but you are wise.
Mirabell. A lord, sir?
Lugier.   Yes, and a noble lord.
Mirabell.   Send her good fortune.
This will not stir her lord. A baroness?
Say ye so; say ye so? By'r lady, a brave title;
Top and topgallant now! Save her great ladyship.   350
I was a poor servant of hers, I must confess, sir,
And in those days I thought I might be jovy,

---

326. *disposes*] whims, purposes.

336. *Savoyan*] Savoyard; an inhabitant or native of Savoy, a region in south-east France.

339. *touch at*] allude to.

344. *poignant metal*] sharp temper, making him quick to take offence.

346. *but*] unless.

348. *This . . . lord*] Mirabell seems to be denying that the 'lord' will take exception to his boorish treatment of Oriana.

350. *Top and topgallant*] 'the ultimate accomplishment', a common expression, short for the nautical expression 'topsail and topgallant sail'; with all sail set, in full array or career (*OED* top n¹ III 9c).

352. *jovy*] jovial (*OED*, citing this line).

And make a little bold to call in to her;
But *basta!* now; I know my rules and distance;
Yet if she want an usher, such an implement,   355
One that is throughly paced; a clean-made gentleman,
Can hold a hanging up with approbation,
Plant his hat formally and wait with patience,
I do beseech you, sir –
Lugier.   Sir, leave your scoffing,
And as ye are a gentleman, deal fairly.   360
I have given ye a friend's counsel; so I'll leave ye.
Mirabell. But hark ye, hark ye, sir; is't possible
I may believe what you say?
Lugier.   You may choose, sir.
Mirabell. No baits, no fish-hooks, sir? No gins, no nooses,
No pitfalls to catch puppies?
Lugier.   I tell ye certain: 365
You may believe; if not, stand to the danger.   *Exit.*
Mirabell. A lord of Savoy, says he? The duke's nephew;
A man so mighty? By'r lady, a fair marriage,
By my faith, a handsome fortune! I must leave prating,
For, to confess the truth, I have abused her,   370
For which I should be sorry; but that will seem scurvy.
I must confess, she was, ever since I knew her,
As modest as she was fair. I am sure she loved me;
Her means good and her breeding excellent,
And for my sake she has refused fair matches: 375

---

353. in to her] *Colman*; into her; *F1.*   357–8. up with approbation, / Plant] *Colman*;
up; with approbation / Plant *F1.*

353. *call in to her*] i.e. consider an amorous liaison with her; possibly linked to the
imagery of love as a journey or voyage and women as ports.
354. *basta!*] Spanish and Italian for 'Enough!', 'No more!' (*OED*).
355. *usher*] a male attendant on a lady (*OED* 2b, quoting this line), sometimes
providing sexual or pimping services (Williams, p. 593).
implement] functionary.
356. *throughly paced*] properly trained.
clean-made] physically attractive.
357. *hold a hanging up*] hanging-holder = an attendant (*OED* 8), cf. Fletcher, *A
Wife for a Month* 1.1.439–40: 'You scurvey usher...'/ thou poore base hanging
holder'.
364. *gins*] traps.
365. *pitfalls...puppies*] 'concealed pits to catch by surprise vain and foolish young
men' (Lister).
366. *stand...danger*] bear the consequences (*OED* contract v. 5a, citing Hobbes:
'You must stand the danger you have contracted').
371. *scurvy*] See 3.1.197n.

I may play the fool finely.

Enter DE GARD [*disguised*], ORIANA, *and* Attendants.

　　　　　　　　　Stay, who are these?
'Tis she, I am sure; and that the lord, it should seem.
He carries a fair port, is a handsome man too.
I do begin to feel I am a coxcomb.
Oriana. Good my lord, choose a nobler: for I know　　　380
　　I am so far below your rank and honour
　　That what ye can say this way I must credit
　　But spoken to beget yourself sport. Alas, sir,
　　I am so far off from deserving you,
　　My beauty so unfit for your affection,　　　　　　385
　　That I am grown the scorn of common railers,
　　Of such injurious things, that, when they cannot
　　Reach at my person, lie with my reputation.
　　I am poor besides.
De Gard.　　　　　Ye are all wealth and goodness;
　　And none but such as are the scum of men,　　　390
　　The ulcers of an honest state, spite-weavers,
　　That live on poison only, like swoll'n spiders,
　　Dare once profane such excellence, such sweetness.
Mirabell. [*Aside*] This man speaks loud indeed.
De Gard.　　　　　　　　　Name but the men, lady;
　　Let me but know these poor and base depravers,　　395
　　Lay but to my revenge their persons open,
　　And you shall see how suddenly, how fully,
　　For your most beauteous sake, how direfully
　　I'll handle their despites. Is this thing one?
　　Be what he will –
Mirabell.　　　　Sir!
De Gard.　　　　　　Dare your malicious tongue, sir –　　400
Mirabell. I know you not, nor what ye mean.
Oriana.　　　　　　　　　Good my lord –
De Gard. If he, or any he –

376SD] *Weber; Enter De-Gard, Oriana, and Attendants.* F1.

　378. *carries a fair port*] has a stately bearing.
　382. *credit*] believe.
　387–8. *when ... reputation*] i.e. when they cannot seduce me, slander my
reputation.
　394. *loud*] forcefully, cf. the 'thundering lord' at l. 412 below.
　396.] Disclose their identities for the sake of my revenge.
　399. *despites*] gossip, cf. 'spite-weavers' at l. 391 above.

Oriana.   I beseech your honour,
This gentleman's a stranger to my knowledge,
And no doubt, sir, a worthy man.
De Gard.   Your mercy.
But had he been a tainter of your honour,   405
A blaster of those beauties reign within ye –
But we shall find a fitter time. Dear lady,
As soon as I have freed ye from your guardian
And done some honoured offices unto ye,
I'll take ye with those faults the world flings on ye,   410
And dearer than the whole world I'll esteem ye.
                    [*Exeunt* DE GARD, ORIANA, *and* Attendants.]
Mirabell. This is a thundering lord; I am glad I 'scaped him.
How lovingly the wench disclaimed my villainy!
I am vexed now heartily that he shall have her;
Not that I care to marry or to lose her,   415
But that this bilbo lord shall reap that maidenhead
That was my due, that he shall rig and top her!
I'd give a thousand crowns now, he might miss her.

                Enter a Servant [Lillia-Bianca's *man*].

Servant. [*Aside*] Nay, if I bear your blows and keep your counsel,
You have good luck, sir; I'll teach ye to strike lighter.   420
Mirabell. Come hither, honest fellow. Canst thou tell me
Where this great lord lies? This Savoy lord? Thou metst him;
He now went by thee, certain.
Servant.   Yes, he did, sir.
I know him, and I know you are fooled.
Mirabell.   Come hither.
Here's all this; [*Gives money.*] give me truth.
Servant.   Not for your money;   425
(And yet that may do much) but I have been beaten,
And by the worshipful contrivers beaten, and I'll tell ye,

---

405. he...a tainter] F2; ye...attaint F1. 411SD] Dyce (subst.); not in F1.
418SD] Bowers; not in F1. 419SD] Fraser and Rabkin; [Speaking to Lugier off-stage]
Lister. 425SD] Lister; not in F1.

---

409. *honoured offices*] ceremonial duties relating to marriage.
    416. *bilbo lord*] (1) bully; a corruption of 'Bilbao', the Spanish city renowned for
the high quality of its swords, which were often sported by swashbucklers (OED 3,
citing this line); (2) sexually suggestive sobriquet since *bilbo* = penis (Williams, p. 106).
    417. *rig ... top*] nautical terms used with the sense of 'to copulate with', see OED
rig v.5 and top v.[1] 11.
    422. *lies*] resides.

This is no lord, no Savoy lord.
Mirabell.   Go forward.
Servant. This is a trick, and put upon ye grossly
　　By one Lugier. The lord is Monsieur De Gard, sir,   430
　　An honest gentleman, and a neighbour here:
　　Their ends you understand better than I, sure.
Mirabell. Now I know him, know him now plain.
Servant. I have discharged my colours; so God by ye, sir.   *Exit.*
Mirabell. What a purblind puppy was I! Now I remember him;   435
　　All the whole cast on's face, though 'twere umbered
　　And masked with patches: what a dunder-whelp
　　To let him domineer thus! How he strutted,
　　And what a load of lord he clapped upon him!
　　Would I had him here again, I would so bounce him,   440
　　I would so thank his lordship for his lewd plot.
　　Do they think to carry it away with a great band made of
　　　　bird-pots,
　　And a pair of pin-buttocked breeches?

　　　Enter DE GARD [*disguised*], ORIANA[, *and* Attendants].

　　　　　　　　　　　　　　　Ha! 'Tis he again;
　　He comes, he comes, he comes; have at him!

---

434. colours] *F1*; choler *Sympson*. cholers *Fraser and Rabkin*.   443SD] *Fraser and Rabkin (subst.); Enter De-Gard, / Oriana, etc. in right margin opp. ll. 444-5 F1.*

434. *discharged . . . colours*] (1) given vent to my anger; 'colour' is an obsolete form of 'choler' (*OED* colour II 8c); (2) an ironic pun on 'colours' = device, badge, or dress identifying allegiance to a particular party (*OED* II 6a). The Servant has, in fact, betrayed his loyalty to his master, by informing Mirabell of the hoax. Cf. 4.1.146.
435. *purblind*] (1) short-sighted (*OED* 2); (2) obtuse (*OED* 3).
436. *umbered*] stained with umber (a brown earth used as pigment), to make it appear darker.
437. *masked . . . patches*] disguised by the pieces of silk used to cover facial imperfections.
　　dunder-whelp] a contemptible blockhead (*OED*, citing this line).
440. *bounce*] beat.
441. *lewd*] villainous, devious.
442. *band*] ruff, collar.
　　bird-pots] (1) Dyce conjectures that this may refer to a neck ornament worn by the 'Savoyan Lord' that 'in its puckers, perhaps' resembled bird-pots; (2) the image may refer to the similarity of bird-pots, the circular wicker cages in which poultry was fattened for the table, to the wicker or wire framework of the 'supportasse'. A supportasse, or 'underpropper' could be affixed around the neck, beneath a large band to hold the ruff out horizontally above the shoulders.
443. *pin-buttocked breeches*] close-fitting trousers, cf. 'pin-buttocked', 1.2.11n.

Sings. My Savoy lord, why dost thou frown on me?   445
And will that favour never sweeter be?
Wilt thou, I say, for ever play the fool?
De Gard, be wise, and Savoy, go to school.

My lord De Gard, I thank ye for your antic,
My lady bright, that will be sometime frantic;   450
You worthy train that wait upon this pair,
Send you more wit, and they a bouncing bairn!
And so I take my humble leave of your honours.   *Exit.*
De Gard. We are discovered; there's no remedy.
Lillia-Bianca's man, upon my life,   455
In stubbornness because Lugier corrected him.
A shameless slave – plague on him for a rascal!
Oriana. I was in a perfect hope; the bane on't is now,
He will make mirth on mirth to persecute us.
De Gard. We must be patient; I am vexed to the proof too.   460
I'll try once more; then, if I fail, here's one speaks.
          [*Grasping his sword*]
Oriana. Let me be lost and scorned first.
De Gard.   Well, we'll consider.
Away, and let me shift; I shall be hooted else.   *Exeunt*

---

452. they] *F1*; them *Colman.*   452. bairn] *Sympson;* Baire *F1.*   457. slave – plague]
Bowers (subst.); Slaves-plague *F1;* Slave's plague *Langbaine;* Slave! Plague *Sympson.*
461SD] *Weber (subst.);* not in *F1.*

---

445. *My Savoy lord*] The opening of Mirabell's song parodies the beginning of the
popular ballad, 'Fortune, my Foe', the first stanza of which is as follows: 'Fortune my
foe, why dost thou frown on me? / And will thy favour never better be? / Wilt thou, I
say, for ever breed my pain? / And wilt thou not restore my joys again?' (cited in Dyce,
2.225). In *F1* only the first four lines of verse are indented, which suggests that, after
'quoting' the well-known ballad, Mirabell modulates from song to spoken verse at
l. 449. Most editors, except Bowers, print ll. 449–52 as a continuation of the song.
     449. *antic*] (1) grotesque or ludicrous trick (*OED* 2); (2) grotesque theatrical display
(*OED* 3).
     452. *bairn*] baby.
     460. *to the proof*] to the extreme.
     463. *shift*] change clothing.

ACT 4

Enter LUGIER, LILLIA-BIANCA, *[and]* Servant
[with a willow garland].

Lugier. Faint not, but do as I direct ye, trust me.
　Believe me too, for what I have told ye, lady,
　As true as you are Lillia, is authentic:
　I know it; I have found it. 'Tis a poor courage
　Flies off for one repulse. These travellers　　　　　5
　Shall find before we have done, a homespun wit,
　A plain French understanding, may cope with 'em.
　They have had the better yet, thank your sweet squire here;
　And let 'em brag. You would be revenged?
Lillia-Bianca.　　　　　　　　　　　　Yes, surely.
Lugier. And married too?
Lillia-Bianca.　　　　　I think so.
Lugier.　　　　　　　　Then be counselled;　　　10
　You know how to proceed. I have other irons
　Heating as well as yours, and I will strike
　Three blows with one stone home. Be ruled and happy;
　And so I leave ye. Now is the time.
Lillia-Bianca.　　　　　　　　I am ready,
　If he do come to dor me.
Servant.　　　　　　　Will ye stand here,　　　15

---

oSD] *Weber; Enter* Leugier, Lelia, *Servants. F1.*　9–10. And . . . surely. / *Lugier.* And
married too?] *Fraser and Rabkin;* And . . . reveng'd? / *Lillia.* Yes, surely. *Bowers.*
14–15. ready, / If . . . me.] *F2;* ready. / If . . . me. *F1;* ready. / If . . . me – *Bowers.*
15. dor me] *Sympson;* do me *F1.*

oSD willow garland] a symbol of unrequited love or grief.
7. *cope with*] prove a match for.
8. *They . . . squire*] i.e. Mirabell and his friends are triumphant, owing to the
servant's betrayal at the end of the previous scene.
11–12. *other . . . Heating*] proverbial; 'to have other irons in the fire' means to have
other opportunities or commitments (Dent I99).
12–13. *strike . . . home*] accomplish three plans with one stratagem, similar in sense
to 'to kill two birds with one stone'.
15. *dor*] mock, make a fool of (*OED* v.[1] 1). F1's 'do' may be construed in the senses
of 'work upon' (*OED* 11), 'undo' (*OED* 11e), 'cheat' (*OED* 11f), or the 'wanton

And let the people think ye are God knows what, mistress?
Let boys and prentices presume upon ye?
Lillia-Bianca.   Prithee hold thy peace.
Servant. Stand at his door that hates ye?
Lillia-Bianca.   Prithee leave prating.
Servant. Pray ye, go to th' tavern; I'll give ye a pint of wine there.
If any of the madcap gentlemen should come by   20
That take up women upon special warrant,
You were in a wise case now.

Enter MIRABELL, PINAC, MARIANA, PRIEST, [*and*] Attendants.

Lillia-Bianca. [*To Servant*]   Give me the garland,
And wait you here.   [Servant *retires.*]
Mirabell.   She is here to seek thee, sirrah.
I told thee what would follow; she is mad for thee.
Show, and advance. – So early stirring, lady?   25
It shows a busy mind, a fancy troubled.
A willow garland too! Is't possible?
'Tis pity so much beauty should lie musty,
But 'tis not to be helped now.
Lillia-Bianca.   The more's my misery. –
Good fortune to ye, lady; you deserve it.   30
To me, too late repentance; I have sought it.
I do not envy, though I grieve a little,
You are mistress of that happiness, those joys
That might have been, had I been wise, but fortune –
Pinac. She understands ye not; pray ye, do not trouble her,   35
And do not cross me like a hare thus, 'tis as ominous.

22SD [*To Servant*]] *Fraser and Rabkin; not in* F1.   23SD] *Fraser and Rabkin; not in*
F1.

---

sense' suggested by Weber, 'copulate' (*OED* 16b). However, 'dor' is supported by
related uses in Fletcher's *The Lovers' Progress* 1.1.28–9: 'I would not / Receive the
Dor', and *A Wife for a Month* 4.5.4: 'To give her such a dor'.
    stand here] i.e. at the doorstep, the traditional operating post for bawds.
    21. *take up*] (1) sieze or take possession of (Lister); (2) arrest (Fraser and Rabkin).
    special warrant] (1) Cf. Mirabell's 'new commission' to 'take up maidenheads' at
3.1.19; (2) possibly a reference to a scandal relating to the press-ganging of young
English women to serve as wives in the new colony of Virginia, which Baldwin Maxwell
discusses in relation to Fletcher's *The Noble Gentleman* (1606, rev. before 1625). See
Maxwell, *Studies in Beaumont, Fletcher, and Massinger* (Chapel Hill: University of
North Carolina Press, 1939), pp. 154–9.
    22. *a wise case*] spoken ironically: 'an advantageous position'.
    25. *Show, and advance*] Present yourself and step forward.
    36. *cross me like a hare*] proverbially a harbinger of bad luck (Dent H150).

Lillia-Bianca. I come not to upbraid your levity,
        Though ye made show of love, and though I liked ye
        To claim an interest (we are yet both strangers;
        But what we might have been, had you persevered, sir!),   40
        To be an eyesore to your loving lady.
        This garland shows I give myself forsaken,
        (Yet she must pardon me, 'tis most unwillingly)
        And all the power and interest I had in ye,
        As I persuade myself somewhat ye loved me,   45
        Thus patiently I render up, I offer
        To her that must enjoy ye, and so bless ye.
        Only, I heartily desire this courtesy,
        And would not be denied: to wait upon ye
        This day, to see ye tied, then no more trouble ye.   50
Pinac. It needs not, lady.
Lillia-Bianca.   Good sir, grant me so much.
Pinac. 'Tis private, and we make no invitation.
Lillia-Bianca. My presence, sir, shall not proclaim it public.
Pinac. Maybe 'tis not in town.
Lillia-Bianca.   I have a coach, sir,
        And a most ready will to do you service.   55
Mirabell. [*Aside to Pinac*] Strike now or never! Make it sure: I tell
        thee,
        She will hang herself if she have thee not.
Pinac. [*Aloud to Mirabell*]   Pray ye, sir,
        Entertain my noble mistress: only a word or two
        With this importunate woman, and I'll relieve ye. –
        Now ye see what your flings are, and your fancies,   60
        Your states and your wild stubborness; now ye find
        What 'tis to gird and kick at men's fair services,
        To raise your pride to such a pitch and glory
        That goodness shows like gnats, scorned under ye.

38-9. ye / To] *F1*; ye) / To *Sympson*; ye, / To *Fraser and Rabkin*.   51. needs] *Colman*;
need *F1*.   56SD] *Weber*; not in *F1*.   57SD] *Lister*; not in *F1*.

38-9. *though . . . interest*] though I liked you sufficiently to claim an interest in you.
41. *eyesore*] cause of annoyance (*OED* 3).
42. *I give myself forsaken*] 'I concede that I have been abandoned'.
50. *tied*] wed.
61. *states*] demeanours, attitudes.
62. *gird*] sneer at (*OED* v² 4b).
64. *shows . . . gnats*] is diminished or rendered inconsequential. Something valueless
is 'not worth a gnat' (Tilley G149).

'Tis ugly, naught; a self-will in a woman,   65
Chained to an overweening thought, is pestilent,
Murders fair fortune first, then fair opinion.
There stands a pattern, a true patient pattern,
                              [*Gesturing to Mariana*]
Humble and sweet.
Lillia-Bianca.   I can but grieve my ignorance.
Repentance, some say too, is the best sacrifice;   70
For sure, sir, if my chance had been so happy
(As I confess I was mine own destroyer)
As to have arrived at you, I will not prophesy,
But certain, as I think, I should have pleased ye,
Have made ye as much wonder at my courtesy,   75
My love and duty, as I have disheartened ye.
Some hours we have of youth, and some of folly,
And being free-born maids we take a liberty,
And to maintain that, sometimes we strain highly.
Pinac.   Now ye talk reason.
Lillia-Bianca. But being yoked and governed,   80
Married, and those light vanities purged from us,
How fair we grow, how gentle, and how tender
We twine about those loves that shoot up with us.
A sullen woman fear, that talks not to ye;
She has a sad and darkened soul, loves dully: 85
A merry and a free wench, give her liberty,
Believe her in the lightest form she appears to ye,
Believe her excellent, though she despise ye,
Let but these fits and flashes pass, she will show to ye
As jewels rubbed from dust, or gold new burnished.   90
Such had I been, had you believed.
Pinac.   Is't possible?

68SD] *This ed.; not in* F1.   82. grow, how gentle, and] F1; grow! how gentle, and
Colman; grow, how gentle; and *Fraser and Rabkin*.

   65. *naught*] wicked.
   73. *to . . . you*] i.e. to have gained Pinac.
   78. *free-born maids*] daughters of a man possessing land in 'free-hold' to the value
of 40 shillings; i.e. someone who was his own master, not having to work for his living.
For Nantolet's daughters, 'free-born' implies possessing the liberty and privileges that
accompany 'gentle' status, such as a private education.
   79. *strain highly*] strive vigorously (*OED* 19).
   82–3. *how tender . . . us*] The plant metaphor builds on the image in ll. 80 above
and 96 below of mutual support within marriage.
   87. *lightest*] most frivolous, capricious.

Lillia-Bianca. And to your happiness, I dare assure ye,
  If true love be accounted so. Your pleasure,
  Your will and your command had tied my motions –
  But that hope's gone. I know you are young and giddy,   95
  And till you have a wife can govern with ye,
  You sail upon this world-sea light and empty,
  Your bark in danger daily. 'Tis not the name, neither,
  Of wife can steer ye, but the noble nature,
  The diligence, the care, the love, the patience.   100
  She makes the pilot and preserves the husband,
  That knows and reckons every rib he is built on.
  But this I tell ye to my shame.
Pinac.   I admire ye,
  And now am sorry that I aim beyond ye.
Mirabell. [*Aside to Pinac*] So, so, so: fair and softly. She is thine
  own, boy,   105
  She comes now, without lure.
Pinac.   But that it must needs
  Be reckoned to me as a wantonness,
  Or worse, a madness, to forsake a blessing,
  A blessing of that hope –
Lillia-Bianca.   I dare not urge ye;
  And yet, dear sir –
Pinac.   'Tis most certain, I had rather,   110
  If 'twere in mine own choice – for you are my countrywoman,
  A neighbour here born by me; she a stranger,
  And who knows how her friends –
Lilia-Bianca.   Do as you please, sir.
  If ye be fast, not all the world . . . I love ye,

105SD] *Weber (subst.); not in F1.*

94. *tied my motions*] guided my behaviour.
97. *this world-sea*] Introduces the image of marriage as a nautical journey.
101-2. *She . . . on*] 'By a rather deft manipulation of the ship-metaphor, "rib" being used of the structure of a ship and the old biblical notion of woman as formed out of man's rib, Lillia-Bianca inverts the usual relationship in which the male marriage partner is the controlling force and the female the controlled party' (Lister).
102. *reckons*] enumerates and appraises (*OED* 2e).
106. *without lure*] i.e. of her own accord. The term derives from falconry and the method of recalling a hawk to the falconer's fist.
107. *reckoned . . . wantonness*] seen as unjustifiable or reckless behaviour on my part.
113. *friends*] relations.
114. *fast*] handfast, contracted to marry, sometimes signified by the joining of hands (*OED* 1).

'Tis most true, and clear I would persuade ye;   115
And I shall love ye still.
Pinac.   Go, get before me:
So much ye have won upon me – do it presently:
Here's a priest ready – I'll have you.
Lillia-Bianca.   Not now, sir.
No, you shall pardon me. Advance your lady,
I dare not hinder your most high preferment: 120
'Tis honour enough for me I have unmasked ye.
Pinac.   How's that?
Lillia-Bianca. I have caught ye, sir. Alas, I am no stateswoman,
Nor no great traveller, yet I have found ye:
I have found your lady too, your beauteous lady;
I have found her birth and breeding too, her discipline,   125
Who brought her over, and who kept your lady,
And, when he laid her by, what virtuous nunnery
Received her in; I have found all these. Are ye blank now?
Methinks such travelled wisdoms should not fool thus,
Such excellent indiscretions.
Mirabell. [Aside]   How could she know this?   130
Lillia-Bianca. 'Tis true she is English born, but most part French now,
And so I hope you will find her, to your comfort.
Alas, I am ignorant of what she cost ye;
The price of these hired clothes I do not know, gentlemen –
Those jewels are the broker's, how ye stand bound for 'em.   135

---

115. true, and clear I] *Dyce;* true: and cleer, I *F1;* true, and clear, I *Sympson;* true and clear, I *Lister.*   121-2. ye. *Pinac.* How's that? / *Lillia.* I] *Lister;* ye. / *Pinac.* How's that. *Lylia.* I *Bowers.*   130SD] *Fraser and Rabkin; not in F1.*   131. 'Tis true she is] *F1;* Tis true, she's *Langbaine.*

---

115. *clear . . . ye*] I would persuade you entirely (*OED* clear B. adv. 5a).

122. *stateswoman*] a woman with an interest, or involvement, in politics and public affairs. Cf. Jonson, *Epicene,* 'be a states-woman, know all the news; what was done at Salisbury . . . what at court' (2.1.113–15).

125. *discipline*] profession.

127. *nunnery*] brothel (*OED* 1b).

128. *blank*] dumbfounded, nonplussed (*OED* 5a).

129. *fool*] be fooled.

130. *excellent indiscretions*] surpassing lack of good judgement.

131. *most . . . now*] i.e. infected with the 'French disease', syphilis. Conversely, to the French syphilis was known as the 'English disease'.

135. *broker's*] pawnbroker's.

how . . . them] what you have paid to take them out of pawn.

Pinac. Will you make this good?
Lillia-Bianca.   Yes, yes, and to her face, sir,
  That she is an English whore! A kind of fling-dust,
  One of your London light o' loves, a right one;
  Came over in thin pumps and half a petticoat,
  One fall, and one smock, with a broken haberdasher: 140
  I know all this without a conjuror.
  Her name is Jumping Joan, an ancient sin-weaver;
  She was first a lady's chambermaid, there slipped
  And broke her leg above the knee; departed
  And set up shop herself, stood the fierce conflicts   145
  Of many a furious term; there lost her colours,
  And last shipped over hither.
Mirabell. [*Aside*]   We are betrayed.
Lillia-Bianca. Do you come to fright me with this mystery?
  To stir me with a stink none can endure, sir?
  I pray ye proceed; the wedding will become ye.   150

---

140. fall] *Bowers;* faith *F1.*   147SD] *Fraser and Rabkin; not in F1.*

137. *fling-dust*] a contemptuous name for a harlot (*OED* fling-dust III.15, quoting
ll. 137–8).
138. *light o' loves*] (1) a fickle woman, a wanton (*OED* 2b); (2) the name of an old
dance-tune (Dyce, 7.227).
139. *thin pumps . . . petticoat*] i.e. poorly dressed; *pump* = a light, close-fitting shoe
(*OED* 1); *petticoat* = skirt worn either externally or beneath the gown or costume.
140. *fall*] a band or collar worn falling flat around the neck (*OED*, fall n.¹ 23a).
Defending his emendation of F1's 'one faith', Bowers notes, 'it is odd indeed to inter-
polate in this series anything but another article of female attire' (*DW*, 6.340).
  smock] a woman's undergarment or chemise (*OED* 1). Both fall and smock would
become grubby quickly.
  broken] bankrupt.
141. *conjuror*] fortune-teller.
142. *Jumping Joan . . . sin-weaver*] jumping = sexual intercourse (Williams, p. 752);
Joan is a common name for a woman engaged in the *ancient* sin of prostitution; proverbially, 'Joan, in the dark, is as good as my Lady' (Tilley J57).
143–4. *slipped . . . knee*] sinned and lost her virginity; the knee was 'conceived as
the penultimate stage in the approach to the genitals' (Williams, pp. 764–5).
145–6. *stood . . . term*] This mock-heroic treatment of Joan's history suggests that
she is one of the disreputable women who frequented the Inns of Court during the four
terms into which the law court year was divided.
146. *lost her colours*] was thoroughly disgraced; from the nautical term 'to strike
one's colours' = to haul down a flag, especially as a sign of surrender (*OED* 17b).
148. *mystery*] (1) personal secret (*OED* 5b); (2) the mystique attached to a trade or
art, cf. the 'discipline' of Joan at l. 125 above.

Who gives the lady? [*To Mirabell*] You? An excellent father,
A careful man, and one that knows a beauty.
[*To Pinac*] Send ye fair shipping, sir, and so I'll leave ye.
Be wise and manly, then I may chance to love ye.
                                        Exit [*with* Servant.]
Mirabell. As I live I am ashamed, this wench has reached me;   155
Monstrous ashamed, but there's no remedy.
This skewed-eyed carrion –   [*Indicating Mariana*]
Pinac.   This I suspected ever. –
Come, come, uncase: we have no more use of ye;
Your clothes must back again.
Mariana.   Sir, ye shall pardon me;
'Tis not our English use to be degraded.   160
If you will visit me and take your venture
You shall have pleasure for your properties;
And so, sweetheart –   [*Exit* MARIANA.]
Mirabell.   Let her go, and the devil go with her!
We have never better luck with these preludiums.
Come, be not daunted: think she is but a woman,   165
And let her have the devil's wit, we'll reach her.   [*Exeunt.*]

SCENE 2

Enter ROSALURA *and* LUGIER.

Rosalura. Ye have now redeemed my good opinion, tutor,
And ye stand fair again.
Lugier.   I can but labour
And sweat in your affairs. I am sure Belleur
Will be here instantly, and use his anger,

151SD] *Lister; not in* F1.   153SD] *This ed.; not in* F1.   154SD] *Fraser and Rabkin;
Exit.* F1.   155. live I am ashamed, this] *F1*; live, I am ashamed this *Sympson.*
157SD] *This ed.; not in* F1.   163SD] *Sympson; not in* F1.   166SD] F2; *Exit.* F1.

153. *fair shipping*] (1) 'safe journey'; (2) continues the metaphoric treatment of
Joan/Mariana as merchandise, begun in ll. 126–7.
155. *reached me*] figuratively, delivered a blow which has 'struck home'.
157. *skewed-eyed*] squint-eyed (OED, skewed a.², citing this line).
carrion] (1) term of contempt; (2) whore (Williams, p. 206).
158. *uncase*] undress.
159. *back again*] be returned to the pawnbroker.
162. *properties*] the pawned clothing that Joan/Mariana is wearing.
164. *preludiums*] preliminaries.
166. *reach*] outsmart.

His wonted harshness.
Rosalura.   I hope he will not beat me.   5
Lugier. No, sure, he has more manners. Be you ready?
Rosalura. Yes, yes, I am, and am resolved to fit him,
With patience to outdo all he can offer.
But how does Oriana?
Lugier.   Worse, and worse still;
There is a sad house for her: she is now,   10
Poor lady, utterly distracted.
Rosalura.   Pity,
Infinite pity! 'Tis a handsome lady.
That Mirabell's a beast, worse than a monster,
If this affliction work not.

                    Enter LILLIA-BIANCA.

Lillia-Bianca.   Are ye ready?
Belleur is coming on, here, hard behind me: 15
I have no leisure to relate my fortune;
Only I wish you may come off as handsomely.
Upon the sign, you know what.
Rosalura.   Well, well; leave me.
                    [*Exeunt* LILLIA-BIANCA *and* LUGIER.]

                    Enter BELLEUR.

Belleur. How now?
Rosalura.   Ye are welcome, sir.   [*Curtsies.*]
Belleur.   'Tis well ye have manners.
That curtsy again, and hold your countenance staidly;   20
That look's too light; take heed – so, sit ye down now,
And to confirm me that your gall is gone,
Your bitterness dispersed – for so I'll have it –
Look on me steadfastly; and whatsoe'er I say to ye,
Move not, nor alter in your face, ye are gone then: 25
For if you do express the least distaste,

---

6. ready?] *Colman;* ready. *F1;* ready! *Weber.*   18SD] *Sympson; Exit. in right margin opp.* 'know what' *F1.*   19SD] *This ed.; not in F1.*

5. *wonted*] customary.
10. *sad house*] 'her situation is sad, and therefore the house is filled with grief and lamentation' (Lister).
17. *come off*] fare.
18. *Upon . . . what*] probably meaning that at l. 70 Rosalura should signal to the women off-stage to enter.
20. *staidly*] soberly (*OED*, citing this line).
21. *too light*] lacking in respect.

Or show an angry wrinkle – mark me, woman!
We are now alone – I will so conjure thee,
The third part of my execution
Cannot be spoke.
Rosalura.   I am at your dispose, sir.   30
Belleur. Now rise, and woo me a little; let me hear that faculty –
But touch me not; nor do not lie, I charge ye.
Begin now.
Rosalura.   If so mean and poor a beauty
May ever hope the grace –
Belleur.   Ye cog, ye flatter
Like a lewd thing, ye lie: 'May hope that grace'!   35
Why, what grace canst thou hope for? Answer not,
For if thou dost, and liest again, I'll swinge thee!
Do not I know thee for a pestilent woman;
A proud at both ends? Be not angry,
Nor stir not o' your life!
Rosalura.   I am counselled, sir.   40
Belleur. Are thou not now – confess, for I'll have the truth out –
As much unworthy of a man of merit,
Or any of ye all, nay, of mere man?
Though he were crooked, cold, all wants upon him;
Nay, of any dishonest thing that bears that figure,   45
As devils are of mercy?
Rosalura.   We are unworthy.
Belleur. Stick to that truth, and it may chance to save thee.
And is it not our bounty that we take ye?
That we are troubled, vexed or tortured with ye;
Our mere and special bounty?

---

28. *conjure*] affect as if by magic (Fraser and Rabkin).

29. *third . . . execution*] (1) third part of my scheme; (2) *execution* as 'the ravaging and destroying of a country that refuses to pay contribution' (Smyth, *Sailor's Word-Book*, 1867 (OED 9), quoting Fletcher's *The Loyal Subject* 5.5.29–30: 'You know his marches, / You have seene his executions: is it yet peace?'); (3) with bawdy sense of *execution* = copulation (Williams, p. 451).

31. *faculty*] ability.

34. *cog*] cheat; a term from dice-play (OED cog v.³ 3).

37. *swinge*] beat, cf. 2.3.86 and l. 51 below.

39. *A . . . ends*] (1) thoroughly proud, from head to tail, with perhaps the inference that Rosalura considers herself intellectually and sexually superior to Belleur; (2) lascivious mentally and physically (Lister); (3) play on *end* = genital area (Williams, p. 438).

50. *mere*] absolute.

Rosalura.   Yes.
Belleur.   Our pity,   50
  That for your wickedness we swinge ye soundly;
  Your stubborness and stout hearts, we belabour ye?
  Answer to that.
Rosalura.   I do confess your pity.
Belleur. And dost not thou deserve in thine own person,
  Thou impudent, thou pert – do not change countenance! –   55
Rosalura. I dare not, sir.
Belleur.   For if ye do –
Rosalura.   I am settled.
Belleur. Thou wagtail, peacock, puppy; look on me.
  I am a gentleman.
Rosalura.   It seems no less, sir.
Belleur. And dar'st thou in thy surquedry –
Rosalura.   I beseech ye!
  It was my weakness, sir, I did not view ye.   60
  I took not notice of your noble parts,
  Nor called your person, nor your proper fashion.
Belleur. This is some amends yet.
Rosalura.   I shall mend, sir, daily,
  And study to deserve.
Belleur.   Come a little nearer.
  Canst thou repent thy villainy?
Rosalura.   Most seriously.   65
Belleur. And be ashamed?
Rosalura.   I am ashamed.
Belleur.   Cry!
Rosalura. It will be hard to do, sir.
Belleur.   Cry now, instantly;
  Cry monstrously, that all the town may hear thee;
  Cry seriously, as if thou hadst lost thy monkey;

---

61. not] *F1*; no *F2*.   62. called] *F1*; culled *Weber*.

---

52. *stout*] arrogant, obstinate.

belabour] (1) thrash; (2) as an extension of the bawdy sense of 'swinge' at ll. 37 and
51 above = cause to go into labour, i.e. childbirth.

57. *wagtail*] (1) familiar or contemptuous epithet applied to a man or young woman
(OED 3a); (2) whore (Williams, pp. 1495–6).

59. *surquedry*] Cf. 3.1.103n.

62. *called*] paid you the respect appropriate to one of your rank.

your proper fashion] your own appearance (Lister).

And as I like thy tears –
Rosalura. [*Signalling to those within*] Now!

       Enter LILLIA-BIANCA *and four* Women[,] *laughing.*

Belleur.   How? How? Do ye jeer me?   70
Have ye broke your bounds again, dame?
Rosalura.   Yes, and laugh at ye;
And laugh most heartily.
Belleur.   What are these, whirlwinds?
Is hell broke loose and all the Furies fluttered?
Am I greased once again?
Rosalura.   Yes, indeed are ye.
And once again ye shall be, if ye quarrel.   75
Do you come to vent your fury on a virgin?
Is this your manhood, sir?
1 Woman.   Let him do his best.
Let's see the utmost of his indignation:
I long to see him angry – Come, proceed, sir.
Hang him, he dares not stir; a man of timber!   80
                  [*The Women display knives.*]
2 Woman. Come hither to fright maids with thy bull-faces,
To threaten gentlewomen? Thou a man? A maypole,
A great dry pudding!
3 Woman.   Come, come, do your worst, sir.

70SD *Signalling . . . within*] This ed.; not in F1. 70SD *Enter . . . laughing.*] *in right margin opp.* 'thy tears', F1; Weber, *following* 'Now!'. 80SD] Fraser and Rabkin; not in F1.

    72. *whirlwinds*] i.e. of violent or tempestuous nature.
    73. *Furies*] The mythical Greek spirits who avenged wrongs and punished crime were represented carrying torches and whips, their hair wreathed in snakes. The chopping-knives wielded by the women make the evocation particularly apposite (see l. 80SDn).
    fluttered] come flying out of Hades (Lister).
    74. *greased*] cheated, flattered (*OED* 4c, citing this line).
    75. *quarrel*] (1) find fault; (2) reprove angrily (*OED* 5).
    80. *man of timber*] (1) physically strong; (2) cf. Rosalura's description of Mirabell as 'a pretty-timbered man' at 1.3.136.
    80SD] At 5.2.44 Belleur says, 'they came with chopping-knives / To cut me into rands and sirloins'. The placing of the stage direction some way into the dialogue heightens the action's shocking effect and gives dramatic point to Belleur's exclamation in l. 84.
    81. *bull-faces*] aggressive expressions.
    82. *maypole*] A tall man, as wooden (cf. l. 80) as the maypole (which of course was also a phallic symbol) (Lister). Cf. *The Convent of Pleasure* 4.1.136SD.
    83. *dry pudding*] (1) *pudding* describes those of stout or thick-set body shape (*OED* 5a); (2) literally, a sausage; (3) bawdy for 'penis', hence a 'dry' pudding would be shrivelled up or impotent.

Be angry if thou dar'st.
Belleur.   The lord deliver me!
4 Woman. Do but look scurvily upon this lady,   85
    Or give us one foul word – we are all mistaken;
    This is some mighty dairymaid in man's clothes.
Lillia-Bianca. I am of that mind too.
Belleur. [*Aside*]   What will they do to me?
Lillia-Bianca. And hired to come and abuse us: a man has manners;
    A gentleman, civility and breeding: 90
    Some tinker's trull with a beard glued on.
1 Woman.   Let's search him,
    And as we find him –
Belleur.   Let me but depart from ye,
    Sweet Christian women.
Lillia-Bianca.   Hear the thing speak, neighbours.
Belleur. 'Tis but a small request: if e'er I trouble ye,
    If e'er I talk again of beating women,   95
    Or beating anything that can but turn to me;
    Of ever thinking of a handsome lady
    But virtuously and well, of ever speaking
    But to her honour – this I'll promise ye:
    I will take rhubarb, and purge choler mainly,   100
    Abundantly I'll purge.
Lillia-Bianca.   I'll send ye broths, sir.
Belleur. I will be laughed at, and endure it patiently;
    I will do anything.
Rosalura.   I'll be your bail then.
    When ye come next to woo, pray ye come not boisterously
    And furnished like a bearward.
Belleur.   No, in truth, forsooth.   105
Rosalura. I scented ye long since.
Belleur.   I was to blame, sure;
    I will appear a gentleman.
Rosalura.   'Tis the best for ye,
    For a true noble gentleman's a brave thing;
    Upon that hope we quit ye. You fear seriously?

88SD] *Sympson; not in F1.*   93. thing] *Colman;* Thing *F1.*

87. *mighty . . . clothes*] i.e. an effeminate coward, a 'big girl's blouse'.
91. *tinker's trull*] i.e. a prostitute catering to the lowest social orders.
96. *turn to me*] retaliate.
100. *mainly*] vigorously (*OED* 1a).
105. *furnished . . . bearward*] perhaps armed with a cudgel or whip, like a keeper of bears.

Belleur. Yes, truly do I; I confess I fear ye,   110
And honour ye, and anything.
Rosalura.   Farewell then.
Women. And when ye come to woo next, bring more mercy!
          Exeunt [ROSALURA, LILLIA-BIANCA, *and four* Women].
Belleur. A dairymaid? A tinker's trull? Heaven bless me!
Sure, if I had provoked 'em, they had quartered me.

                    Enter two Gentlemen.

I am a most ridiculous ass, now I perceive it: 115
A coward, and a knave too.
1 Gentleman.   'Tis the mad gentleman.
Let's set our faces right.
Belleur.   No, no, laugh at me,
And laugh aloud.
2 Gentleman.   We are better mannered, sir.
Belleur. I do deserve it; call me Patch and Puppy,
And beat me if you please.
1 Gentleman.   No, indeed: we know ye.   120
Belleur. Death, do as I would have ye!
2 Gentleman.   Ye are an ass then,
A coxcomb and a calf.
Belleur.   I am a great calf.
Kick me a little now: why, when? [*They kick him.*] Sufficient!
Now laugh aloud, and scorn me. So goodbye;
And ever when ye meet me, laugh.
Gentlemen.   We will, sir.   *Exeunt.* 125

SCENE 3

          Enter NANTOLET, LA CASTRE, DE GARD, LUGIER,
                    and MIRABELL.

Mirabell. Your patience, gentlemen; why do ye bait me?
Nantolet. Is't not a shame you are so stubborn-hearted,

112SD] *Lister; Exeunt. F1.*   123SD] *Dyce; following l. 123 Weber.*   124. goodbye]
This ed.; good buy'ye *F1;* good b'ye *F2;* God b'ye *Sympson;* God b' wi' ye! *Weber;* God
by ye! *Fraser and Rabkin.*

114. *quartered*] cut into quarters, the punishment of traitors or criminals.
119. *Patch and Puppy*] generic names for a fool, an empty-headed young man.
121. *Death*] an exclamation, an abbreviation of 'God's death' (*OED* 10).
122. *calf*] a stupid fellow; sometimes a meek, inoffensive person (*OED* 1c).

  1. *bait*] harass (*OED* 4).

So stony and so dull to such a lady,
Of her perfections, and her misery?
Lugier. Does not she love ye? Does not her distraction　　　5
For your sake only, her most pitied lunacy
Of all but you, show ye; does it not compel ye?
Mirabell. Soft and fair, gentlemen; pray ye proceed temperately.
Lugier. If ye have any feeling, any sense in ye,
The least touch of a noble heart –
La Castre.　　　　　　　　　　Let him alone;　　　　　10
It is his glory that he can kill beauty –
Ye bear my stamp, but not my tenderness –
Your wild unsavoury courses set that in ye!
For shame, be sorry; though ye cannot cure her,
Show something of a man, of a fair nature.　　　　　15
Mirabell. Ye make me mad.
De Gard.　　　　　　　Let me pronounce this to ye,
You take a strange felicity in slighting
And wronging women, which my poor sister feels now;
Heaven's hand be gentle on her. Mark me, sir,
That very hour she dies (there's small hope otherwise),　　20
That minute, you and I must grapple for it;
Either your life or mine.
Mirabell.　　　　　　　Be not so hot, sir,
I am not to be wrought on by these policies,
In truth, I am not. Nor do I fear the tricks
Or the high-sounding threats of a Savoyan.　　　　25
I glory not in cruelty, ye wrong me;
Nor grow up watered with the tears of women.
This let me tell ye, howsoe'er I show to ye
Wild, as you please to call it, or self-willed,
When I see cause, I can both do and suffer　　　　30
Freely, and feelingly, as a true gentleman.

---

13. set] *F1;* let *Dyce.*

5. *distraction*] insanity.
6–7. *her . . . you*] her lunacy which is pitied immensely by all but you.
7. *show ye*] prove to you that she loves you.
12. *stamp*] physical similarity.
13. *unsavoury courses*] loose behaviour.
20. *there's . . . otherwise*] there's small hope of any other outcome.
21. *grapple*] (1) take revenge by duel or fight; (2) engage in a tussle.
22. *hot*] hot-tempered.
28. *show*] appear.

Enter ROSALURA *and* LILLIA-BIANCA.

Rosalura. Oh, pity, pity; thousand thousand pities!
Lillia-Bianca. Alas, poor soul! She will die, she is grown senseless;
    She will not know nor speak now.
Rosalura.   Die for love,
    And love of such a youth? I would die for a dog first.   35
    He that kills me, I'll give him leave to eat me;
    I'll know men better ere I sigh for any of 'em.
Lillia-Bianca. Ye have done a worthy act, sir, a most famous;
    Ye have killed a maid the wrong way; ye are a conqueror.
Rosalura. A conqueror? A cobbler; hang him, souter!   40
    Go hide thyself for shame; go lose thy memory,
    Live not 'mongst men. Thou art a beast, a monster,
    A blatant beast!
Lillia-Bianca.   If ye have yet any honesty,
    Or ever heard of any, take my counsel:
    Off with your garters, and seek out a bough,   45
    A handsome bough (for I would have ye hang like a gentleman),
    And write some doleful matter to the world,
    A warning to hard-hearted men.
Mirabell.   Out, kitlings!
    What caterwauling's here; what gibbing?

---

41. hide] *F2*; hid *F1*.

33. *senseless*] (1) unconscious (*OED* 1b); (2) incapable of feeling or perception (*OED* 2).
    35–6. *die ... eat*] For the linguistic nexus of sex and death, and the bawdy use of *die* as orgasm and *eat* as enjoy sexually see Williams, pp. 374, 430. Cf. 'killed a maid the wrong way' at l. 39 below.
    39. *killed ... wrong way*] i.e. through lack of love, as opposed to the 'right' way, through coitus (see l. 36 above); cf. the proverb 'to kill a maid with kindness' (Dent K51).
    40. *souter*] (1) cobbler; often used to denote a type of workman of little or no education; (2) a term of abuse (*OED* 1, 1b).
    41. *lose thy memory*] 'forget what you have done if you want to have any peace' (Lister). Memory was considered a critical determinant of self-knowledge since our sense of identity depends on what we recall of ourselves and our past.
    42. *Live not ... beast*] Rosalura evokes the figure of the Wild Man of medieval literature, modelled on the biblical figure Nebuchadnezzar, who was cast out into the desert to live amongst animals as a punishment for pride.
    43. *blatant beast*] A phrase used by Spenser in *The Faerie Queene* (Book 5, Canto 12, Stanza 37) as an epithet for the thousand-tongued monster symbolising slander.
    46. *hang*] bawdy use of 'hang' with allusion to male genitals.
    48. *kitlings*] applied to persons acting like a kitten (*OED* 3, citing this line).
    49. *gibbing*] cat-like behaviour (*OED* 1, citing this line).

Do you think my heart is softened with a black santis?   50
Show me some reason.

Enter ORIANA *on a bed.*

Rosalura.   Here then, here is a reason.
Nantolet. Now, if ye be a man, let this sight shake ye.
La Castre. Alas, poor gentlewoman! – Do ye know me, lady?
Lugier. How she looks up and stares!
Oriana.   I know ye very well:
You are my godfather; and that's the monsieur.   55
De Gard. And who am I?
Oriana.   You are Amadis de Gaul, sir.
Oh, oh, my heart! – Were you never in love, sweet lady?
And do you never dream of flowers and gardens?
I dream of walking fires. Take heed; it comes now.
Who's that? [*Pointing to Mirabell*] Pray stand away. I have seen
   that face, sure.   60
How light my head is!
Rosalura.   Take some rest.
Oriana.   I cannot,
For I must be up tomorrow to go to church,
And I must dress me, put my new gown on,
And be as fine to meet my love – Heigh-ho!
Will not you tell me where my love lies buried?   65
Mirabell. He is not dead. [*Aside*] Beshrew my heart, she stirs me.
Oriana. He is dead to me.

51SD] *F1; [Servants bring in]* ORIANA *on a bed. Lister.*   60SD] *This ed.; not in
F1.*   66SD] *Sympson, in right margin opp. l. 66; not in F1.*

---

50. *black santis*] obsolete form of 'sanctus'; a kind of burlesque hymn, the discordant, 'rough music' accompanying public shaming rituals.
51SD.] 'A stage direction like "*Enter X upon a bed*" may mean either that the bed was pushed out onto the stage or that it was discovered' (Gurr, p. 188).
51. *reason*] (1) grounds or cause; (2) a pun on *reason* as 'sanity' (*OED* 11a).
56-9. *Amadis . . . fires*] Lister points out that, in feigning madness, Oriana appears to identify with her namesake in the romantic novel *Amadis of Gaul*, in which Oriana takes up residence at the castle of Miraflores, 'in a wood by the side of a mountain, surrounded with orchards and gardens that abounded with fruits and flowers' (*Amadis of Gaul*, trans. Robert Southey, London: J.R. Smith, 1872, vol. 2, p. 8). Whilst estranged from Oriana, the hero, Amadis, now calling himself 'Beltenebros', dreams of Oriana being 'surrounded with a great flame of fire, [he] ran through the fire to save her, feeling no hurt, and took her in his arms and carried her into a garden' (Vol. 1, p. 284).

Mirabell. [*Aside*]   Is't possible my nature
Should be so damnable to let her suffer? –
Give me your hand.
Oriana.   How soft you feel; how gentle!
I'll tell ye your fortune, friend.
Mirabell.   How she stares on me!   70
Oriana. You have a flattering face, but 'tis a fine one;
I warrant you may have a hundred sweethearts.
Will ye pray for me? I shall die tomorrow;
And will ye ring the bells?
Mirabell.   I am most unworthy –
I do confess, unhappy. Do you know me?   75
Oriana. I would I did.
Mirabell. [*Aside*]   Oh, fair tears, how ye take me!
Oriana. Do you weep, too? You have not lost your lover?
You mock me; I'll go home and pray.
Mirabell.   Pray ye, pardon me,
Or, if it please ye to consider justly,
Scorn me, for I deserve it. Scorn and shame me,   80
Sweet Oriana.
Lillia-Bianca.   Let her alone; she trembles.
Her fits will grow more strong if ye provoke her.
La Castre. Certain, she knows ye not, yet loves to see ye.
How she smiles now!

[*Enter* BELLEUR.]

Belleur. Where are ye? Oh, why do not ye laugh? Come, laugh at me.   85
Why a devil art thou sad and such a subject,
Such a ridiculous subject as I am,
Before thy face?
Mirabell.   Prithee put off this lightness;
This is no time for mirth, nor place. I have used too much on't.
I have undone myself and a sweet lady   90
By being too indulgent to my foolery,

70. *I'll . . . fortune*] Cf. the resemblance to the disordered speech of the lovesick Jailer's Daughter in a scene attributed to Fletcher in *TNK*: 'Give me your hand . . . I can tell your fortune' (3.5.79).
71. *flattering*] insincere.
76. *take*] overwhelm.
86. *a devil*] the devil, an exclamation of irritation (*OED* 20).
88. *lightness*] levity.

Which truly I repent. Look here!   [*Pointing to Oriana*]
Belleur.   What ails she?
Mirabell. Alas, she is mad.
Belleur.   Mad?
Mirabell.   Yes, too sure; for me too.
Belleur. Dost thou wonder at that? By this good light, they are all so.
   They are cozening mad, they are brawling mad, they are proud
      mad;   95
   They are all, all mad. I came from a world of madwomen,
   Mad as March hares. Get 'em in chains, then deal with 'em.
   There's one that's mad [*Pointing to Rosalura*]; she seems well,
      but she is dog mad.
   Is she dead, dost think?   [*Turning to Oriana*]
Mirabell.   Dead? Heaven forbid!
Belleur.   Heaven further it!
   For till they be key-cold dead, there's no trusting of 'em.   100
   Whate'er they seem, or howsoe'er they carry it;
   Till they be chap-fall'n and their tongues at peace,
   Nailed in their coffins sure, I'll ne'er believe 'em.
   Shall I talk with her?
Mirabell.   No, dear friend, be quiet,
   And be at peace awhile.
Belleur.   I'll walk aside,   105
   And come again anon. But take heed to her:
   You say she is a woman?
Mirabell.   Yes.
Belleur.   Take great heed;
   For if she do not cozen thee, then hang me.
   Let her be mad, or what she will, she'll cheat thee.   *Exit.*
Mirabell. Away, wild fool. – How vile this shows in him now!   110

92SD] *This ed.; not in F1.* 93. sure; for] *Colman;* sure for *F1.* 98SD] *This ed.; not in F1.* 99SD] *This ed.; not in F1.* 110. vile] *F2;* vild *F1.*

---

   92. *What ails she?*] What's wrong with her?
   93. *for me too*] because of me; on my account.
   97. *Mad as March hares*] proverbial (Dent H148). During March, the breeding season, hares behave with energetic aggression that appears absurd and mad (*OED* 1b).
   98. *dog mad*] suffering from the viral disease of rabies which makes dogs and other animals viciously excitable.
   100. *key-cold dead*] proverbial: 'As cold as a key' (Tilley K27), especially in relation to cold in death (*OED*).
   101. *carry it*] behave (*OED* 22b).
   102. *chap-fall'n*] with the lower jaw hanging down, esp. as a result of death (*OED*, *chap-fallen* 1, citing this line).

[*To Oriana*] Now take my faith – before ye all I speak it –
And with it, my repentant love.
La Castre.   This seems well.
Mirabell. Were but this lady clear again, whose sorrows
My very heart melts for; were she but perfect
(For thus to marry her would be two miseries),   115
Before the richest and the noblest beauty
France, or the world, could show me, I would take her.
As she is now, my tears and prayers shall wed her.
De Gard. This makes some small amends.
Rosalura.   She beckons to ye,
To us too, to go off.
Nantolet.   Let's draw aside all.   120
                    [*Exeunt all but* ORIANA *and* MIRABELL.]
Oriana. Oh, my best friend! I would fain –
Mirabell. [*Aside*]   What? She speaks well,
And with another voice.
Oriana.   But I am fearful,
And shame a little stops my tongue –
Mirabell.   Speak boldly.
Oriana. Tell ye, I am well; I am perfect well – pray ye mock not –
And that I did this to provoke your nature,   125
Out of my infinite and restless love,
To win your pity. Pardon me.
Mirabell.   Go forward.
Who set ye on?
Oriana.   None, as I live, no creature;
Not any knew, or ever dreamed what I meant.
Will ye be mine?
Mirabell.   'Tis true, I pity ye;   130
But when I marry ye, ye must be wiser.
Nothing but tricks? Devices?
Oriana.   Will ye shame me?

111SD] *This ed.; not in F1.*   120SD] *Colman; not in F1.*   121SD] *Dyce; not in F1.*

113. *clear*] in good health.
115. *two miseries*] i.e. the institution of marriage is unappealing to Mirabell and marriage to a demented woman would compound this misery.
121. *well*] as if in normal health.
126. *restless*] unceasing.
128. *set ye on*] Cf. 2.1.25.
None] no one.

Mirabell. Yes, marry, will I. [*Calling to the others*] Come near, come
    near; a miracle!
The woman's well; she was only mad for marriage,
Stark mad to be stoned to death. Give her good counsel.   135
Will this world never mend? – Are ye caught, damsel?

    Enter BELLEUR, LA CASTRE, LUGIER, NANTOLET,
      DE GARD, ROSALURA, *and* LILLIA-BIANCA.

Belleur. How goes it now?
Mirabell.   Thou art a kind of prophet;
The woman's well again, and would have gulled me;
Well, excellent well, and not a taint upon her.
Belleur. Did not I tell ye? Let 'em be what can be,   140
Saints, devils, anything, they will abuse us.
Thou wert an ass to believe her so long, a coxcomb;
Give 'em a minute, they'll abuse whole millions.
Mirabell. And am not I a rare physician, gentlemen,
That can cure desperate minds?
De Gard.   Be not insolent.   145
Mirabell. [*To Oriana*] Well, go thy ways. From this hour I disclaim
    thee,
Unless thou hast a trick above this; then I'll love thee.
Ye owe me for your cure. [*To De Gard*] Pray, have a care of her,
For fear she fall into relapse – Come, Belleur,
We'll set up bills to cure diseasèd virgins.   150
Belleur. Shall we be merry?
Mirabell.   Yes.

133SD] *Lister; not in F1.*   146SD] *Lister; not in F1.*   148SD] *Lister; not in F1.*
149. into relapse] *F1*; into a relapse. *Weber.*

133. *marry*] (1) exclamation implying surprise that a question should be asked
(*OED* a); (2) wordplay on *marry* at l. 131 above.
   135. *Stark . . . death*] avid for coitus, since 'stone' = testicles (Williams, p. 374).
   136. *caught*] caught out (in a deception).
   damsel] (1) young, unmarried woman; sometimes used slightingly or playfully (*OED*
2); (2) common appellation in chivalric romances, used by Mirabell to taunt Oriana
for her performance as a 'mad' heroine.
   139. *taint*] (1) stain on her character, spoken ironically (*OED, taint* C.1a); (2) pun
on *taint* as a trace of disease in its latent state (*OED* C.2b).
   147. *trick above this*] better ruse.
   150. *set up bills*] post up written or printed notices advertising a service.
   diseasèd virgins] i.e. women suffering from love melancholy, sometimes known as
'green-sickness' or 'the virgins' disease'.

Belleur.   But I'll no more projects.
If we could make 'em mad, it were some mastery.
                              Exeunt [MIRABELL *and* BELLEUR].
Lillia-Bianca. I am glad she is well again.
Rosalura.   So am I, certain. –
Be not ashamed.
Oriana.   I shall never see a man more.
De Gard. Come, ye are a fool! Had ye but told me this trick,   155
He should not have gloried thus.
Lugier.   He shall not long, neither.
La Castre. Be ruled, and be at peace. Ye have my consent,
And what power I can work with.
Nantolet.   Come, leave blushing.
We are your friends – an honest way compelled ye.
Heaven will not see so true a love unrecompensed.   160
Come in, and slight him too.
Lugier.   The next shall hit him.   *Exeunt.*

152SD] Dyce; *Exeunt. F1.*

152. *it . . . mastery*] (1) it would be a commendable achievement; (2) pun on *mastery*
as the superior role of a 'master' to his 'mistress'.
153. *certain*] certainly.
161. *The . . . him*] i.e. the next plan to 'catch' Mirabell will succeed.

ACT 5

SCENE I

Enter DE GARD *and* LUGIER

De Gard. 'Twill be discovered.

Lugier.   That's the worst can happen.
If there be any way to reach, and work upon him,
Upon his nature suddenly, and catch him – that he loves,
Though he dissemble it and would show contrary,
And will at length relent, I'll lay my fortune;   5
Nay more, my life.

De Gard.   Is she won?

Lugier.   Yes, and ready,
And my designments set.

De Gard.   They are now for travel,
All for that game again; they have forgot wooing.

Lugier. Let 'em; we'll travel with 'em.

De Gard.   Where's his father?

Lugier. Within. He knows my mind too, and allows it,   10
Pities your sister's fortune most sincerely,
And has appointed, for our more assistance,
Some of his secret friends.

De Gard.   Speed the plough!

Lugier.   Well said;
And be you serious too.

De Gard.   I shall be diligent.

Lugier. Let's break the ice for one, the rest will drink too,   15
Believe me, sir, of the same cup. My young gentlewomen
Wait but who sets the game afoot; though they seem stubborn,

---

5. *lay*] wager.

6. *won*] i.e. willing to co-operate in the execution of Lugier's plan.

7. *designments*] arrangements (*OED* 3).

10. *allows*] sanctions.

13. *secret friends*] i.e. the young man disguised as a factor who enters at 5.2.71SD and the two merchants at 5.4.0SD.

Speed the plough] (1) a corruption of 'God speed the plough', an expression of good luck; (2) the title of a ballad (*c.*1500).

15–16. *Let's . . . same cup*] A conjunction of two proverbs. If we prepare the way for one (potential suitor) the others will follow (Tilley I3, Dent C908).

157

Reserved and proud now, yet I know their hearts,
Their pulses, how they beat, and for what cause, sir,
And how they long to venture their abilities   20
In a true quarrel. Husbands they must and will have,
Or nunneries and thin collations
To cool their bloods. Let's all about our business,
And if this fail, let nature work!
De Gard.   Ye have armed me.   *Exeunt.*

SCENE 2

Enter MIRABELL, NANTOLET, [*and*] LA CASTRE.

La Castre. Will ye be wilful then?
Mirabell.   Pray, sir, your pardon,
For I must travel. Lie lazy here,
Bound to a wife, chained to her subtleties,
Her humours and her wills, which are mere fetters?
To have her today pleased, tomorrow peevish,   5
The third day mad, the fourth rebellious?
You see before they are married what moriscoes,
What masques and mummeries they put upon us:
To be tied here and suffer their lavoltas!
Nantolet. 'Tis your own seeking.
Mirabell.   Yes, to get my freedom.   10
Were they as I could wish 'em –
La Castre.   Fools and meacocks,
To endure what you think fit to put upon 'em.
Come, change your mind.
Mirabell.   Not before I have changed air, father.
When I know women worthy of my company
I will return again and wait upon 'em.   15

---

9. lavoltas!] *Dyce;* Lavalto's? *F1.*

---

21. *true quarrel*] honest contest of a sexual nature.
22. *nunneries . . . collations*] i.e. an ascetic existence; a collation was the light, usually cold, meal traditionally served in monasteries.
24. *armed*] prepared.

4. *mere*] nothing short of (OED mere *a²* and *adv.*).
7. *moriscoes*] morris dances (OED 4).
8. *mummeries*] acts in dumb-show (OED).
9. *lavoltas*] (voltas); dances of Provençal origin, popular at the English court between 1550 and 1650.
11. *meacocks*] effeminate or cowardly persons (OED 1).

Till then, dear sir, I'll amble all the world over,
And run all hazards, misery, and poverty,

          Enter PINAC *and* BELLEUR.

So I escape the dangerous Bay of Matrimony.
Pinac. Are ye resolved?
Mirabell.   Yes, certain; I will out again.
Pinac. We are for ye, sir; we are your servants once more: 20
Once more we'll seek our fortune in strange countries;
Ours is too scornful for us.
Belleur.   Is there ne'er a land
That ye have read or heard of – for I care not how far it be,
Nor under what pestiferous star it lies –
A happy kingdom, where there are no women,   25
Nor have been ever? Nor no mention
Of any such lewd things, with lewder qualities?
For thither would I travel; where 'tis felony
To confess he had a mother; a mistress, treason.
La Castre. Are you for travel too?
Belleur.   For anything,   30
For living in the moon, and stopping hedges,
Ere I stay here to be abused and baffelled.
Nantolet. Why did ye not break your minds to me? They are my
          daughters;
And sure I think I should have that command over 'em,
To see 'em well bestowed. I know ye are gentlemen,   35
Men of fair parts and states; I know your parents;
And had ye told me of your fair affections –
Make but one trial more, and let me second ye.
Belleur. No; I'll make hob-nails first, and mend old kettles.

---

18. Bay of Matrimony] *F1*; bay of matrimony *Colman.*   23. heard] *Langbaine*; head
F1.   27. things] *F2*; Things *F1.*   29. he] *F1*; ye *Langbaine.*

18. *dangerous ... Matrimony*] a metaphor based on the navigational uncertainty of
sailing close to shore, as opposed to the relative security of a craft in mid-ocean.
  19. *out*] Cf. 'went out' at 1.1.54.
  24. *pestiferous star*] ill-fated astrological sign, cf. 2.3.54.
  25. *kingdom ... women*] Cf. the academe proposed by the King of Navarre in *LLL*,
from which women are banned for a three-year period (1.1.15–18, 36–7).
  31. *living ... stopping hedges*] (1) *stopping* = mending hedges; (2) 'The man in the
moon carried a bundle of sticks' (Fraser and Rabkin).
  32. *baffelled*] (1) insulted (*OED* 2); (2) disgraced; originally a punishment of infamy,
inflicted on recreant knights, one part of which was hanging them up by the heels.
  39. *hob-nails*] nails with a large head used on the soles of boots and shoes
(*OED* 1).

Can ye lend me an armour of high proof to appear in,   40
And two or three field-pieces to defend me?
The king's guard are mere pygmies.
Nantolet.   They will not eat ye.
Belleur. Yes, and you too, and twenty fatter monsieurs,
If their high stomachs hold. They came with chopping-knives
To cut me into rands and sirloins, and so powder me.   45
Come, shall we go?
Nantolet.   You cannot be so discourteous,
If ye intend to go, as not to visit 'em,
And take your leaves.
Mirabell.   That we dare do, and civilly,
And thank 'em too.
Pinac.   Yes, sir; we know that honesty.
Belleur. I'll come i' th' rear, forty foot off, I'll assure ye,   50
With a good gun in my hand; I'll no more Amazons –
I mean, no more of their frights. I'll make my three legs,
Kiss my hand twice, and if I smell no danger,
If the interview be clear, maybe I'll speak to her;
I'll wear a privy coat too, and behind me,   55
To make those parts secure, a bandog.
La Castre. You are a merry gentleman.
Belleur.   A wary gentleman. I do assure ye,
I have been warned, and must be armed.

57–8. gentleman. I . . . ye, I] *This ed.*; Gentleman; I . . . ye, / I *F1*; gentleman, I . . . ye;
/ I *Colman.*

---

40. *high proof*] high degree of impenetrability (*OED* proof 10a).
41. *field-pieces*] cannons used on a battlefield (*OED* field 21).
44. *high stomachs hold*] audacity prevails.
45. *rands and sirloins*] slices of meat.
powder] preserve with salt or spices (*OED* 2a), cf. 1.3.206.
49. *honesty*] (1) manner of honourable behaviour (Lister); (2) Dyce suggests the
French concept of '*honnêteté*', defined by Erica Veevers as 'the standard of virtuous
yet civilised behaviour advocated for men, and particularly for women' (*Images of Love
and Religion: Queen Henrietta Maria and Court Entertainments* (Cambridge University Press, 1989), p. 21). This meaning is plausible in the cultural context of the 1630s,
when *honnêteté* became influential at the Caroline court.
51. *Amazons*] i.e. behaviour befitting the mythical race of Scythian warrior women.
Belleur's choice of analogy is apt, linking his mock-castration in 4.2 to the self-
mutilation of Amazons, who allegedly removed their right breast so it would not
impede their use of a bow.
52. *make my three legs*] bow.
54. *clear*] propitious, favourable.
55. *privy coat*] coat of mail worn under the ordinary dress (*OED* 8b).
56. *bandog*] Cf. 3.1.169.
58. *warned . . . armed*] (1) Proverbial: 'Forewarned, forearmed' (*The Oxford Dictionary of English Proverbs*, comp. W. G. Smith, 3rd edition, rev. F.P. Wilson (Oxford:
Clarendon Press, 1970), H54); (2) cf. 'armed' at 5.1.24.

La Castre.   Well, son,
    These are your hasty thoughts: when I see you are bent to it,
    Then I'll believe and join with ye. So we'll leave ye.   60
    [*Aside*] There's a trick will make ye stay.
Nantolet. [*Aside*]   I hope so.
                              Exeunt [LA CASTRE *and* NANTOLET].
Mirabell. We have won immortal fame now, if we leave 'em.
Pinac. You have, but we have lost.
Mirabell.   Pinac, thou art cozened;
    I know they love ye; and to gain ye handsomely,
    Not to be thought to yield, they would give millions.   65
    Their father's willingness, that must needs show ye.
Pinac. If I thought so –
Mirabell.   Ye shall be hanged, ye recreant!
    Would ye turn renegado now?
Belleur.   No, let's away, boys,
    Out of the air and tumult of their villainies!
    Though I were married to that grasshopper,   70
    And had her fast by th' legs, I should think she would cozen me.

            Enter a Young [Man, *disguised as a*] Factor.

Young Man. Monsieur Mirabell, I take it?
Mirabell.   You're i' th' right, sir.
Young Man. I am come to seek ye, sir. I have been at your father's,
    And understanding you were here –
Mirabell.   Ye are welcome.
    May I crave your name?
Young Man.   Foss, sir, and your servant.   75
    That you may know me better, I am factor
    To your old merchant, Leverdure.
Mirabell.   How does he?

61SD *La Castre. Aside*] *Dyce; not in* F1.   61SD *Nantolet. Aside*] *Dyce; not in* F1.
61SD *Exeunt* LA CASTRE *and* NANTOLET.] *Dyce; Exeunt.* F1.   68. now?] *F2; no?*
F1.   71SD] *Weber; Enter a young Factor* F1.   72SP *Young Man.*] *Lister; Fac.* F1.
75. *Foss*] *F2; Fosse* F1.

68. *renegado*] Spanish form of 'renegade' = turncoat, especially used of a Christian
who becomes a Muslim.
    69. *air and tumult*] atmosphere of noisy confusion, such as one might experience
on the battlefield.
    71SD *Factor*] an agent in financial affairs. The Young Man pretends to deputise for
Alberto's sister (the disguised Oriana), who wishes to deliver her brother's bequest to
Mirabell.
    75. *Foss*] (1) ditch; (2) one of the great Roman roads in Britain; (3) possibly an
oblique allusion to the trap Mirabell will fall into.

Young Man. Well, sir, I hope; he is now at Orléans,
    About some business.
Mirabell.   You are once more welcome.
    Your master's a right honest man, and one   80
    I am much beholding to, and must very shortly
    Trouble his love again.
Young Man.   You may be bold, sir.
Mirabell. Your business, if you please now?
Young Man.   This it is, sir.
    I know ye well remember in your travel
    A Genoa merchant.
Mirabell.   I remember many.   85
Young Man. But this man, sir, particularly. Your own benefit
    Must needs imprint him in ye. One Alberto,
    A gentleman you saved from being murdered
    A little from Bologna.
    I was then myself in Italy, and supplied ye,   90
    Though haply you have forgot me now.
Mirabell.   No, I remember ye,
    And that Alberto too – a noble gentleman.
    More to remember were to thank myself, sir.
    What of that gentleman?
Young Man.   He is dead.
Mirabell.   I am sorry.
Young Man. But on his deathbed, leaving to his sister   95
    All that he had, beside some certain jewels,
    Which, with a ceremony, he bequeathed to you
    In grateful memory, he commanded strictly
    His sister, as she loved him and his peace,
    To see those jewels safe and true delivered;   100
    And with them, his last love. She, as tender
    To observe this will, not trusting friend nor servant

---

78. Orléans] *This ed.;* Orleance *F1;* Orleans *Colman.*   81. to] *F2;* too *F1.*   91.
haply] *F2;* happely *F1;* happily *Dyce.*   102. this] *F1;* his *F2.*

86–7. *Your own ... ye*] 'As a consequence of your noble act, you must remember
him'.
90. *supplied ye*] furnished your requirements.
91. *haply*] perhaps.
93. *More ... myself*] 'Were I to remember more I would have to thank myself.'
96. *beside*] other than (*OED* 3).
97. *with a ceremony*] formally, solemnly.
101. *last love*] i.e. affection harboured in the last years of his life.
tender] anxious.

With such a weight, is come herself to Paris,
And at my master's house.
Mirabell.   You tell me a wonder.
Young Man. I tell ye a truth, sir. She is young and handsome,   105
And well-attended; of much state and riches;
So loving and obedient to her brother,
That, on my conscience, if he had given her also,
She would most willingly have made her tender.
Mirabell. May not I see her?
Young Man.   She desires it heartily.   110
Mirabell. And presently?
Young Man.   She is now about some business,
Passing accounts of some few debts here owing,
And buying jewels of a merchant.
Mirabell.   Is she wealthy?
Young Man. I would ye had her, sir, at all adventure:
Her brother had a main state.
Mirabell.   And fair, too?   115
Young Man. The prime of all those parts of Italy,
For beauty and for courtesy.
Mirabell.   I must needs see her.
Young Man. 'Tis all her business, sir. Ye may now see her,
But tomorrow will be fitter for your visitation,
For she is not yet prepared.
Mirabell.   Only her sight, sir;   120
And when you shall think fit for further visit.
Young Man. Sir, ye may see her, and I'll wait your coming.
Mirabell. And I'll be with ye instantly – I know the house.
Meantime, my love and thanks, sir.
Young Man.   Your poor servant.   *Exit.*
Pinac. Thou hast the strangest luck. What was that Alberto?   125
Mirabell. An honest noble merchant, 'twas my chance
To rescue from some rogues had almost slain him;
And he in kindness to remember this!
Belleur.   Now we shall have you,

---

104. *at*] is at.
109. *made her tender*] included herself as part of the reward.
112. *Passing*] approving.
114. *at all adventure*] in any case (*OED* adventure 3c).
115. *main state*] a sizeable estate (*OED* main 3a).
116. *prime*] unexcelled.
125. *What*] of what condition or rank (see Abbott 254).

For all your protestations and your forwardness,
Find out strange fortunes in this lady's eyes,   130
And new enticements to put off your journey;
And who shall have honour then?
Mirabell.   No, no, never fear it.
I must needs see her to receive my legacy.
Belleur. If it be tied up in her smock, heaven help thee!
May not we see too?
Mirabell.   Yes, afore we go.   135
I must be known myself ere I be able
To make thee welcome. Wouldst thou see more women?
I thought you had been out of love with all.
Belleur.   I may be,
I find that with the least encouragement.
Yet I desire to see whether all countries   140
Are naturally possessed with the same spirits,
For if they be, I'll take a monastery
And never travel; for I had rather be a friar,
And live mewed up, than be a fool, and flouted.
Mirabell. Well, well, I'll meet ye anon; then tell you more, boys.   145
Howe'er, stand prepared, pressed for our journey;
For certain we shall go, I think, when I have seen her,
And viewed her well.
Pinac.   Go, go, and we'll wait for ye;
Your fortune directs ours.
Belleur.   Ye shall find us i' th' tavern,
Lamenting in sack and sugar for our losses.   150
If she be right Italian, and want servants,
You may prefer the properest man.
How I could worry a woman now!
Pinac.   Come, come, leave prating;
Ye may have enough to do, without this boasting.   *Exeunt.*

---

137. thee] *F2*; thou *F1*.   152–3. man. / How I could . . . now!] *F1*; man. How I /
Could . . . now? *Bowers.*

---

134. *tied up in her smock*] conditional upon a sexual relationship.
135. *afore*] before.
142. *take*] enter.
144. *mewed up*] caged up, a term from falconry.
146. *pressed*] ready.
148. *viewed her well*] inspected her thoroughly.
150. *sack and sugar*] sweetened wine.
151. *right Italian . . . servants*] i.e. conforms to the stereotype of lascivious Italian
womanhood and encourages lovers.
152. *prefer . . . man*] recommend the most handsome man, cf. 1.1.46.
153. *worry*] (1) kiss or hug vehemently (OED 3c); (2) 'have a go at', cf. Fletcher's
The Woman's Prize 3.3.162–5: 'had I ever / A pull at this same poor sport men

SCENE 3

    Enter LUGIER, DE GARD, ROSALURA, *and* LILLIA[-BIANCA.]

Lugier. This is the last adventure.
De Gard.　　　　　　　　　And the happiest,
  As we hope, too.
Rosalura.　　　　　　We should be glad to find it.
Lillia-Bianca. Who shall conduct us thither?
Lugier.　　　　　　　　　　Your man is ready,
  For I must not be seen; no, nor this gentleman;
  That may beget suspicion. All the rest　　　　　　　　　　5
  Are people of no doubt. I would have ye, ladies,
  Keep your old liberties, and do as we instruct ye.
  Come, look not pale. You shall not lose your wishes,
  Nor beg 'em neither, but be yourselves, and happy.
Roslaura. I tell ye true, I cannot hold off longer,　　　　　10
  Nor give no more hard language.
De Gard.　　　　　　　　You shall not need.
Rosalura. I love the gentleman, and must now show it;
  Shall I beat a proper man out of heart?
Lugier.　　　　　　　　There's none advises ye.
Lillia-Bianca. Faith, I repent me too.
Lugier.　　　　　　　Repent, and spoil all.
  Tell what ye know, ye had best!
Lillia-Bianca.　　　　　I'll tell what I think.　　　　　15
  For if he ask me now if I can love him,
  I'll tell him yes, I can. The man's a kind man,

---

7. and do as] *Langbaine;* and as *F1.*

---

run mad for, / But like a cur I was faine to shew my teeth first, / And almost worry
her?'

  1. *happiest*] having the most favourable outcome.
  6. *of . . . doubt*] i.e. whose identity is unknown to Mirabell.
  7. *Keep . . . liberties*] behave as freely as in the past. Cf. the reference to 'freedom'
at l. 25 below.
  10. *hold off*] remain aloof.
  11. *hard*] harsh, acerbic.
  13. *proper*] true, genuine.
  14. *Faith*] In faith.
  15. *Tell . . . best*] Lugier is daring the girls to divulge the next plan.

And out of his true honesty affects me;
Although he played the fool, which I requited,
Must I still hold him at the stave's end?
Lugier.   You are two strange women.   20
Rosalura. We may be, if we fool still.
Lugier.   Dare ye believe me?
Follow but this advice I have set you in now,
And if ye lose – would ye yield now so basely?
Give up without your honours saved?
De Gard.   Fie, ladies!
Preserve your freedom still.
Lillia-Bianca.   Well, well, for this time.   25
Lugier. And carry that full state –
Rosalura.   That's as the wind stands:
If it begin to chop about, and scant us,
Hang me, but I know what I'll do! Come, direct us;
I make no doubt we shall do handsomely.
De Gard. Some part o' th' way we'll wait upon ye, ladies;   30
The rest your man supplies.
Lugier.   Do well, I'll honour ye.   *Exeunt.*

SCENE 4

Enter [Young Man, *disguised as a*] Factor *and* MIRABELL,
ORIANA [*above, disguised as an Italian lady*], *and* [*also above*]
two [Men *disguised as*] Merchants.

Young Man. Look ye, sir, there she is; you see how busy.
Methinks you are infinitely bound to her for her journey.

18. affects] *F2*; affect *F1*.   20. women] *F2*; woman *F1*.

oSD *Lister; Enter Factor and Mirabel, Oriana and two Merchants. F1.*

18. *out of . . . me*] loves me sincerely.
20. *at . . . end*] on unfriendly terms (*OED* staff 5b).
strange] odd, singular.
26. *full state*] independent spirit, cf. the 'state' of women at 2.1.2 and 'states' at
4.1.61.
26–7. *That's . . . scant us*] i.e., depending on conditions and whether they are
favourable; a wind that chops and scants is changeable in direction and diminishes in
force, making it difficult for a boat to hold course under sail.
28. *direct*] guide, act as the 'pilot'.

oSD ORIANA . . . *above*] Oriana, in disguise, and two of La Castre's 'secret friends'
(see 5.1.13), disguised as merchants, appear on the upper stage.

Mirabell. How gloriously she shows! She is a tall woman.
Young Man. Of a fair size, sir. My master not being at home,
     I have been so out of my wits to get her company: 5
     I mean, sir, of her own fair sex and fashion.
Mirabell. Afar off, she is most fair, too.
Young Man.   Near, most excellent. –
     At length, I have entreated two fair ladies
     (And happily you know 'em): the young daughters
     Of Monsieur Nantolet.
Mirabell.   I know 'em well, sir.   10
     What are those? Jewels?
Young Man.   All.
Mirabell.   They make a rich show.
Young Man. There is a matter of ten thousand pounds, too,
     Was owing here: you see those merchants with her;
     They have brought it in now.
Mirabell.   How handsomely her shape shows!
Young Man. Those are still neat: your Italians are most curious.   15
     Now she looks this way.
Mirabell.   She has a goodly presence.
     How full of courtesy! Well, sir, I'll leave ye;
     And if I may be bold to bring a friend or two,
     Good noble gentlemen –
Young Man.   No doubt ye may, sir,
     For you have most command.
Mirabell.   I have seen a wonder!   *Exit.*   20
Oriana. Is he gone?
Young Man.   Yes.

---

16. goodly] *F2; gooly F1.*

---

  3. *tall*] (1) comely, elegant (*OED* 2b); (2) Oriana may have assumed built-up
footwear as part of her disguise. Moryson noted that 'the women of *Venice* weare chop-
pines or shoos three or foure hand-bredths high, so as the lowest of them seeme higher
than the tallest men' (Moryson, *Itinerary*, Part 3, Bk 4, Ch. 1, p. 172).
  6. *fashion*] rank, cf. 4.2.62.
  8. *At length*] After some effort.
  14. *brought it in*] i.e. perhaps from a ship moored on the river Seine.
  15. *Those . . . neat*] i.e. Italian women are always elegantly dressed.
  curious] fastidious in matters of taste and appearance (*OED* 2).
  16. *goodly*] impressive.
  20. *wonder*] The Renaissance dramatic *topos* of 'wonder' included elements of surprise, strangeness, admiration, amazement, and self-forgetfulness. (See, for example,
Dolora Cunningham, 'Wonder and Love in the Romantic Comedies', *SQ*, 35 (1984),
262–6.)

Oriana.   How?
Young Man.   Taken to the utmost;
    A wonder dwells about him.
Oriana.   He did not guess at me?
Young Man. No, be secure; ye show another woman.
    He is gone to fetch his friends.
Oriana. Where are the gentlewomen?

    Enter [below] ROSALURA, LILLIA[-BIANCA, *and*] Servant.

Young Man.   Here, here; now they are come,   25
    Sit still, and let them see ye.
Rosalura.   Pray ye, where's my friend, sir?
Young Man. She is within, ladies, but here's another gentlewoman,
    A stranger to this town. So please you visit her,
    'Twill be well taken.
Lillia-Bianca.   Where is she?
Young Man.   There, above, ladies.
Servant. Bless me, what thing is this? Two pinnacles   30
    Upon her pate! Is't not a glade to catch woodcocks?
Rosalura. Peace, ye rude knave.
Servant.   What a bouncing bum she has too!

25SD] *Weber; in right margin opp. 'are come' F1; following 'see ye', l.26. F2.*
31. *glade] Dyce; glode F1.*

---

21. *Taken . . . utmost*] (1) thoroughly infatuated; (2) completely fooled.
23. *show*] appear.
30–1. *Two pinnacles . . . pate*] (1) two peaks on her head. The servant's description suggests the style of head-dress consisting of two pointed cones, fabricated with the help of wires and covered by a caule or hairnet; (2) 'With suggestion of her future husband's cuckold horns' (Fraser and Rabkin).
31. *glade*] snare (*OED* glode 1b, citing ll. 30–1). 'The Servant compares the space between the pinnacles on her pate to a *glade* cut in a wood, in which it is usual to spread nets for woodcocks' (Mason, cited in Dyce). Fletcher may have drawn inspiration from Moryson's observation that 'Italian Gentlemen much delight in the art to catch birds, and in Gardens fitted to that purpose, with nets, bushes and glades' (Moryson, *Itinerary*, Part 3, Bk 2, Ch. 5, p. 111) and from his description of Venetian women who 'raise up their haire on the forehead in two knotted hornes'. The 'gold netted cawle' Moryson noted women wearing over these appendages enforces the bird snare imagery in l. 31 (Moryson, *Itinerary*, Part 3, Bk 4, Ch. 1, pp. 172–3).
    woodcocks] birds easily caught in a snare, hence applied allusively to a simpleton (*OED* 2).
32. *bouncing bum*] i.e. jaunty movement of the posterior, exacerbated by padding, popularly known as a 'bum-roll', worn under the very full farthingale skirt. For contemporary illustrations of the farthingale, bum-roll, and trunk-hose (l. 58, below) see Janet Arnold, *Patterns of Fashion: The Cut and Construction of Clothes for Men and Women c.1560–1620* (London and New York: Macmillan, 1985), pp. 10–14.

There's sail enough for a carrack.
Rosalura.   What is this lady?
For, as I live, she's a goodly woman.
Young Man.   Guess, guess!
Lillia-Bianca. I have not seen a nobler presence.   35
Servant. 'Tis a lusty wench. Now could I spend my forty pence,
     With all my heart, to have but one fling at her,
     To give her but a swashing blow.
Lillia-Bianca.   Ye rascal.
Servant. Ay, that's all a man has for's good will. 'Twill be long enough
     Before ye cry, 'Come Antony, and kiss me!'   40
Lillia-Bianca. I'll have ye whipped.
Rosalura.   Has my friend seen this lady?
Factor. Yes, yes, and is well known to her.
Rosalura. I much admire her presence.
Lillia-Bianca.   So do I too.
     For, I protest, she is the handsomest,
     The rarest, and the newest to mine eye   45
     That ever I saw yet.
Rosalura.   I long to know her;
     My friend shall do that kindness.
Oriana.   So she shall, ladies:
     Come, pray ye come up.
Rosalura.   O me!
Lillia-Bianca.   Hang me if I knew her!
     Were I a man myself, I should now love ye,
     Nay, I should dote.
Rosalura.   I dare not trust mine eyes,   50
     For, as I live, ye are the strangest altered.
     I must come up to know the truth.
Servant.   So must I, lady,
     For I am a kind of unbeliever too.
Lillia-Bianca.   Get ye gone, sirrah;
     And what ye have seen, be secret in: you are paid else!

---

38. swashing] *Colman;* washing *F1.*

33. *carrack*] type of galleon that carried copious sails.
36. *forty pence*] customary amount for a wager (*OED* forty A.c).
37. *fling*] (1) passing attempt or attack upon something (*OED* 2a); (2) fit or spell of unrestrained indulgence in one's impulses (*OED* 5); cf. 4.1.60.
38. *swashing blow*] (1) applied to a particular blow in fencing: slashing with great force (*OED, swashing* 2); (2) for 'copulatory meanings' of the phrase see Williams, p. 116, citing this line.
54. *you ... paid else*] you will be punished otherwise.

No more of your long tongue.
Young Man.   Will ye go in, ladies,   55
And talk with her? These venturers will come straight.
Away with this fellow!
Lillia-Bianca.   There, sirrah; go disport ye.
                              [*Gives money to* Servant.]
Servant. I would the trunk-hosed woman would go with me.
              [*Exeunt, on one side,* ROSALURA, LILLIA-BIANCA,
              and the Young Man; *on the other,* Servant; ORIANA *and*
                              Men *disguised as* Merchants, *above.*]

SCENE 5

              Enter MIRABEL, PINAC, [*and*] BELLEUR

Pinac. Is she so glorious handsome?
Mirabell.   You would wonder.
Our women look like gypsies, like Jills, to her;
Their clothes and fashions beggarly and bankrupt –
Base, old, and scurvy.
Belleur.   How looks her face?
Mirabell.   Most heavenly,
And the becoming motion of her body   5
So sets her off.
Belleur.   Why, then we shall stay.

57SD] Lister; *not in* F1.   58SD] *This ed.*; *Exit* F1; *Exeunt, on one side,* ROSALURA,
LILLIA-BIANCA *and the* Young Man *disguised as a Factor; on the other,* Servant. *Dyce.*

---

55. *long tongue*] loquacity (*OED* A.1.c, quoting lines 54–5).
56. *straight*] straight away.
58. *trunk-hosed*] (1) i.e. dressed in an old-fashioned manner (*OED* b, citing this
line). Trunk-hose were onion-shaped breeches, usually mid-thigh length and more frequently an item of men's apparel. Full, flared breeches came into fashion in Britain from
about 1613 after the death of Henry, Prince of Wales. Trunk-hose were, therefore,
considered out of date by the second decade of the seventeenth century; (2) interpreted
literally, the phrase suggests that Oriana wears breeches visible beneath her gown, a
fashion Moryson observed among Italian 'City Virgins, and . . . Gentlewomen' who 'in
many places weare silke or linnen breeches under their gownes' (Moryson, *Itinerary*,
Part 3, Bk 4, Ch. 1, p. 172). An English fashion of cross-dressing was current at the
time of *The Wild-Goose Chase*'s composition, issuing in the satirical pamphlets *Hic-
Mulier, or, The Man-Woman*, and *Haec-Vir, or, The Womanish Man*, both published
in 1620.
2. *gypsies . . . Jills*] See 1.3.6n for *gypsies*; see 3.1.296n for *Jills*.
3. *bankrupt*] destitute (*OED* 2c).
5. *becoming motion*] gracefulness.

Mirabell.   Pardon me,
That's more than I know. If she be that woman
She appears to be –
Belleur.   As 'tis impossible.
Mirabell. I shall then tell ye more.
Pinac.   Did ye speak to her?
Mirabell. No, no, I only saw her, she was busy: 10
Now I go for that end. And mark her, gentlemen,
If she appear not to ye one of the sweetest,
The handsomest, the fairest in behaviour:
We shall meet the two wenches there too. They come to visit her,
To wonder, as we do.   15
Pinac. Then we shall meet 'em.
Belleur.   I had rather meet two bears.
Mirabell. There you may take your leaves, dispatch that business,
And, as ye find their humours –
Pinac.   Is your love there, too?
Mirabell. No, certain, she has no great heart to set out again.
This is the house; I'll usher ye.
Belleur.   I'll bless me,   20
And take a good heart if I can.
Mirabell.   Come, nobly.   *Exeunt.*

SCENE 6

Enter [*Young Man disguised as a*] Factor, ROSALURA,
LILLIA-BIANCA, [*and*] ORIANA [*disguised as before*].

Young Man. They are come in. Sit you two off, as strangers.

[*Enter Boy.*]

[*To Oriana*] There, lady. – Where's the boy? – Be ready, sirrah,

---

13. fairest in behaviour:] *F2*; fayrest, in behaviour, *F1*; fairest in Behaviour – *Sympson*,
fairest in behaviour. *Lister.*

oSD] *Dyce; Enter Factor, Rosaluce, Lillia, Oriana. F1*   1SD] *Sympson; not in F1.*

---

11. *for that end*] i.e. to court her.
17. *dispatch . . . business*] resolve that matter you have become engaged in.
18. *Is your . . . too?*] 'Is the woman (Oriana in disguise as "Alberto's sister") agreeable to travelling with us?' Pinac is teasing Mirabell for his extolling a woman whose
acquaintance he has not yet made.
21. *take . . . heart*] act bravely.
nobly] courageously.

And clear your pipes. The music now.   *Music.*
                            They enter.

            Enter MIRABELL, PINAC, *and* BELLEUR.

Pinac. What a state she keeps! How far off they sit from her!
    How rich she is! Ay, marry, this shows bravely.   5
Belleur. She is a lusty wench, and may allure a good man.
    But if she have a tongue, I'll not give twopence for her.
    There sits my fury; how I shake to see her!
Young Man. [*To Oriana*] Madam, this is the gentleman.
                            [*Mirabell kisses Oriana.*]
Mirabell.   How sweet she kisses!
    She has a spring dwells on her lips, a paradise.   10
    This is the legacy?
            [*Boy sings, while he presents a casket to Mirabell.*]
            From the honoured dead I bring
            Thus his love and last off'ring.
            Take it nobly, 'tis your due,
            From a friendship ever true,   15
            From a faith, etc.
Oriana.   Most noble sir,
    This from my now dead brother, as his love
    And grateful memory of your great benefit:
    From me my thanks, my wishes, and my service.
    Till I am more acquainted I am silent;   20
    Only I dare say this, you are truly noble.
Mirabell. What should I think?
Pinac.   Think ye have a handsome fortune;
    Would I had such another.

3SD *Music.*] *This ed.; Musick. then* / *Enter Mirabell . . . Bellure. in right margin opp.*
ll. 3–5 F1; *Music* [*within*] *in right margin opp.* 'The music now' *Lister.* 9SD *To
Oriana.*] *This ed.; not in* F1.   9SD *Mirabell kisses Oriana*] *Lister (subst.); not in* F1.
11. *legacy?*] *Fraser and Rabkin; legacy.* F1.   11SD] *Dyce (subst.); Song.* F1.   16.
noble sir] F2; *noble, Sir* F1.

3. *clear . . . pipes*] clear your throat (in preparation for song).
    4. *state*] Cf. 2.1.2.
    5. *rich*] opulently dressed.
    shows bravely] is a propitious start.
    8. *fury*] (1) threateningly ferocious woman, cf. 'Furies' at 4.2.73; (2) adversary.
    10. *spring* (1) source or origin of pleasure or delight; (2) as this is the last trap to
catch Mirabell, the 'wild goose', a pun on *spring* = 'trap to catch birds', cf. Middleton
and Dekker, *The Roaring Girl* 3.3.73–4: 'Here's the springe / I ha' set to catch this
woodcock in'.
    19. *service*] respect.

Rosalura.   Ye are well met, gentlemen;
    We hear ye are for travel?
Pinac.   Ye hear true, lady,
    And come to take our leaves.
Lillia-Bianca.   We'll along with ye.   25
    We see you are grown so witty by your journey,
    We cannot choose but step out too. This lady
    We mean to wait upon as far as Italy.
Belleur. [*Aside*] I'll travel into Wales, amongst the mountains;
    I hope they cannot find me.
Rosalura.   If you go further,   30
    So good and free society we hold ye,
    We'll jog along too.
Pinac.   Are ye so valiant, lady?
Lillia-Bianca. And we'll be merry, sir, and laugh.
Pinac.   It may be
    We'll go by sea.
Lillia-Bianca.   Why, 'tis the only voyage:
    I love a sea voyage and a blust'ring tempest,   35
    And let all split!
Pinac. [*Aside*]   This is a dainty damosel!
    [*To her*] I think 'twill tame ye. Can ye ride post?
Lillia-Bianca. O excellently! I am never weary that way;
    A hundred mile a day is nothing with me.
Belleur. I'll travel underground. – Do you hear, sweet lady?   40
    I fear it will be dangerous for a woman.
Rosalura. No danger, sir, I warrant; I love to be under.
Belleur. I see she will abuse me all the world over! –
    But say we pass through Germany, and drink hard?

29SD] *Lister; not in F1*; *l.* 29 *Fraser and Rabkin.*   29–30. Wales, amongst the mountains; / I hope . . . me.] *F1*; Wales, amongst the mountains, / In hope . . . me. *Colman;*
Wales; amongst the mountains, / I hope . . . me. *Bowers.*   36SD] *Lister; not in F1.*
37SD] *Lister; not in F1.*

---

29. *Wales . . . mountains*] considered a primitive, inhospitable country.

31. *free society*] agreeable company.

32. *jog along*] (1) accompany you on horseback; (2) double entendre; for *jog* 'as
imitative of coital motion', see Williams, p. 744.

34. *'tis . . . voyage*] it's the best way to travel.

36. *let . . . split*] (1) let the sails rip or the ship break up, conveying the sense of
'throwing caution to the wind'; (2) with bawdy subtext of *split* alluding to 'woman's
open-legged coital posture' (Williams, p. 1290).

37. *post*] (1) with post-horses, hence with haste; (2) a bawdy quibble on 'ride post'.

40. *underground*] (1) in secrecy or concealment, although the first use of the phrase
in this sense in OED is dated 1632; (2) sets up Rosalura's sexually implicit reply, 'I
love to be under', at l. 42.

Rosalura. We'll learn to drink and swagger too.
Belleur. [*Aside*]   She'll beat me!   45
   Lady, I'll live at home.
Rosalura.   And I'll live with thee,
   And we'll keep house together.
Belleur.   I'll keep hounds first –
   And those I hate right heartily.
Pinac.   I go for Turkey,
   And so it may be, up into Persia.
Lillia-Bianca. We cannot know too much. I'll travel with ye.   50
Pinac. And you'll abuse me?
Lillia-Bianca.   Like enough.
Pinac.   'Tis dainty!
Belleur. I will live in a bawdy-house.
Rosalura.   I dare come to ye.
Belleur. Say I am disposed to hang myself?
Rosalura. There I'll leave ye.
Belleur.   I am glad I know how to avoid ye.
Mirabell. May I speak yet?
Young Man.   She beckons to ye.   55
Mirabell. Lady, I could wish I knew to recompense,
   Even with the service of my life, those pains
   And those high favours you have thrown upon me.
   Till I be more desertful in your eye,
   And till my duty shall make known I honour ye,   60
   Noblest of women, do me but this favour,
   To accept this back again, as a poor testimony.
                     [*Offering the casket*]
Oriana. I must have you, too, with 'em; else the will,
   That says they must rest with ye, is infringed, sir;
   Which, pardon me, I dare not do.
Mirabell.   Take me, then,   65
   And take me with the truest love.
Oriana.   'Tis certain,
   My brother loved ye dearly, and I ought

45SD] Fraser and Rabkin; *not in* F1.   50. too] F2; to F1.   62SD] Dyce; *not in* F1.

48. *Turkey*] Eating turkey was reputed to excite lust (Williams, p. 1440).
49. *Persia*] homophonic wordplay on *Persia* and 'purse' = vagina (Williams, p. 1116).
51. *'Tis dainty*] 'Fine!'
56. *to*] how to.
59. *desertful*] deserving.
62. *testimony*] proof.

As dearly to preserve that love. But, sir,
Though I were willing, these are but your ceremonies.
Mirabell. As I have life, I speak my soul.
Oriana.   I like ye: 70
But how you can like me, without I have testimony,
A stranger to ye –
Mirabell.   I'll marry ye immediately;
A fair state I dare promise ye.
Belleur.   Yet she'll cozen thee.
Oriana. Would some fair gentlemen durst promise for ye.
Mirabell. By all that's good –

    Enter LA CASTRE, NANTOLET, LUGIER, *and* DE GARD.

All.   And we'll make up the rest, lady.   75
Oriana. Then Oriana takes ye; nay, she has caught ye!
If ye start now, let all the world cry shame on ye!
I have out-travelled ye.
Belleur.   Did not I say she would cheat thee?
Mirabell. I thank ye. I am pleased ye have deceived me;
And willingly I swallow it, and joy in't;   80
And yet perhaps I knew ye. Whose plot was this?
Lugier. He is not ashamed that cast it: he that executed
Followed your father's will.
Mirabell.   What a world's this,
Nothing but craft and cozenage!
Oriana.   Who begun, sir?
Mirabell. Well, I do take thee upon mere compassion –   85
And I do think I shall love thee. As a testimony,
I'll burn my book, and turn a new leaf over.
But these fine clothes you shall wear still.
Oriana. I obey you, sir, in all.
Nantolet.   And how,
How, daughters? What say you to these gentlemen?   90

---

74. gentlemen] *F1*; Gentleman *F2*.   81. knew] *Sympson*; know *F1*.   89–90. how, /
How . . . gentlemen?] *Lister*; how! How . . . Gentlemen? *F1*.

74. *promise for ye*] i.e. act as witnesses to Mirabell's promise of marriage.
77. *start*] recoil in alarm (*OED* 2e).
85. *I . . . compassion*] reminiscent of *MAdo*, 5.4.92–3: 'by this light, I take thee for
pity'.
87. *burn my book*] (1) a reference to Mirabell's book of conquests at 2.1.146; (2)
an allusion to Marlowe's *Doctor Faustus*, 19.190: 'I'll burn my books!'; and a possible echo of Prospero's renunciation of his magic, *Temp.* 5.1.56–7: 'deeper than did ever
plummet sound / I'll drown my book'. 'The powers abjured by Mirabell are those of
unrestrained sexual license' (Lister).
    turn . . . over] change my ways; proverbial (Dent L146). Lister notes that Mirabell
is being clever, 'he would burn his book first, and then turn over a new page'.

What say ye, gentlemen, to the girls?
Pinac. By my troth – if she can love me –
Lillia-Bianca.   How long?
Pinac. Nay, if once ye love –
Lillia-Bianca.   Then take me,
And take your chance.
Pinac.   Most willingly. Ye are mine, lady;
And if I use ye not, that ye may love me –   95
Lillia-Bianca. A match, i' faith.
Pinac.   Why, now ye travel with me.
Rosalura. How that thing stands!
Belleur.   It will, if ye urge it.
Bless your five wits!
Rosalura.   Nay, prithee stay; I'll have thee.
Belleur. You must ask me leave first.
Roslaura.   Wilt thou use me kindly,
And beat me but once a week?
Belleur.   If ye deserve no more.   100
Rosalura. And wilt thou get me with child?
Belleur. Dost thou ask me seriously?
Rosalura.   Yes, indeed do I.
Belleur. Yes, I will get thee with child. Come, presently,
And't be but in revenge, I'll do thee that courtesy.
Well, if thou wilt fear God and me, have at thee!   105
Rosalura. I'll love ye and I'll honour ye.
Belleur.   I am pleased then.
Mirabell. This wild-goose chase is done; we have won o' both sides.
[*To De Gard*] Brother, your love – And now to church, of all hands,
Let's lose no time.
Pinac.   Our travelling lay by.
Belleur. No more for Italy; for the Low Countries, I.   *Exeunt.*   110

---

110. Low Countries, I.] *Sympson;* Low-Countries, *F1.*

98. *five wits*] the five bodily senses; the perceptions or mental faculties generally
(*OED* 3b).
 108. *of . . . hands*] on the part of everyone (Lister).
 110. *Low Countries*] (1) the region now forming the kingdoms of the Netherlands
and Belgium, and the grand duchy of Luxembourg (*OED* 2a); (2) sexual innuendo
arising from *low countries* in reference to female pudenda (see Williams, pp. 830–2).

The Bird in a Cage
James Shirley

edited by Julie Sanders

The title page of the 1633 quarto reads as follows 'THE / BIRD IN A / CAGE. / A *Comedie*. / As it hath beene Presented at the / *Phoenix* in *Drury-Lane*. / The *Author* IAMES SHIRLEY, / Servant to Her Majesty. / IUVEN. Satyra. 7. / *Et Spes, & ratio Studiorum, in Caesaretantum.* / LONDON / Printed by *B. Alsop.* and *T. Fawcet.* for *William* / *Cooke*, and are to be sold at his Shop neere / *Furnivals-Inne* Gate, in *Holborne.* / 1633.'

The epigram is from Juvenal, *Satires*, 7: 'On Caesar alone hang all the hopes and prospects of the learned' (Loeb). Senescu notes that this compliments Henrietta Maria and her patronage of Shirley's work, thereby aligning the playwright explicitly on the queen's side in the debate over women and theatre that had recently been enflamed by William Prynne's publication of *Histriomastix*, a fact confirmed by the ironic dedication of the playtext to the Puritan pamphleteer (see Introduction, p. 23). On the significance of William Cooke as a publisher of Shirley's dramatic writings see the Introduction, p. 22.

[THE DEDICATION]

To Master WILLIAM PRYNNE, Utter-Barrister of Lincoln's Inn.

SIR,

The fame of your candour and innocent love to learning, especially to that musical part of human knowledge, poetry, and in particular to that

---

o. PRYNNE . . . Inn] William Prynne (1600–69) was an Inns of Court lawyer, and a notorious Puritan pamphleteer, who at the time when Shirley published *The Bird in a Cage* was incarcerated in the Tower of London. There is, therefore, an ironic angle to Shirley's dedication of his play to this alternative 'bird in a cage'. Prynne was awaiting trial on charges of libel following his late 1632 publication of the thousand-page pamphlet, *Histriomastix: The Player's Scourge; Or, The Actor's Tragedy* (published by Michael Sparke in November of that year). The tract, in addition to railing against theatre in general, using to support its claims numerous scriptural and classical authorities, suggested that theatre was a corrupting force both for those who performed in it and for those who spectated, stating on its title page: 'the profession of play-poets, of stage players, together with the penning, acting, and frequenting of stage-plays, are unlawful, infamous, and misbeseeming Christians'.

Prynne, a member of Lincoln's Inn, the most puritanical of the otherwise theatre-loving Inns of Court, was particularly disturbed throughout the pamphlet by theatre's deployment of cross-dressing: 'this putting on of woman's array (especially to act a lascivious, amorous, whorish, lovesick play upon the stage), must needs be sinful, yea abominable' (Prynne, 1632, Dd4v, p. 208). He did not limit his comments to boy actors, however, also indicting female performers who disguised themselves as men. What saw him tried in the Star Chamber in 1634, however, was his index entry equating 'Women Actors' with 'notorious whores'. Archbishop Laud and Charles I's attorney Noy argued that this was a direct statement against Henrietta Maria, who at the time when *Histriomastix* was published was in rehearsals for Montagu's pastoral *The Shepherds' Paradise* (see Introduction, p. 23). Prynne argued in his trial that the reference could not have been specific to the queen since he had begun work on the pamphlet in the 1620s and it was licensed as early as 1630, but the index was clearly a later addition to the publication and so the imputation held (William M. Lamont, *Marginal Prynne, 1600–69*, London: Routledge, 1963, p. 29). He was sentenced to have his ears cropped in public, fined £5000, and imprisoned for life. His publisher, Sparke, was also fined and his stocks of the offending work confiscated. A full list of the charges against Prynne is contained in PRO, S.P. 16/534 and the fullest account of the trial is in BL Add. MS 11764. Shirley would go on to win the commission to write *The Triumph of Peace* in 1634, a masque intended by the Inns of Court to apologise to the king and queen for any offence taken from Prynne's outburst in print.

o. *Utter-Barrister*] 'In the Inns of Court, the Utter or Outer Barristers [were] the Masters of Arts', *Shakespeare's England*, 1.409.

which concerns the stage and scene – yourself, as I hear, having lately
written a tragedy – doth justly challenge from me this dedication. I had   5
an early desire to congratulate your happy retirement, but no poem
could tempt me with so fair a circumstance as this; in the title wherein
I take some delight to think – not without imitation of yourself, who
have ingeniously fancied such elegant and apposite names for your own
compositions, as *Health's Sickness, The Unloveliness of Love-locks*, etc.   10
– how aptly I may present you, at this time, with *The Bird in a Cage*,
a comedy, which wanteth, I must confess, much of that ornament which
the stage and action lent it. For it comprehending also another play or
interlude, personated by ladies, I must refer to your imagination the
music, the songs, the dancing, and other varieties, which I know would   15
have pleased you infinitely in the presentment. I was the rather inclined
to make this oblation that posterity might read you a patron to the

---

11–12. *Cage*, a] *This ed.*; *Cage*. A Q.   13. it. For] *This ed.*; it, for Q.

4–5. *lately . . . tragedy*] The full title of *Histriomastix* was *The Player's Scourge; Or
Actor's Tragedy*; Prynne also mocked the dramatic genre by dividing his pamphlet into
acts and scenes with a prologue, choruses, and a closing 'catastrophe'.

5. *challenge . . . dedication*] Shirley decided on the dedication after writing his play,
and appears to have retitled it in order to point up the allusions to Prynne. It is believed
that *The Bird in a Cage* is the play licensed on 21 January 1633 under the title *The
Beauties* (spelt *Bewties*) (see Bawcutt, p. 178 [No. 248]). The revised title still has relevance to the play proper, since it reflects both Eugenia's incarceration and Philenzo's
method of penetrating her prison, and the playtext appears to allude to other Prynne
pamphlets at 1.1.23–5 (see Dedication, 10). Shirley's motives for intervention in the
debate over female theatricals are discussed in more detail in the Introduction, pp. 25–9.

6. *retirement*] Prynne's imprisonment in the Tower of London in 1633.

9–10. *fancied . . . compositions*] Prynne was notorious for his archly titled pamphlets, which played with puns and antithetical constructions, such as *The Unloveliness of Love-locks* (1628) or *Lame Giles His Haltings* (1630).

10. *Health's Sickness*] This tract, published in 1628, was ironically dedicated to
Charles I.

The . . . Love-locks] Also published in 1628, this tract concerned itself with the
Caroline vogue for men wearing their hair very long. Shirley refers to the fashion in
The Bird in a Cage at 1.1.23–5. Ironically, following public ear-croppings in 1634 and
1637, Prynne would wear his hair long until his death.

11. *The . . . Cage*] On the change in title from *The Bewties*, see Dedication 5n.

11–16.] The awkward syntax of these sentences in Q is a product of erratic punctuation, possibly caused by the hasty production of these sections in the printing-house
(see Introduction, pp. 43–5 and 1.1.226–8n below).

14. *interlude . . . ladies*] 'The New Prison' – the Jupiter–Danae playlet within a play,
performed by Eugenia and her female companions at 4.2. This specific reference to
female theatricals suggests Shirley was well aware of the reasons behind Prynne's arrest
and that a defence of female theatricals in part spurred his retitling of the playtext.

15. *music . . . dancing*] Prynne specifically condemns these arts in *Histriomastix*.

17. *oblation*] thing offered to a divine being (OED 1).

Muses, and one that durst, in such a critical age, bind up the wounds
which ignorance had printed upon wit and the professors. Proceed,
inimitable Maecenas, and, having such convenient leisure, and an inde-   20
fatigable Pegasus – I mean your prose, which scorneth the road of
common sense, and despiseth any style in his way – travel still in the
pursuit of new discoveries, which you may publish, if you please, in
your next book of digressions. If you do not happen presently to
convert the organs, you may in time confute the steeple, and bring every   25
parish to one bell –

This is all I have to say at this time, and my own occasions not per-
mitting my personal attendance, I have entreated a gentleman to deliver
this testimony of my service. Many faults have escaped the press, which
your judgement will no sooner find than your mercy correct; by which   30
you shall teach others a charity to your own volumes, though they be
all errata. If you continue where you are, you will every day enlarge
your fame, and beside the engagement of other poets to celebrate your
Roman constancy, in particular oblige the tongue and pen of your
devout honourer,   35

JAMES SHIRLEY.

---

29. service. Many] *Senescu;* Seruice, many *Q*.

---

18. *such . . . age*] Shirley refers to the ongoing pamphlet war waged against the
theatre by puritan writers.
19. *ignorance*] Senescu notes that in his commendatory verse attached to the printed
edition of Ford's *Love's Sacrifice* in 1633 Shirley describes Prynne as 'voluminously
ignorant'.
20. *Maecenas*] Patron of the Roman writer Horace.
21. *Pegasus*] winged horse of classical literature, though here the sarcastic allusion
is to the flights of fancy taken by Prynne's prose.
21-2. *prose . . . sense*] Prynne's prose style was renowned for its deployment of long
sentences and complex legal phraseology.
22. *style*] with pun on 'stile'.
25-6. *convert . . . bell*] a reference to Puritan opposition to Laudian church ceremony, including the use of bells and organs, which were regarded by Prynne and others
as 'popish devices'.
32. *If . . . continue*] Prynne had not yet been formally tried or sentenced.
33. *other poets*] Jasper Mayne's *The City Match* (1638) and Thomas Heywood's
The English Traveller (1633) also ridiculed Prynne.
34. *Roman constancy*] The use of the initial capital on 'Roman' clearly invokes
Roman Catholicism, Prynne's paranoid obsession in *Histriomastix*, although the surface
reference is to stoicism.
pen] Shirley alludes to Prynne elsewhere in his work; see, e.g., Dedication 19n, on
the aforementioned commendatory verse to Ford's *Love's Sacrifice*, also published in
1633, and his 1633 revision of Fletcher's *The Nightwalker* 3.4: 'They are so pat upon
the time, as if / He studied to answer the late *Histriomastix*.'

THE PERSONS

DUKE of MANTUA.
PERENOTTO, *Captain of his Guard.*
PHILENZO, *lover of Eugenia, under the disguise and name of*
  ROLLIARDO.
FULVIO,
ORPIANO. } *Noblemen.*   5
MORELLO,
DONDOLO, } *Courtiers.*
GRUTTI.
AMBASSADOR *of Florence.*
BONAMICO, *a mountebank, or decayed artist.*   10
[CARLO, *Bonamico's*] Servant.
Guard.
Attendants.
EUGENIA, *the duke's daughter.*
DONELLA,   15
KATHERINA,
MARDONA,   } *Ladies, attendant on the princess.*
FIDELIA,
CASSIANA.

---

6. MORELLO] a sour dark cherry (from the Italian for 'blackish').
7. DONDOLO] from *dondolore* (Ital.), meaning 'idler' or 'loafer'.
10. BONAMICO] 'good friend' (Ital.); Bonamico's pseudonym when he plays the mountebank is 'Altomaro' meaning 'deep sea' (Ital.).

ACT I

Enter FULVIO [*and*] ORPIANO.

Orpiano. He does not mean this building for a college, I hope?

Fulvio. That were an ill foundation, there are more scholars than can live one by another already; 'tis pity we should have more plenty of learned beggars.

Orpiano. 'Tis past all my conjecture why he built it.   5

Fulvio. Signor Perenotto, captain o' the guard, is of counsel only with the duke in't.

Enter MORELLO.

Morello. Signor Orpiano, and Fulvio.

Fulvio. My spark! Whither in such haste? Let us change air a little.

Morello. You are travelling to your mistress.   10

Orpiano. Madam Donella is newly returned to court.

Fulvio. With the princess?

Orpiano. She was but late retired into the country. What's the matter?

Morello. Your lordships I hope have heard. The duke sent post for them, as they say: there is something in't.   15

Fulvio. What?

Morello. Does not your lordship know?

Fulvio. Not I.

Morello. Your lordship's wisdom and mine is much about a scantling

---

o] *A Room in the Duke's Palace. G; no scene locations in Q.*   oSD] *Qc (subst.); Enter Fulvio, Orpiano, passing. Qu.*   2. there] *Qc; therc Qu.*   10. Morello] *Q (subst.); Orp. Senescu.*   11. Orpiano] *Q (subst.); Mor. Senescu.*   15. say:] *G; say, Q.*

---

o.] The scene takes place in a reception room that is freely accessible to courtiers, including Morello who is en route to the 'princess's lodging' (22). It is used later by the duke as a presence chamber for the reception of court officials and business.

1. *this building*] the palatial tower constructed by the duke for the purposes of incarcerating his daughter, referred to later as the 'New Prison' (174).

9. *spark*] young man of elegant or foppish character (OED 2).

change air] discourse (exchange air). Cf. *LLL* 5.2.238.

10SP] Senescu reassigns this line to Orpiano suggesting that it makes sense only if referring to Morello's suit to the princess. However, if Morello speaks the line the implication is that he refers to Orpiano's suit to Donella.

14. *post*] courier, messenger.

19. *much . . . scantling*] much of a muchness (OED 2d).

then; yet, for aught I hear, there be others of the court as ignorant   20
as we – your honour's pardon, I beseech you, I must in all haste
to the princess's lodging.

Orpiano. Farewell, signor. Your amorous lock has a hair out of order.

Morello. Um! What an oversight was this of my barber! I must
return now and have it corrected, dear signor.   *Exit.*   25

Fulvio. Here's a courtier that will not miss a hair of his compliment
when he is to appear before his mistress: every morning does this
fellow put himself upon the rack with putting on's apparel, and
manfully endures his tailor when he screws and wrests his body
into the fashion of his doublet. But that the court cannot subsist   30
without a fool, I should marvel what this fellow does to follow
it.

Orpiano. There are more have much about his parcel of brains; the
benefit of youth and good clothes procured their places, and ignorance and impudence have since maintained 'em.   35

Fulvio. Two great helps, as the world goes.

Enter Gentlemen Ushers, D O N D O L O, [*and*] G R U T T I.

Gentlemen Ushers. Clear the presence, the duke is entering.

Enter D U K E, E U G E N I A, P E R E N O T T O, [*and*] *Attendants.*

Eugenia. I ever was obedient –

Duke. 'Tis for thy honour, which I know,
Is to thy self a precious sound – that building   40
I late erected, then, shall be thy palace.

Eugenia. Or my prison, sir,
If I do rightly understand.

---

24. barber!] G; barber, Q.   25. signor] *This ed.*; signior G; Sign. Q.   42–3. Or . . .
understand.] G; *one line in* Q.

---

23. *amorous lock*] lock of hair worn on the left side by men, and considerably longer
than the rest of the hair at the front; a 1630s court fashion since Charles I sported the
style. The fashion spurred William Prynne's scorn in his *The Unloveliness of Love-locks*
(London, 1628), a text which Shirley invokes in his ironic dedication of *The Bird in a
Cage* to Prynne (10).

26. *compliment*] formal courtesy (*OED* II.2). Morello regards being in the court
fashion as a means of paying respect to Eugenia. Shirley, who made his own tributes
to his courtly patron Henrietta Maria as we have seen, was not averse to mocking this
courtly tradition; see his *Love-Tricks, or The School of Complement* (1625).

28. *rack*] instrument of torture; a comic reference to Morello being tortured into his
clothing (29–31).

30–1. *court . . . fool*] prefiguring Morello's later role as official court fool (see Act
4).

33. *There . . . about*] There are many (at court) that share.

33. *parcel*] fragment (*OED* 5b).

Duke.   That name
Is too unworthy of it, my Eugenia.
Nor will it seem restraint to my loved daughter,   45
Since, free to all delights, thy mind shall be
Its own commander; every day shall strive
To bring thee in fresh rarities. Time shall be
Delighted with thy pleasures, and stay with thee.
Eugenia. Indeed, I shall think Time has lost his wings   50
When I am thus caged up.
Duke.   Thou shalt give
To him feathers when thou pleasest. Mantua
Shall pour her raptures on thee – why have I
A crown but to command what thou canst wish for,
My dear Eugenia?
Eugenia.   A deer, it seems,   55
For as you had suspicion of my wildness
You'll measure out my walk.
Duke.   I am thy father,
Who, by example of the wisest kings,
But build a place to lay my treasure in
Safe from the robber, where I'll place a guard –   60
Eugenia. Do you suspect I shall break prison?
Duke. To keep off violence and soliciting
Which may disturb thy pleasures. Until we
Shall find out one to match thy birth and virtues –
My dukedom is too poor that way – maintain   65
Thy father's soul: thou hast no blood to mix
With any beneath prince. Forget, as I shall,
Thy love was ever falling from thy greatness

---

61. prison?] Q *(subst.)*; prison [sir?] G.   63. pleasures. Until] *This ed.*; pleasures,
untill *Q*; pleasures; until G.   64. virtues –] *This ed.*; virtues, G; Vertues, *Q*.   65. My
... way] *This ed.*; My ... way, *Q*; (My ... way) G.

---

50. *Time ... wings*] Proverbial image of time as a winged figure (Dent T327).
    51-2. *Thou ... feathers*] continuing the image of winged Time begun at l. 50, but
also ironically prefiguring the liberating impact of the caged birds in Act 4.
    58. *by ... kings*] In John Barclay's prose romance *Argenis* (1621), the king confines
his daughter in a castle while he procures her a husband (Senescu).
    61. *prison*] Gifford's addition of 'sir' to the end of Eugenia's line was a response to
her formal addresses to her father elsewhere in the scene, and served to create a metrical line. However, Shirley regularly deploys lines of nine syllables and it is feasible
that he sought to indicate that the Duke's response should follow swiftly after Eugenia's
statement (Senescu).
    62. *soliciting*] There is a sexual undertone to the sense.

Into the arms of one carries but style of honour.
Eugenia. Sir, I am your daughter.   70
Duke. Thou'st deserved my blessing; and thy obedience
In this new crowns thy father. I see I need not
Urge what I am to move thee, and lay force.
Thy understanding does appear convinced
And loving duty teaches thee to more   75
Than the command – Perenotto!
Eugenia. [*Aside*] What narrow ground I tread! I know he is
Too passionate to be denied his will
And yet to yield will make me miserable.
'Tis my misfortune to be born so great.   80
Each common man and woman can enjoy
The air, when the condition of a princess
Makes me a prisoner. But I must obey
In hope it will not last – [*To the duke*] I have a soul
Is full of grateful duty, nor will suffer me   85
Further dispute your precept: you have power
To steer me as you please.
Duke.   All the graces
Speak in my girl. Each syllable doth carry
A volume of thy goodness. All my cares
So well rewarded do convert to sweetness.   90
I thank thy filial piety. Know, my girl,
That place wherein I lock so rich a jewel,
I do pronounce again, shall be thy paradise:
Thy paradise, my Eugenia, saving that
In this man only finds no being. Other   95
Delights shall stream themselves into thy bosom
And those that pass shall flow again t' invite
Thy sense to tasting – Perenotto!
Perenotto.   Your grace's pleasure?
Duke. Admit those ladies that attend –   [*Exit* PERENOTTO.]
Fulvio. The duke shows much indulgence.   100
Orpiano. Observe the issue.
Duke. We will not limit thy companions.
Elect what Mantuan beauties thou canst best

---

69. style . . . honour.] Q *(stile of Honour);* style / Of . . . honour. G. 71. Thou'st]
This ed.; Thou hast G; Th'ast Q. 71.] Q; Thou hast / Deserv'd G. 76. Perenotto!]
G; *Perenotto –* Q. 77SD] *This ed.; not in* Q. 84SD] *This ed.;* [*Aside.*] – G. 99SD]
G; *not in* Q.

---

69. *arms*] (with pun on heraldic arms).
95. *In . . . being*] No man enters there.
103. *beauties*] The use of this phrase to refer to Eugenia's ladies adds credence to
Fleay's suggestion that *The Bewties* was the earlier title (see Introduction, p. 23).

Delight in, they shall serve thee: or, if some
Of your own train whom we have thought most proper   105
To be your personal guard affect you, they
Attend our pleasures.

Enter [PERENOTTO,] DONELLA, KATHERINA, MARDONA,
and FIDELIA.

See, they are ignorant
Yet of our purpose; if to any thy
Affection be not free thy breath discharge them
And 'point thy own attendants.   110
Eugenia. I shall be pleased with your appointment.
                                        She goes to the ladies.
Ladies, I know you love me.
Donella. Doth your grace hold suspicion any of us
Serve you not with our heart?
Eugenia.   I do not doubt,
Or if I did, you now approach a trial.   115
For my sake can you be content to be
All prisoners?
Ladies.   Prisoners?
Eugenia. Yes, shut up close prisoners, and be barred
The conversation, nay, the sight, of men.
Katherina. Marry, heaven defend; wherein have we offended   120
That we must lose the sweet society
Of men?
Mardona.   How have we forfeited our freedom?
Duke. No man argue – 'tis our pleasure.
Donella. 'Las, madam, I am new contracted to a handsome signor.
Katherina. I have but newly entertained a servant   125
That gave me these gloves;
They smell of him still, a sweet courtier.
Donella. Not one man among so many ladies?
Not a gentleman usher? Nor a page?
How shall we do, madam?   130

107SD] G; *positioned in right margin* Q.   109. not] Qc; more Qu.   124.] Q; 'Las,
madam / I . . . signior. G.   125-7.] *This ed.; prose in* Q.   128-30.] Q; *prose in* G.

---

106. *affect*] appeal to.
110. *'point*] appoint.
111. The appointment of ladies in waiting to attend the queen consort was a high
profile political issue, as debates around the companions of Henrietta Maria and her
predecessor Anna of Denmark indicate; see, e.g., Barbara Kiefer Lewalski, *Writing
Women in Jacobean England* (Cambridge, Massachusetts: Harvard University Press,
1993), p. 23.
124. *contracted*] engaged.
125. *servant*] suitor. This was a common usage of the term in neoplatonic discourse.
130. *do*] cope (with bawdy sense of 'be sexually satisfied').

Mardona. I beseech your grace, let me be exempted.
    If I have committed an offence deserves your anger,
    Let one of your lords cut off my head rather – Signor Dondolo?
Fidelia. Shall we express
    So cold a duty to her highness? Fie, ladies.   135
Eugenia. You shall but suffer with me: I partake
    As much severity as any of you shall.
Duke. I will expect your duties, lords, in silence.
    Orpiano, you shall to Florence with
    Our daughter's picture; your commission's sealed –   140
    Now, fair ladies,
    I hope you're fixed to wait upon Eugenia.
    If your restraint be a burden, it shall be
    In her power to enlarge you and elect
    New friends into your places.
Ladies.   'Tis our duties   145
    To obey your grace and her.
Duke. Perenotto, are all things prepared?
Perenotto. They are, my lord.
Duke.   For once then let us usher you.
                                    [*Exit with* EUGENIA.]
Katherina. Whither do we go?
Perenotto.   I'll tell you.
Donella. Whither?
Perenotto.   To take physic, madam.   150
    The duke has prepared to stay all looseness in your bodies. You
    must be all fast: stone walls and mortar will bind.
Fidelia. Come, follow with a courage.
Donella. I hope we shall be allowed our little dogs and monkeys.
Dondolo. Sweet madam –   155
            Exit [DONELLA, KATHERINA, MARDONA,
                and FIDELIA, *with* PERENOTTO].

133. Dondolo?] *Q (Dondalo.).*   139. Florence] *Qc on Errata sheet (Ferrara).*
148SD] *G; not in Q.*   149–50.] *Q; prose in G.*   155. madam –] *G;* madam. *Q.*
155SD] *This ed.;* [Exeunt ladies.] *G;* Exit omn. man. Fulv. Orp. Dond. Grutti. *Q.*

133. *Signor Dondolo*] Dondolo entered at 36SD but has not spoken until this point
and does not respond to Mardona. Presumably she turns to address him at this point.
    139–40.] Orpiano is dispatched to take Eugenia's picture to the Prince of Florence,
whom her father intends her to marry. The sending of portraits was common practice
in early modern courtly marriage negotiations.
    150. *physic*] medicine.
    151. *looseness*] moral laxity.
    152. *fast*] confined (i.e. contained within the tower). At 150–2 Perenotto is also
making jokes about constipation.
    154. *dogs and monkeys*] the traditional pets of Caroline aristocratic women, fea-
tured in many contemporary portraits.

Grutti. Madam Katherina – They are gone, signor.
Dondolo. Would I had known this afore!
Fulvio. The duke will be censured for this act.
Orpiano. 'Tis very strange. Good lady,
    I read a forced obedience in her eye,   160
    Which hardly held up rain.

                Enter MORELLO.

Morello. Save you, dear signor, which way went the ladies?
Grutti. News, signor, news.
Morello. I beseech you I may partake.
Fulvio. Have you forgot there was suspicion she affected Signor 165
    Philenzo, the cardinal's nephew?
Orpiano. Alas, poor gentleman, he suffers for't.
Fulvio. By this restraint he would make her sure. His jealousy is not
    yet over – Signor Morello, is your lock rectified? You have missed
    your lady but a hair's breadth.   170
Morello. Nay, but my lords and gentlemen, where are the ladies gone
    indeed?
Grutti. We ha' told you.
Morello. What, committed to New Prison?
Fulvio. Very true, signor.   175
Dondolo. Our dancing days are done; shut up close, not a man must
    enter.
Morello. Would I were a mouse then! Why, but is the duke mad?
Orpiano. Take heed what you say, signor: though we be no informers,
    yet walls have ears.   180
Morello. Ears? Would I had left mine behind me. Here's news indeed!
Fulvio. And you'd come a little sooner, you might ha' taken your leave,
    but 'twas your barber's fault.
Morello. Would he had left me i' th' suds an hour ago! What shall we

---

156. Katharina –] *This ed.*; Catherina: – G; *Katherina*, Q.   178. then!] G; then – Q.
182. you'd] *This ed.*; An you had G; y'ad Q.

161. *hardly . . . rain*] barely avoided tears.

   174. *New Prison*] Probably a reference to the tower intended for the women. 'New
Prison' becomes the title for the dramatic interlude they perform there (4.2). Senescu
suggests a possible pun on Newgate Prison, which had been restored in 1628 and was
subsequently referred to as 'new' by Londoners. A statement made by Archbishop Laud
to the Court of High Commission on 21 June 1632 observed that three nonconformists
convicted of holding false opinions should be sent to three prisons other than 'the new
prison' (S.R. Gardiner, ed., *Reports of Cases in the Courts of Star Chamber and High
Commission* (London: Camden Society, 1886–87, pp. 270–1).
   180. *walls . . . ears*] Proverbial (Dent W19). Cf. Marston, *The Malcontent* 3.3.3:
'Suspect that hedges, walls, and trees, have ears.'

do, gentlemen? 'Tis a hard case, when a man that has an intention   185
to marry and live honest –

      Enter [PHILENZO *disguised* as] ROLLIARDO.

How now, what art thou?
Philenzo. Anything, nothing: yet a man, yet no man, for I want.
Morello. What? Th' art no capon, I hope.
Philenzo. Money, sir. Will you spare any from your precious sins?   190
Grutti. Th' art very free.
Philenzo. Yet, sir, I am in debt.
Dondolo. What dost owe?
Philenzo. Nobody harm.
Fulvio. Whence cam'st?   195
Philenzo. I dropped from the moon.
Orpiano. So methinks, thou talkst very madly – thou'st much humour
    in thee.
Philenzo. Ha' you any thing to do that you account impossible,
    gentlemen?   200
Fulvio. Why, wilt thou do't?
Philenzo. And you'll pay for't. Let me have money enough and I'll do
    anything.
Orpiano. Hold, hold.
Philenzo. Yes, I will hold.   205
Morello. I'll lay with thee; what wilt hold –
Philenzo. Why, paradoxes.
Grutti and Dondolo. Paradoxes!
Morello. I hold you a paradox.
Fulvio. Let's hear some.   210
Philenzo. There are no beasts, but cuckolds and flatterers; no cold
    weather but i' the dog-days; no physic to a whore; no fool to an

188SP] *This ed.; Rolliardo (subst.) throughout in Q.*

186SD] Despite listing Philenzo as 'PHILENZO ... under the disguise and name of
ROLLIARDO' in the 'Persons' of the play, Q refers to him as 'Rolliardo' in all subsequent stage directions and speech prefixes. We have amended this throughout to 'Philenzo', collating only this first instance. Intriguingly, Shirley chooses not to accord the audience any privileged knowledge of Philenzo's true identity.

189. *capon*] Morello's figurative sense is that Philenzo seeks fattening up by means of financial patronage (a capon is a cockerel fattened for the table).

196-7. *I ... madly*] the moon was traditionally associated with madness, hence 'lunacy'.

202. *And*] If (this usage occurs throughout the play; e.g. 2.1.65, 3.3.20).

212. *dog-days*] about the time of the rising of the dog-star (c. July 3 to August 15); noted from ancient times as the hottest, most unwholesome period of the year. Cf. H8 5.3.42.

alderman; no scholar to a justice of peace; nor no soldier to a belt
and buff jerkin.

Orpiano. A smart fellow.   215

     Enter DUKE.

Morello. The duke.

Duke. So, my fears are over. In her restraint I bury all my jealousies –
how now, what fellow's this?

Fulvio. Such an humorist as I never before conversed withal. It seems
he makes himself free of all places.   220

Duke. What would he have?

Philenzo. Thy pardon, mighty man. If it be no treason to pray for thee,
save thee, wilt employ me? 'Tis vacation, and I want work. Ask me
not what I can do; let me have money enough and I'll do anything.

Duke. You have your senses?   225

Philenzo. Five, I take it: I can see greatness big with an impostume, yet,
towering in the air like a falcon, the small birds dare not peep for
him. I can hear a man swear 'I am thy eternal slave, and will serve
thee', when, if opportunity were offered, for price of a plush cloak
he will be the first shall strip thee to the very soul. I can taste wine   230
that another man pays for and relish anything that comes of free
cost. I can smell a knave through a barred gown; a politician

---

215SD] G; *not in* Q.   226–9. Five . . . cloak] Qc *unique*; Five, the small Birds dare
not peepe for him, I take it: I can see greatnesse big with an Impostume, yet towring
in the Ayre like a Falcon: Qu.   228–9. 'I . . . thee,'] *This ed.; in italics* G.   229. when]
Qc; whē Qu.   229. for price] Q; for [the] price G.   229. cloak] Qu *(subst.);* Cloake
Qc.

---

213. *alderman*] city dignitary, next in line of importance to the mayor.

213–14. *belt . . . jerkin*] Soldiers' clothes, the 'belt' being a leather girdle used to
carry weapons; 'jerkin', a sleeveless upper garment.

219. *humorist*] person subject to 'humours' or fancies (OED 1); cf. 2.1.41 and
4.1.134.

223. *vacation*] period between terms at the Inns of Court. Traditionally it was a time
when the young men training in law at the Inns were seen on the streets of London in
search of entertainment. Many Jacobean and Caroline city comedies include such characters; see, e.g., Brome, *The Sparagus Garden*. Shirley had trained at Gray's Inn.

224. *money enough*] Philenzo's persistent repetition of this phrase echoes Iago's
refrain 'put money in thy purse', *Oth.* 1.3.339–51.

226–8.] The existence of three versions of this passage in extant copies of Q indicates a compositor attempting to make sense of difficult formes while the printing
job was in progress, redistributing the word order until the sense seemed right (see
Introduction, p. 44).

226. *impostume*] swelling or cyst (OED 1).

229. *plush*] soft silk or cotton.

232. *barred gown*] Judges and other officers of the law wore broad stripes or bars
of gold lace on the front of their gowns (Gifford).

through a surplice; a fool through a scarlet outside. I can touch a
wench better than a lute, and tell money with a secretary to show
I ha' not lost my feeling. Tush, all's nothing; I have a humour to   235
do something to be talked on. Nothing can come amiss to me.
Let me have money enough and, my life to a cheese-paring, I'll do
anything.
Duke. You'll except somewhat.
Philenzo. Not to do o'er the seven wonders of the world and demol-   240
ish 'em when I ha' done. Let me have money enough, what star so
high but I will measure by this Jacob's staff? Divine money, the
soul of all things sublunary. What lawyer's tongue will not be
tipped with silver; and will not money with a judge make it a plain
case? Does not gouty greatness find ease with *aurum palpabile?*   245
And he's a slight physician cannot give a golden clyster at a dead
lift. Money, I adore thee! It comes near the nature of a spirit, and
is so subtle it can creep in at a cranny, be present at the most inward
councils and betray 'em. Money – it opens locks, draws curtains,
buys wit, sells honesty, keeps courts, fights quarrels, pulls down   250
churches, and builds almshouses.
Duke. A wild fellow.

---

235. ha' not lost] G; ha'lost Q.   241–2. Let . . . staff. Divine] *This ed.*; let . . .
enough. What . . . staff, divine G; let . . . enough, what . . . *staffe,* divine Q.   246. lift.]
This ed.; lift – Q.   249. Money –] *This ed.*; Money, Q.

---

233. *surplice*] loose vestment of white linen, with wide sleeves, worn (usually) over
a cassock) by clerics and choristers.
scarlet] the colour of those in the legal profession, especially judges.
233–4. *touch . . . lute*] punning on the fact that playing the lute was called
'fingering'.
234. *tell*] count.
secretary] often responsible for household accounts.
235. *ha' not lost*] Gifford's emendation here clarifies the sense and is further evidence that this particular speech appeared in a muddled state in the copy from which
the printers were working (see 226–8 above).
237. *cheese-paring*] thin portion of cheese, shaved off the surface; sometimes the
rind.
240. *do o'er*] remake (do over again).
242. *Jacob's staff*] instrument used for measuring the altitude of the sun and other
stars (*OED* 2).
243. *sublunary*] existing or situated beneath the moon (*OED* 1).
244. *plain*] simple or easily understood (in a legal context).
245. *gouty*] swollen (gout is a disease that involves inflammation of the small joints).
aurum palpabile] touchable gold (Lat.); cf. *Volpone* 1.4.73.
245–6. *he's . . . lift*] 'He is a poor doctor who cannot prescribe a golden clyster
(enema) at the final juncture': 'dead lift' is the position at which one can do no more
(*OED* 2; cf. Shirley, *The Maid's Revenge* 3.2). Philenzo's cynical implication is that
money can prove a solution even at a point of impasse.

Fulvio. Will your grace have him punished for this insolence?
Duke. No, his humour is good mirth to us – Whence art?
Philenzo. I am of no country.   255
Duke. How?
Philenzo. I was born upon the sea.
Duke. When?
Philenzo. In a tempest, I was told –
Morello. A blustering fellow.   260
Duke. Thy name?
Philenzo. Rolliardo.
Duke. And how long hast thou been mad thus?
Philenzo. Your highness may be merry, and if you have no employment
    for me, I am gone.   265
Duke. Stay, we command you, and bethink again
    What to except in your bold undertaking.
Philenzo. I except nothing. Nothing, duke. It were no glory not to be
    general, active in all. Let me have money enough and I'll do
    anything.   270
Duke. You shall.
Fulvio. Will your grace set him awork?
Philenzo. Name the action.
Duke. What say you to a lady?
Philenzo. I will fall upon her, as Jupiter on Danae. Let me have a   275
    shower of gold, Acrisius' brazen tower shall melt again. Were there
    an army about it, I would compass her in a month or die for't.
Duke. Ha? A lady without guard would try your wit and money to get
    her love.
Philenzo. A toy, a toy.   280
Duke. Through a credulity, you may too much
    Traduce the sex, and merit such a justice
    No money will buy off. Admit some branches
    Grow not so straight and beautiful as Nature

---

254. us –] G; vs; Q.   268. nothing. Nothing] *This ed.*; nothing, nothing Q.

---

272. *awork*] to work.

275–6. *I . . . again*] The allusion is to Jupiter's metamorphosis into a shower of gold in order to penetrate the tower in which Acrisius had imprisoned his daughter, Danae. Acrisius had been informed by an oracle that a grandchild would kill him, so he sought to prevent Danae from bearing children. Impregnated by Jupiter, she gave birth to Perseus who duly fulfilled the oracular prediction. Shirley does not deploy the oracle aspect of the story, but otherwise exploits to the full its associations with sexual penetration and gold of a literal and figurative quality. Philenzo's reference to the myth here prefigures its choice as the subject of the women's dramatic interlude in the tower.

277. *compass*] encompass, gain.

month] The time-scheme of a month is akin to the wager in Fletcher's *Women Pleased*.

282. *Traduce*] misrepresent.

Intended them, will you disgrace the stem   285
Or for some woman's lenity accuse
That fair creation? Money buy their love?
Promise a salary of that sacred flame
Themselves cannot direct, as guided by
Divine intelligence.   290
Philenzo. Your highness, pardon. If you prohibit, I must not undertake;
but let me have freedom and money enough (for that's the circle I
walk in) and, if I do not conjure up a spirit hot enough to inflame
a frozen Lucrece's bosom, make mummy of my flesh, and sell me
to the apothecaries. Try me with some masterpiece. A woman's   295
love is as easy as to eat dinner without saying grace, getting of chil-
dren, or going to bed drunk. Let me have money enough and tax
me to the purpose.
Fulvio and Orpiano. He's constant.
Duke. Admit there be a lady whom a prince   300
Might court for her affection, of a beauty
Great as her virtue; add unto them birth
Equal to both; and all three but in her
Not to be matched. Suppose this miracle,
Too precious for man's eye, were shut up where   305
A guard more watchful than the dragons did
Forbid access to mankind – men picked out
Between whose souls and money were antipathy
Beyond that which we know, and you as soon
Might bribe to be a saint – what would you do   310

---

286. lenity] Q; levity G.   296. eat dinner] Qc (subst.); eate a dinner Qu.   305. Too
. . . eye,] This ed.; (Too . . . eye) Q.   306. dragons did] This ed.; Dragons; did Q.
310. Might . . . saint] Q; Might bribe . . . to be a saint G, *suggesting a dropped line.*

286. *lenity*] act of mercy (used ironically). This reading renders Gifford's emendation to 'levity' unnecessary.

287–90.] The Duke implies that his daughter cannot be bought except with a
payment ('salary') procured from heaven.

292. *circle*] circuit, compass (echoing the reference at 277). Philenzo also puns on
the circle in which devils and spirits were claimed to be conjured. Cf. 2.1.94, and
Jonson, *Devil Is an Ass* 1.2.21, 26–7.

294. *Lucrece*] Roman woman who committed suicide following her rape by Tarquin
owing to the shame she represented for her husband. She became an emblem of chastity.

mummy] medicinal preparation of dead flesh (*OED* 1a); cf. Donne, 'Love's
Alchemy'; *MWW* 3.5.16–17.

295. *masterpiece*] a piece of work produced by an apprentice in order to be admitted to a guild as an acknowledged master (*OED* 1a).

306. *dragons*] possibly a reference to the dragon who guarded the golden apples in
the garden of the Hesperides, or that which guarded the golden fleece.

310. *Might . . . saint*] A paradox; you cannot bribe someone to be a saint, since the
very act of bribery denies the outcome. Gifford questioned the sense here and suggested

With your enough of money, were your life
Engaged to win her love?
Philenzo. The sky may fall, and aldermen cry larks
About the city.
Duke. The fellow's impudent. Sirrah, thou hast landed thyself upon a   315
rock; you shall have sense of what you would contemn, a life. Put
on a most fortified resolution, you shall need it. We have a daugh-
ter thus locked up –
Fulvio. What does the duke mean?
Duke. A virgin.   320
Orpiano. He is in passion.
Duke. Shalt not engage thee on a work so much
Impossible as procurement of her love?
Make it appear with all the art thou canst
Get but access to her; a month we limit.   325
But take heed, boaster: if you fail, your life
Shall only satisfy our charge and teach
All other mountebanks to be at distance
With such bold undertakings. You shall expect
A severe justice.   330
By this, I shall try the fidelity of those are trusted.
Philenzo. 'Tis a match. I shall have money enough?
Duke. You shall. What d' ye call enough?
Philenzo. I will not be particular and agree o' the sum. You look I
should die if I perform not, and I'll look to be merry and want   335
nothing while I live. I'll not take the advantage on you, because I
hope to receive credit by it: if I use now and then a round sum set
me up o' the ticket for't. But who shall pass his word, if I do this
feat, you'll let me keep my head o' my shoulders?

313–14. The . . . larks / About . . . city.] *Q*; The . . . fall / And . . . city. *G*.   331. By]
Q; [*Aside.*] By *G*.   333. enough?] *Qc on Errata page*; 'enough, yet it shall be under
20. thousand Crownes: I will not leave the Pawne here, for twice so much'. *Qu.*
339. o'] *This ed.*; a *Q*; on *G*.

a line may have been dropped from the press. Senescu posits the following: 'Might bribe
[the Guard as hope that gold convert / The devil] to be a saint.'
    313–14.] Proverbial phrase for an impossibility (Dent S517: 'When the sky falls we
shall have larks'). Cf. *Tim.* 2.5.1044.
    328. *mountebanks*] pretenders to skill or knowledge (*OED* 2). See 2.1.0SD for an
alternative use of the word.
    333. *enough?*] The lines that were deleted in retrospect in *Q* by means of the inclu-
sion of an errata page (K4r) are further indication that the first act was delivered to
the printing-house while still in a process of correction and that these initial pages were
printed hastily (see Introduction, p. 44).
    337–8. *if . . . for't*] if I spend a certain amount now and then, set me up a credit note
(a 'ticket' being a tradesman's bill or note of indebtedness, *OED* 7a).

Duke. Our royal word secure thee.   340
Philenzo. 'Tis enough.
Fulvio. What security can your grace expect for his forthcoming, if
    he fail?
Duke. We ha' studied that.
    'Tis but the loss of some superfluous crowns.
    Let the end carry what success fate please,   345
    All the expense will not be lost to try
    The faith of those we shall employ in this.
    Our city's strong; the river that environs
    On three parts shall be carefully attended;
    A wall makes safe the fourth, which shall be guarded.   350
    Our vigils shall be so exact he shall
    Deserve his liberty if he escape us.
    We are constant, sir.
Fulvio. [*Aside*] Would he might pay for his curiosity.
Philenzo. I'll wait upon your highness for some earnest. I have a month   355
    – good. Let me have fair play and my bargain, money enough. If
    I do come short, let my head be too heavy for my shoulders. If I
    do more than is expected, you'll believe it possible hereafter: when
    a man has money enough, he may do anything.
Duke. Maintain your humour still. Attend us.   360
        Exeunt [DUKE, PHILENZO, FULVIO, *and* ORPIANO].
Morello. Here's a mad fellow; does he mean to get into the ladies?
Dondolo. It seems so.
Grutti. Or I would not be in his taking when the moon changes.
Morello. Our best course then is to observe and humour him. He may
    have a trick more than we know. He seems to be a good fellow.   365
    Let's be drunk together, and get him to confess it – ha?
Dondolo and Grutti. A match.
Morello. Like errant knights, our valiant wits must wrestle
    To free our ladies from the enchanted castle.   *Exeunt.*

354SD] G; *not in* Q.   355–6. month –] *This ed.*; Moneth: good Q.   361SD] G;
Exeunt. Manent Morello, Dondolo, and Grutti. Q.   363. changes] G; chãges Q.

---

  355. *earnest*] sum of money paid as an instalment (*OED* 1); cf. *Cym.* 1.5.65. *The
Bird in a Cage* plays with several meanings of the phrase 'earnest': see Introduction,
p. 32.
  357. *let . . . shoulders*] let me be beheaded.
  363. *when . . . changes*] continues suggestions of lunacy begun at 194–5.
  368–9.] Morello's closing couplet plays with common plotlines and motifs of
medieval romances. Cf. Shirley, *The Witty Fair One* (1633), 'By all means, let's see the
doughty Knight that must free the Lady from her enchanted castle' (2.2 D4r).

ACT 2

Enter [from the house] BONAMICO *[disguised as a mountebank,]*
and [CARLO].

Carlo. D' ye think this hair
And habit will sufficiently disguise you
From your inquiring creditors?
Bonamico. No question.
Have you dispersed my bills about the city?   5
Does every public place carry the scroll
As I commanded?
Carlo.   I have been careful.
Bonamico. What do they say abroad? Do they not wonder?
Carlo. They are stricken dumb at reading; he that has
The use of tongue employs it to express   10
His admiration of your art, your deep,
Invisible art.
Bonamico. There's hope, then, we shall prosper
In this believing age. Italy is full
Of juggling mountebanks that show tricks with oils   15
And powders. Here, an empiric dares boast

---

o] *A ... House, with a painted sign over the door.* G.   oSD] G; *Enter Bonamico and*
a Servant. Q.   8. abroad?] G; abroad, Q.

oSD *mountebank*] itinerant quack doctor, who appealed to audiences, often from a
raised platform in the street, by means of stories, tricks, and juggling. Frequently they
were accompanied by a professional clown or fool. That role is performed here by
Carlo; cf. Volpone as Scoto of Mantua, attended by Mosca, in *Volpone* 2.2.

1SP] Q has the generic *Seruant* as the speech heading for Carlo's speeches, but, since
he is named directly in the play, we have followed Gifford's lead in assigning him
this name both in the Persons of the Play and all subsequent speech prefixes and stage
directions.

5. *bills*] paper advertisements publicising Bonamico's mountebank trade. These presumably carry the name of Altomaro, since this is deployed without prompting by
Dondolo at 2.1.338.

6–7. *Does ... commanded*] Public notices were conventionally placed on market
crosses and similar prominent locations.

8. *abroad*] in the wider community.

14–15. *Italy ... mountebanks*] Mountebanks were particularly associated with Italy
(see oSD).

16. *empiric*] one who evidences things by empirical practice.

Himself a Paracelsian and daub
Each post with printed follies when he went
O' the ticket with some midwife or old woman
For his whole stock of physic; here, a fellow　　　　20
Only has skill to make a handsome periwig
Or to sow teeth i' the gums of some stale madam,
Which she coughs out again when so much phlegm
As would not strangle a poor flea provokes her,
Proclaims himself a rectifier of nature　　　　25
And is believed, so getteth more by keeping
Mouths in their quarterly reparations,
Than knowing men for all their art and pains
I' th' cure of the whole body. Shall we doubt
To be made rich, rich, Carlo, by our art,　　　　30
Whereof I am the first and bold professor
In Italy? We shall grow fat and purchase;
Dost not think so?
Carlo.　　　　　　To go invisible
Who will not learn at any rate?
Bonamico.　　　　　True, Carlo.
There may be in the throng of our admirers,　　　　35
Some will presume't above the power of art
To make men walk and talk invisible;
But we can clear the mystery and make
Mantua, in the proof, acknowledge it
A matter feasible – here's some customer.　　　　40

　　　Enter [PHILENZO *disguised* as] ROLLIARDO.

Ha! 'Tis the humorist, the undertaker,
The bird I spread my art for: he has money
Enough and's apt to prove a fortune to me.

---

19. O' the] *This ed.*; On the G; A'th Q.　26. believed, so] G; believed so, Q.
29. body.] *This ed.*; body – Q.　40SD] *in right margin* Q.　43. and's] *This ed.*; and
is apt G; and 's apt Q.

---

17. *Paracelsian*] Follower or adherent of the Swiss physician, chemist, and natural
philosopher Paracelsus (1490–1541) or of his medical and philosophical principles.
　19. O' *the ticket*] See 1.1.338.
　27. *reparations*] repairs.
　31. *first . . . bold*] boldest.
　32. *purchase*] get rich.
　41. *humorist*] See 1.1.219.
　undertaker] one who takes up a challenge (OED 3c); cf. *TwN* 3.4.349.
　42–3. *money / Enough*] Philenzo's phrase is here turned back on him.

Philenzo. So the covenants are sealed: I am like a famous cathedral
    with two ring of bells, a sweet chime o' both sides. Now 'tis noised   45
    I ha' money enough, how many gallants of all sorts and sexes court
    me. Here's a gentleman ready to run himself in the kennel for haste
    to give me the wall. This cavalier will kiss my hand, while th' other
    signor crinkles i' th' hams as he were studying new postures against
    his turn comes to salute me. As I walk, every window is glazed   50
    with eyes, as some triumph were in the street. This *madonna* invites
    me to a banquet for my discourse; t' other *bona-roba* sends me a
    spark, a third a ruby, a fourth an emerald; and all but in hope to
    put their jewels to usury, that they may return again with precious
    interest. Thus far it goes well, very well; what's next?   55
Bonamico. [*Coming forward*] Save you, signor.
Philenzo. What art thou?
Bonamico. One appointed by fate to do you service, sir.
Philenzo. But I gave fate no commission to take you up for me; I ha'
    more followers than the duke already. Prithee, have me com-   60
    mended to the lady Destinies, and tell 'em I am provided.
Bonamico. Mistake me not, he speaks to you, has power
    To make you happy.
Philenzo. Prithee, make thyself happy with a warm suit first; thy house
    is but poorly thatched. And thou be'st so good at making happy,   65
    why hast no better clothes?

---

45. o'] *This ed.*; a Q; on G.   51. *madonna*] Q *(Madova)*.   55. interest. Thus] interest – thus Q.   55. next?] G; next – Q.   56SD] G; *not in* Q.   65. thatched. And]
This ed.; thatched, and Q.

---

44. *covenants*] legal agreements.
    47–8. *in . . . wall*] into the gutter ('kennel'; according to the OED, this phrase for a
surface street drain was used figuratively from 1630 onwards) in his eagerness to defer
to me ('give me the wall').
    48. *cavalier*] swaggering fellow; cf. Shakespeare, *2H4* 5.3.62; Brome, *The Weeding
of Covent Garden*, where Captain Driblow assists Clotpoll with his desire for initiation into the 'Brotherhood of the Blade' (1.1.10). The term had not yet been affixed to
followers of Charles I or Caroline courtiers more generally.
    49. *crinkles . . . hams*] bows obsequiously (OED's first recorded usage). Cf. Shirley,
A Contention for Honour and Riches 6.302.
    against] in preparation for when.
    51. *triumph*] public procession or pageant; cf. Shirley's *Triumph of Peace* (1634).
    madonna] Italian lady (OED 1b); cf. *TwN* 1.5.72.
    52. bona-roba] wench, 'showy wanton' (OED); cf. *2H4* 3.2.26. See Jonson, *The
Alchemist* 2.6.30; *New Inn* 3.2.271.
    53. *spark*] small diamond (OED 4a).
    61. *lady Destinies*] Clotho, Lachesis, and Atropos, the three Fates, who span the
thread of human destiny, but could also cut it off with shears when they pleased
(Senescu).

Bonamico. 'Tis no felicity; or admit, the sun
   Dispenseth a rich warmth about the world
   Yet hath no heat itself.
Philenzo.   Philosophy!
Bonamico. To omit circumstance, I know what you   70
   Have undertaken to the general
   Amazement: upon penalty of death,
   You must procure access to the fair princess.
   'Tis in my art to help – to perfect what
   The duke holds so impossible.   75
Philenzo. How canst thou assist me?
Bonamico. Although my outside promise not, my brain
   Is better furnished. I ha' gained by study
   A secret will advance the work you labour with:
   I'll teach you, sir, to go invisible –   80
Philenzo. How? thou'st no cloven foot, I scent no brimstone; and thou
   be'st a devil, tell me.
Bonamico. I trifle not. I am a man whose fame
   Shall outlive time in teaching you this mystery,
   For which I must expect reward. You are –   85
   Loud noise proclaims it – able and can pay me
   Out of the duke's exchequer, being yourself
   His walking treasury.
Philenzo. You'll teach me to go invisible, you say?
Bonamico. I can, and with your safety, for I deal not   90
   With magic to betray you to a faith
   Black and satanical: I abhor the devil.
Philenzo. Very like so.
Bonamico. Which some have conjured into a ring

---

81. thou'st] *This ed.*; thou hast *G*; t'hast *Q*.   81. scent no brimstone] *This ed.*; sent no
brimstone *G*; sent brimstone *Q*.   82. devil,] *Qu* (Diuell,); Diuell *Qc*.   85. reward.]
This ed.; reward – *Q*.   85. are –] *This ed.*; are, *G*; are *Q*.   86. Loud . . . it –] *This
ed.*; (Loud . . . it) *Q*.   89. invisible,] *Qu*; invisible *Qc*.

---

  67. *felicity*] happiness.
  70. *circumstance*] surrounding context (*OED* I.1c).
  81. *cloven foot*] traditional attribute of Satan; cf. *Oth.* 5.2.292.
  scent no] Gifford added this negative, which clarifies the reading slightly, but he
retained 'sent' rather than emending to 'scent' as we have done for sense. Seventeenth-
century printing-house compositors did frequently skip over 'no' as errata pages in
several editions attest (Senescu).
  brimstone] sulphur, associated with the devil: see Genesis, 19.24; Revelations, 19.20.
  91–2. *faith / Black*] Black magic, associated with diabolic intentions.
  94. *conjured . . . ring*] magic trick which gave power over the devil by confining him
within a circle (*OED* 9c); cf. *Devil Is an Ass* 1.2.21, 26–7. This continues a series of
references to circles and conjuring, begun at 1.1.292.

To effect the wonder. I admit of no   95
Suffumigation, incense offered to
Infernal spirits, but by art, whose rules
Are lawful and demonstrative –

Philenzo. You think I admire you all this while – Hark, when did you
eat? Or do you hope again that you are put to this pitiful and des-   100
perate exigent? I see you, my would-be-invisible, fine knave.

Bonamico. D' ye mock me, sir?

Philenzo. I'll tell you a better project wherein no courtier has prefooled
you. Stick your skin with feathers and draw the rabble of the city
fourpence a piece to see a monstrous bird brought from Peru.   105
Baboons have passed for men already, been taken for usurers, i'
their furred gowns and night-caps. Keep a fool in pay to tell the
multitude of a gentle faith that you were caught in a wilderness
and thou mayst be taken for some far-country owlet.

Bonamico. Do you despise my art?   110

Philenzo. Art? But such another word, and I shall mar the whole expectation of your invisible traffic. In, to your nest, and leave me; distinguish men before you practise on 'em: 'tis wholesome caution.

Bonamico. I leave you to the misery of your unbelief. When you hear
of me hereafter, you will curse your fortune to have thus neglected 115
me. Fare you well, sir.   [*Exeunt* BONAMICO *and* CARLO.]

   Enter PERENOTTO, *with three or four of the* Guard.

Philenzo. This is Perenotto, captain of the guard.

Perenotto. Not yet attempted, you?

1 Guard. We have not seen him, my lord.

Perenotto. He's here.   120

2 Guard. Is that he that has gold enough? Would I had some of his
yellow hammers!

Philenzo. D' ye hear, you are one of the list?

1 Guard. A poor halberdman, sir.

Philenzo. Poor? Hold thee, there's gold for thee. [*Offers him money.*] 125

---

101. you . . . knave.] Qc2; you would be / Invisible, my fine Knave. *Qu*; you would be
/ Invisible, fine my Knave. *Qc1.*   102. D' ye] *This ed.*; D'ee *Q.*   105. fourpence] *This
ed.*; for pence *Q.*   116SD Exeunt . . . CARLO] *G*; *Exit. Q.*   123. D' ye] *This ed.*; D'ee
Q.   125SD] *G (subst.); not in Q.*

96. *Suffumigation*] Burning of herbs in witchcraft to excite evil spirits (*OED* 1b).
101. *exigent*] urgent need (exigence).
105. *bird . . . Peru*] Senescu suggests the condor.
112. *traffic*] trade (*OED* I.1).
122. *yellow hammers*] slang reference to gold coins.
123. *one . . . list*] one employed to keep trespassers out of the tower in which
Eugenia is incarcerated.
124. *halberdman*] one who carries a halberd, a combined spear and battle-axe.

Thou wilt be honest now?

1 Guard. Oh, yes, sir.

Philenzo. [*Retracts the money.*] Not a penny. And thou hadst not been
   a fool, thou wouldst ha' been a knave, and so thou mightst have
   got by me. Yet, by those scurvy legs, there's some hope thou'lt be   130
   converted: at all adventures, take it.   [*Gives him the money.*]

1 Guard. I will be what you please, sir.

Philenzo. Tell me what condition is that signor of? Is he rich?

1 Guard. He loves money.

Philenzo. Come, shalt be my pensioner – here's more gold for thee   135
   [*Gives him more money.*] – and will he take a bribe?

1 Guard. D' ye make question of that, sir? He bought his office and
   therefore may sell his conscience; he has sold two hundred on's
   twice over. He was brought up at court and knows what belongs
   to his place, I warrant you.   140

Philenzo. Good.

1 Guard. Am I not a knave now, sir?

Philenzo. I like thee.

1 Guard. [*Aside*] To your cost – I hope you won't tell him what I say:
   but if you do, and he chance to turn me out of my office, your gold   145
   is restorative.

Perenotto. To your stations, and be circumspect.   *Exeunt* Guard.

Philenzo. Noble sir, you are the only man I have ambition to honour.

Perenotto. I should be proud to merit such a phrase.

Philenzo. 'Tis in your power to oblige my soul – we're private;   150
   I am jealous of the wind lest it convey
   Our noise too far. This morn I had some traffic
   With a jeweller and, if my judgement err not,
   He's richly furnished me.
   What says your lordship to this diamond?   155

Perenotto. 'Tis a glorious one.

Philenzo. Does it not sparkle most divinely, signor?
   A row of these stuck in a lady's forehead
   Would make a Persian stagger in his faith

---

126. wilt] G; woo't Q.   128SD] *This ed.*; *not in* Q.   130. thou'lt] *This ed.*;
thou wilt G; thou't Q.   131SD] G *(subst.)*; *not in* Q.   136SD] *This ed.*; *not in* Q.
138. on's] Q; of his G.   144SD] G; *not in* Q.   144. won't] *This ed.*; wo'not Q.
154. He's] *This ed.*; H'as Q.

135. *pensioner*] paid or hired soldier (*OED* I.1). The term was frequently used in
the seventeenth century, as here, to suggest one with base motives.

138. *on's*] of his consciences.

152. *traffic*] See 112 above.

159. *Persian . . . faith*] Persians were thought to worship the sun.

And give more adoration to this light   160
Than to the sunbeam. I ha' fellows to 'em –
A nest of bright ones.
Perenotto. This box is studded like a frosty night with stars.
Philenzo. You have outbid their value. Make me a gainer
In changing them for your commends.   165
Perenotto. How, sir?
Philenzo. I'm serious.
Perenotto. I never shall deserve this bounty. If
You'd point me out some service to begin my gratitude –
Philenzo. You have a noble soul;   170
I'll teach you how to merit more.
Perenotto. I am covetous of such a knowledge.
Philenzo. Make but my path a smooth one to the princess –
I am brief: you know my undertaking.
Perenotto. So I should be a traitor.   175
Philenzo. It comes not near the question of a life: do't, I'll enable you
to buy another dukedom, state, and title.
Perenotto. Although 'twere necessary in the affairs
Of such high consequence to deliberate,
Yet, for this once, I'll be as brief as you: 180
I won't do't.
Philenzo. How?
Perenotto. No, indeed, signor. You shall pardon me
At this time, and I'll keep your jewels too,
For they are gifts. Hereafter you will know me,   185
So fare you well, sir.   *Exit.*
Philenzo. Was I not told this officer was corrupt?
I want faith to believe the miracle.
Sure he does but jest with me, ha?

Enter MORELLO, DONDOLO, [*and*] GRUTTI.

Morello. The guard will accept no money.   190
Dondolo. What an age do we live in, when officers will take no bribes.
Grutti. Not the golden one.
Dondolo. Here's Rolliardo.
Philenzo. I'm quite lost.
Grutti. 'Tis he.   195
Philenzo. Yet he keeps my jewels; there may be some hope.

---

161. 'em –] *This ed.; not in* Q.   164SP] *G; assigned to Per* Q.   173. princess –] *G
(subst.);* Princesse, Q.   181. won't] *This ed.;* wo'not Q.   196. keeps] Qc *(subst.);*
keepe Qu.

---

165. commends] commendations (*OED* 2); cf. Heywood, *Fair Maid of the West*
(1631), 2.302: 'To vouchsafe some few commends / Before his death.'

I'll to him again. 'Tis but his modesty
At first not to seem easy; he must be courted.
Statesmen, like virgins, first should give denial;
Experience and opportunity make the trial –   200
Save you, gallants!
Morello. And you go there to. Save yourself, you are in a worse pickle
    then we are.
Dondolo. And how is't wi' ye, signor?
Grutti. Do you thrive in your hopes?   205
Philenzo. I do not despair, gentlemen. You see, I do not wear my hat
    in my eyes, crucify my arms, or entreat your lordships' brain to
    melt in a petition for me.
Morello. I did but jest. I know you have a way to the wood in your
    pericranium. What is't? We are honest, simple-minded lords.   210
Philenzo. I think so.
Grutti. Nay, nay, impart.
Dondolo. We tell no tales.
Morello. Would we were whipped and we do.
Philenzo. Why shall I tell you? You are three –   215
Morello. Very secret –
Philenzo. Coxcombs.
All. How?
Philenzo. A miserable leash of court mimics.
Morello. 'Mimics', what's that?   220
Philenzo. You perfumed goats!
Morello. Oh, is that it? I never heard what a mimic was before.
Philenzo. D' ye think I am so wretched in a point that concerns my life
    and honour to trust my ways and purposes to you that have no
    souls?   225
Dondolo. No souls?
Morello. Peace, how comes he to know that?
Grutti. Why hast thou none?

---

204. wi' ye] *This ed.;* with you G; wee Q.   205. hopes?] Qc; hopes. Qu.
215. you?] G; you – Q.   215. three –] G; three. Q.   223. D' ye] *This ed.:* Dee Q.

206–7. *wear . . . eyes*] commonly read as a sign of despair.
207. *crucify . . . arms*] cross my arms. A sign of resignation. OED notes this as the
only instance of this usage (4).
209. *way . . . wood*] Proverbial; 'There be more ways to the wood than one' (Dent
W179); cf. Middleton, *Family of Love* 3.4.3.
210. *pericranium*] brain, as a seat of thought (OED 2b).
217. *Coxcombs*] Fools (OED 3); cf. *Oth.* 5.2.234.
219. *leash*] set of three, originally a sporting term used of hounds, etc. (OED 2).
221. *perfumed*] musk and civet were commonly used as perfumes at court.
goats] renowned as lascivious creatures.

Morello. 'Twas more than ever I could see in myself yet.

Philenzo. Things that have forfeited their creation, and had not your   230
    tailors took compassion on you, you had died to all men's
    thoughts, who long since would ha' forgotten that ever there were
    such things in nature.

Dondolo. Shall we suffer this?

Philenzo. Yes, and make legs in token of your thankfulness. If I were   235
    at leisure, I would make you show tricks now –
                               [*Seizes Morello and squeezes him.*]

Morello. Do I look like a Johnanapes?

Philenzo. But I won't.

Morello. It were not your best course.

Philenzo. How?   240

Morello. Alas, sir, I should but shame myself, and be laughed at afore
    all this company.

Philenzo. When you see me next avoid me, as you would do your poor
    kindred when they come to court. Get you home, say your prayers,
    and wonder that you come off without beating, for 'tis one of my   245
    miracles.   [*Exit.*]

Morello. Had we not better a' gone to tavern, as I plotted at first? He
    could not ha' been more valiant in his drink.

Grutti. I'm glad he's gone.

Dondolo. I know not what to make on him.   250

Morello. 'Make on him', quotha? He made little reckoning of us but,
    and he had not gone as he did, I should ha' made –

Dondolo. What?

Morello. Urine in my breeches – he squeezed me. I think I was ready
    to melt o' both sides.   255

Grutti. But hark you, signor, we forget the ladies still.

Morello. Well remembered.

Dondolo. Let's consult to purpose about that, shall we?

Morello. No, every one think what he can by himself. My thoughts
    shall be private and not free at this time; every one scratch his own   260
    head.

Grutti. And he that gets the first hint, communicate –

---

236. now –] *This ed.; now. Q.*   236SD] *G (subst.); not in Q.*   238. won't] *This ed.;*
wo'not *Q.*   246SD] *G; not in Q.*   247SP] *Q; Dond. G.*   247. to tavern] *Q (subst.);*
to a tavern *G.*   249. I'm] *G;* Im'e *Q.*   252. made –] *G;* made *Q.*   255. melt o'] *This
ed.;* melt on *G;* melt'o, *Q.*   258. that,] *This ed.;* that – *Q.*

  235. *make legs*] bow.

  237. *Johnanapes*] Jackanapes; applied pejoratively to a person in order to imply
apelike behaviour. This is *OED*'s first recorded usage of the rarer form.

  251. *quotha?*] said he?

Dondolo. A match.
Morello. Let me see – umh.
Dondolo. What if I did – nothing; my brains are dull.   265
Grutti. Ten to one, but if I did – let it alone, a pox on't. I were best
   drink some sack; they say it helps invention.
Morello. O rare!
Both. Rub, rub; out with it.
Morello. No, 'tis gone back again. I drunk buttered sack this morning   270
   and it slipped back when 'twas almost at my tongue's end – but it
   was a delicate project, whatsoever it was.
Grutti. Recover it with thy finger.
Dondolo. Follow it, Morello.
Morello. Now, now, now, let me alone – make no noise, 'tis coming   275
   again. I ha't! I ha't! –
Dondolo. Hold it fast now!
Grutti. Lose it not! Thou art great with wit, let us deliver thee. What
   is't?
Morello. Some wiser than some.   280
                    They follow him up and down for discovery.
Dondolo. Wilt not tell us?
Grutti. Didst not promise?
Morello. No haste – as occasion serves – it cost more than so, yet you
   may know't.
Dondolo. Well said.   285
Morello. Hereafter, but not now – away, do not tempt me; I will eat
   the sweat of my own brain. O rare! Never was such a strain of
   wit invented! D' ye hear, gentlemen? If you will command me
   any service to the ladies, I do purpose to visit 'em with quirk –
   hey!   290
Grutti. How?
Morello. Marry, do I.
Dondolo. Nay, Morello.

281SD] *in right margin in* Q.   288. D' ye] *This ed.*; Dee Q.   290. hey!] G; hey.
Q.

263. *match*] compact, bargain (*OED* 11).
267. *sack*] generic term for a class of white wine formerly imported from Spain and
the Canary Islands (*OED* 1a); cf. *The Wild-Goose Chase* 1.1.107; *TwN* 2.3.206.
269. *Rub, rub*] Stir up the memory or recollection (*OED* 2b); cf. Lyly, *Euphues* 248:
'I will rub my memory.'
270. *buttered*] served with butter (*OED* 2b).
273.] Rub the brain and so stir up the recollection; see 2.1.269.
278. *Thou ... thee*] playing on the idea of being pregnant with thought.
283. *more than so*] much to think of.
289. *with quirk*] with, or by means of, a trick (*OED* 4).

Morello. Gentlemen, as I told you, if you have anything to the ladies,
    before I go, I am the messenger – there is a crotchet and so forth;   295
    a carwhichet is found out – your ears – I will do such a stratagem
    as never the like was heard of in the world. O rare! –   *Exit.*
Dondolo. He's mad!
Grutti. So am I, that he is so reserved. What shall's do?

Enter BONAMICO, *disguised.*

Bonamico. Save you, signors; pray, whereabouts is the sign of the invis-   300
    ible man?
Dondolo and Grutti. The invisible man?
Bonamico. Cry you mercy, now I see it.

Exit [*entering into the house*].

Dondolo. See't? He does more than we can. The gentleman's mistaken;
    here's no such sign, yet he went in there.   305
Grutti. He has better eyes than we to distinguish it –

Enter [CARLO], *disguised.*

Carlo. This, ay, this is it.
Dondolo. What is it, pray?
Carlo. What's that to you?
Grutti. In courtesy we ask.   310
Carlo. Then, by the sign, this is the house, whither I am going to
    enquire for a gentleman that teaches men to walk invisible.
Grutti. That would be seen; this is news.
Carlo. News? Either you have slept long, or you are gentlemen of very
    small intelligence; examine the next paper you see advanced and   315
    inform yourselves. Farewell, gallants.

Exit [*entering into the house*].

Dondolo. He's entered there too.
Grutti. Teach men to walk invisible! A very fine trade.
Dondolo. Would 'twere true; we should desire no other device to get
    in to the ladies.   320

---

297. rare! –] G; rare. – Q.   299SD] Qc; *Enter Bonanico. Qu; Enter* BONAMICO, *in
another habit.* G.   303SD] *This ed.; Exit.* Q; *Enters the house.* G.   306SD] *This ed.;
Enter Servant to Bon: disguised.* Q; *Enter* CARLO. G.   308. pray?] Qc; pray. *Qu.*
316SD] *This ed.; Exit.* Q; *Enters the house.* G.

295. *crotchet*] whimsical fancy (*OED* 9a).
296. *carwhichet*] pun, quibble, or conundrum; cf. Jonson, *Bart. Fair* 5.1.69.
299. *reserved*] secretive (about his plan).
300–01. *whereabouts . . . man*] Gifford's suggestion that the sign should be visible
on stage is surely misleading as Dondolo and Grutti should not be able to see it in this
exchange (see, e.g., 2.1.305), enhancing their perception of Bonamico's powers.

Enter BONAMICO *and* [CARLO] *in other disguises.*
[*They pass over the stage and enter the house.*]

Grutti. 'Tis impossible. See, see, more gentlemen. Prithee, let's to him;
this will be a trick worth our learning.

Dondolo. Stay, we are not acquainted. Let's knock first.   [*Knocks.*]

Enter [CARLO, *disguised*].

Carlo. Your pleasures, gentlemen?
Dondolo. Pray, sir, what sign is this?   325
Carlo. The invisible man, sir.
Grutti. Man? I see no man.
Dondolo. Here's nothing but a cloud.
Carlo. Right, sir, and he's behind it: the man's invisible.
Dondolo. Pretty faith; it may be the man i' the moon for ought we   330
know.
Carlo. Would ye anything with my master?
Grutti. He does teach to walk invisible, they say.
Carlo. He is the only professor of the miraculous invisible art.
Dondolo. May we change a little discourse with him?   335
Carlo. There are some gentlemen with him, but I'll tell him – I am pre-
vented: he's coming forth himself.

Enter BONAMICO [*in his mountebank disguise*].

Dondolo. Signor Altomaro, I take it.
Bonamico. 'Tis my name, sir. A poor artist, not warm in these parts of
Italy.   340
Grutti. And you were not too busy, sir –
Bonamico. Please you, walk in. I am now alone; your persons will grace
my poor habitation.
Dondolo. We saw four or five enter but now.

320SD] *This ed.; Enter Bonamico and Seruant in other disguises. Qc; Enter Bonanico
and Seruant. Qu;* BONAMICO *and* CARLO *pass over the stage, in other dresses, and
enter the house. G.*   321. him;] *G;* him, *Qc;* him *Qu.*   323. acquainted.] *This ed.;*
acquainted, *Qc;* acquainted *Qu;* acquainted; *G.*   323SD *Knocks.*] *G;* omitted in *Q.*
323SD *Enter . . . disguised*] *G; Enter Seruant. Q.*   325. sign] *G;* signes *Q.*   325.
this?] *Qc;* this. *Qu.*   330. faith;] *G;* faith, *Qc;* faith *Qu.*   333SP] *Q (Gurt.).*   336.
him,] *G;* him – *Q.*   336. him –] *G;* him, *Q.*   336–7. prevented:] *Qc (subst.);*
preuented, *Qu.*   337SD] *G; Enter Bonamico. Q.*

---

328. Senescu speculates that this could imply a sign with a cloud painted on it being
present on stage, but it is more likely that the term means 'Here's nothing but the sky'.
330. *man . . . moon*] proverbial for a fanciful or preposterous idea.
335. *change . . . discourse*] See 1.1.9.
338. *Altomaro*] 'Deep sea'. Senescu conjectures that this is a reference to Bonamico's home in southern Italy, near the Meditarranean. Presumably Dondolo addresses
him by this name because he has seen the posted advertisements referred to at 2.1.5.
339–40. *not warm . . . Italy*] i.e. in the colder north in which Mantua is located.

Bonamico. I ha' dispatched 'em. They are fresh departed.   345
Dondolo. Which way?
Grutti. Here's not a man. Are they not sunk? Came they out here?
Bonamico. Upon my credit, sir, no other way.
Dondolo. Then they went invisible.
Bonamico. Right, sir; they came hither to that purpose. Their designs   350
required haste.
Grutti. This man can do't; I see already.
Dondolo. Sir, if you can assure us this invisible walking, for we are not
so ignorant as we seem: we ha' seen the play of *The Invisible
Knight*, and –   355
Bonamico. That of *The Ring* too, ha' ye not?
Dondolo. Yes.
Bonamico. The one was magic and t' other an imposture. What I do
is by art fair and natural. Are you in debt and fear arresting? You
shall save your money in protections, come up to the face of a   360
sergeant, nay walk by a shoal of these mankind horse-leeches,
and be mace-proof. If you have a mind to rail at 'em, or kick some
o' their loose flesh out, they shall not say 'blacks your eye', nor
with all their lynxes' eyes discover you. Would you see within the
mercer's abroad, how his man plays the merchant at home with   365
his mistress Silkworm, and deals underhand for commodity?
Would yourself talk with a lady in secret, sit down, play with her,
ravish a diamond from her finger, and bind her soft wrist with a

352. do't;] *This ed.*; doot *Q*; do it, *G*.   352. see already] *Q*; see, already. *G*.
363. o'] *This ed.*; a *Q*.   363. shall not] *G*; shannot *Q*.   364. lynxes'] *G (subst.)*;
linces *Q*.

354-5. The Invisible Knight] This text has not been traced.
356. The Ring] Robert Dodsley conjectured this play was *The Two Merry Milk-
maids* (1620) (*Select Collection of Old Plays*, London, 1745).
360. *protections*] money paid usually to criminals on a regular basis to purchase
security.
361. *mankind*] furious (possibly from 'mankeen' meaning fierce or savage).
horse-leeches] literally 'blood-suckers', therefore rapacious or intractable individuals (*OED*, 3). Cf. *The Lady of Pleasure* 3.2.284.
362. *mace-proof*] safe from arrest (although *OED* only records this sense from the
nineteenth century). A mace was a staff of office.
363. *they ... eye*] they shall not find any accusation against you; cf. Jonson, *The
Staple of News* Act 1, Intermean, 25.
364. *lynxes' eyes*] Lynxes were renowned for keen sight (*OED* 1b).
365. *mercer's*] one who deals in textiles and fabrics, especially a dealer in silks,
velvets, and other costly materials (*OED* 1a).
365-6. *how ... commodity?*] how his servant deceives him by sleeping with the
mercer's wife ('mistress Silkworm') and steals his goods (sexual and material) from him
while he is away.

bracelet; kiss her abroad, at home, before her servants, in the
presence of her jealous husband, nay, truss her up when the tame   370
lord is abed with her, and to his eyes be undiscovered as the wind,
signor? Do you suspect your mistress plays double? Would you
hear how she entertains the t' other's love, and know what she does
i' the closet with the smooth page? Would you be present at secret
counsels, betray letters, see how such a lord paints his thighs, this   375
perfume his breath, t' other marshal his fine French teeth; see this
statesman's eyes put out with a bribe; how that officer cozens the
duke, and his secretary abuses 'em both; this lawyer takes fees o'
both sides, while the judge examines the fertility and price of the
manor before the witnesses and then decrees who shall have the   380
land? Would you see justice employ her scales to weigh light gold
that comes in for fees or corruption and flourish with her sword
like a fencer to make more room for causes i' the court?

Dondolo. All this and more may be done if we can but go invisible;
but how can you assure us of that?   385

Grutti. I would fain see any man go invisible once.

Bonamico. See him, sir?

Grutti. Video pro intelligo, I mean, sir.

Bonamico. Nay, sir, you need not distinguish; for it is possible to see a
man invisible. Observe me: you see me now perfectly in every part;   390
if I should walk before you without a body –

Grutti. How?

Bonamico. My head only visible and hanging in the air like a comet.

Dondolo. That were a strange sight!

Bonamico. Sometimes nothing shall be seen but my arm; another while   395
one of my legs, hopping without a body.

Grutti. This is admirable.

Bonamico. When I please I will have nothing conspicuous but my hand,
nay, perhaps my little finger.

Dondolo. Do not you conjure then?   400

Grutti. Come, you will cast a mist before our eyes.

Bonamico. 'Tis a mystery, indeed, but a safe one, signors.

---

373. entertains the t' other's] *Q (subst.)*; entertains t'other's *G.*   386SP] *Senescu; not
in Q and line assigned to Don.*

---

370. *truss . . . up*] tie her up (with the implication of sexual bondage).
374. *smooth*] free from hairs or bristles (*OED* 2a).
375. *paints . . . thighs*] wears exotic leggings.
376. *French teeth*] Possibly a figurative reference to speaking in affected French.
French fashions were commonly aped at court.
381. *light gold*] below the standard, legal weight (i.e. forged) (*OED* I.1b).
388. *Video . . . intelligo*] Lat. 'I see for I know'.
400. *conjure*] play tricks.

Dondolo. Why, look you, sir, if you will be pleased that we may see
  you first walk invisible, we shall not only credit your art, but at
  any rate be ambitious to be your disciples.   405
Bonamico. Why, gentlemen, you speak but justice; you shall have
  experiment. I will be invisible first, but as to other in this kind, I
  will not demonstrate without half in hand. Let me have fifty crowns
  apiece, I'll 'point you a day when I will be invisible.
Grutti. Can you not do it presently?   410
Bonamico. I can be invisible in a twinkling, but what assurance can
  you have, that I am here at the same instant? When you see no
  part of me, I may deceive you.
Dondolo. He says true.
Bonamico. I do purpose therefore to give you reality and proof, for I   415
  will walk invisible all but – my hand.
Both. Your hand?
Bonamico. Only my hand. You shall touch it, see every line in't, and
  the rest of my body be to you invisible. This will require a little
  time for preparation, and when, with the consent of your eyes   420
  and understandings, I keep my promise in this point, you will think
  your moneys well expended to be taught the mystery.
Dondolo. This is very fair.
Grutti. The crowns shall be ready, sir.
Dondolo. Expect 'em within this hour.   425

           Enter [PHILENZO *disguised as*] ROLLIARDO.

Bonamico. At your own pleasures – Ha, Rolliardo? – [*Aside to
  Dondolo and Grutti*] I must not be seen, gentlemen.   *Exit.*
Grutti. Farewell, incomparable signor. What luck had we to light upon
  this artist! He shall not publish it; we'll buy the whole secret at
  any value, and then get him remove into some other province.   430
  Who's this?
Philenzo. Am not I mad? Sure I am, though I do not know it, and all
  the world is but a Bedlam, a house of correction to whip us into
  our senses. I ha' known the time when jewels and gold has some

---

405. disciples] *Qc (subst.)*; Disciple *Qu*.   407. to other] *Qc*; t'other *Qu, G.*   424.
shall be] *Qc*; are *Qu, G.*   426–7SD *Aside.*] *G; not in Q.*   428SP] *This ed.*; *Both Q.*

409. *'point*] appoint.
410. *presently*] immediately.
429. *publish*] make it known publicly (*OED* I.1a).
430. *remove*] move.
433. *Bedlam*] Hospital of St Mary of Bethlehem, London. Founded as a priory in
1247, it became a hospital in 1330 and in 1407 a hospital for lunatics.
433–4. *whip . . . senses*] a figurative statement that nevertheless has its roots in the
harsh treatment of insanity in the seventeenth century.

virtue in 'em. The generation of men now are not subject to cor-   435
ruption: Democritus, the world's refined!
Dondolo. 'Tis Rolliardo! He looks melancholy; let's have a fling at him.
Give you joy of the great lady, sir! Which is the next way to the
moon, pray?
Philenzo. Bolt upright, musk-cat, and if you make haste you may be   440
one of her calves. Next time she appears, you shall see her beckon
to you with a pair of horns just o' the size of those are preparing
for your forehead, my precious animal.
Dondolo. Ha, ha, ha! The fellow's mad!
Grutti. Can you tell, sir, what became of all the swallows, cuckoos, and   445
small birds we had here last summer?
Philenzo. Marry, sir, they went to sea to aid the cranes and there have
been mustering ever since; but for want of a woodcock they ha'
left behind 'em, they dare not venture upon the pygmies. You may
do well to overtake the buzzard and relieve the army, sir.   450

---

442. o'] *This ed.*; a *Q.*

---

436. *Democritus*] Greek philosopher of the fifth century BC who was known as the
'laughing philosopher', a reference to his sceptical method of laughing at everything.

437. *melancholy*] one of the four primary humours (along with blood, phlegm, and
choler), an imbalance of which in the individual was believed to cause or promote
certain temperaments. Robert Burton's monumental treatise on the subject, *The
Anatomy of Melancholy*, first published in 1621, went through several editions (the
third edition was published in 1628). The figure of the melancholic, usually dressed in
black and depicted in a state of contemplation, was regularly satirised on the early
modern stage.

440. *musk-cat*] civet cat, an animal from which musk was obtained for use in perfumes. The phrase was frequently used as a term of reproach to a fop: cf. Philenzo's
comment at 2.1.221. See also, *AWW* 5.2.21; Shirley's *A Contention for Honour and
Riches* (1633) 6.302.

441. *one . . . calves*] i.e. a mooncalf; the phrase was idiomatic for a fool or someone
born with an undeveloped brain. Cf. *Temp.* 2.2.104, and Jonson's character of the same
name in *Bart. Fair.*

442. *pair . . . horns*] proverbial horns of a cuckold.

445-6. *swallows / . . . birds*] Senescu conjectures this is a reference to cuckoldry
extending the allusions at 2.1.441-3. Cuckolds were proverbially referred to as 'summer
birds' and cuckoos are birds renowned for laying eggs in the nests of other birds. These
lines need to be understood in the context of seventeenth-century beliefs, which did not
countenance the idea of migration.

447-9. *cranes . . . pygmies*] referring to a battle mentioned in several classical texts,
including Homer and Aristotle. Shirley may have encountered the tale in Antonio de
Torquemada's *The Spanish Mandeville of Miracles* (1618), which refers to riverside
battles where the pygmies came to destroy the nests of cranes.

448. *woodcock*] fool or gull (because woodcocks were easily caught in snares).

450. *overtake . . . army*] The buzzard is a predatory bird. Philenzo may be
suggesting that, by overtaking it, Dondolo and Grutti could save the smaller birds,

Grutti. Ha, ha, ha!   *Exeunt* [DONDOLO *and* GRUTTI].
Philenzo. I shall be grinned to death as I walk the streets – 'Tis no
policy to be dull and modest. But, let me see, which way to compass
my work and put myself out of the common laughter? The very
children will jeer me shortly, I think, and point me out with stones: 455
'the precious undertaker'. I might have had more wit than to run
myself into this calamity. Who have we next?

Enter the DUKE, AMBASSADOR, FULVIO, DONDOLO,
GRUTTI, *Attendants* [and] Courtiers.

The duke? What stranger's that? I must not seem dejected.
Ambassador. Is this he your highness discoursed of?
Duke. This is the piece made up of all performance,   460
The man of any thing, without exception.
Give him but gold, kings' daughters, and their heirs,
Though locked in towers of brass, are not safe from him.
Nay, though I play the chemist with my trust
And from a million of sure confidences   465
I draw the spirit of honesty into a few,
He can corrupt 'em.
Philenzo. You are my prince, great sir, and you have spoke
Not much unlike a brave one.
Dondolo. He'll jeer the duke too –   470
Philenzo. If my head
Come to be paid to you before sunset
That day when it is forfeit, I ha' cleared with you
And shall depart out of your royal debt.
There's all you can demand; a good, sharp sword   475
Will make an even reckoning.
Ambassador. He seems confident.
1 Courtier. With your grace's leave, let me come to him.
Philenzo. Now, a fierce dog.
1 Courtier. What came into thy mind, thou daring madman –   480
fool is a word of favour to thee –
Philenzo. So, sir.

451SD] *G; Exit. Q.*   454. laughter?] *G;* laughter *Q.*

---

but there is also a sense in which he is suggesting they are vultures themselves by this
comparison.
   456. *precious*] worthless, good-for-nothing (*OED* 4b); cf. Fletcher, *The Mad Lover*
(1619) 3.3.
   undertaker] See 41 above.
   462–3. *kings' . . . brass*] a further allusion to the Jupiter-Danae myth.
   464. *play the chemist*] play the alchemist (by sublimating my trust). The tower in
which Eugenia (and Danae before her) is imprisoned relates to the symbolism of towers
in alchemy which often represented the site for experimentation and transformation,
extending the significance of gold in both narratives.

1 Courtier. To undertake such an impossible task?
Philenzo. Mushroom, I'll cast away a few words on thee.
    Had I another life, I'd undertake yet,   485
    Though I be low in all opinion,
    To venture it, with the riches I have spread
    To corrupt others, to make thee my parasite;
    I would engage my life to wear no steps
    To thy white daughter. Thou and thy grave matron   490
    Most humbly should present her, when I was pleased to,
    For fear I should refuse the sport you brought me.
Duke. I never knew man bear his scorn so high: to him, some other.
Grutti. Not I, sir; you shall excuse me, 'twas the last thing I did.
2 Courtier. In the position general, I'll not touch him,   495
    For money may be said to purchase all things
    But to aspire to my good sovereign's daughter
    Of blessed memory –
Philenzo. She's not dead, I hope?
2 Courtier. There gold and trash was impudently inferred   500
    And 'twas a task too insolent; in that point
    You'd willingly give a pound of your proud flesh,
    To be released.
Philenzo. I heard a pound of flesh a Jew's demand once –
    'Twas gravely now remembered of your lordship. Released?   505
    Fortune and courtesy of opinion
    Gives many men nobility of birth
    That never durst do nobly, nor attempt
    Any design, but fell below their honours.
    Cased up in chambers, scarcely air themselves   510
    But at a horse-race or i' th' Park with puppets.

---

484. Mushroom,] G; Mushroumpe – Q.   490. daughter. Thou] *This ed.*; daughter, thou Q.   496. money] Qc; *many* Qu.   497. aspire to my] Qc; aspire my Qu.   500. There] Qc; Theyr Qu.

---

484. *Mushroom*] person who has suddenly sprung into notice, an upstart; frequently used in early Stuart drama to refer to someone who has purchased their nobility following James I's sale of titles to bolster a bankrupt treasury.

490. *white*] pure, virginal.

492. *For . . . me*] 'Out of anxiety I should decline the [marital] match you proposed.' Philenzo's use of the contemptuous phrase 'sport' to refer to the courtier's daughter concurs with the role of cynical misogynist he is performing.

502. *pound . . . flesh*] invoking the plotline of Shylock and the pound of flesh in *MerVen.*, as Philenzo makes explicit at 504 below.

511. *horse-race*] Horse-races were becoming highly fashionable pursuits in the Caroline period. See, e.g., 4.3 in Shirley's *Hyde Park* (1632).

Park . . . puppets] Puppet plays performed in canvas booths in parks and fairs were a common form of entertainment in the seventeenth century; cf. Jonson, *Bart. Fair*, Act 5; Shirley, *The Lady of Pleasure* 3.2.230–6. Like horse-races, they were common in Hyde Park, which is therefore the likely specific reference here.

That for which I'm your laughter – I speak to
You, flattering tribe of courtiers, to you, glow-worms –
Is my chief glory. That, perhaps, being sprung
From humble parentage, dare yet attempt   515
A deed so far above me, that sets all
Your wisdoms in combustion. You may think
I've made a sorry bargain for my life:
Let scorners know in aiming at her only,
My memory after death receives more honour   520
Than all your marble pinnacles can raise you,
Or alabaster figures, whiter far
Than e'er your souls were; and, that hour I die,
If you dare look upon me without fainting –
Which I much fear – you shall see death so scorned,   525
I mean for any terror, you shall think him
My slave to take my upper garment off.
Dondolo. I told your highness how you should find him.
Ambassador. A brave resolution.
Duke. Be this the prologue to the mirth, my lord   530
Attends to entertain you; set on, we'll leave him. Ha, ha, ha!
                    Exeunt [all but PHILENZO *as* ROLLIARDO,
                    [*who*] *pulls* FULVIO *back.*
Philenzo. Sir, I observed you noble and not apt
To throw derision on me with the rest,
Which does encourage me to ask you a question.
Fulvio. Name it, sir.   535
Philenzo. Pray, what stranger's that walked with the duke?
Fulvio. 'Tis an ambassador from Florence, sir.
Philenzo. An ambassador? His design, I pray?
Fulvio. To treat of marriage betwixt our princess
And the great duke's son, desired much by our master 540
Who has some hope 'twill be effected too.
He's brought rich presents to her.
Philenzo. This is all?

---

524. fainting –] *This ed.*; fainting, Q.   525. Which . . . fear –] *This ed.*; (Which . . .
fear) Q.   531SD] G; *Exeunt. Roll. pulls Fulvio backe.* Qc; *Florish. in left margin.
Exeunt. Roll. pulls Fulvio backe. in right margin.* Qu.

513. *glow-worms*] (applied contemptuously to individuals in the seventeenth
century).
521–2. *marble . . . figures*] common forms of funerary monument in the period. Cf.
Philenzo imagining his own monument at 561–2.
527. *upper garment*] the body, clothing of the soul. Cf. Shirley, *The Wedding* (1629)
4.4.

Fulvio. You have it freely.   *Exit.*

Philenzo. You've honoured me – married to Tuscany? So, if my ambi-   545
tion had been fortunate, I might have been his taster; but my stars
want influence, they are too dull and weary of my fate. Rolliardo
then must forfeit. Why that's the worst on't: I will make a glorious blaze in death and, while I live, make the duke's treasure pay
for't; nor shall he accuse me, I exhaust him poorly. I'll study out   550
some noble way to build me a remembrance. Ha! – A church or
college? Tedious; my glass has but few sands: I must do something
I may live to finish. I ha't: I will send to all the prisons i' th' city
and pay the poor men's debts for 'em; the world wants such a
precedent. I ha' money enough since I fail in my other ends. I will   555
do some good deeds before I die, so shall I be more sure of prayers
than if I built a church, for they are not certain to continue
their foundation. Fate, I despise thee. I sink under no cheap and
common action, but sell my life to fame, in catching my death by
so brave an aspiring.   560
    If I obtain a monument, be this all,
    Write on my grave: *This man climbed high to fall.*   *Exit.*

---

555. precedent] Q (President).   562. Write] Q; Writ G.

547. dull] inert, inactive.
552. *glass . . . sands*] proverbial reference to time as sand slipping through an hour-
glass (Dent G132).
562. This . . . fall.] Proverbial (Dent C413: 'Hasty climbers have sudden falls').

ACT 3

Enter Guard.

1 Guard. Come, gentlemen, we must watch still, that none run away
   with the princess.
2 Guard. He must have an excellent stomach, that can break these
   stone walls to come to her.
3 Guard. Beside this moveable wall of flesh which we carry.   5
2 Guard. One makes towards us – 'tis a lady.

Enter MORELLO, [*disguised*] *like a lady.*

Morello. So, now am I as valiant as Hercules, when he turned spinster!
   Great Jupiter, the patron of scapes, assist my petticoat, and, at my
   return, I will sacrifice my linen breeches to thee – here be the men,
   the men of mettle. Now, Venus, I beseech thee, and they be men,   10
   they will let a lady enter without many questions.
1 Guard. Save you, sweet lady; your affair's this way?
Morello. I go but in to the princess.
2 Guard. From whom?
Morello. From the duke's grace.   15
1 Guard. What may be your ladyship's name?
Morello. [*Aside*] I never thought to give myself a name! – [*To Guard*]
   my name is Madam – um . . . My name is something, an odd name,
   but – I do not stand upon't – my name's Thorn.
1 Guard. Indeed, Madam Thorn, if his grace have sent you to such a   20

---

7. valiant] Qc; *turned* 'n' Qu.   7. spinster] spnister Q.   17SD *Aside*] *This ed.; not
in* Q.   17SD *To Guard*] *This ed.; not in* Q.   19, 20. Thorn] G; *Thorne* Q.

---

3. *have . . . stomach*] be brave.
   7. *valiant . . . spinster*] Hercules, whose bravery was legendary, fell in love with Iole,
princess of Oechalia, but in pursuit of her killed her brother. He did penance for this
crime by being enslaved to Omphale, queen of Libya, who dressed him as a woman
and made him spin wool.
   8. *Jupiter . . . scapes*] Morello compares his disguise in a romantic cause to Jupiter's
metamorphoses in pursuit of sexual encounters with Io, Leda, Europa, etc. The intertextual relevance of the Danae story surfaces again here. Thomas Heywood's 1611 play
The Golden Age re-enacted Jupiter's seduction of Danae. In 1623 a version of this play
conflated with Heywood's *The Silver Age* was performed at the Cockpit theatre (the
same theatre in which *The Bird in a Cage* was first performed) under the title *The
Escapes of Jupiter* (Bawcutt, p. 87 (No. 50)).
   scapes] transgressions, especially breaches of chastity (Onions); cf. *WT* 3.3.70.

216

purpose, you must show something for our discharge.

Morello. Why, hark you, it was but forgotten of the duke to send his
signet – but I ha' brought some of his highness' deputies wi' me, I
hope that will satisfy.

As he takes out money, [he] discovers [his] breeches.

2 Guard. By this gold, breeches!   25
3 Guard. No, they are but silk – here will be sport; I have a hint already.
1 Guard. Say you so? 'Tis very well – but, madam, we are many, and
we would be loath to venture – deal ingeniously, sweet lady, have
you no more gold in your breeches?
Morello. Not a doit, as I am virtuous and sinful.   30
1 Guard. Pass – but d' ye hear? – and you should not be secret now.
Morello. As I am a gentleman.
3 Guard. A gentleman? Dost hear him? I'll put him to't.
Morello. I have left some crowns with your fellow.
2 Guard. Tush, that won't satisfy me.   35
Morello. Indeed, I ha' no more money.
2 Guard. You have commodity. Hang this transitory gold – give me . . .
[*Tugs at Morello's gloved hand.*] What's this?
Morello. Nothing but a wart o' my little finger.
2 Guard. A wart? Let me see't.   *Pulls off his glove.*   40
Morello. 'Tis a diamond; 'twas my mother's legacy, or else . . .
2 Guard. Is it your will I should have it?
Morello. It was my mother's will I should wear it. Her ghost will haunt
me, and I should give it away.
2 Guard. You know the way back, lady.   45
Morello. You will give me my gold again?
1 Guard. Not a doit, as I am virtuous and sinful. Stand with him for
a toy, and know you've no warrant from the duke. 'Tis in our
power –
Morello. D' ye hear, sir, and it were a diamond of gold you should have   50
it.   [*Hands over the ring.*]

23. wi' me] *This ed.*; with me G; wo'mee Q.   31. d'ye] *This ed.*; d'ee Q.   33. gentleman? . . . him?] Qc; gentleman, . . . him, Qu.   35. won't] *This ed.*; wo'not Q.
38SD] *This ed.*; Feeling his hand G; omitted in Q.   39. o' my] *This ed.*; on my
G; a'my Q.   41. legacy,] G; Legacy – Q.   41. else . . .] *This ed.*; – G; else Q.
49. power –] G; power.Q.   50. D' ye] *This ed.*; D'ee Q.   51SD] *This ed.*; not in
Q.

30. *doit*] former Dutch coin, equivalent to half a farthing; used figuratively to refer
to a small sum (Onions). See also 47 below.
    41. *mother's legacy*] Wills written by women specifically intended for their children
were common in this period.
    42. *will*] (1) wish; (2) pun on the 'legacy' mentioned at 41.
    47–8. *Stand . . . toy*] Haggle with him for a trifle.
    50. *diamond . . . gold*] diamond of exceptional value (Senescu).

2 Guard. Lady, I kiss your hand.

Morello. You've kissed the ring off o' my finger, I'm sure.

2 Guard. Use your fortune, pass.

Morello. [*Aside*] If I get to the ladies, somebody shall pay for this; that's   55
my comfort.

3 Guard. Can you wrestle, madam?   *Takes him by the shoulder.*

Morello. Ah, wrestle, sir? Ladies do not use to wrestle.

3 Guard. They are thrown down with their good wills then. Come, you
and I will have a bout; I must hug your little body.   60

1 Guard. Humour him, and you're past danger.

Morello. Would you ha' me tear my clothes?

1 Guard. I'll persuade him.

2 Guard. To tell you true, madam, this fellow is an abominable lecher,
there is no 'scaping him without a fall; a very satyr, he leaps all   65
comes near him. If your ladyship's modesty can dispense with a
private favour – you understand, for our parts, we are satisfied
otherwise, and our lips are sewed up. Take him o' one side, and
see how you can mollify him. He's a cock at the game, and will
tread you, and you were ten thorns.   70

Morello. Mollify him! Doth he use ladies so? He will mollify me.

2 Guard. And you were his sister, all's one to him: the devil is not more
hot and robustious, where he finds opposition to the sport. Therefore the duke made choice of him, as suspecting some lord might
come disguised o' this fashion: to prevent dishonour to the princess   75
and ladies. Use your own discretion.

Morello. [*Aside*] What will become of me? If he be such a wencher,
he'll ravish me, and discover all; what a rascal was I to venture
thus. I'll give thee my fan to persuade him – [*Aloud*] Help, help!

3 Guard. Nay, then.   80
          He throws him down, and discovers his breeches.
Why how now? Breeches?

1 Guard. This is a man!

2 Guard. Sure, 'tis a woman!

55SD] *This ed.; not in* Q.   57SD] *Q; Takes him by the shoulders* G.   62. clothes?]
Qc; clothes. Qu.   68. up.] *This ed.; up:* G; up, *Q*   68. o' one side] *G; a 'toside* Q.
70. thorns] *G (subst.);* Thornes *Qc;* Thornes *Qu.*   71. him!...so?] *G (subst.);* him,
...so, *Q*.   73. sport.] *This ed.;* sport: *G;* sport; *Qc;* sport, *Qu.*   75. o'] *This ed.; in*
G; *a* Q.   76. ladies.] *This ed.;* ladies – *Q*.   77SD] *G; not in* Q.   79SD] *This ed.; not*
in Q.

---

65. *fall*] The figurative sense here is sexual; cf. *Rom.* 1.3.58.
satyr] half-man, half-goat, usually associated with sexual promiscuity or lechery.
leaps] copulates with (*OED* 9).
73. *robustious*] boisterous, noisy.
77. *wencher*] one who consorts with prostitutes.

Morello. To tell you true, gentlemen, I am neither a man nor a woman:
   I am an hermaphrodite.   85
1 Guard. How? An hermaphrodite? What would you do among the
   ladies then?
2 Guard. An hermaphrodite?
3 Guard. Let's search him.
Morello. Ah.   90
1 Guard. Stay, let's be advised; if he be such a monster, our best way
   is to carry him to the duke.
2 and 3 Guard. Agreed.
Morello. [*Aside*] I shall be undone. [*To Guard*] D' ye hear, noble
   friends? 'Tis but a folly to dissemble: I am no such thing, I am no   95
   hermaphrodite; I am a friend of yours.
All. Of ours?
2 Guard. Your name, I beseech you?
Morello. I did but jest all this while. The duke himself put me upon't,
   to see whether I could cozen you; my name's Morello.   100
1 Guard. Signor Morello? 'Tis not possible.
Morello. As I am virtuous, I am. I am no hermaphrodite. No matter
   for the gold or diamonds, 'tis your own. I'll acquaint his grace how
   careful I found you, and if he do not reward you beside, I'll say
   he's the poorest duke in Christendom: I'll tell him presently.   105
3 Guard. Noble signor, we'll wait upon you to him.
Morello. No, no; 'tis better for me to go alone.
1 Guard. Your pardon. You shall tell him how careful you found us;
   we'll relate to him how cunningly you carried the business.
Morello. Nay, d' ye hear, gentlemen?   110
All. It must be so, sir; come, sweet, effeminate signor!   *Exeunt.*

[3.2]

           Enter FULVIO [*and*] AMBASSADOR.

Ambassador. You've done me a noble office, signor, in this discovery:
   where now lives her banished lover?
Fulvio. My kinsman lives in Florence – but two days since I received
   letters from him.
Ambassador. In Florence too?   5
Fulvio. Sir, you may censure me,

94SD *Aside*] *This ed.; not in* Q. 94. undone.] *This ed.;* undone – Q. 94SD *To
Guard*] *This ed.; not in* Q. 94. D' ye] *This ed.;* d'yee Q. 102. hermaphrodite. No]
This ed.; hermaphrodite, no Q. 103. own.] *This ed.;* owne – Q. 110. d' ye] *This
ed.;* d'yee Q.

o.] G; *no scene division* Q.

   6. Shirley switches back to verse here presumably to indicate the shift to a courtly
setting and the more formal nature of the dialogue with the ambassador in this scene.

But my affection to the injured lord,
And not without respect unto the honour
Of your master, too, hath been the cause of
My free language.   10
Ambassador. Trust me, signor,
We are all engaged to study you a recompense.
But Mantua was unjust to banish him
For being too much a servant.
Fulvio. Sir, when princes resolve to punish –   15
Ambassador. Virtue shall be treason.
'Twas tyranny – why now is she thus caged?
Fulvio. I can conjecture nothing but his jealousy,
Which will be ever active; by that love
We interchanged at Pisa, when we grew   20
Together in our studies, I conjure
Your nobleness to silence me.
Ambassador. You will dishonour me by suspicion: I am charmed.

      Enter PERENOTTO, DONDOLO, [*and*] GRUTTI.

Perenotto. My honoured lord.
Ambassador. Signor Perenotto.   25
Fulvio. My gentle sparks.
Dondolo and Grutti. Your servants.
Fulvio. You are all courtship.
Perenotto. Is your lordship for this wonder?
Ambassador. What wonder, my lord?   30
Perenotto. These pair of gentlemen have discoursed me into admira-
    tion: there's one has undertaken to go invisible.
Ambassador. Invisible?
Perenotto. This hour expected, and in this place.
Fulvio. How?   35
Dondolo. With a trick that he has.
Fulvio. Do you believe him, gentlemen?
Grutti. You shall see't.
Dondolo. We were heretics in that point, but our understandings are
    convinced: he did demonstrate.   40
Grutti. And because you shall know the truth of his art, he will be

---

15. punish –] G; punish. Q.   21. studies,] G; studies – Q.

12. *study . . . recompense*] devise a reward for you.
23. *charmed*] cast by a spell (into silence). The terminology of magic and conjura-
tion indulged in by Fulvio and the Ambassador here (21–3) prefigures the discussion
of Bonamico's invisibility in the lines immediately following (31–48).
26. *gentle sparks*] See 1.1.9.

invisible all but his hand. What think you of that? The rarest fellow
in Christendom!
Ambassador. Nothing visible but his hand?
Dondolo. As sure as we have given him a hundred crowns in hand.   45
Ambassador. Why is not the duke presented with this novelty?
Dondolo. He's travelling to the emperor first; only, as he goes, for our
sake, he will show us a figary of his art.

Enter [PHILENZO *disguised* as] ROLLIARDO.

Here's Rolliardo. He's somewhat costive on t' other side; wants
faith.   50
Philenzo. Save you, nest of courtiers; smooth faces, rich clothes, and
sublime compliments make you amorous in sight of your ladies.
Donzel del Phebo and Rosicleer, are you there? What pestilent dis-
eases have you got, that you wear so much musk and civet about
you? O for a priest of Cupid to sacrifice you now! How your   55
breeches would burn, like incense, and your hair, disguised in sweet
powder, leave your bodies in a mist, while your bones were
inwardly consuming with the fire of Dame Venus's altar.
Dondolo. The same humorist, still.
Philenzo. I heard say, we shall have strange apparitions i' th' air, and   60
yet invisible wonders: a hand must appear as fatal to some as that
hung o'er the Capitol; for there is a suspicion some purses will be
juggled empty, and as silent as the moon: no bright Sol appearing,
not a piece of pale faced silver in your silken hemispheres.
Grutti. He is an infidel.   65

49. on t' other] G; a'tother Q.   53. Donzel . . . Phebo] *This ed.; in italics* Q.
53. Rosicleer] *This ed.; in italics* Q.

48. *figary*] vagary or eccentric act. OED provides no evidence for Shirley's spelling
variant, but Donella later deploys the plural version to mean 'dances' (3.3.24) (perhaps
playing on the additional sense of 'caprice').
49. *costive*] impervious to belief.
51. *nest*] another of Philenzo's anti-court statements, so presumably he means a
wasps' or hornets' nest.
53. *Donzel . . . Rosicleer*] Heroes of the chivalric romance *Espejo de principes y
cavelleros* by Ortuñez de Calahorra, translated into English by Margaret Tyler as *The
Mirror of Princely Deeds and Knighthood*, and published in parts between 1578 and
1601. This book was famously in Don Quixote's library of romances. It was a frequent
focus for mockery in early modern drama; see, e.g., Jonson, *New Inn* 1.6.124.
54. *musk . . . civet*] Cf. 2.1.440.
59. *humorist*] As 'Rolliardo' Philenzo plays the role of cynic; his 'humour' is that
of the melancholic and sceptic; cf. 2.1.41.
61–2. *as . . . Capitol*] an allusion to the prodigies which were said to have filled the
night sky on the eve of Julius Caesar's murder in the Roman Capitol; cf. *JC* 2.2.15–24.
63. *Sol*] (1) the sun; (2) French coin of the same name.
64. *silken hemispheres*] punning on the shape of their silk purses (Senescu).

Philenzo. Right, Yehochanan, right, my precious Jew; we are all infidel
   that won't believe the court catechism. My lord ambassador, you
   are welcome from Florence. Does the great duke pick salads still
   – I mean, continue his assize, return into his exchequer once in
   seven years the wealth of Tuscany? Vespasian was held covetous   70
   for ordaining vessels to receive the beneficial public urine, but 'tis
   heathenism among Christians not to hold *Dulcis odor lucri e re*
   qualibet.
Ambassador. He's mad!
Philenzo. Signor Perenotto, it has puzzled my understanding how you   75
   can subsist at court without making use of the common sins,
   flattery, and corruption. Take heed, you're a great man, and 'tis
   ominous to die in your bed: a sign your children are like to inherit
   but weak brains. Thou must go to heaven, but thy heir had rather
   thou shouldst make a journey to Erebus, for the proverb's sake: 80
   happy is that son whose father goes to the devil. Why, when comes

---

66. Yehochanan] *This ed.*; *Jehochanan Q.*   67. won't] *This ed.*; wo'not *Q.*   67 catechism.] *This ed.*; catchisme – *Q.*   68–9. still –] *This ed.*; still, *Q.*   80. proverb's] *G*;
proverbe *Q.*   81. devil.] *This ed.*; Divell. – *Q.*

---

66. *Yehochanan*] This Hebrew name appears frequently in the Bible, also occurring
in a shortened form as Johanan or John. Shirley appears to use it here as an archetypal
Jewish name, but Senescu speculates that there may be a more precise reference to
Johanan, 'one of the captains of the remnant of Judah' who refused to accept the
warning of the prophet Jeremiah that the tribe would be destroyed if it went to Egypt
(Jeremiah, 40–3). She argues that 'Johanon was the real infidel and Philenzo, by using
his name, is returning the opprobrious epithet with keen point'.
   68. *great duke*] Cosimo I (Cosimo de Medici) was the first to be titled Grand Duke
of Tuscany in 1569, but Shirley's reference does not appear to refer to a specific historical figure.
   pick salads] collect produce (used here in a financial sense)
   69. *assize*] the statutory price of bread and ale.
   exchequer] government department charged with receipt and custody of revenue.
   70. *wealth . . . Tuscany*] Tuscany's wealth was legendary in the Renaissance.
   Vespasian] Titus Flavius Vespasianus, Roman emperor, AD 70–9. He put his energies into domestic government, leaving his son Titus to wage foreign wars on his behalf.
In order to improve the financial condition of Rome he renewed old taxes and insti-
tuted new ones. There may be a contemporary parallel intended by these references to
taxation to Charles I's policies during the period of Personal Rule (1629–40).
   72–3. *Dulcis . . . qualibet*] 'The smell of gain is good, come from what it may'. Vespasian is reputed to have made this reply to his son Titus when he questioned the imposition of a tax on urine (Senescu). The quotation as given in the play is deployed twice
in the correspondence of Archbishop Laud in relation to the soap monopoly: H.R.
Trevor-Roper, *Archbishop Laud, 1573–1645* (London: Macmillan, 1940), pp. 222–3.
   80. *Erebus*] Place of darkness between earth and Hades.
   81. *happy . . . devil*] Proverbial (Dent C305); cf. *3H6* 2.2.47–8.

out my Don invisible? Maybe he's here already, for we cannot
see him: what says my squirrel? Thou lookst dull and physical,
methinks; the crowns will return again invisibly, never fear it.
And how does any grave gymnosophist, whose ambition is to be regis-   85
tered an honest lord? Though thou be'st buried upon alms, carried
to church with four torches, and have an inscription on thy marble
worse than the ballad of the devil and the baker, and might be sung
to as vile a tune too. Gentlemen, I'll invite you shortly to see my
head cut off; and do only entreat you would not laugh at me when   90
I am dead. 'Twill show but poorly in you, and I shall revenge it
with my ghost-walking.

Fulvio. Either he is very confident to achieve his design, or late grown
desperate, he talks so wildly.

Dondolo. I wonder Signor Altomaro forgets us.   95

Enter [CARLO].

Now, now, ye shall hear: this is his servant. I know he is not far
off. [*To Carlo*] Where is thy master?

Carlo. He is invisible – this letter is directed to you.

[*Hands the letter to Dondolo.*]

Dondolo. [*Reads*] 'Gentlemen, that you may perceive I deal plainly
with you, I am now invisible, all but my hand; and here it is – you   100
may with ease read every line – as I promised upon the receipt of
your crowns.' – His hand?

Carlo. Ay, sir, 'tis his own hand, I can assure you.

All. Ha, ha, ha.

Dondolo. He does not mean to serve us so; thou dost but jest. Where   105
is he invisible?

89. too.] *This ed.*; too. – Q.   95SD] *This ed.*; *Enter* CARLO. *centred at l.* 100 G;
Enter Seruant. in right margin at l. 94 Q .   97SD] *This ed.*; *not in* Q.   98SD] *This
ed.*; *Gives Dondolo a letter* G; *not in* Q.   99SD] G; *The Letter.* Q.   99–102. 'Gentlemen . . . crowns.'] *This ed.*; *in italics* Q.   100. invisible,] *This ed.*; *invisible* – G;
invisible; Q.   100. is –] *This ed.*; *is*; G; *is*, Q.   101. line –] *This ed.*; *line*, Q.   102.
hand?] *This ed.*; hand! G; hand. Q.   104SP] *This ed.*; *Omnes* Q.

83. *squirrel*] epithet usually deployed as a patronising insult.
physical] full of physic; i.e. sick.
85. *gymnosophist*] member of an ancient Hindu philosophical sect whose adherents
go near-naked and are given to contemplation.
86. *upon alms*] by means of charitable funds.
86–7. *carried . . . torches*] signifiers of a pauper's funeral.
88. *ballad . . . baker*] Shirley refers to the same ballad in *Hyde Park* at 2.4: 'And then
puzzle / Your brain to make an elegy, which shall be sung / To the tune of the Devil and
the Baker; good!', but no trace of it has been found in extant ballad collections.
91–2. *revenge . . . ghost-walking*] This was a common device in revenge drama; see
e.g., *Sp.Trag*. This play is also referred to by Bonamico at 3.4.35–6.
94. *desperate*] in despair.

Carlo. Here, I think, for I cannot see him, nor do I know when I shall, or where he will be visible again. Upon diligent search I found this paper, but my master is not to be found.

Fulvio. Then he is invisible, indeed.   110

Philenzo. All but his hand. Ha, ha.

Grutti. I do incline to believe that we are cheated.

Perenotto. With a trick that he has! Ha, ha, ha.

Ambassador. You were heretics in that point, till he did demonstrate! Ha, ha, ha.   115

Philenzo. I cannot contain my merry spleen. Ha, ha.

Fulvio. Come, my lord, let's leave them now to be their own derision.

                         Exeunt AMBASSADOR [*and*] FULVIO.

             Enter [*members of the*] Guard, *with* MORELLO
                        [*disguised as before*].

Dondolo. Signor Morello, ha, ha, ha! How came he in a petticoat?

Morello. Carry me away quickly, they will laugh me out of my little wit.   120

Philenzo. No, no, do not, gentlemen, remember yourselves.

Grutti. We won't then.

Perenotto. Morello? I'll wait upon him to the duke myself.

Morello. What wise man in Italy would be in my coat now?

                Exit [PERENOTTO *and* Guard, *with* MORELLO].

Philenzo. I was costive, and an infidel, you are Christian coxcombs;   125
and so, while I see what will become of the mirth that is gone before, I leave your wise signorships to the mercy of your garters, which is a speedy way, after a little time, to make yourselves invisible indeed. Fare you well.   *Exit.*

Dondolo. Signor Grutti, we are gulled.   130

Grutti. I always thought he would cheat us; what shall's do, to prevent more laughter?

Carlo. I am resolved – [*Aside*] I shall get no more money by him – Gentlemen, be not head-hung. Droop not; 'tis in this sconce to revenge yourselves, and, it may be, recover your crowns too.   135

117SD *Enter ... before.*] G; *Enter ... Morello.* Q.   122. won't] *This ed.*; wo'not Q.
124SD] G; *Exit.* Q.   131. shall's] Q; shall we G.   133SD] G; *not in* Q.   133. him
–] G; him, Q.

---

116. *merry spleen*] The spleen was considered to be the seat of laughter.

125. *costive*] see 49 above.

127. *mercy ... garters*] Garters were made of very coarse wool, encouraging puns on their being 'cruel' to the skin; cf. *Lear* 2.2.190.

134. *head-hung*] disconsolate, ashamed (i.e. do not hang your heads in shame).
sconce] head.

Dondolo. How, prithee?
Carlo. My master –
Dondolo. Is invisible: we know't too well.
Carlo. What will you give me if I discover him to your eyes again –
   nay, give him to your possession.   140
Dondolo. Gives him money. This.
Grutti. [*Also gives him money.*] And this – oh, quickly.
Carlo. Then first know my master is not that man you took him for,
   no Altomaro he, but Bonamico, the decayed artist; he that made
   properties, and grew poor for want of pictures; who for fear of his   145
   creditors left his dwelling, and, in this quaint disguise, set up the
   trade of cozening such wise gentlemen as you are.
Grutti and Dondolo. Bonamico!
Carlo. The same.
Dondolo. Oh, that we could reach him again.   150
Carlo. Follow me close, and I will bring you within an hair's breadth
   of his false beard immediately.
Grutti. That will be excellent.
Dondolo. Nimbly, good Mercury, nimbly.   *Exeunt.*

[3.3]

      Enter EUGENIA, FIDELIA, MARDONA, DONELLA,
          KATHERINA, [*and*] CASSIANA.

Fidelia. Madam, you are too passive; if you be dejected what must we,
   whose hopes and blisses depend upon your fortune?
Donella. Oh liberty, liberty! Are all the Roman spirits extinct? Never
   a Brutus in nature, to deliver poor ladies from this captivity?
Cassiana. Since there is no probability of our enlargement, let's be   5

---

139. again –] *This ed.*; agen, Q.   141SD] *Q (subst.).*   142SD] *This ed.*; *not in* Q.

o.] G; *no scene division* Q.   oSD KATHERINA] *This ed.*; CATHERINA G; *Catarina*
Q.   oSD CASSIANA] G; *Cassiava* Q.   3. liberty! Are] *This ed.*; liberty; are Q.

154. *Mercury*] Messenger of the gods.

oSD KATHERINA] Q spells this name both Katherina and Catarina. We have silently
corrected all instances to read 'Katherina' for consistency.

CASSIANA] Cassiana is not listed among the ladies-in-waiting onstage in 1.1 whom
Eugenia chooses for her companions in incarceration, but makes her entry here in the
apartments of the 'New Prison'.

3. *Roman spirits*] the proverbial association of Romans with a love of liberty is
invoked.

4. *Brutus*] Marcus Brutus, who assassinated Julius Caesar with the aim of liberating Rome from tyranny.

5. *enlargement*] liberation from captivity.

merry, and despise our sufferings: laugh, tell tales, sing, dance, anything to cozen our melancholy.

Eugenia. There are some thoughts that stick upon my memory, I would fain discharge.

Katherina. Shall we try our lutes, madam?   10

Eugenia. And voices, if you please.

Donella. Yes, you may try; they say music built the walls of Thebes. It were a greater miracle if you could charm these to fall. I shall never endure to live an anchorite thus; and it were not for the happiness that I do sometimes dream of a man, I should leap the battlement.   15 Now would I give all my jewels for the sight of a pair of breeches, though there were nothing in 'em.

                            [The women sing a] song.

This but feeds our dullness; shall we dance, madam, and stir ourselves?

Cassiana. I am for that. Music! We shall grow to the ground and we   20 use no more activity.

Eugenia. With all my heart.

Donella. None o' your dull measures; there's no sport but in your country figaries. A nimble dance will heat, and make us merry.

                          They dance, which done, a bell rings.

Eugenia. Hark, the bell!   25

    Exit DONELLA, *and enters again with a letter.*

Donella. Some news from the duke. A letter, madam, and these jewels.

Eugenia. Ha! Whence? – from Florence?   *Reads*

    This is my father's practice; I'll peruse the paper.   *Exit.*

Donella. I have an excellent hint, ladies, of a mirth cannot but please the princess.   30

17SD] *This ed.; A Song by the ladies. G; Song. Q.*   20. that. Music! We] *This ed.;* that Musicke. We *Q.*   23. o' your] *This ed.;* of your *G;* a your *Q.*   24. and make] *G;* and and make *Q.*

---

12. *music . . . Thebes*] Ancient Greek city in Boetia, 44 miles from Athens. One legend told how the king of Thebes, Amphion, made stones form themselves into a wall by the power of his lyre music (Senescu).

14. *anchorite*] religious recluse.

17SD] No lyrics are provided for the song but previous comments by Donella suggest it had a melancholy theme and tone (see 3.3.18).

20. *Music*] Cassiana's call is not for mere effect. Donella's comment at 4.2.30 suggests the women play musical parts in the interlude. It would not be unusual for women of their status to have musical capabilities. Their access to instruments in their space of imprisonment is surely confirmed by the SD at 4.2.33. Since Mardona and Fidelia are behind the arras at the point when music is called for (see 4.2.29SD), they may well perform this additional role.

24. *figaries*] dances (see 3.2.48 above).

Fidelia. What is't?
Donella. It will require everyone's endeavour. What if we play some
    pretty comic story?
Katherina. A play?
Cassiana. Shall we?   35
Donella. We? Do not distrust your own performance. I ha' known men
    ha' been insufficient, but women can play their parts.
Mardona. I like it; 'twill be new.
Donella. We will not present it to the princess, but engage her person
    in the action; we shall be too few else. Some pretty interlude, to   40
    square with our number – d' ye allow it?
All. Willingly.
Donella. Come, I'll acquaint you with a plot, then, instantly: refer
    yourselves to me for your parts. We can receive no disparagement;
    our spectators cannot jeer us, for we'll speak but to the people in   45
    the hangings and they have as much judgement as some men that
    are but clothes, at most but walking pictures.
Fidelia. I shall be on't.
Cassiana. What part will you give me? I'll be a king.
Katherina. Thou'lt play a tyrant bravely!   50
Donella. Let me alone; I'll fit you all, I warrant you.   *Exeunt*

---

36. We?] *Q (subst.)*; [Shall] we? *G.*   37. been] *Q (bin).*   37. can play] *Q*; can
[always] play *G.*   38. 'twill be] *G*; 'twilbe *Q.*   39–41.] *G; in verse Q.*   41. d' ye]
This ed.; d'yee *Q.*   43. plot, then,] *G*; plot, then *Q.*   48. on't] *Q*; of it *G.*

32–3. *What . . . story?*] The genre most associated with Henrietta Maria's court theatricals was pastoral.

37. *parts*] roles; though with obvious sexual pun on 'genitalia'; cf. *The Wild-Goose
Chase* 1.3.29–30.

39–40. *We . . . action*] The care taken by Shirley to make Eugenia a participant but
not an instigator of the interlude is discussed in the Introduction, p. 28.

40–1. *interlude . . . number*] The women do not consider staging a full play since
there are only six of them to take part.

44–5. *We . . . us*] According to Prynne's *Histriomastix*, in 1629 there had been harsh
reactions to French professional women actors who had appeared on the stage at the
Blackfriars theatre. Firm evidence for this claim has not been traced; see Michael
Shapiro, 'The Introduction of Actresses in England: Delay or Defensiveness?', in Viviana
Comensoli and Anne Russell (eds), *Enacting Gender on the English Renaissance Stage*
(Urbana and Chicago: University of Illinois Press, 1999), p. 198 n43.

46. *hangings*] arrases or tapestries that presumably decorate the walls of the
women's tower and provide an alternative audience.

49. *I'll . . . king*] Mardona's wish to play what emerges as the part of Acrisius draws
attention to Shirley's careful attribution of parts in the interlude; although he does allow
his women actors to play male roles (but not to cross-dress: Donella is careful to stress
that Mardona's beard will only be imagined; see 4.2.17–18), Eugenia, the princess, plays
a female role equivalent to her social status.

[3.4]

Enter DONDOLO *and* GRUTTI.

Dondolo. Now our invisible merchant is caged, we may redeem our
opinion and pass again in the rank of discreet courtiers.

Grutti. I think now, to most of the beholders, he is invisible all but his
head, for he has but a small grate to look out at.

Dondolo. He shall gull no more with his art, I warrant him.   5

Grutti. Nay, he is like to lie by't, for I hear since all his creditors, like
so many crows, have light upon him, and they'll leave him but a
thin carcass.

Dondolo. Let 'em pick out his eyes, what care we?

Grutti. He sent me an epistle, to take pity on him.   10

Dondolo. But I hope thou hast more wit than to show thyself a
Christian to such a rascal as he is?

Grutti. I returned him my court compliment, that I was sorry I could
not serve him: I would do him any office that stretched not to mine
own prejudice; that we had taken order with his keeper, upon   15
payment of our sums disbursed, he might be enlarged.

Dondolo. Which is impossible.

Enter BONAMICO [*behind them, richly dressed*].

Prithee, let me see his letter, in what submissive language that
rogue does beseech us – [*Reads.*] 'Most heroic signors' – good – 'I
throw myself at the feet of your mercy; for to your justice, I beg I   20
may not be made a sacrifice' – nay, we'll make him beg ere we ha'
done.

Grutti. At the grate.

Dondolo. [*Reads on.*] 'I confess I ha' done you wrong' – does he so?

0.] G; *no scene division* Q.   7. light] Q; lit G.   14. stretched] Q *(strecth'd).*   17SD]
This ed.; Enter behind, BONAMICO, *brave.* G; *Enter Bonamico brave. in right margin*
Q.   19SD] G; *not in* Q.   19. 'Most . . . signors'] *This ed.; in italics* G; *no quotation marks* Q.   19–21. 'I . . . sacrifice'] *This ed.; in italics* G; *no quotation marks* Q.
21. ha'] *This ed.;* h'a Q; have G.   24SD] *This ed.; not in* Q.   24. 'I . . . wrong'] *This
ed.; in italics* G; *no quotation marks* Q.

4. *grate*] grating, grille. See also 3.4.114 and *The Convent of Pleasure* 2.1.53.

6–7. *creditors . . . crows*] Bonamico's creditors are compared to carrion feeders;
cf. the legacy hunters Corvino, Corbaccio, and Voltore in Jonson's *Volpone*.

7. *light*] alighted.

17SD] Q's SD reads '*Enter Bonamico brave*' with 'brave' carrying the sense of richly
or well dressed.

It shall not serve the turn! – 'there is no hope I shall ever satisify   25
you' – all the better, lie and rot! – 'if I be known a prisoner to my
creditors I am irrecoverably lost. Oh, compassionate a miserable
man, who otherwise must soon forfeit his daylight, and die in a
dungeon.' – Ha, ha, ha!
Bonamico. [*Coming forward*] Save you, noble signors.   30
Grutti. Ha!
Dondolo. 'Tis he.
Grutti. Did he not die in prison, and his ghost haunts us? Brave! – 'Tis
not he.
Bonamico. When this eternal substance of my soul   35
Did live imprisoned in my wanton flesh . . .
and so forth? And how d' ye like Don Andrea, gentlemen? Poor
snake, but he has cast his skin, and recovered a new coat o' th'
Destinies' spinning. The bird is flown again!
Dondolo. How the devil came he at liberty?   40
Grutti. And thus gallant?
Bonamico. The slave does not beg your heroic signorship a court
compassion: debts must be paid. There is no danger of the grate
as the case goes, nor of 'forfeiting his daylight in a dungeon', if I
mistake not, my illustrious pair of wigeons, my serene, smooth-   45
faced coxcombs, whose brains are curdled this hot weather. Will
your neat worship sell your cloak, ha? Or you that superfluous
double-hatched rapier? There be sums in nature to lend you, upon
security that I shall like of.
Dondolo. He jeers us!   50
Grutti. Would we durst beat him!
Bonamico. You see me now, gentlemen, perfectly; what if I should

---

25–6. 'there . . . you'] *This ed.; in italics G; no quotation marks Q.*   26–9. 'if . . .
dungeon.'] *This ed.; in italics G; no quotation marks Q.*   30SD] *G; not in Q.*   33.
us?] *G; vs, Q.*   35–6. *When . . . flesh*] *G; not in italics in Q.*   44. 'forfeiting . . .
dungeon'] *This ed.; in italics G; no quotation marks Q.*

27. *compassionate*] have pity on (*v.*).
35–6. When . . . flesh] The opening lines of *Sp. Trag* when the Ghost of Don Andrea
appears onstage.
39. *Destinies' spinning*] A reference to the three Fates; see 2.1.61.
44. *'forfeiting . . . dungeon'*] Bonamico is quoting Dondolo and Grutti's scornful
tone (see 28–9 above) back at them.
45. *wigeons*] ducks, proverbially held to be caught easily by hunters.
46. *curdled*] congealed.
48. *double-hatched*] marked with narrow stripes or strokes in two directions.
Bonamico's description of this rapier as 'superfluous' (47) suggests that Dondolo and
Grutti wear such items purely for the purposes of fashion.

'walk before you without a body, my head hanging in the air like
a comet'?

Grutti. Would thou wert hanged anyway!   55

   Enter [PHILENZO *disguised* as] ROLLIARDO.

Dondolo. Here's Rolliardo, too. Let's be gone.

Bonamico. Or shall I appoint you a day 'when I will be invisible all
but my hand'?

Dondolo. No, I thank you, sir; we have some business at this present.

Grutti. Let's to the prison, and know the wonder better – noble signor –   60

Bonamico. For your crowns –

Dondolo. We are glad we had 'em for you, dear signor, talk no more
on 'em.   *Exeunt* [DONDOLO *and* GRUTTI].

Bonamico. Farewell, phantasmas, then – ha? 'tis he! – Sir –

Philenzo. Keep your way.   65

Bonamico. You do not know me,
 But I ha' brought a life, which by your means
 Has been preserved from wretchedness; your bounty
 Deserves you should dispose it.

Philenzo. What are you?   70

Bonamico. I was the object of a charity
 We seldom meet in mankind: from a prison
 You sent a sum to free me.

Philenzo. Prithee, friend, if thou'st received a benefit, go home, and say
 thy prayers: I would forget it.   75

Bonamico. 'Mong many whom your nobleness enlarged,
 I came to make you tender of my service:
 Despise not, sir, my gratitude.

Philenzo. D' ye mock me?

Bonamico. May my soul want heaven's mercy then! To you,   80
 Next my Creator, I do owe my thus being.
 I have a soul is full of thanks; but name
 Employment to assure you, and you make me twice happy.

Philenzo. I ha' nothing to say to you.

Bonamico. Then I ha' something to say to you.   85

Philenzo. How?

53–4. 'walk . . . comet'] *This ed.; in italics G; no quotation marks Q.*   55SD] *This
ed.; l. 56 and in right margin Q.*   63SD] *G; Exeunt. Q.*   74–5.] *Q (subst.); verse
in G.*   79. D' ye] *This ed.;* D'yee *Q.*   81. my thus] *This ed.;* my this *Q;* this my *G.*
83. me twice] *Q;* me / Twice *G.*

 53–4, 57–8. 'walk . . . comet', 'when . . . hand'] Bonamico now quotes his own
earlier lines which deceived Dondolo and Grutti; see 2.1.393, 416.

 64. *phantasmas*] apparitions (Bonamico is implying that Dondolo and Grutti lack
substance).

Bonamico. And you shall hear it, too, and give me thanks.
You've sowed your charity in a fruitful ground,
Which shall return it tenfold – nay, one hundred.
What you have done for me you shall acknowledge   90
I will deserve to th' height.
Philenzo. Thou'rt liberal in language.
Bonamico. I'll be active – off with this sullen face,
It scurvily becomes you; d' ye hear?
I studied for you, since you paid my debts;   95
I'll do you a courtesy, and save your life,
Which your attempt upon the princess has
Left desperate; a happy fancy, sir,
If heaven will please to prosper it, and you
Not be your own enemy to refuse it.   100
Philenzo. Ha, ha, ha! What meanst?
Bonamico. Nay, you shall laugh, and heartily, ere I ha' done wi' ye:
The duke does love his daughter, sends her all
Rarities are presented to him.
Philenzo. His soul's not dearer to him – what of that?   105
Bonamico. Why, then, you shall be admitted into the castle of comfort,
that's all; the conceit is in my brain, and would you could as prob-
ably get her consent to untie her virgin zone, as I dispose your
access to her. It shall not cost you much, if I fail; instead of saying
of my prayers, I'll curse the Destinies, and die with you.   110
Philenzo. D' ye hear? I ha' bestowed three hundred crowns already to
set your heels at liberty; if you do mock me, it shall cost me five
hundred, but I'll ha' you clapped up again, where you shall howl
all day at the grate, for a meal at night from the basket.

---

89. tenfold –] *This ed.*; tenfold; *Q.*   91. to th'] *This ed.*; toth' *Q*; to the *G.*   93SP]
Qc (Bo.); *not in Qu.*   94. scurvily] *Qc*; scur *in italics Qu.*   94. d' ye] *This ed.*;
d'yee *Q.*   102.] *Q*; Nay . . . laugh, / And . . . you: *G.*   102. wi' ye] *This ed.*; w'e *Q*;
with you *G.*   111. D' ye] *This ed.*; D'yee *Q.*   111. three hundred] *G*; 300. *Q.*
112–13. five hundred] *G*; 500. *Q.*

---

106. *castle . . . comfort*] another mock-chivalric allusion; cf. Shirley, *The Witty Fair
One* 3.4.
      107. *conceit*] idea.
      108. *virgin zone*] literally a chastity belt, though it also alludes to the impenetrable
space and circumstances in which the Duke has confined his daughter.
      110. *Destinies*] See also 2.1.67.
      112. *set . . . liberty*] common phrase for setting someone free, deriving from a time
when leg shackles were frequently used to hold prisoners.
      113. *clapped*] locked.
      113–14 *howl . . . grate*] Cf. Malvolio's reaction to his imprisonment in *TwN* 4.2.
      114. *meal . . . basket*] Prisoners were traditionally sent left-overs in a basket.

Bonamico. You are in earnest now?   115
Philenzo. Yes.
Bonamico. By all that you have threatened, so am I; have but the
    patience to walk and hear me.
Philenzo. Can thy art procure this?
Bonamico. My art? Why, look you, I made this watch: I'll bestow it   120
    on you.
Philenzo. What to do? To reckon the hours I ha' to live?
Bonamico. It shan't cost me so much trouble as that toy did, to make
    you master of your wishes still, if heaven prosper it: come, let's talk
    privately, you shall ha' the plot.   125
        He that doth many good deeds, it may fall,
        Among the rest, one may reward them all.
    I long to be discoursing it; pray, lead the way.
Philenzo. Provide again, you mock me not. Come on, sir.   [*Exeunt.*]

---

118. me.] *Q; me. [They discourse aside.* G.   123. shan't] *This ed.;* sha'not *Q.*
129. not.] *This ed.;* not – *Q.*   129SD] G; *not in* Q.

115. *in earnest*] serious. For the significance of this phrase and its variant meanings
see Introduction, p. 32.
126–7.] Proverbial (cf. Dent T616: 'One good turn asks another').

ACT 4

Enter DONDOLO *and* GRUTTI.

Dondolo. Rolliardo pay his debts? Sure the fellow, that never saw much
money in's life, now by the duke made master of so many sums, is
grown mad with 'em.

Grutti. Many other he hath discharged, they say.

Dondolo. He'll undo the exchequer, and he hold on; he shall be   5
chronicled for't.

Grutti. He has some cause to imagine himself short-lived, and that
makes him so desperately charitable toward his end. Signor
Perenotto –

Enter PERENOTTO.

Perenotto. Dondolo and Grutti, news, news for ye!   10

Dondolo. What, we beseech you?

Perenotto. You have lost the best mirth in Italy in your absence; your
companion, Morello –

Dondolo. Was carried to the duke in a petticoat, in which he attempted
a passage to the sequestered ladies – what's the issue?   15

Perenetto. Mirth in abundance.

Grutti. How came he off?

Perenotto. Nay, 'tis on still. The duke, to make himself sport, would call
a council, before whom the poor signor must be arraigned. Not to
hold you in circumstance, the business was merrily discussed, and   20
the pitiful projector was judged –

Dondolo. How, how?

Perenotto. To wear the petticoat for a month; if he appear without it
during the term, he incurs his perpetual exile from court.

Dondolo and Grutti. Ha, ha, ha!   25

Perenotto. You may imagine with what variety of lamentable faces the
courtier heard his unexpected sentence; some would have pleaded
for him but for laughter, which continued so long and so high, that

---

0.] *A Part of the Palace.* G.   19. council] *Q* (Counsell).   19. arraigned.] *This ed.*;
arraigned; *Q*.

---

5. *exchequer*] See 3.2.69.
6. *chronicled*] recorded in the historical chronicles.
18, 54. *sport*] On the significance of the language of sports see Introduction, p. 4.

233

he had time to collect his scattered senses, and instead of swooning, which was expected, he grew fortified, and most humbly   30
besought the duke, since his sentence had passed so definitive, he
would be so merciful to admit him that course of a moon to be his
jester, that since he could not shake off the fool's coat, that he might
have that favourable pretence to keep it on.

Grutti. Very good –   35

Perenotto. 'Twas easily granted, but ever since, to the astonishment of
the hearers, he is grown so jocund and airy. Nay, as if he had been
born with a song in's head, he talks everlasting ballad. No man
laughs at him, but he lashes him in rhyme worse than a satyr. The
duke has privileged his mirth, made him fool-free, and now he   40
plays the tyrant – he's here already.

Enter MORELLO, *like a jester.*

Morello. O yes, o yes, o yes.
    If there be anyone, in city or in town,
    Can show me a wise man, I'll please him for his pain.

Perenotto. Disgrace has made him witty.   45

Dondolo. What will you say to him, will show you a wise man?

Morello. Marry, if he go far, he is not so wise as he should be. Dondolo,
    Grutti! Old acquaintance, how is't, how is't?

Grutti. The case is altered with you.

Morello. It does appear so, but nothing can make me proud; I'll know   50
    my fellows.

Perenotto. How do you mean, Morello?

29–30. *swooning*] Q *(sowning)*.   41SD] Q *(subst.)*; Enter MORELLO, *in his former
disguise*. G.

    32. *course of a moon*] a month, the time period that Morello must remain in his
petticoat and wear the fool's coat (see 33–4). This time period already has significance
as the timespan of Philenzo's wager with the duke. This phrase also picks up on earlier
associations of his character with lunacy; see 90 below.
    37. *airy*] flippant.
    39. *satyr*] satire. 'The confusion between the words *satiric* and *satyric* gave rise to
the notion that the satyrs who formed the chorus of the Greek satiric drama had to
deliver "satirical speeches". Hence in the sixteenth and seventeenth centuries, the frequent attribution to the satyrs of censoriousness as a characteristic quality' (*OED* 1c).
    40. *privileged . . . fool-free*] Court fools were licensed to speak more freely than
other courtiers.
    41SD] Morello presumably appears in the conventional long coat and 'motley'
(multi-coloured, often red and yellow) of the fool, in addition to his petticoat. He specifically refers to his 'new coat' at 68.
    43–4.] Proverbial (Dent C111).

Morello. Your lordship may make one at football,
  'Tis all the sport nowadays.
  What other is the world than a ball,   55
  Which we run after with whoop and with hollow?
  He that doth catch it is sure of a fall;
  His heels tripped up by him that doth follow.
Dondolo. Do not women play too?
Grutti. They are too light, quickly down.   60
Morello. Oh yes, they are the best gamesters of all,
  For though they often lie on the ground,
  Not one amongst a hundred will fall,
  But under her coats the ball will be found.
  With a fading.   65
  But we be three of old, without exception to your lordship, only
  with this difference: I am the wisest fool, for you play the fool in
  your old clothes, and I have a new coat on.
Perenotto. Does it not become him?
Dondolo. Rarely well; do you ever mean to resign it?   70
Grutti. 'Twere pity, but he should have patent for't, to him and his
  posterity.
Morello. Hark you, gentlemen, d' ye hear the news?
Dondolo. News? What news?
Morello. D' ye not hear on't yet? Why, 'tis in a ballad already. 75
Grutti. And thou canst sing it?
Morello. 'Twas well guessed, and I can but hit o' th' tune:
  [*Sings*] *There was an invisible fox, by chance,*
  Did meet with two visible geese,
  He led 'em a fine invisible dance,   80
  For a hundred crowns apiece.
  Invisible, all but his hand, he would go,
  But when it came to be tried,
  Not only his hand, which was left, he did show,
  But a fair pair of heels beside.   85
  Invisible since their wits have been,

53–4.] *Q; prose in G.*   54.] *G adds* [Sings. *in right margin.*   55–8.] *Q; G prints in
italics to indicate a song.*   61SP] *Q; Mor.* [sings.] *G.*   61–4.] *Q (subst.); G prints
in italics to indicate a song.*   64. will be] *G;* will *Q .*   73. d' ye] *This ed.;* d'yee *Q.*
75. D' ye] *This ed.;* Dee *Q.*   78SD] *G in right margin; not in Q.*   79. visible] *Qc
(subst.) on errata page;* Jnvisible *Qu.*

---

53. *make . . . football*] Proverbial; a variation on the phrase 'All fellows at football'.
Senescu comments on the fact that this sport had become more popular with the elite
classes in the 1630s.
  65. With . . . fading] 'The refrain of a popular song of an indecent character' (*OED*).

> *But yet there is hope of either,*
> *Their wit and their crowns may return again,*
> *Invisible altogether.*   *Exit.*

Grutti. And he continue thus but a moon, he'll make the court mad.   90
Perenotto. Oh, 'twill be excellent, since it is not safe for a wise man to
   speak truth, 'twere pity fools should lose their privilege – the duke.

Enter DUKE, FULVIO, *and courtiers.*

Fulvio. My lord.
Duke. What is't?
Fulvio. Here's an important suitor, calls himself   95
   An artist, humbly craves admittance with
   A present, which he'd tender to your acceptance,
   And if my judgement err not, a most pleasing one.
Duke. Let us see him, and his present;
   It will reward my daughter's patience,   100
   Love, and obedience. All the rarities
   Ten kingdoms yield shall not be thought too weighty,
   That she may shift each solitary hour
   With a fresh object.

Enter BONAMICO *[with servants drawing in a large cage*
filled with various species of bird].

Dondolo. Bonamico?   105
Grutti. 'Tis he.
Duke. By my love to goodness,
   It is a masterpiece: 'twill feed the eye
   With plenty of delight.
Bonamico. *[Aside]* I am as jocund since I am admitted; I talk as glib,   110
   methinks, as he that farms the monuments.
Duke. Is't not, sirs?

---

95. important] *Q*; importunate *G.*   104SD] *G (subst.); Enter Bonamico. A Cage dis-*
covered. Q.   110SD] *G; not in Q* .

90.] Continues the proverbial association of the moon and madness.
   95. *important*] importunate. Gifford modernises it to this, but this creates metrical
difficulties.
   104SD *large . . . bird*] a considerable stage property, resembling some of the engines
of the court masques in its complexity. It needs to be large enough to conceal the actor
playing Philenzo in one of its pillars and it is clearly moved on wheels (see 4.2.175).
The birds themselves, described in detail by Bonamico at 154–73 and Eugenia at
4.2.191–205, may have been real since there is no evidence of automata being owned
by theatre companies at this time, no doubt owing to their prohibitive cost.
   111. *he . . . monuments*] person with the right to show the monuments at St Paul's
and Westminster for a fee (Gifford).

Perenotto. My lord, I ha' not seen so much delight in any piece these
    seven years.
Duke. Where's the master of the work?   115
Bonamico. My lord, I am the constable that put all these in the cage,
    and you may call it a point of injustice, for they never kept late
    hours. Though they all wear feathers, there's not a roarer amongst
    'em, and yet were they suffered, they'd fly high, for some of 'em
    are very lofty minded.   120
Duke. A pleasant fellow too.
Bonamico. Oh, my lord, we're all born in our degrees to make one
    another merry. The birds make me merry; I make my wife merry;
    the fool makes your courtiers merry; and the courtiers make your
    grace merry.   125
Duke. And whom do I make merry?
Bonamico. The whole commonwealth, if you govern handsomely.
Duke. There's salt in's mirth –
    I'll ha' this fellow wait i' th' court.
Bonamico. I shall be kicked out by the pages.   130
Duke. Why so?
Bonamico. Because I cannot flatter.
Duke. A conceited thing.
    We lack the humorist Rolliardo here.
Dondolo. We saw him i' th' court ere while, my lord.   135
Duke. This humour would ha' been a gadfly to him
    And stung him to the quick.
Bonamico. [*Aside*] Not altogether so, duke.
Grutti. Fellow, what bird is that?
Bonamico. Fellow? – Cry mercy, I'd forgot you; fellow, I'll tell thee. D'   140
    ye not know him? 'Tis an Arabian woodcock; the same that carried
    a bunch of grapes in January last to Bethlem Gabor.

113–14.] *This ed.*; My . . . delight / In . . . yeares. *Q.*   135. saw] *G*; see *Q.*   138SD]
G; *not in Q.*   140–1. D' ye] *This ed.*; d'ee *Q.*

---

118. *feathers*] (1) literally, the birds are all feathered; (2) humorous comparison to
courtiers who wore feathers in their caps and were associated with free-spirited or
riotous behaviour. *OED* does not give this meaning, but the word became synecdochal
for 'cavaliers' in the 1630s. Cf. the 'Brotherhood of the Blade' in Richard Brome's *The
Weeding of Covent Garden* (1.1.10).
    118. *roarer*] reveller or roisterer (*OED* 1b).
    133. *conceited*] full of wit or conceits.
    136. *gadfly*] fly which bites and goads cattle.
    141–2. *Arabian . . . Gabor*] The woodcock was a bird proverbially associated with
foolishness because it was believed easily caught. Bethlem Gabor, who had died after
being poisoned by a Hungarian Jesuit in 1629, was a military adventurer who became
Prince of Transylvania and King of Hungary. He had been an ally of the Elector

Dondolo. And what call you this?
Bonamico. This was the duke of Venice, his own bullfinch,
    And taken by the Turks.   145
Duke. By the Turks, sayst thou? He droops, indeed.
Bonamico. Since his captivity, the wretch endured
    Much misery by the infidel; it had nothing
    But bread and water for three months.
Fulvio. A shrewd calamity.   150
Duke. I do affect this fellow's prate.
Perenotto. What's this?
Bonamico. This is the blackbird, which was hatched that day
    Gondomar died, and, which was ominous,
    About that time Spinola's thrush forsook him.   155
Perenotto. Was this he?
Bonamico. Yes.
Duke. And what was this?
Bonamico. This was the pigeon was so shrewdly handled
    For carrying letters at the siege of Bergen.   160
Perenotto. Alas, pretty bird –
Bonamico. This a wagtail of the city, which a silkman
    So dearly loved, he called it wife, but could not –
    Though in much jealousy he had caged her up –

---

156. he?] *This ed.*; he? – G; he – Q.

Palatine during the Palatinate crisis. Senescu (p. liii) speculates that the 'bunch of grapes' is an allusion to his poisoning.

    144–5. *duke . . . Turks*] The Doge of Venice had led famous battles against the Turks in the late sixteenth century. Venice was assisted in this by the Vatican, and Senescu speculates that the bullfinch with its reddish plumage might therefore be intended to resemble the Pope or a cardinal.

    154. *Gondomar*] Don Diego Sarmiento, made Count Gondomar in 1618, was Spanish ambassador to the Jacobean court and a promoter of the 'Spanish Match' – the proposed but failed attempt to secure a marriage between Prince Charles and the Spanish Infanta – in the early 1620s. Gondomar was represented by the Black Knight in Middleton's *A Game at Chess* (1624), which may explain the connection with the blackbird here. He died in 1625.

    155. *Spinola*] Marquis Ambrosio Spinola, a Genoese general who governed the Spanish forces in the Low Countries in the early 1600s. The relevance of 'Spinola's thrush' forsaking him remains unclear, but may refer to his political or military eclipse.

    159. *shrewdly*] maliciously, malignly.

    160. *siege of Bergen*] The Dutch achieved a great victory at Bergen-ap-Zoom between 8 September and 14 October 1631. Senescu uses this reference as a means of dating the composition of *The Bird in a Cage*.

    162. *wagtail*] proverbial for gossips or promiscuous women in the seventeenth century.

Keep her from flying out. This was a rail,   165
Bred up by a zealous brother in Amsterdam,
Which, being sent unto an English lady,
Was ta'en at sea by Dunkirks. Name but Rome,
And straight she gapes, as she would eat the pope.
A bird to be made much on: she and the horse   170
That snorts at Spain by an instinct of nature,
Should ha' shown tricks together. I could run over –
But your gracious pardon.
Duke. How, our pardon?
Bonamico. I'm now another man, and know my distance.   175
Duke. This man is good at all.
Bonamico. My buffoon face is off; I did but show
The impudent condition of a mountebank,
That sets off base toys with miraculous lies.
Thus far I'll boast: they are the only choice   180
Italy and other parts of Europe yield.
For the work, if it prove so fortunate
To receive grace from your divine acceptance,
The workmanship, so duty suffer not,
I freely tender –   185
Duke. No, that were to quench
The fire in all deservers – Fulvio.
Fulvio. My lord.
Duke. Pay the cost double; I'll send it to my daughter.
Bonamico. [*Aside*] It takes, as art could wish it.   190
Duke. I know it is a present the sweet soul
Will raise much joy in: Signor Perenotto –
Perenotto. My lord.
Bonamico. [*To Dondolo and Grutti*] There are two birds I ha' not
    named.

---

168. Dunkirks.] *This ed.*; Dunkirks – Q.   177SP] Q *(Brn.)*.   190SD] G; *not in* Q.
193.] Q; G adds [*Walks aside with the duke. in right margin.*

---

165. *rail*] small marsh bird, but here also a pun on the ranting of extreme Protestant sects from Amsterdam (see 166 below).

166. *zealous . . . Amsterdam*] fundamentalist Puritans from Amsterdam were a
common stage representation; cf. Ananias and Tribulation Wholesome in Jonson's *The
Alchemist.*

168. *Dunkirks*] pirates who used the port of Dunkirk as a base, preying on shipping in the English Channel. Their piracy had only very recently been brought under
control with the Treaty of Spain in 1630, adding to the topicality of this passage.

170–1. *horse . . . Spain*] an unidentified reference.

194–7.] These lines form a side conversation between Bonamico, Dondolo, and
Grutti, in which Bonamico continues his mockery of the gullible courtiers.

Dondolo. What are they?   195
Bonamico. [*To Dondolo and Grutti*] A pair of gulls, which you may
    share between you.
Perenotto. It shall, my lord.
Duke. If Florence now keep touch, we shortly shall
    Conclude all fear with a glad nuptial.   *Exeunt.*

[4.2]

> *Enter* EUGENIA, FIDELIA, MARDONA, DONELLA, CASSIANA,
> [*and*] KATHERINA.

Donella. You like this story best then?
Eugenia. That of Jupiter and Danae comes near our own.
Donella. Be it so; we are all perfect in the plot, I think.
Eugenia. You shall dispose the rest.
Donella. You will not be ambitious, then, and quarrel about the parts,   5
    like your spruce actor, that will not play out of the best clothes,
    and the fine young prince, who, if he fight, 'tis six to four he kills
    all and gets the lady?
Fidelia. We are constant; you shall appoint 'em.
Donella. Then, madam, without ceremony, you shall play Danae, that   10
    is shut up in the brazen tower.
Eugenia. Well, I'm contented; 'twill suit with my present fortune.
Donella. I need not to instruct you in the character. [*To Mardona*] You
    shall be the king Acrisius, her father, a jealous, harsh, crabbed man,
    who, in fear of the oracle, commands her to be thus enclosed.   15
Mardona. So – I'll fit you for a vinegar king.
Donella. No matter for properties – we'll imagine, madam, you have
    a beard.

0.] G; *no scene division in* Q.   0.] *The Castle.* – Eugenia's *Apartments.* G.   0SD
KATHERINA] *This ed.; Katerina* Q.   5. about] *Senescu;* About Q.   10. play] Q;
pl y *and* ply *Qu.*   13SD] G; *not in* Q.

196. *pair of gulls*] mocking the gullibility of Dondolo and Grutti.

2. *comes . . . own*] Eugenia recognises the parallels between her own story and that
of Danae; see also 12, 23, 57.

3. *plot*] in the theatrical sense of plotline, though there is at least a hint that Donella
may have ulterior plans to seduce Eugenia.

6. *spruce*] smart in appearance (*OED* 2); cf. Jonson, *Every Man Out*, Charact.
Persons: 'A neat, spruce, affecting courtier'.

14. *crabbed*] sour, bitter (i.e. like the taste of a crab-apple).

16. *vinegar*] sour (in behaviour).

17–18. *No . . . beard*] There are no stage properties or costumes; emphasis is laid
on the fact that the women are not putting on a fully realised production: beards will
be imagined. In this way, Shirley protects his female performers from some of Prynne's
particular charges about transvestism and the stage.

Fidelia. What shall I play?
Donella. You must be ladies whom the king leaves to keep her   20
    company. Entertain what humour you please.
Cassiana and Katherina. This is our own parts, indeed.
Donella. You will play it the more naturally. And let me alone to play
    the Thunderer: I'll wanton Jove it. Now, whet your inventions and
    about it: imagine our scene expressed, and *The New Prison*, the   25
    title, advanced in form.
Eugenia. The New Prison! Why?
Donella. Oh, 'tis an excellent name, where spectators throng together,
    as ours do, methinks, in the arras already.

        [MARDONA and FIDELIA *hide behind the arras.*]

    The music ha' their part; dispose yourselves for your entrances,   30
    while I speak the prologue to our mixed audience of silk and cruel
    gentlemen in the hangings – [*Clears throat.*] Hem!
Katherina. Let it be a confident prologue, howsoever.   *Music.*
Donella. You're welcome to New Prison! We have still
    Our ancient keeper, and we fear he will   35
    Speak in his old key too. But do not look for

---

24. it.] *This ed.*; it: – Q.   25. *The . . . Prison*] *This ed.*; *no italics in* Q.   27. *The
. . . Prison*] G; *no italics* Q.   29SD] *This ed.*; *not in* Q.   32SD] *This ed.*; *not in* Q.
34SP] *This ed.*; *Don.* Q; *Donel.* [*coming forward.*] – G.   34–56.] G; *no italics* Q.

24. *Thunderer*] Jupiter was god of thunder.
    wanton Jove] Jupiter was depicted in texts such as Ovid's *Metamorphoses* taking on
numerous disguises to satisfy his sexual whims. The Danae story is one of many in this
respect. See also 138.
    25. *New Prison*] The title chosen for the women's interlude is a further reference to
their own position.
    26. *advanced . . . form*] Play titles were displayed on placards from playhouses as a
form of advertisement.
    28–9. *spectators . . . arras*] imagining the wall tapestries as an audience (see also the
'silk and cruel gentlemen' at 31, and the 'Judicious hangings' at 41). There are interesting links to the staging of drama in early modern households and to the particular
genre or mode of closet drama (see Introduction, p. 9). On the use of hangings in the
Cockpit theatre, see T.J. King, 'Staging of Plays at the Phoenix in Drury Lane, 1617–42'.
Theatre Notebook 19 (1964–5), 146–60.
    29SD] The stage direction allows for Mardona and Fidelia to be positioned behind
the arras when later in the scene Cassiana and Katherina refer to them laughing behind
the arras and therefore causing the hangings to shake (65–6). See also the additional
SD at 66.
    30. *music . . . part*] it was traditional for music to be played between the acts in
private theatre performances (such as those at the Cockpit theatre where *The Bird in
a Cage* was first staged).
    31. *cruel*] punning on 'crewel' embroidery; see 3.2.127; Jonson, *New Inn* 2.1.31.

Choice diet, for alas, we play the cook for
All you are like to feed on. Let your palate
Expect at most, then, but a root or salad,
Picked from the prison garden. We know you are   40
Judicious hangings, and well seen; nor dare
We lift you up – too bold – lest we incense
Your green and spreading wits with impudence.
As I began, let me conclude in rhyme:
Hang still you learnèd critics of the time.   45
Now: Danae and the ladies.
Eugenia. *Was ever father to his child*
So unkind? It makes me wild,
When to beguile a tedious hour,
From the top of this high tower,   50
I see every other creature
Enjoy a liberty by nature.
Can the silver-running fountains,
And the cloud-aspiring mountains,
Every grove, and flowery field,   55
But a new affliction yield?
Donella. This is excellent! She has played the part before.
Cassiana. *Waste not yourself in woeful plaint;*
Sorrow will not help restraint.
Think, madam, all is but a dream   60
That we are in – Now I am out – 'beam', 'cream' . . .
Help me, Katherina, I can make no sense rhyme to't.
Donella. 'Cream' is as good a rhyme as your mouth can wish – Ha,
ha, ha!
Cassiana. Does not the arras laugh at me? It shakes, methinks.   65
Katherina. It cannot choose: there's one behind does tickle it.
                    [MARDONA *and* FIDELIA *come forward from*
                                        behind the arras.]

47SP] *This ed.; Eug.* Q; Eug. [coming forward.] – G.   47–56.] G; *no italics* Q.   58SP]
This ed.; Cass. Q; Cas. [coming forward.] – G.   58–61. *Waste . . . in*] G; *no italics* Q.
61. 'beam', 'cream'] *This ed.; beam, cream.* G; *no italics* Q.   63. 'Cream'] *This ed.;*
Cream G; *no italics* Q.   66SD] *This ed.; not in* Q.

37–8. we . . . on] Comparisons between the staging of a play and cooking and the
feeding of an audience's appetite were commonplace; see, e.g., Jonson, *New Inn*
Prologue.

41. Judicious hangings] Shirley seems to be consciously guying Jonson's complaint
that spectators in the public theatres were no more engaged than hangings and arras
cloths: see *New Inn* 'The Dedication to the Reader'.

62. can . . . to't] The women are ad-libbing their lines, improvising, in contrast to
Henrietta Maria and her ladies, who clearly spent several weeks learning lines for court
performances. See also ll.75.86, and 121 below.

66SD] See 29SD above.

Eugenia. A dream! Alas, 'tis no relief
  For us to flatter so much grief;
  Fancy wants power to delight,
  Or if we could think it might,   70
  Such a dream so sad would make us,
  That it could not choose but wake us.
Donella. My lady has helped her pretty well out of her dream.
Katherina. The sun, with glittering golden rays,
  May appear one of these days.   75
  You know always after winter
  Comes the spring and pleasant summer.
Donella. 'Winter' and 'summer', ha, ha, ha!
Mardona. Winter and summer? By my faith, that's well, there's but half
  a year between. There be some call themselves poets, make their   80
  rhymes straddle so wide a twelvemonth will hardly reconcile 'em,
  and, I hope, a lady may straddle a little by poetical licence.
Cassiana. Madam, your father King Acrisius.
Mardona. Must I enter already? – [*Clears throat.*] Hem!
Eugenia. This is his hour to visit us.   85
Mardona. How fares our daughter?
Cassiana. What voice is that?
Donella. The king speaks through a trunk.
Mardona. How is't, heroic birth? What dullness, cold
  As Saturn's, dwells on thy forehead? Be bold   90
  To give thy grief a tongue; instruct, child,
  My paternal nature, lest I grow wild
  As the rude north: thought of thee makes my hairs
  Silver, my blood is curdled with my cares.
Donella. Most high and mighty nonsense! Sure the king has swallowed   95
  pills, and his stomach, not able to digest 'em, does vomit 'em up
  again.
Mardona. Is thy organ dumb?
  Or am I grown cheap in majesty? Trivial fool,
  Shall I reap crabbed thistles in neglect for rich love?   100

67–72.] G; *no italics* Q.   74SP] *This ed.*; *Kat.* Q; Cath. [coming forward.] – G.
74–7.] G; *no italics* Q.   78. 'Winter' . . . 'summer'] *This ed.*; *Winter* and *summer* G;
Winter . . . Summer Q.   81. twelvemonth] G; 12. Moneth Q.   83.] G; *no italics* Q.
84SD] *This ed.*; *not in* Q.   85.] G; *no italics* Q.   86SP] *This ed.*; *Mard.* Q; Mard.
[coming forward.] – G.   86.] G; *no italics* Q.   89–94.] G; *no italics* Q.   93. *north:*]
This ed.; North: – Q.   98–100.] G; *no italics* Q.

89–90. cold . . . Saturn's] the planet Saturn was believed to consist largely of the cold
element, therefore those considered to have a saturnine complexion were traditionally
melancholic.
  101. *crabbed*] See 14 above.

Cassiana. Crabbed language, I am sure!
Donella. Sure my lady does not understand him.
Eugenia. *If my brow so sad appear,*
  My fortune's livery I wear.
Mardona. *Weep no more, thy eyes pave the ground with pearl.*   105
  My power is razed, my crown thy tribute, girl;
  Here is nothing to want.
Eugenia. *Nothing to want, indeed! To be*
  A prisoner speaks all misery.
Mardona. *Curse not thy soft stars, but take thy fair bliss*   110
  With comfort; free from loud noise and fear is
  Thy gaudy station. *When I have unscrewed*
  Mystic oracles, which not understood
  Do perplex with involved sense, I shall then
  Enlarge thy person, Danae. *Till when,*   115
  If aught else do clog thy thoughts, with unkind
  Thoughts, unload the dark burden of thy mind.
  Pronounce thy grief aloud, my amorous darling,
  And I will –
Cassiana. Let him choose his rhyme, I beseech you, madam.   120
Mardona. Uh, uh! – cold phlegm obstructs my language – 'barling',
  'carling' . . .
Donella. Ha, ha! 'Tis time to make an end;
  He was almost choked with his own phrase.
Mardona. And you get me to play an old man again –   125
Donella. We'll have a young one for thee; twenty-one and a coat is a
  double game – my turn comes next.   [*Exit.*]
Eugenia. *He's gone and leaveth us behind*
  To tell our passions to the wind.
  Ha? What o' th' sudden doth surprise   130
  My active motion? On my eyes
  What dark and heavy cloud doth sit
  To persuade me it is night?
  It is some charm: I cannot keep
  These windows open; I must sleep.   135

103–19.] G; *no italics* Q.   106. *razed*] G; rac'd Q.   114. *sense,*] G; sense, – Q.
125.] Q; G adds [*Exit. in right margin.*   127SD] This ed.; not in Q.   128–35.] G;
no italics Q.   132. *sit*] Q; light, G.

---

112. unscrewed] 'opened up' (since oracles were often carried in sealed containers),
with the additional sense of 'interpreted' or 'solved'.

126–7. twenty-one . . . coat] There was a French card game known as *vingt-et-un* to
which Donella presumably refers.

Enter [DONELLA, *as*] *Jupiter.*

Cassiana. This was well passionated. Now comes Jupiter to take my
    lady napping: we'll sleep too. Let the wanton have her swing –
    would she were a man for her sake.

Donella. Let the music of the spheres,
    Captivate these mortal ears,   140
    While Jove descends into this tower
    In a golden streaming shower.
    To disguise him from the eye
    Of Juno, who is apt to pry
    Into my pleasures, I today   145
    Have bid Ganymede go play,
    And thus stole from heaven to be
    Welcome on earth to Danae.
    And see where the princely maid
    On her easy couch is laid,   150
    Fairer than the Queen of Love's
    Drawn about with milky doves.
    To thee let Paphian altars smoke;
    Priests thy better name invoke.
    When Hymen lights his holy fires,   155
    Thou that canst infuse desires
    In the gods, from thy lip
    Let Jove heavenly nectar sip;
    And translate, by kissing thee,
    Into thy breast his deity –   160
    But I rob myself of treasure:
    This is but the gate of pleasure.
    To dwell here, it were a sin,

135SD] *This ed.; not in* Q. 136–8.] Q; This . . . Jupiter / To . . . too, / Let . . . sake!
G. 139SP] *This ed.;* Donel. [coming forward.] – G; *Jupit.* Q. 139–66.] G; *no italics*
Q. 160. *deity –*] *This ed.;* Deity: Q.

136–8. There a hint here that the women suspect at least a degree of homoerotic
intent on Donella's part. This may be part of the 'plot' as alluded to earlier in the scene
(3).

  137. *have . . . swing*] have liberty to follow her feelings.

  144. Juno] Jupiter's wife, renowned for her jealousy.

  146. Ganymede] Jupiter's young male cupbearer and object of his homoerotic interest, hence the significance of the name adopted by Rosalind when cross-dressed in *AYL*.
Donella's claim here (albeit as Jupiter) to have dismissed any rival love-interest adds to
the homoerotic undertones of the scene.

  151. Queen of Love] Venus.

  153. Paphian] Paphos was where an altar to Venus was located.

  155. Hymen] god of marriage.

When Elysium is within.
Leave off then this flattering kisses,   165
To rifle other greater blisses.   Bell [*rings*] *within.*
Eugenia. The bell – news from my father.
Cassiana. Then your play is interrupted, Jove – Madam, I'll see.
                                                    [*Exit.*]
Donella. Beshrew the bell-man! And you had not waked as you did,
     madam, I should ha' forgot myself and played Jupiter indeed   170
     with you. My imaginations were strong upon me, and you lay so
     sweetly – How now?

                    [*Re-enter* CASSIANA.]

Cassiana. A present, madam, from the duke – one of the finest pieces
     of pageantry that e'er you saw: 'tis a cage with variety of birds in
     it. It moves on wheels – your assistance, ladies, to bring it in.   175
                                          [*Exeunt* Ladies.]
Eugenia. A cage – if from Florence it shall to the fire;
     Or whencesoe'er, it cannot be intended
     But as a mockery of my restraint.
     I'm very sad o' th' sudden –

               [*Re-enter* Ladies, *drawing the cage.*]

                    Ha, 'tis so;
     Break it to pieces!   180
Donella. 'Twere pity, madam, to destroy so much art.
Eugenia. Yet spare the workmanship; in the perusal
     There's something pleads for mercy. I feel within
     Some alteration, I know not what.
     Let me entreat your absence for some minutes.   185
     I am in earnest; pray do, without reply.
     Your eyes shall feed with plenteous satisfaction
     On this gay object, when I call you.
Ladies. We obey you.   [*Exeunt.*]
Eugenia. Yet, can't I say I am alone, that have   190

---

165. this] Q; thes G.   166SD] G; *Bell within.* Q.   168SD] G; *not in* Q.   172SD]
G; *not in* Q.   173. duke –] *This ed.*; Duke: Q.   175SD] G; *not in* Q.   179SD] G
(*subst.*); *not in* Q.   183. mercy.] *This ed.*; Mercy: – Q   187. shall] G; shell Q.
189SD] G; *not in* Q.

---

166. rifle] steal.
168. *play*] Literally the performance is interrupted, but there are further puns on
the sexual connotation of 'play'.
174. *pageantry*] The wheeled birdcage is being explicitly compared to the pageant
wagons familiar from medieval drama and in the early modern period from civic
pageantry such as the Lord Mayor's show. Shirley's *The Triumph of Peace* in 1634
would involve the use of several wagons or 'chariots'.
186. *in earnest*] serious (*OED* 1.2). See 3.4.115 and Introduction, p. 32.

So many partners in captivity?
Sweet fellow prisoners, 'twas a cruel art,
The first invention to restrain the wing.
To keep th' inhabitants o' th' air close captive
That were created to sky-freedom. Surely,   195
The merciless creditor took his first light,
And prisons their first models, from such bird-loops?
I know yon nightingale is not long lived;
See how that turtle mourns, wanting her mate.
And doth the duke, my father, think I can   200
Take comfort either in restraint, or in
The sight of these that every moment do
Present it to me? Were these tendered me?
They shall no more be prisoners to please me,
Nor shall the woods be robbed of so much music –   205

She opens the cage [and the birds fly out], and
[PHILENZO *disguised as*] ROLLIARDO *comes from the pillar.*

Philenzo. I take you at your word, fair princess;
   I am the truest prisoner. Tremble not,
   Fear flies the noble mind, for injury dares not come near.
Eugenia. Sir, what are you?
Philenzo. The humblest of your servants.   210
Eugenia. You are not mine; for in this bold attempt
   You have undone me.
Philenzo. You see I keep at distance.
Eugenia. You're too near; I will discover you,
   Though I fall myself by your presumption.   [*Starts to leave.*] 215
Philenzo. Hold, be counselled rather
   But to calm silence for a pair of minutes,
   And none shall perish: you shall save him, too,
   That would, for your sake, lose himself for ever.
Eugenia. For my sake? What relation has my birth,   220
   Or any passion I call mine to you?
Philenzo. Nor doom me unto scorn. I am a gentleman,

---

195. sky-freedom] *This ed.*; Skye freedome Q.   197. bird-loops?] *This ed.*; Bird
Loopes; Q; bird-loops; G.   203. Were] Q *(subst.)*; Why were G.   214-15. You're
. . . you, / Though . . . presumption.] *This ed.*; *prose in* Q; You . . . near, / I . . . myself /
By . . . presumption. G.   215SD] *This ed.*; [*Going.* G; *not in* Q.

192ff.] Eugenia identifies with the birds as fellow prisoners.
197. *bird-loops*] the hoops or wires of the cage.
198. *nightingale*] a bird often linked to melancholy, partly owing to its role in the
myth of Philomel. Having been raped by Tereus she metamorphosed into a nightingale
to sing of her plight.
199. *turtle*] turtle dove, proverbial for loyalty and monogamy (Dent T624).

And when my inimitable resolution
In those attempts, whose very sounds breeds earthquakes
In other hearers, shall your knowledge fill   225
With wonder and amaze, you will at least
Think I fall too low, if I love beneath you.
Eugenia. Ha? This is a strange accident.
Philenzo.   Was it less
Than death, dear princess, to adventure hither?
Eugenia. It will be death, however.   230
Philenzo. You're deceived, lady.
Eugenia. How I'm perplexed!
Philenzo.   It had been death.
Your sight gives me a lease of longer life.
My head stands fast.
Eugenia. [*Aside*]   He speaks all mystery;
I shall not get him off, I fear, without some stain.   235
Philenzo. The truth is, princess, if you now discover me –
Though I made nice at first to put your fright by –
You cannot harm me much: I ha' done my task.
Do you fear me still? Why is there such a space
Betwixt us, lady? Can you keep that man   240
At so unkind a distance, that for your sake
Has in his undertaking swallowed danger,
Robbed death of all his fears?
Eugenia.   For my sake?
Philenzo. Yours – fair princess, dare you so far trust me yet
To let me kiss your hand?
Eugenia.   Audacious sir,   245
I shall grow loud if you forget your distance,
Nor that you may hold long –
[*Aside*] I'm studying how I should be rid of him
Without their knowledge; yet that's dangerous too,
And might show guilt in me, for he will boast on't.   250
Philenzo. Such was the duke your gracious father's care,
He would put confidence in none about him,

---

224. breeds] *Q; breed G.*   232. death.] *Q; death to fail. G.*   234SD] *G; not in Q.*
234–5. He . . . mystery; / I . . . stain.] *G; prose in Q.*   235. shall not] *This ed.;* sha'
not *Q.*   236–7. me – / Though . . . by –] *This ed.;* me, / (Tho . . . by) *Q.*   240. lady?
Can] *This ed.;* lady? – Can *Q.*   243. sake?] *G; sake. Q.*   245. hand?] *G; hand. Q.*
248SD] *G (subst.); not in Q.*   248–50.] *This ed.;* I'm . . . theyr / Knowledge . . . might
/ Shew . . . on't. *Q.*

---

226. *amaze*] amazement.
235. *get him off*] get away from him.
237. *made nice*] pretended.
247.] Or continue too long.

But saw me brought himself.
Eugenia. This is a fine paradox –
Philenzo. Which must be to high purpose. Come, be wise,   255
    And keep me while you have me; 'tis but reaping
    This fruitless harvest from my cheek and chin,
    And you can form the rest. You're young and beautiful:
    Lose not the blessing of your youth, sweet princess:
    Fair opportunity waits upon your pleasure.   260
    You want but the first knowledge of your joy.
    Your blood is ripe; come, I am confident
    Your will is but controlled by upstart fears.
    Like advanced beggars, that will shock their princes,
    My safest way is yours – now to conceal me.   265
    It may be thought I have enjoyed you else;
    Ill censure soon takes fire. Nay, perhaps
    To be revenged of your stern cruelty,
    I'll swear myself I have possessed you freely.
    Play your game wisely, then; your honour lies   270
    Full at my mercy. Come, 'tis in your love
    To lead me to a secret couch.
Eugenia.   Bold villain,
    For these uncivil, most unhallowed words,
    I'll die, but I'll undo thee.   *[Starts to leave again.]*
Philenzo. Stay, and let me circle in mine arms   275
    All happiness at once; I have not soul
    Enough to apprehend my joy: it spreads
    Too mighty for me. Know, excellent Eugenia,
    I am the prince of Florence, that owe heaven
    More for thy virtues, than his own creation.   280
    I was born with guilt enough to cancel
    My first purity, but so chaste a love
    As thine, will so refine my second being
    When holy marriage frames us in one piece,
    Angels will envy me.
Eugenia.   Ha! the prince of Florence?   285

---

254. paradox –] *This ed.*; Paradoxe. Q.   265. yours –] *This ed.*; yours, Q.   274SD]
This ed.; [*Going. G; not in Q.*

---

258. *You're . . . beautiful*] Philenzo deploys *carpe diem* rhetoric, which was preva-
lent in Caroline poetry, as part of his testing of Eugenia's chastity.

263. *will*] desire.

264. *advanced*] brought forward (presumably for a monarch to see).

270. *game*] continues the complicated discourse of sports, games, and play in *The
Bird in a Cage*; see Introduction, pp. 31–2.

285. *prince . . . Florence*] Eugenia at this point believes Philenzo to be the Prince of
Florence, to whose father her father has promised her hand in marriage (see 299).

Philenzo. I ha' made no travel for so rich a blessing.
Turn me to pilgrimage, divinest beauty,
And when I ha' put a girdle 'bout the world,
This purchase will reward me.
Eugenia. Purchase? – I am not bought and sold I hope?   290
Philenzo. Give it what name you will, you're mine, Eugenia.
Eugenia. Yours, prince? I do not know
By what title you pretend this claim;
I never yet remember that I saw you,
And if you had any interest in myself,   295
Produce your witness, when I gave it you.
I have possession yet; ere I deliver it,
You must show stronger evidence.
Philenzo. Are we not contracted?
Eugenia. Contracted? When? Where? –   300
Good prince, I pity your abuse.
Philenzo. 'Tis firm between our fathers.
Eugenia. Mine cannot give away my heart.
Philenzo. Cannot?
Eugenia.   Shall not.
Prince, it is not your travel and your trouble   305
With this conceit to boot, were it your own
Invention, with all your birds about you,
That can take me.
Philenzo.   Is it my person, madam,
You hold unworthy? For my birth and fortune
Cannot deserve your scorn.
Eugenia.   It takes not from   310
The greatness of your state, or blood, my lord,
To say I cannot love you, since affection

292–4. Yours . . . know / By . . . claim; / I . . . you,] *This ed.*; Your's . . . not / Know . . .
claim; / I . . . you; *G; prose in Q.*   294. you] *This ed.*; I Q.   300–1. Contracted? . . .
Where? – / Good . . . abuse.] *This ed.*; Contracted? / When? . . . abuse. *G; prose in Q.*
304–5. Shall not. / Prince, it . . . travel] *G (subst.)*; Shall, not Prince, your travaile *Q.*

Philenzo, already performing the part of Rolliardo, here takes on a further layer of representation. He does not reveal the truth until Eugenia declares her unswerving loyalty
to Philenzo at 321–3.
   286. *travel*] (1) journey; (2) travail or hardship.
   288. *put . . . world*] made a circuit of the earth (*OED* 3b); cf. Shakespeare, *MND*
2.1.175.
   294. *you*] Q's 'I' is unclear, and has been presumed erroneous.
   305.] Gifford's additions (which I have retained) improve the metre and sense of this
passage.
   travel . . . trouble] Eugenia echoes Philenzo's double meaning at 286.

Flows uncompelled, and rests in the clear object.
Nor do I rob your person of just value,
If to me other seem as fair and comely.   315
Form may apparel, and become what we
Affect, not cause true love. You have enough
To promise you a happier choice; attempt
A nobler fate, and leave me to myself
And humble destiny. For know, Florentine,   320
I have but one faith, one love, and, though my father
Lock up my person, 'tis beyond his will
To make me false to him I gave my faith to.
And you're not noble now if you proceed;
Be, then, what you were born, and do not tempt   325
A woman to commit a sacrilege:
For when I give my heart to any other
Than my Philenzo, I commit that sin.
Philenzo. If you'll not pardon, I'll deliver up
Philenzo to be punished for this trial –   *Discovers himself.*
                                See, lady.   330
Eugenia. My dear banished Philenzo!   [*Kneeling before him*]
Philenzo. Oh, let not such a glorious building stoop:
It is my duty.   [*Kneeling too*]
Eugenia.   I will make it mine.   [*Both standing up*]
Philenzo. I have a double duty, for I owe
Your constancy as much respect and reverence,   335
As your most princely person.
Eugenia.   What for our safety?
Philenzo. Oh, with what willingness could I be lost
In this distracted wilderness of joy.
Tomorrow, madam, I go to my arraignment.
Eugenia. How?
Philenzo.   Spend no fear upon't,   340
Your story shall be pleasing – I ha' much
To tell you. For your ladies –
Eugenia. They are mine. What should our innocence
Fear in their knowledge? I desire to hear
The circumstance of this wonder
Philenzo.   It attends: 345
The story past, we must some counsel find;
The puzzle of our fate is still behind.   *Exeunt.*

330SD] *This ed.; He discovers himselfe. at l. 328 in Q;* [*Pulls off his false beard and hair. G.* 331SD] *This ed.; not in Q.* 333SD *Kneeling too] This ed.; not in Q.*
333SD *Both . . . up] This ed.; not in Q.* 342. *you. For] This ed.; you – for Q.*

---

332. *building*] body; cf. Shirley, *The Duke's Mistress* 1.1.
345. *attends*] follows.

ACT 5

SCENE I

Enter DONDOLO, MORELLO, [*and*] GRUTTI.

Dondolo. We are sorry we gave thee distaste. Come, let's be friends;
    you did apprehend too nicely.
Morello. Nicely? It might ha' been your own case.
Grutti. Come, you were unkind to rub us before the duke so.
Morello. Be wise hereafter, and make the fool your friend; 'tis many an   5
    honest man's case at court. It is safer to displease the duke than
    his jester: every sentence the one speaks, flatterers make an oracle,
    but let the impudent fool bark never so absurdly, other men ha'
    the wit to make a jest on't. 'Tis policy in state to maintain a fool
    at court to teach great men discretion.   10
Dondolo and Grutti. Great men? We are none!
Morello. No, but you may be, by the length of your wit and shortness
    of your memory; for if you have but wit enough to do mischief,
    and oblivion enough to forget good turns, you may come to great
    places in time. Keep a fool o' your own, and then you are made –   15
Dondolo. Made what?
Morello. Cuckolds, if my lady take a liking to the innocent. Oh, your
    fool is an excellent fellow upon all occasions.
    [*Sings*] *Among all sorts of people*
        The matter if we look well to,   20
    The fool is the best, he from the rest
    Will carry away the bell too.
    All places he is free of,
    And fools it without blushing.

0.] *A Part of the Palace. G.*   1. distaste. Come] *This ed.*; distaste: come, *G*; distaste,
come *Q.*   7. jester:] *This ed.*; jester; *G*; jester, *Q.*   9. on't.] *This ed.*; on't; *G*; on't,
Q.   11. men? . . . none!] *This ed.*; men! . . . none. *G*; men, . . . none. *Q.*   19SD] *This
ed.*; *Song Q.*

---

    4. *rub us*] rub our noses in our gullible behaviour.
    5. *make . . . friend*] Proverbial; see Dent F469: 'A Fool may sometimes give a wise
man counsel.' Cf. Jonson, *A Tale of a Tub* 2.3.56.
    9–10. *'Tis . . . discretion*] Proverbial (cf. Dent F530.12).
    17. *innocent*] half-witted, imbecilic (*OED* 3b).
    22. *carry . . . bell*] win the prize. Bells were given as prizes at horse races.

At masques and plays is not the bays   25
  Thrust out to let the plush in?
Your fool is fine; he's merry,
  And of all men doth fear least.
At every word he jests with my lord
  And tickles my lady in earnest: 30
The fool doth pass the guard now;
  He'll kiss his hand and leg it.
When wise men prate, and forfeit their state,
  Who but the fine fool will beg it?
He without fear can walk in   35
  The streets that are so stony;
Your gallant sneaks, your merchant breaks,
  He's a fool that does owe no money.

          Enter [PHILENZO disguised as] ROLLIARDO.

Philenzo. The duke, where is the duke?
Morello. He's forthcoming: there's no more money i' th' exchequer.   40
Philenzo. I come to give up my accounts, and reckon with him; some-
    body tell him so.
Morello. And you do not reckon well with him, he'll be even with you.
    I'll do your message.   [Exit.]
Philenzo. Do, and say I sent a fool o' my errand, prithee. Cry mercy,   45
    such an office would ha' become either of you gentlemen.

39SP] This ed.; Rol. G; Boll. Q.   43SP] This ed.; Mor. G; Mor, Q.   44SD] G; not in
Q.

25-6. At ... in?] The implication is that the self-display of courtiers in velvet
('plush') is favoured over genuine wit or literary skills (as represented by the 'bays', a
laurel wreath usually awarded as a prize in literary or intellectual competitions) in court
theatre. Gifford suggested a possible allusion to the Jacobean and Caroline court jester
Archibald Armstrong who eventually lost his privileged position at court after openly
mocking Archbishop Laud. Morello's lyrics suggest, however, that the fool often escapes
the dismissal endured by literary counterparts, enjoying instead the ear of the court
(29-30).
    30. in earnest] with all seriousness (though with a bawdy inference in this context).
The oxymoronic idea of tickling with serious intent extends the ethical role Morello
assigns the court fool throughout this exchange. It is familiar from many Shakespearean
plays, especially King Lear. Morello's use of this phrase in his song also underscores
its significance in the play as a whole (see 3.4.115, 4.2.187, and Introduction, p. 32).
    31.] The image rewrites Morello's failure to access Eugenia's tower earlier in the play.
    32. leg it] bow.
    37. breaks] becomes bankrupt.
    38.] Presumably a proverbial defence of the credit system, although it has not been
traced. On credit generally in this period see Ceri Sullivan, The Rhetoric of Credit:
Merchants in Early Modern Writing (London: Associated University Presses, 2002).
    40. exchequer] see 4.1.5.

Dondolo. His tongue moves circular in abuses.
Grutti. The duke.

    Enter DUKE, FULVIO, PERENOTTO, *and* [*Attendants*].

Duke. How now, what day is't?
Philenzo. 'Tis holiday.   50
Duke. How?
Philenzo. Therefore we are preparing a morris to make your grace
    merry. They have chosen me for the hobby-horse, and if I do not
    deceive their expectation, they will laugh at me extremely before I
    die.   55
Duke. Do you come like one prepared for death?
Philenzo. Not so well, I hope, as I may be hereafter, unless you will be
    unjust, and have a desire to be clapped into the chronicles with
    some o' your predecessors for cutting off heads when you do not
    like their complexion. 'Tis but laying one block upon another, and   60
    I am quickly sent of a headless errand.
Duke. Unjust? Do you remember what sums you owe for? Do not jest
    away your life.
Philenzo. I crave no longer day for't, and I prove not myself free from
    my engagements.   65
Duke. How?
Philenzo. For, although I had not the art to go invisible as these wise
    courtiers, nor could counterfeit another sex so becomingly as t'
    other gaudy signor to introduce me to the ladies, yet, with your
    princely licence, I may say 'tis done.   70
Duke. Done? What is done?
Perenotto. He's mad, sir.
Philenzo. I come not to petition for a mercy,
    But to cry up my merit for a deed

48SD] *G; &c Q.*   53. if I do] *G;* if doe *Q.*   62. Unjust] *This ed.;* Iniust *Q.*

47. *moves . . . in*] never rests from making.

52. *morris*] morris dance; English folk dance that often included characters such as
Robin Hood and Maid Marion and the hobby-horse (53).

53. *hobby-horse*] created by a performer inside a wooden frame fitted with the head
and tail of a horse, with material often covering the actor's body and legs (similar to
modern pantomime horses). Miniature versions were popular as children's toys: Lantern
Leatherhead makes a living selling these in Jonson's *Bart. Fair.*

60. *one . . . another*] punning on the slang word for a head.

67–9. *although . . . ladies*] Philenzo here recalls the various follies of the play, including Bonamico's gulling of Dondolo and Grutti, and Morello's failed attempt at
cross-dressing.

74. *cry up*] proclaim in public.

Shall drown all story; and posterity,   75
When it shall find in her large chronicle
My glorious undertaking, shall admire it
More than a Sibyl's leaf, and lose itself
In wonder of the action. Poets shall
With this make proud their muses, and apparel it   80
In ravishing numbers, which the soft-haired virgins,
Forgetting all their legends, and love-tales
Of Venus, Cupid, and the scapes of Jove,
Shall make their only song and in full choir
Chant it at Hymen's feast.   85
Duke. What means this boasting?
Fulvio. Rolliardo?
Philenzo. You think I am a lost man, and your gay things,
   That echo to your passions, and see through
   Your eyes all that's presented, do already   90
   Tickle their very souls with expectation
   To see me beg most miserably for life.
   But you are all deceived. Here I pronounce
   The great work done that cancels all my debts:
   I have had access unto the fair Eugenia,   95
   Your princely daughter; stayed, discoursed with her;
   More, she has entertained me for her servant.
Perenotto. Sir, do you believe him?
Duke. Thou hast profaned a name will strike thee dead.
Philenzo. It cannot be; for, if you mean your daughter,   100
   'Tis that is my preserver: blessed Eugenia,
   To whose memory my heart does dedicate
   Itself an altar; in whose very mention
   My lips are hallowed, and the place a temple
   Whence the divine sound came. It is a voice   105

---

84. choir] *This ed.;* quire Q.   93. deceived. Here] *This ed.;* deceiu'd – here Q.

---

76. *chronicle*] As with his earlier obsession with his epitaph, Philenzo is deeply concerned with the way posterity and history will portray him.

78. *Sibyl's leaf*] The Sibyl was a classical prophetess. She inscribed people's fate on leaves and if the wind blew them away their fates would rest unknown.

83. *scapes . . . Jove*] echoing Morello at 3.1.8.

85. *Hymen*] God of marriage.

88. *gay things*] courtiers (continuing Philenzo's earlier exposure of the vanity of courtiers in his role as Rolliardo the cynic).

101–5. *blessed . . . came*] Philenzo's religious vocabulary here and his description of himself at 97 as Eugenia's 'servant' deploy the language of neoplatonic worship of women which was highly fashionable at the Caroline court at this time.

Which, should our holy churchmen use, it might,
Without addition of more exorcism,
Disenchant houses, tie up nightly spirits
Which fright the solitary groves. Eugenia,
When I have named, I needs must love my breath   110
The better after it.
Duke.   Thou hast undone
Thyself i' th' repetition, and in this
Wherein thou cunningly wouldst beg our pity,
Thou hast destroyed it, and not left a thought   115
To plead against our anger. Where before
Thy life should have been gently invited forth,
Now with a horrid circumstance death shall
Make thy soul tremble, and, forsaking all
The noble parts, it shall retire into   120
Some angle of thy body, and be afraid
To inform thy eyes, lest they let in a horror
They would not look on.
Philenzo.   I am still the same, and let me be so bold
To plead your royal word, 'twas my security;   125
Nor shall you take mine to induce your faith
To what is done. I have more pregnant evidence:
                              [*Hands the duke a letter.*]
Your highness knows that character.
Duke. Ha? 'Tis not so – I'll not believe my eyes.
Come hither, Fulvio, Perenotto: read,   130
But not too loud. Does she not write to me
It is unjust you let Rolliardo die,
Unless Eugenia bear him company?
Give me the paper.
Perenotto.   'Tis counterfeit, my lord. Cut off my head   135
If this be not a jig of his invention.
Duke. My soul is in a sweat. I feel my blood
Heave in my veins – he looks as he had seen her.
More, my prophetic thoughts do whisper to me –
Fulvio. Believe it not, sir.   140
Duke. I won't – Perenotto –   [*Takes Perenotto aside.*]

---

112. undone] G; vndone. Q.   127SD] *This ed.; Presents a paper.* G; *not in* Q.
129. so –] *This ed.;* so, Q.   132–3.] Q *(subst.); in italics* G.   141. won't] *This ed.;*
wo'not Q.   141SD] G; *not in* Q.

---

108. *Disenchant*] Remove a spell from, exorcise.
   127SD] The stage property of the letter in Eugenia's hand is an intriguing reworking of Bonamico's earlier trick with the letter at 3.2. A further letter appears and is read aloud onstage at 299ff.

Dondolo. I know not what to think.

Grutti. The duke's perplexed: observe.

Philenzo. Will either of you speak for me, gentlemen, if the justice of
my cause should fail me? I'll pay you for't. I know courtiers, that   145
live upon countenance, must sell their tongues: what is the price
of yours, pray?

Grutti. Humble yourself, you coxcomb.

Duke. Away –   [*Exit* PERENOTTO.]
    and let not him stir, I charge you.
[*Aside*] This does entrench too much upon her person.   150
Have my endeavours to preserve Eugenia,
Of whom I thought so many men unworthy,
Ruined themselves? Human invention
Could not instruct me to dispose her where
She could be more defenced from all men's eyes: 155
An anchorite lives not prisoned in a wall
With more security. 'Tis not possible.
Why am I troubled thus? My fear abuses me;
In such a cause I would check an oracle.
And shall his dextrous forgery unsettle   160
My confidence? I won't show a guilt
Of so much weakness in me. [*To the court*] Fulvio –
And gentlemen – we'll speak to you anon.

Philenzo. [*Aside*] I ha' spoke too much already, it seems. Sure he has
sent for her; I dare repose my life on her, to whose trust I gave my   165
heart. She is a thousand witnesses in herself.

Fulvio. [*To the duke*] It will be mirth, sir.

Philenzo. [*Aside*] I like not this consulting: they break off pleasantly.
Now, in the name of Mercury, what crotchet?

Duke. I see it is in vain   170
To interrupt our fate; what is decreed
Above becomes not mortals to dispute.
[*To Philenzo*] Sit there   [*Gestures towards the throne.*]

---

143. duke's] *G*; Duk's *Q*.   149SD] *G*; *not in Q*.   149. not him] *Q*; him not *G*.
150SD] *This ed.*; *not in Q*.   159. check an] *Q (subst.)*; check [at] an *G*.   161. won't]
This ed.; wo' not *Q*.   162SD] *This ed.*; *not in Q*.   164SD] *G*; *not in Q*.   164–6.]
Q; *verse in G*.   166. thousand] *G*; tbousand *Q*.   167SD] *This ed.*; *not in Q*.
168SD] *This ed.*; *not in Q*.   168–9.] *Q*; *verse in G*.   173SD To Philenzo] *This ed.*;
not in Q.   173SD *Gestures . . . throne*] *This ed.*; *not in Q*.

---

155. *defenced*] preserved, defended.

156. *anchorite*] religious hermit; echoing Donella's earlier use of this phrase at
3.3.14.

169. *crotchet*] See 2.1.295.

173SD, 174SD] Philenzo's immediate impulse to remove his hat (indicated by the
duke's order he remain covered at 174) suggests that the gesture must be to the throne

             – nay, be not modest, you were born to't,
And therefore take your place. [*Philenzo starts to remove his hat.*]
           Nay, nay, be covered;
Imagine that a crown, and these your subjects;   175
As when I die, you know 'twill come to that,
In right of my sole daughter. So, does he not
Look like a prince indeed? Appears he not
A pretty lamp of majesty?
Dondolo. He's studying some speech, I'll lay my life –   180
Duke. Against his coronation, to thank all
His loving subjects, that, as low as earth,
Thus offer him their duties.
        [*The courtiers*] *draw their swords* [*against Philenzo.*]

        Enter EUGENIA *and* PERENOTTO.

Eugenia. Hold, I beseech you.
    Let not my duty suffer misconstruction   185
    If, while my knee doth beg your blessing, here
    I throw my arms, and circle, next to heaven,
    What must be dearest to me.   [*Embraces Philenzo.*]
Duke. Ha?
Eugenia. My joy of life.   190
Duke. Destroy me not.
Eugenia. Alas, I would preserve all; am so far from killing
    That I would die myself rather than see
    One drop of blood forced from his crimson fountain,
    Or but one tear racked from your eye. Oh, hear me,   195
    And after let your anger strike two dead –
    So you would let us dwell both in one grave;
    And did you know how near we were in life
    You would not think it fitting that in death
    Our ashes were divided. You have heard   200
    When the poor turtle's ravished from her mate,
    The orphaned dove doth groan away her life
    In widow's solitude; let me call him husband

174SD] *This ed.; not in* Q.   183SD *The ... Philenzo.*] *This ed.; Draw their Swords.*
Q.   188SD] *G; not in* Q.   191. not.] *G; not?* Q.   195. from] *G; frow* Q.

as seat of power. This stage business is difficult to decipher since courtiers were usually
expected to be hatless in the presence of a ruler. Philenzo's covered head may be a mark
of defiance, underscored by the duke's insistence that he remain covered at this point
in the action.
   201–3. *turtle ... solitude*] Turtle doves were proverbially loyal to their mates; cf.
4.2.199.

And tell yourself the rest.
Duke. Kill not thy father with one word, Eugenia –   205
   Thy husband?
Eugenia. I do beseech you, hear me.
Duke. Beg thou mayst be forgotten; 'tis sin
   'Bove my forgiveness: this a match for thee?
   What man can bring me a certificate   210
   He had a father, or was christened? He?
   We all are in a dream; awake me, thunder!
Philenzo. Temper your passion, sir.
Duke. Some tortures, to enforce confession from him
   How he procured access.   215
Philenzo. They sha' not need; you sent me, sir, yourself.
Duke. We?
Philenzo. The cage was my conveyance.
Perenotto. That was presented lately with the birds – you gave
   command.
Duke. Be dumb! I dare not hear you.   220
Dondolo. This was a bird in a cage, indeed!
Duke. Search for the traitor Bonamico, presently.
   He has betrayed me.   [*Exit* GRUTTI.]
             They shall suffer both,
   Before the noise be spread to our dishonour.
Eugenia. Yet will you hear me?   225
Duke. I hear too much. Thou hast forgot thy birth,
   Thy fortunes, and thy father; were my cares
   So wondered at abroad, censured at home,
   Worthy of nothing but contempt from thee
   For whom they were begotten? Thou hast ploughed   230
   Upon my face; canst thou undo a wrinkle,
   Or change but the complexion of one hair?
   Yet thou hast greyed a thousand; taken from me,
   Not added to my comforts, more than what
   Like an indulgent parent I have flattered   235
   Myself into.

       Enter [GRUTTI *with*] BONAMICO.

205. Eugenia –] G; Eugenia, Q.   206. husband?] Q *(subst.); husband?* G.   208. 'tis
sin] Q *(subst.);* 'tis a sin G.   221. bird . . . cage] Q; *in capitals* G.   223SD] G; *not
in* Q.   236SD] G *(subst.).*

221.] It was common in Caroline plays to include the title in the closing lines (see,
e.g., Ford's *'Tis Pity She's a Whore*). Shirley's play may not have been called this for
the original performance (see Introduction, p. 23), but Dondolo's line still refers to the
central plot device of the cage of birds so is unlikely to have been a late addition.
   230. *Thou . . . ploughed*] written lines or wrinkles (i.e. ploughed furrows).

Grutti. Here is the other traitor, sir.
Duke. Away with 'em to death.
Eugenia. Let me go too.
Duke. It needs not, thou art dead already, girl,   240
    And, in thy shame, I and the dukedom suffer.
    Thou mayst remember – false to thy own vow –
    Philenzo, whom I banished for thy sake.
    The title of my subject, and thy love
    To him, pulled our displeasure on him. Since,   245
    We studying to add more height to thee,
    Thou hast made thyself less, and, for aught we know,
    Clasped with the son of earth to cool the fever
    Of hot sin in thy veins, ungrateful to
    Philenzo, cold already in thy memory.   250
Philenzo. 'Tis happiness enough that you have mentioned him,
    And whither to your mercy, or your justice,
    See that Philenzo kneel.   [*Reveals himself and kneels.*]
All. Lord Philenzo!
Fulvio. My noble cousin, so near me, and concealed!   255
Eugenia. Your daughter's knees join with his bended heart
    To beg your pardon.   [*Kneels.*]
Duke. Philenzo? Were not you banished, sir?
Philenzo. It was your sentence.
Duke. In pain of death not to return. Blessed fate,   260
    Thou hast relieved me. Hadst thou died before
    By our command, it would have been thought tyranny,
    Though none durst tell us so; now we have argument
    Of justice, and our every breath is law
    To speak thee dead at once. We sha' not need   265
    To study a divorce. Thy second exile
    Shall be eternal: death.
Philenzo. You do me honour.

---

242. remember – . . . vow –] *This ed.;* remember (. . . vow) *Q.* 246.] *Q (subst.); in
parentheses G.* 248. the] *Q;* this *G.* 253SD] *This ed.; Discovers himself. G.*
254SP] *This ed.; Omnes. Q.* 254. Philenzo!] *G; Philenzo. Q.* 257SD] *G; not in Q.*
258. Philenzo? Were . . . sir?] *this ed.;* Philenzo! – / Were . . . sir? *G; Philenzo?
were . . . Sir. Q.* 259SP] *This ed.; Roll. Q; henceforth G substitutes 'Phil.' for 'Rol.'.*
260. In] *Q;* On *G.* 260. return. Blessed] *This ed.;* return? – Blest *G;* returne, blest
Q. 261. me. Hadst] *This ed.;* me. – Hadst *G;* mee, had'st *Q.* 265. once. We] *G;*
once, wce *Q.* 266. divorce. Thy] *This ed.;* divorce, thy *Q.*

---

246. *add . . . thee*] raise your status (by marriage into the ruling family of Florence).
248. *Clasped . . . earth*] Had sexual intercourse with someone of lower social status.

Duke. [*To Bonamico*] Be it your punishment, as you preferred him
    By art to her, now by another art   270
    Forever to divide 'em: be's executioner.
    And, after, make him higher by the head
    To cure's ambition: see't advanced.
Philenzo. Ere I go, dread sir,
    I have an humble suit. It is not life   275
    I'll ask, for that I give up willingly,
    And call it mercy in you to immortalize
    The affection I shall owe Eugenia.
    Your other banishment is only death;
    You new create me now. It was my aim.   280
    And my attempt you thought so bold I made
    To serve this end, that since I could not live
    I might die for her. Pray, reprieve my breath
    But till I take my leave. One minute does it;
    It shall be a very short and silent farewell.   285

                  Enter AMBASSADOR.

Duke. 'Tis granted.
Fulvio. My lord ambassador.
Duke. [*Aside to Fulvio*] Not the least whisper of Philenzo, as you value
    our regard – Oh, my good lord, welcome.
Ambassador. Letters to your grace.   290
Duke. They are grateful as my comfort. Perenotto, let them withdraw;
    her vein will be discovered – [*Aside to Fulvio*] Fulvio, follow and
    part 'em. Give order for his execution; off with his head instantly.
    I can read no more for joy – Perenotto, use your best oratory on
    my daughter to forget that traitor and prepare to marry Florence: 295
    'tis concluded to be solemnised by proxy.
          [*Exit* PERENOTTO *with* EUGENIA *and* PHILENZO,
              with FULVIO *and* BONAMICO *following*.]
Dondolo. I'll see the execution.   *Exit.*

269SD] *G; not in Q.*   288SD] *G; not in Q.*   291. comfort.] *This ed.*; comforte – *Q.*
292. vein] *Q* (vaine).   293. instantly.] *This ed.*; instantly – *Q.*   296SD] *G; not in Q.*

   269. *preferred*] transported, carried.
   272–3. *make . . . ambition*] the heads of executed persons were frequently displayed
on poles to serve as warnings to others.
   280–3. *It . . . her*] Philenzo suggests the duke answers his wish ('aim') by executing
him, since if he could not marry Eugenia he intended to be martyred for her sake. Slight
repunctuation of this passage clarifies *Q*'s ambiguity.
   291. *grateful*] gratefully received.
   292. *vein*] intention, disposition of mind.

Duke. Now, to the rest.

[*Reads.*] 'Your last letters were acceptable, and our son before had
intention to finish the marriage in his person; but lately, receiving   300
intelligence that one Philenzo of noble birth, now in exile, though
without your consent, had long since interest in your daughter's
affection, we thought meet rather to advise for his repeal than
proceed to our dishonour. Where the hearts meet, there only mar-
riages are sacred, and princes should be exemplary in all justice.   305
Although we disclaim in this design, on our parts we will continue
all other princely correspondence.'
I am justly punished and have run myself
Into a labyrinth from whence no art
Can bring me off with safety. [*To Ambassador*] My lord, you may   310
Please to retire yourself –   [*Exit* AMBASSADOR.]
                    a thousand wheels
Do move preposterous in my brain. What cure?
I lose myself – run with a haste thou wouldst
Preserve my life, and stay the execution.
I will not have a drop of blood fall from   315
Philenzo for my dukedom. Fly, I say;
Thou shouldst be there already.   [*Exit Attendant.*]

                    Enter DONDOLO.

How now? Has Philenzo still a head on?
Dondolo. Yes, my lord.
Duke. Follow him, and with that nimbleness thou wouldst   320
Leap from thy chamber when the roof's a-fire,
Proclaim aloud our pardon to Philenzo,
And bring him back to us.   [*Exit* GRUTTI.]
Dondolo. 'Tis too late, sir, Philenzo's dead already:
He saved the executioner that trouble.   325
The voice is he is poisoned.

                    Enter FULVIO.

299SD] *G; not in Q.* 299–307. 'Your . . . correspondence.'] *This ed.; in italics G; no
quotation marks Q.* 310. safety.] *This ed.; safety – Q.* 310SD] *This ed.; not in Q.*
311. yourself –] *G; yourself, Q.* 311SD] *This ed.; not in Q.* 313. myself – Run] *G
(subst.); my selfe, runne Q.* 316. dukedom. Fly] *This ed.; dukedom. – Fly G; Duke-
dome, flye Q.* 317SD] *G; not in Q.* 323SD] *G; not in Q.*

303. *advise . . . repeal*] sue for the annulment of his banishment.
306. *disclaim . . . design*] renounce our claims in this matter.
310–11. *My . . . yourself*] The duke appears to instruct the ambassador to leave at
this point, though Q makes no provision for an exit.
312. *preposterous*] contrary to reason.
313–14. *with . . . execution*] as if you were running to save my life, and thereby stop
the execution of Philenzo taking place.
326. *voice*] word, rumour.

Duke. Poisoned? How? –
    Where is Philenzo?
    This fool reports him poisoned; what circumstance?
Fulvio. He had no sooner parted from Eugenia,   330
    But suddenly he fainted; at which fall
    Of his own spirit, he seemed grieved with shame
    To show so little courage near his death,
    Which he called martyrdom, and presently –
    Whether supplied by other, or prepared   335
    By himself, we know not – he had a vial
    Of water sovereign, as was pretended,
    To enliven his dull heart. He drank it up,
    And soon showed cheerful in his eyes. We led
    Him smiling forward, but before we could   340
    Approach the place of death, he sunk again,
    But irrecoverably, for in vain we applied
    Our help; by which we did conclude he had
    Drunk poison.
Duke. All this talk is such, and through   345
    My ear I take it in with as much danger;
    I feel it active in my brain already.
    Call our physicians. I will hang 'em all,
    Unless they can recover him. It shall be
    Death to save any man hereafter, if   350
    They suffer him to perish.

            Enter PERENOTTO [*and*] EUGENIA.

Fulvio. Sir, your daughter:
    It seems the accident has arrived at her.
Duke. Arrived at her? Fame will soon spread it, Fulvio,
    About the world, and we shall be their mockery.   355
    He's dead they tell me, girl; poisoned they say, too.
Eugenia. Oh, my Philenzo.

        Enter GRUTTI [*and* BONAMICO]. PHILENZO's *body is*
        brought in, and laid upon a carpet.

---

327. Poisoned?] G; Poyson'd, Q.   327. How?] G *(subst.)*; how – Q.   329. poisoned; what] Q *(subst.)*; poison'd; what's the G.   334. presently –] *This ed.*; presently, G; presently Q.   336. not –] not, Q.   336. vial] Q *(Violl)*.   338. enliven] Q *(inlifne)*.   351SD] Q *(subst.)*; Re-enter PERENOTTO *and* EUGENIA, *followed by the ladies.* G   357SD] *This ed.*; Re-enter GRUTTI *and* BONAMICO, *followed by officers bringing in* PHILENZO's *body, which is laid upon a carpet.* G; Enter Grutti, *Philenzoes Body is brought in, and layd vpon a Carpet.* Q.

---

337. *sovereign*] possessing special power or potency.
345. *such*] the same (i.e. poison to him).

Duke. Eugenia, sha' not marry Florence now,
 Nor any other, since Philenzo's dead:
 But, thou wilt not believe me, had he lived,   360
 He had been thine. That minute took him hence,
 Wherein I first resolved to ha' given thee to him.
Eugenia. Oh, do not mock me, sir, to add to my
 Affliction; you ne'er would give me to him.
Duke. May heaven forgive me never then! But what 365
 Avails too late compunction? Noble gentleman,
 Thou shalt have princely funeral, and carry
 On thy cold marble the inscription of
 Our son in death, and my Eugenia's husband.
Fulvio. Madam, this sorrow for his loss is real.   370
 We met the Florentine ambassador,
 Who told me the expectation of that prince
 Was now dissolved, and messengers were sent
 To stay the execution.
Duke.   Who now
 Shall marry my Eugenia? I have undone   375
 The hope of our posterity.
Eugenia.   Not so, sir;
 If yet you'll give me leave to make my choice,
 I'll not despair to find a husband.
Duke.   Where?
Eugenia. Here, royal sir; Philenzo is not dead,
 But made by virtue of a drink to seem so,   380
 Thus to prevent his suffering, that I might,
 Or other friend by my confederacy,
 By begging of his body fit for burial,
 Preserve him from your anger.
Duke. Dost not mock me?   385
Eugenia. Let me beg your pardon;
 Confident of your change to mercy, I have
 Confessed what terror could not force me to.

    Enter MORELLO, *and* Ladies.

---

358. sha' not] *This ed.*; 'shalt G; 'shat Q. 360. wilt not] G; wo't Q. 364. ne'er]
Q *(nere).* 388SD] Q; G *omits 'and Ladies.'.*

367–9. *carry . . . husband*] Here the duke himself writes an epitaph for Philenzo.
379–80. *Philenzo . . . so*] The plotline of the feigned death by poisoned drink is a
conscious echo of Shakespeare's *Rom.*

Grutti. This is pretty, Dondolo.
Duke. Blessings fall doubly on thee!
Eugenia.   He expects   390
   Not such a full stream of happiness; heaven dispose him
   To meet it quickly.
Perenotto. Here are strange turnings; see, he stirs!
Philenzo. [*Awakening*] Where am I now? No matter where I be,
   'Tis heaven if my Eugenia meet me here.   395
   She made some promise sure to such a purpose.
   This music sounds divinely; ha, Eugenia!
   'Tis so; let's dwell here for eternity.
   If I be dead, I wo' not live again;
   If living –   [*Sees the duke.*]
       ha! I'm lost, lost for ever.   400
Duke. Not found till now; take her, a gift from me,
   And call me father.
Philenzo.   I am not yet awake.
Eugenia. Thou art, Philenzo, and all this is truth.
   My father is converted.
Philenzo.   'Tis a miracle.
Duke. You must believe it.   405
   In sign how we are pleased, proclaim this day
   Through Mantua a pardon to all offenders,
   As amply as when we took our crown.
Morello. Then my petticoat is discharged.
Dondolo. Now, lady, you are free.   410
Grutti. Make me happy to renew my suit.
Morello. And mine; shall's to barley-break?
   I was in hell last, 'tis little less to be in a petticoat, sometimes.
Philenzo. [*Indicating Bonamico*] Madam, vouchsafe him kiss your
   hand,
   We owe him much.   415

390–1. expects / Not such] *Q*; expects not / Such *G*.   392. quickly.] *This ed.*; quickly!
G; quickly, *Q*.   394SD] *G* (*subst.*); not in *Q*.   400SD] *G* (*subst.*); not in *Q*.
404.] *Q*; *G adds SD* 'Rising'.   412. shall's] *Q*; shall we *G*.   412. barley-break?] *G*;
Barlibreake. *Q*.   414SD] *This ed.*; not in *Q*.

397. *music*] Music may have been played at this point; alternatively it could be a
metaphorical allusion to the sweet news Philenzo has awakened to.

   412. *barley-break*] a game, also known as 'last-in-hell'. It was played by six people,
three of each sex, and involved the ground being divided into three sections, with
the middle section designated 'hell'. The couple condemned to hell try to catch the
others, but are not allowed to lose contact with each other as they do so, and if they
succeed they swap places. The last couple to be caught were called the 'last in hell'
(*Shakespeare's England*, 2.479). Cf. Middleton, *The Changeling* 3.3.165; 5.3.163.

Duke. We'll take him to our service.

Bonamico. I am too much honoured.

Duke. [*To Philenzo*] And you into our bosom. This day shall
    Be consecrate to triumph, and may time,
    When 'tis decreed the world shall have an end,   420
    By revolution of the year make this
    The day that shall conclude all memories.   *Exeunt.*

417SP] G; Dond. Q.   418SD] *This ed.; not in* Q.   422SD] G; *Exeunt Omnes.* Q.

The Convent of Pleasure
Margaret Cavendish

edited by Hero Chalmers

1. Since *The Convent of Pleasure* was not written for or performed in the public playhouses, the printed text does not have a title page comparable to those in *F1* of *The Wild-Goose Chase* or *Q* of *The Bird in a Cage*.

THE ACTORS' NAMES

Three Gentlemen.
LADY HAPPY.
MADAM MEDIATOR.
MONSIEUR TAKE-PLEASURE.
DICK HIS MAN.   5
MONSIEUR FACIL.
MONSIEUR ADVISER.
MONSIEUR COURTLY.
LADY AMOROUS.
LADY VIRTUE.   10
THE PRINCESS.
MIMIC, *a fool.*
Servant to Lady Happy.
The Ladies of the Convent.
Two Mean Women.   15

---

3. MADAM] *F;* MADAME *Shaver.* 10. VIRTUE] *F (*Vertue*).* 11.] *F;* THE PRINCE *Shaver.* 12.] *This ed.;* MIMICK THE FOOL *Shaver; not in F.* 13.] *Shaver; not in F.* 14.] *Shaver; not in F.* 15–27.] *not in Shaver.*

The Actors' Names] Cavendish places the dramatis personae at the end of her play as she does in all but one of the pieces in *Plays, Never Before Printed* (1668) although not in *Playes* (1662). Unlike Shaver, this edition follows *F* in listing the characters from the Act 3 playlets – who are played by the ladies of the convent – since such a decision appears to reflect the way in which the multiple impersonations throughout the play seem to take on a life of their own. Characters who appear in the play, but whom Cavendish has omitted from her list, have also been added here. For characters who recur from her play *The Bridals* see Introduction, p. 35. *F* offers almost no specific indications of location beyond those implied in the dialogue, except in the stage direction which opens the final scene where the wedding party is imagined coming from the church. Otherwise, the action takes place inside the convent of pleasure or in its environs. The period of the play remains similarly unspecificied in *F*. Despite the church wedding, the characters sometimes speak loosely of classical-sounding 'gods' (e.g. 1.2.39, 40), yet, as our introduction and commentary demonstrate, many aspects of the play bind it overwhelmingly to the seventeenth-century context of its composition.

3. *MEDIATOR*] Suggests the way in which Madam Mediator moves between the various groups of characters although, ironically, sometimes stirring up strife as much as pursuing mediation or reconciliation.

6. *FACIL*] (1) Affable or courteous; (2) easily led.

15. *Mean*] of low social status.

A Lady and her Maid.
Two Ladies.
A Distracted Lady and her Maid.
A Citizen's Wife and Two Gentlemen.
A Lady in Labour and a Company of Women.   20
Two Ancient Ladies.
A Gentleman and a Young Lady.
Two Shepherds.
Sea-Nymphs.
An Ambassador.   25
Men.
Magistrates.

---

19. and . . . Gentlemen] *This ed.; not in* F.   20.] *This ed.; not in* F.   23.] *This ed.;* A
Shepherd F.

19. *Citizen's Wife*] This title establishes her social rank as beneath, or distinct from,
that of the landed nobility or gentry.

ACT I

Enter Three Gentlemen

1 Gentleman. Tom, where have you been, you look so sadly of it?

2 Gentleman. I have been at the funeral of the Lord Fortunate who has left his daughter, the Lady Happy, very rich, having no other daughter but her.

1 Gentleman. If she be so rich, it will make us all young men spend all 5
our wealth in fine clothes, coaches, and lackeys to set out our wooing hopes.

3 Gentleman. If all her wooers be younger brothers, as most of us gallants are, we shall undo ourselves upon bare hopes without probability. But is she handsome, Tom? 10

2 Gentleman. Yes, she is extreme handsome, young, rich, and virtuous.

1 Gentleman. Faith, that is too much for one woman to possess.

2 Gentleman. Not if you were to have her.

1 Gentleman. No, not for me, but in my opinion too much for any other man. *Exeunt.* 15

SCENE 2

Enter LADY HAPPY *and one of her* Attendants.

Servant. Madam, you being young, handsome, rich, and virtuous, I hope you will not cast away those gifts of nature, fortune, and heaven upon a person which cannot merit you?

Lady Happy. Let me tell you that riches ought to be bestowed on such as are poor and want means to maintain themselves, and youth on 5
those that are old, beauty on those that are ill-favoured, and virtue on those that are vicious. So that if I should place my gifts rightly,

---

11. extreme] *This ed.;* extream *F;* extremely *Rowsell.*

oSD LADY HAPPY] *This ed.; the lady* Happy *F.*

---

6. *lackeys*] footmen.

8. *younger brothers*] those who do not stand to inherit the family fortune owing to the principle of primogeniture.

9–10. *undo . . . probability*] ruin ourselves because of our unrealistic expectations.

6. *ill-favoured*] ugly.

7. *vicious*] guilty of vice.

I must marry one that's poor, old, ill-favoured, and debauched.
Servant. Heaven forbid!
Lady Happy. Nay, heaven doth not only allow of it but commands it,   10
for we are commanded to give to those that want.

Enter MADAM MEDIATOR.

Madam Mediator. Surely, madam, you do but talk and intend not to
go where you say.
Lady Happy. Yes, truly, my words and intentions go even together.
Madam Mediator. But surely you will not incloister yourself as you say.   15
Lady Happy. Why, what is there in the public world that should invite
me to live in it?
Madam Mediator. More than if you should banish yourself from it.
Lady Happy. Put the case I should marry the best of men, if any best
there be; yet would a married life have more crosses and sorrows   20
than pleasure, freedom, or happiness. Nay, marriage to those that
are virtuous is a greater restraint than a monastery. Or, should I
take delight in admirers, they might gaze on my beauty and praise
my wit and I receive nothing from their eyes nor lips. For words
vanish as soon as spoken, and sights are not substantial. Besides,   25
I should lose more of my reputation by their visits than gain by
their praises. Or, should I quit reputation and turn courtesan, there
would be more lost in my health than gained by my lovers; I should
find more pain than pleasure. Besides, the troubles and frights I
should be put to, with the quarrels and brouilleries that jealous   30
rivals make, would be a torment to me. And 'tis only for the sake
of men when women retire not. And since there is so much folly,
vanity, and falsehood in men, why should women trouble and vex
themselves for their sake? For retiredness bars the life from nothing
else but men.   35
Madam Mediator. Oh, yes, for those that incloister themselves bar
themselves from all other worldly pleasures.
Lady Happy. The more fools they.
Madam Mediator. Will you call those fools that do it for the gods' sake?
Lady Happy. No, madam, it is not for the gods' sake, but for opinion's   40

11SD] *This ed.; Enter Madam* Mediator *to the Lady* Happy *F.*   15. incloister] F
*(*incloyster*).*   23. admirers,] *This ed.;* Admirers? *F.*

11. *we . . . want*] a sentiment frequently reiterated in the New Testament, e.g.
Matthew, 19.21, Mark, 10.21, Luke, 14.13, Galatians, 2.10.
27. *quit*] renounce.
courtesan] prostitute.
30. *brouilleries*] disputes, turmoils.
32. *retire*] retreat from the world.

sake. For can any rational creature think or believe the gods take
delight in the creature's uneasy life? Or, did they command or give
leave to nature to make senses for no use, or to cross, vex, and
pain them? For what profit or pleasure can it be to the gods to
have men or women wear coarse linen or rough woollen, or to flay   45
their skin with hair-cloth, or to eat or saw through their flesh with
cords? Or what profit or pleasure can it be to the gods to have men
eat more fish than flesh, or to fast, unless the gods did feed on such
meat themselves? For then, for fear the gods should want it, it were
fit for men to abstain from it. The like for garments, for fear the   50
gods should want fine clothes to adorn themselves, it were fit men
should not wear them. Or, what profit or pleasure can it be to the
gods to have men to lie uneasily on the hard ground, unless the
gods and nature were at variance, strife and wars as if what is dis-
pleasing unto nature were pleasing to the gods and to be enemies   55
to her were to be friends to them?
Madam Mediator. But being done for the gods' sake, it makes that
   which in nature seems to be bad, in divinity to be good.
Lady Happy. It cannot be good if it be neither pleasure nor profit to
   the gods. Neither do men anything for the gods' but their own   60
   sake.
Madam Mediator. But when the mind is not employed with vanities,
   nor the senses with luxury, the mind is more free to offer its ado-
   rations, prayers, and praises to the gods.
Lady Happy. I believe the gods are better pleased with praises than   65
   fasting. But, when the senses are dulled with abstinency, the body
   weakened with fasting, the spirits tired with watching, the life
   made uneasy with pain, the soul can have but little will to worship.

---

45. flay] F *(flea)*.

---

41. *rational creature*] Lady Happy here reflects Cavendish's consistent support in
her writings on natural philosophy for the idea that men and women have 'rational
souls', e.g. *Philosophical and Physical Opinions* (London, 1655), sig. B2v; *Philosophical Letters* (London, 1664), p. 112; *Observations upon Experimental Philosophy*,
second edition (London, 1668), pp. 301–6.
   43. *nature*] here, as elsewhere in her writings, Cavendish figures nature as a benign
feminine figure, 'the Infinite Servant of God', as she writes in *Observations Upon Experimental Philosophy*, sig. e2v. See also e.g. *Poems and Fancies* (London, 1653), p. 1;
Philosophical Letters, p. 302; *Observations Upon Experimental Philosophy*, p. 102.
For a discussion of this phenomenon see Rebecca Merrens, 'A Nature of "Infinite Sense
and Reason": Margaret Cavendish's Natural Philosophy and the "Noise" of a Femi-
nised Nature', *Women's Studies*, 2 (1996), 421–38.
   46. *hair-cloth*] fabric made of hair, used for a variety of purposes such as tents,
towels, and most relevantly here, the shirts of penitents or ascetics.
   63. *luxury*] (1) indulgence in what is choice or costly; (2) lasciviousness or lust.

Only the imagination doth frighten it into active zeal, which devotion is rather forced than voluntary, so that their prayers rather   70
flow out of their mouth than spring from their heart, like rainwater that runs through gutters or like water that's forced up a hill
by artificial pipes and cisterns. But those that pray not unto the
gods, or praise them more in prosperity than adversity, more in
pleasures than pains, more in liberty than restraint, deserve neither   75
the happiness of ease, peace, freedom, plenty, and tranquillity in
this world, nor the glory and blessedness of the next. And if the
gods should take pleasure in nothing but in the torments of their
creatures, and would not prefer those prayers that are offered with
ease and delight, I should believe the gods were cruel. And what   80
creature that had reason or rational understanding would serve
cruel masters when they might serve a kind mistress, or would
forsake the service of their kind mistress to serve cruel masters?
Wherefore, if the gods be cruel, I will serve nature. But the gods
are bountiful and give all that's good, and bid us freely please our-   85
selves in that which is best for us: and that is best what is most
temperately used and longest may be enjoyed. For excess doth
waste itself and all it feeds upon.
Madam Mediator. In my opinion your doctrine and your intention do
not agree together.   90
Lady Happy. Why?
Madam Mediator. You intend to live incloistered and retired from the
world.
Lady Happy. 'Tis true, but not from pleasures, for I intend to incloister myself from the world to enjoy pleasure, and not to bury myself   95
from it; but to incloister myself from the encumbered cares and
vexations, troubles, and perturbance of the world.
Madam Mediator. But if you incloister yourself, how will you enjoy
the company of men, whose conversation is thought the greatest
pleasure?   100
Lady Happy. Men are the only troublers of women, for they only cross
and oppose their sweet delights and peaceable life. They cause their
pains but not their pleasures. Wherefore those women that are
poor and have not means to buy delights and maintain pleasures
are only fit for men. For, having not means to please themselves,   105
they must serve only to please others. But those women, where
fortune, nature, and the gods are joined to make them happy, were
mad to live with men, who make the female sex their slaves. But
I will not be so enslaved, but will live retired from their company.

69–70. *devotion*] religious observance, devoutness.
96. *but to*] only
99. *conversation*] (1) interaction; (2) sexual intercourse, intimacy.

Wherefore, in order thereto, I will take so many noble persons   110
of my own sex as my estate will plentifully maintain – such
whose births are greater than their fortunes, and are resolved to
live a single life and vow virginity. With these I mean to live inclois-
tered, with all the delights and pleasures that are allowable and
lawful. My cloister shall not be a cloister of restraint but a place   115
for freedom, not to vex the senses but to please them.
For every sense shall pleasure take,
And all our lives shall merry make.
Our minds in full delight shall joy,
Not vexed with every idle toy.   120
Each season shall our caterers be
To search the land and fish the sea,
To gather fruit and reap the corn
That's brought to us in plenty's horn,
With which we'll feast and please our taste   125
But not luxurious make a waste.
We'll clothe ourselves with softest silk,
And linen fine as white as milk.
We'll please our sight with pictures rare,
Our nostrils with perfumèd air,   130
Our ears with sweet melodious sound
Whose substance can be nowhere found,
Our taste with sweet delicious meat
And savoury sauces we will eat.
Variety each sense shall feed   135
And change in them new appetites breed.
Thus will in pleasure's convent I
Live with delight and with it die.   *Exeunt.*

---

113. *live . . . virginity*] Cf. Montagu, *The Shepheard's Paradise*, p. 22, where the
inhabitants 'vow chastity and single life'.

117–38. *For . . . die*] reminiscent of Christopher Marlowe's poem, 'The Passionate
Shepheard to his love', printed in *England's Helicon* (London, 1600), with which this
passage shares a structure of rhyming couplets and iambic tetrameters, and which opens
with the famous lines: 'Come live with me and be my love, / And we will all the pleasures prove.'

124. *plenty's horn*] the mythical cornucopia or horn of plenty, traditionally represented in art as a goat's horn overflowing with flowers, fruit, and corn.

126. *luxurious*] (1) indulgently; (2) lasciviously.

133. *meat*] food.

ACT 2

    Enter MONSIEUR TAKE-PLEASURE *and his man,* DICK.

Take-Pleasure. Dick, am I fine today?
Dick. Yes, sir, as fine as feathers, ribbons, gold, and silver can make
    you.
Take-Pleasure. Dost thou think I shall get the Lady Happy?
Dick. Not if it be her fortune to continue in that name.   5
Take-Pleasure. Why?
Dick. Because, if she marry your worship she must change her name;
    for the wife takes the name of her husband and quits her own.
Take-Pleasure. Faith, Dick, if I had her wealth I should be happy.
Dick. It would be according as your worship would use it, but, on my   10
    conscience, you would be more happy with the lady's wealth than
    the lady would be with your worship.
Take-Pleasure. Why should you think so?
Dick. Because women never think themselves happy in marriage.
Take-Pleasure. You are mistaken, for women never think themselves   15
    happy until they be married.
Dick. The truth is, sir, that women are always unhappy in their
    thoughts, both before and after marriage: for before marriage they
    think themselves unhappy for want of a husband, and after they
    are married they think themselves unhappy for having a husband.   20
Take-Pleasure. Indeed, women's thoughts are restless.

    Enter MONSIEUR FACIL *and* MONSIEUR ADVISER *to* MONSIEUR
      TAKE-PLEASURE, *all in their wooing accoutrements.*

Take-Pleasure. Gentlemen, I perceive you are all prepared to woo.
Facil. Yes, faith, we are all prepared to be wooers. But whom shall we
    get to present us to the Lady Happy?
Adviser. We must set on bold faces and present ourselves.   25
Take-Pleasure. Faith, I would not give my hopes for an indifferent
    portion.
Facil. Nor I.

---

16. happy] *Rowsell, Shaver*; happpy *F.*

---

8. *quits*] renounces.
26–7. *indifferent portion*] moderately large dowry.

Adviser. The truth is we are all stuffed with hopes, as cushions are with
   feathers.   30

Enter MONSIEUR COURTLY

Courtly. Oh, gentlemen, gentlemen, we are all utterly undone.
Adviser. Why, what's the matter?
Courtly. Why, the Lady Happy hath incloistered herself with twenty
   ladies more.
Adviser. The devil she hath!   35
Facil. The gods forbid!
Courtly. Whether it was the devil or the gods that have persuaded her
   to it I cannot tell, but gone in she is.
Take-Pleasure. I hope it is but a blast of devotion which will soon flame
   out.   40

Enter MADAM MEDIATOR

Take-Pleasure. Oh, Madam Mediator, we are all undone: the Lady
   Happy is incloistered.
Madam Mediator. Yes, gentlemen, the more is the pity.
Adviser. Is there no hopes?
Madam Mediator. Faith, little.   45
Facil. Let us fee the clergy to persuade her out for the good of the
   commonwealth.
Madam Mediator. Alas, gentlemen, they can do no good, for she is not
   a votress to the gods but to nature.
Courtly. If she be a votress to nature, you are the only person fit to be   50
   lady prioress and so by your power and authority you may give us
   leave to visit your nuns sometimes.
Madam Mediator. Not but at a grate, unless in time of building or when
   they are sick. But, howsoever, the Lady Happy is lady prioress
   herself and will admit none of the masculine sex, not so much as   55
   to a grate, for she will suffer no grates about the cloister. She has
   also women physicians, surgeons, and apothecaries, and she is the
   chief confessor herself, and gives what indulgences or absolutions

---

39. *devotion*] See 1.2.69–70. The men appear initially to assume that Lady Happy has
withdrawn from the world for religious reasons, until Madam Mediator corrects them.

46. *fee*] pay.

50. *votress*] woman under a vow.

53. *grate*] grating, grille.

58. *confessor*] continues Madam Mediator's emphasis on women taking up male
professions in the 'convent' by implying that Lady Happy will take on the traditional
priest's role of hearing confessions of sin.

indulgences] in the Roman Catholic tradition, the Church's remission of a punishment still considered due for sin after sacramental absolution.

absolutions] remissions or forgivenesses of sin.

she pleaseth. Also her house, where she hath made her convent, is
so big and convenient and so strong as it needs no addition or   60
repair. Besides, she has so much compass of ground within her
walls as there is not only room and place enough for gardens,
orchards, walks, groves, bowers, arbours, ponds, fountains,
springs, and the like, but also conveniency for much provision, and
hath women for every office and employment. For though she hath   65
not above twenty ladies with her, yet she hath a numerous company
of female servants, so as there is no occasion for men.
Take-Pleasure. If there be so many women, there will be the more use
for men. But pray, Madam Mediator, give me leave rightly to
understand you by being more clearly informed. You say the Lady   70
Happy is become a votress to nature, and if she be a votress to
nature she must be a mistress to men.
Madam Mediator. By your favour, sir, she declares that she hath avoided
the company of men by retirement merely because she would enjoy
the variety of pleasures which are in nature of which, she says, men 75
are obstructors. For, instead of increasing pleasure, they produce
pain, and instead of giving content, they increase trouble. Instead
of making the female sex happy, they make them miserable, for
which she hath banished the masculine company for ever.
Adviser. Her heretical opinions ought not to be suffered, nor her doc-   80
trine allowed; and she ought to be examined by a masculine synod
and punished with a severe husband or tortured with a debauched
husband.
Madam Mediator. The best way, gentlemen, is to make your complaints
and put up a petition to the state with your desires for a redress.   85
Courtly. Your counsel is good.
Facil. We will follow it and go presently about it.   *Exeunt.*

---

82. debauched] F *(deboist)*.

60. *convenient*] favourable to the comfort of its inhabitants, commodious.
64. *conveniency . . . provision*] suitable conditions for providing an ample supply of
food to the household.
71–2. *if . . . men*] Take-Pleasure implies that it is simply acting in accordance with
nature for women to take male suitors.
80. *heretical*] contrary to orthodox doctrines.
81. *synod*] ecclesiastical council.
85. *petition*] Cavendish may be satirising the men's outrage further by implictly
linking it to the upsurge of political and religious petitions to Parliament which had
occurred around the English civil war: see Derek Hirst, *Authority and Conflict: England
1603–58* (London: Edward Arnold, 1986), pp. 194, 202–3, 219–20, 228, 273, 308,
315.

SCENE 2

Enter LADY HAPPY *with her* Ladies *and* MADAM MEDIATOR.

Lady Happy. Ladies, give me leave to desire your confession, whether
or no you repent your retirement.

Ladies. Most excellent lady, it were as probable a repentance could be
in heaven amongst angels as amongst us.

Lady Happy. Now, Madam Mediator, let me ask you, do you condemn   5
my act of retirement?

Madam Mediator. I approve of it with admiration and wonder, that
one that is so young should be so wise.

Lady Happy. Now, give me leave to inform you how I have ordered
this our convent of pleasure. First, I have such things as are for our   10
ease and conveniency; next for pleasure and delight, as I have
change of furniture for my house according to the four seasons of
the year, especially our chambers: as in the spring, our chambers
are hung with silk-damask and all other things suitable to it and
a great looking-glass in each chamber that we may view ourselves   15
and take pleasure in our own beauties whilst they are fresh and
young. Also, I have in each chamber a cupboard of such plate
as is useful, and whatsoever is to be used is there ready to be
employed. Also, I have all the floor strewed with sweet flowers. In
the summer I have all our chambers hung with taffety and all other   20
things suitable to it and a cupboard of porcelain and of plate, and
all the floor strewed every day with green rushes or leaves, and
cisterns placed near our bed-heads wherein water may run out of
small pipes made for that purpose. To invite repose in the autumn,
all our chambers are hung with gilt leather or frangipane, also beds   25
and all other things suitable, and the rooms matted with very fine
mats. In the winter our chambers must be hung with tapestry and
our beds of velvet lined with satin and all things suitable to it, and

---

0SD LADY HAPPY] *This ed.; the Lady* Happy *F.*   0SD Ladies *and*] *This ed.; Ladies; as
also F.*   21. porcelain] *This ed.;* Purseline *F;* Porcelaine *Rowsell.*

7. *admiration*] amazement.

14. *silk-damask*] rich silk fabric, woven with elaborate designs and figures; often in
a variety of colours and taking its name from Damascus where it was originally manufactured.

17. *plate*] valuable household utensils.

20. *taffety*] taffeta: a fine, diaphanous silk fabric.

25. *gilt*] coated wholly or in part with a thin layer of gold.

25. *frangipane*] sweet-smelling flowers of red jasmine.

all the floor spread over with Turkey carpets, and a cupboard of
gilt plate, and all the wood for firing to be cypress and juniper, and   30
all the lights to be perfumed wax. Also, the bedding and pillows
are ordered according to each season, viz. to be stuffed with feathers in the spring and autumn and with down in the winter, but in
the summer to be only quilts either of silk or fine holland, and our
sheets, pillows, tablecloths, and towels to be of pure fine holland   35
and every day clean. Also, the rooms we eat in and the vessels we
feed withal I have according to each season, and the linen we use
to our meat to be pure fine diaper and damask and to change it
fresh every course of meat. As for our galleries, staircases, and passages, they shall be hung with various pictures and, all along the   40
wall of our gallery, as long as the summer lasts, do stand upon
pedestals flower-pots with various flowers and in the winter orange
trees. And my gardens to be kept curiously and flourish in every
season of all sorts of flowers, sweet herbs and fruits, and kept so
as not to have a weed in it. And all the groves, wildernesses,   45
bowers, and arbours pruned and kept free from dead boughs,
branches, or leaves. And all the ponds, rivulets, fountains, and
springs, kept clear, pure, and fresh. Also, we will have the choic-
est meats every season doth afford, and that every day our meat
be dressed several ways and our drink cooler or hotter according   50
to the several seasons, and all our drinks fresh and pleasing.
Change of garments are also provided, of the newest fashions for
every season, and rich trimming so as we may be accoutred properly and according to our several pastimes. And our shifts shall be
of the finest and purest linen that can be bought or spun.   55
Ladies. None in this world can be happier.
Lady Happy. Now, ladies, let us go to our several pastimes, if you
    please.   *Exeunt.*

---

30. *juniper*] The seeds and wood of this tree were formerly burnt as purifiers of the
air and the coal of juniper wood was fabled to have a wonderful power of remaining
glowing.
    34. *holland*] linen fabric originating in the Netherlands.
    37–8. *linen . . . meat*] table-linen.
    38. *diaper*] a linen or cotton fabric woven with a simple pattern consisting of lines
crossing diamond-wise.
    43. *curiously*] skilfully, with great care.
    50. *dressed*] prepared.
    54. *shifts*] chemises.

SCENE 3

Enter [LADY AMOROUS *and* LADY VIRTUE].

Lady Amorous. Madam, how do you since you were married?
Lady Virtue. Very well, I thank you.
Lady Amorous. I am not so well as I wish I were.

Enter MADAM MEDIATOR.

Madam Mediator. Ladies, do you hear the news?
Lady Virtue. What news?   5
Madam Mediator. Why, there is a great foreign princess arrived, hearing
    of the famous convent of pleasure, to be one of nature's devotees.
Lady Amorous. What manner of lady is she?
Madam Mediator. She is a princely brave woman truly, of a masculine
    presence.   10
Lady Virtue. But, Madam Mediator, do they live in such pleasure as
    you say? For they'll admit you, a widow, although not us, by
    reason we are wives.
Madam Mediator. In so much pleasure as nature never knew before
    this convent was. And for my part, I had rather be one in the   15
    convent of pleasure than empress of the whole world. For every
    lady there enjoyeth as much pleasure as any absolute monarch can
    do, without the troubles and cares that wait on royalty. Besides,
    none can enjoy those pleasures they have unless they live such a
    retired or retreated life free from the world's vexations.   20
Lady Virtue. Well, I wish I might see and know what pleasures they
    enjoy.
Madam Mediator. If you were there you could not know all their plea-
    sure in a short time for, their varieties will require a long time to
    know their several changes. Besides, their pleasures and delights   25
    vary with the seasons, so that, what with the several seasons and
    the varieties of every season, it will take up a whole life's time.
Lady Virtue. But I could judge of their changes by their single
    principles.
Madam Mediator. But they have variety of one and the same kind.   30
Lady Virtue. But I should see the way or manner of them.
Madam Mediator. That you might.   *Exeunt.*

oSD] *This ed.; Enter Two* Ladies. F.   3SD] *This ed.; Enter . . .* Mediator *to them.* F.
28. judge] *Rowsell;* judg F.

    7. *devotees*] worshippers.
    28–9. *single principles*] own general rules.

SCENE 4

Enter MONSIEUR ADVISER, MONSIEUR COURTLY, MONSIEUR
          TAKE-PLEASURE, *and* MONSIEUR FACIL.

Courtly. Is there no hopes to get those ladies out of their convent?
Adviser. No, faith, unless we could set the convent on fire.
Take-Pleasure. For Jupiter's sake, let us do it! Let's every one carry a
     fire-brand to fire it.
Courtly. Yes, and smoke them out as they do a swarm of bees.   5
Facil. Let's go presently about it.
Adviser. Stay, there is a great princess there.
Take-Pleasure. 'Tis true, but when that princess is gone we will surely
     do it.
Adviser. Yes, and be punished for our villainy.   10
Take-Pleasure. It will not prove villainy for we shall do nature good
     service.
Adviser. Why, so we do nature good service when we get a wench with
     child, but yet the civil laws do punish us for it.
Courtly. They are not civil laws that punish lovers.   15
Adviser. But those are civil laws that punish adulterers.
Courtly. Those are barbarous laws that make love adultery.
Adviser. No, those are barbarous that make adultery love.
Facil. Well, leaving love and adultery, they are foolish women that vex
     us with their retirement.   20
Adviser. Well, gentlemen, although we rail at the Lady Happy for retir-
     ing, yet if I had such an estate as she and would follow her example,
     I make no doubt but you would all be content to incloister your-
     selves with me upon the same conditions as those ladies incloister
     themselves with her.   25
Take-Pleasure. Not unless you had women in your convent.
Adviser. Nay, faith, since women can quit the pleasure of men, we men
     may well quit the trouble of women.
Courtly. But is there no place where we may peek into the convent?
Adviser. No, there are no grates, but brick and stone walls.   30

---

3. *Jupiter's*] This may well be another instance of Cavendish having *The Bird in a
Cage* in mind since the incarcerated ladies in that play choose to act out the story of
Jupiter's appearance to Danae in a shower of gold.
    6. *presently*] immediately.
    14. *civil laws*] laws of any city or state regulating the private rights and duties of
the inhabitants. In the next line Courtly puns on another sense of civil, i.e. humane,
gentle, or kind, thereby implying the apparent incivility of the civil law in punishing
people for supposed acts of love; see also the pun in l. 16.
    27. *quit*] renounce.
    30. *grates*] gratings, grilles.

Facil. Let us get out some of the bricks or stones.

Adviser. Alas, the walls are a yard thick!

Facil. But nothing is difficult to willing minds.

Adviser. My mind is willing but my reason tells me it is impossible –
wherefore I'll never go about it.   35

Take-Pleasure. Faith, let us resolve to put ourselves in women's apparel
and so by that means get into the convent.

Adviser. We shall be discovered.

Take-Pleasure. Who will discover us?

Adviser. We shall discover ourselves.   40

Take-Pleasure. We are not such fools as to betray ourselves.

Adviser. We cannot avoid it, for our very garb and behaviour, besides
our voices, will discover us. For we are as untoward to make curtsies in petticoats as women are to make legs in breeches, and it will
be as great a difficulty to raise our voices to a treble-sound as for   45
women to press down their voices to a bass. Besides, we shall never
frame our eyes and mouths to such coy, dissembling looks, and
pretty simpering mopes and smiles as they do.

Courtly. But we will go as strong lusty country wenches that desire to
serve them in inferior places and offices as cook-maids, laundry-   50
maids, dairy-maids, and the like.

Facil. I do verily believe I could make an indifferent cook-maid, but
not a laundry- nor a dairy-maid, for I cannot milk cows nor starch
gorgets. But I think I could make a pretty shift to wash some of
the ladies' night-linen.   55

Take-Pleasure. But they employ women in all places in their gardens
and for brewing, baking, and making all sorts of things. Besides,
some keep their swine, and twenty such like offices and employments there are which we should be very proper for.

Facil. Oh, yes, for keeping of swine belongs to men: remember the   60
prodigal son.

Adviser. Faith, for our prodigality we might be all swine-herds.

Courtly. Also, we shall be proper for gardens, for we can dig and set
and sow.

Take-Pleasure. And we are proper for brewing.   65

---

33. *nothing . . . minds*] proverbial (Dent N299).
38. *discovered*] revealed.
44. *legs*] obeisances made by drawing back one leg and bending the other.
48. *mopes*] grimaces, face-pulling.
54. *gorgets*] articles of female dress covering the neck and breast.
54–5. *I . . . night-linen*] a bawdy pun on the two senses of shift: (1) a stratagem or
expedient where 'make shift to' means contrive to; (2) a chemise as at 2.2.54 above.
See also l. 69.
60–1. *keeping . . . son*] the prodigal son appears as a swineherd in Luke, 15.15–16.

Adviser. We are more proper for drinking, for I can drink good beer
     or ale when 'tis brewed. But I could not brew such beer or ale as
     any man could drink.
Facil. Come, come, we shall make a shift one way or other. Besides,
     we shall be very willing to learn and be very diligent in our ser-   70
     vices, which will give good and great content. Wherefore, let us go
     and put these designs into execution.
Courtly. Content, content.
Adviser. Nay, faith, let us not trouble ourselves for it, 'tis in vain.

                                                                    Exeunt.

66–7. *beer or ale*] both malt liquors, but beer had hops added.
70–1. *services*] probably punning on the underlying meaning of sexual attentions.

ACT 3

Enter the PRINCESS *and* LADY HAPPY *with the rest of the*
Ladies *belonging to the convent.*

Lady Happy. Madam, your highness has done me much honour to
come from a splendid court to a retired convent.

Princess. Sweet Lady Happy, there are many that have quit their
crowns and power for a cloister of restraint. Then well may I quit
a court of troubles for a convent of pleasure. But the greatest plea-   5
sure I could receive were to have your friendship.

Lady Happy. I should be ungrateful should I not be not only your
friend but humble servant.

Princess. I desire you would be my mistress and I your servant, and
upon this agreement of friendship I desire you will grant me one   10
request.

Lady Happy. Anything that is in my power to grant.

Princess. Why then, I observing in your several recreations, some of
your ladies do accoutre themselves in masculine habits and act
lovers' parts, I desire you will give me leave to be sometimes so   15
accoutred and act the part of your loving servant.

Lady Happy. I shall never desire to have any other loving servant than
yourself.

Princess. Nor I any other loving mistress than yourself.

Lady Happy. More innocent lovers never can there be   20
Than my most princely lover that's a she.

Princess. Nor never convent did such pleasures give,
Where lovers with their mistresses may live.

Enter a Lady.

---

oSD LADY HAPPY] *This ed.; the Lady* Happy *F.*   20–3.] F; *prose in Rowsell.*   23SD]
This ed.; Enter a Lady, *asking whether they will see the play F.*

3. *quit*] renounced, abdicated.
9. *mistress . . . servant*] Lady Happy appears to have used the term 'servant' in a
more neutral sense, but the princess subtly redirects it to mean a lover where 'mistress'
means female love-object within the language of courtly love on which she draws here.
See also l. 16.
20–3. *More . . . live*] In addition to their proleptic irony (given the princess's ultimate revelation as a prince) these lines touch on the play's concern with the acceptable
boundaries of female same-sex relations: see Introduction p. 39.

Lady. May it please your highness, the play is ready to be acted.

> THE PRINCESS *and* LADY HAPPY *sit down to watch the play.*
> *Enter a woman dressed as a man who speaks the prologue.*

[*Prologue*]. Noble spectators, you shall see tonight   25
   A play which though't be dull yet's short to sight.
   For since we cannot please your ears with wit,
   We will not tire your limbs long here to sit.

SCENE 2

> *Enter* Two Mean Women.

1 Woman. Oh, neighbour, well met. Where have you been?

2 Woman. I have been with my neighbour, the cobbler's wife, to comfort her for the loss of her husband who is run away with Goody Mettle, the tinker's wife.

1 Woman. I would to heaven my husband would run away with Goody   5
Shred, the botcher's wife, for he lies all day drinking in an alehouse like a drunken rogue as he is. And when he comes home, he beats me all black and blue, when I and my children are almost starved for want.

2 Woman. Truly, neighbour, so doth my husband, and spends not   10
only what he gets but what I earn with the sweat of my brows; the whilst my children cry for bread, and he drinks that away that should feed my small children which are too young to work for themselves.

1 Woman. But I will go and pull my husband out of the alehouse or   15
I'll break their lattice-windows down.

24SD] *This ed.; The Scene is opened, the* Princess *and* L. Happy *sit down, and the Play is Acted within the Scene; the* Princess *and the* L. Happy *being Spectators. Enter one drest like a Man that speaks the Prologue. F.*

24SD] The phrase '*The Scene is opened*' in the original SD was conventionally used to indicate the beginning of the action of a play or of an act or scene. However, Cavendish's additional instruction that '*the Play is Acted within the Scene*' shows that she is also using the term 'scene' to signify the place where the action is located. Yet she gives no specific locations for the series of short scenes that follow and the very rapidity with which the action shifts from one place to another calls on spectators or readers to imagine changed locations.

4. *Goody*] Goodwife: a term of civility applied to a woman, usually a married woman of lowly social station.

Mettle] spirit, vivacity, and therefore may be sexually suggestive in this context. Also puns on 'metal' since she is the tinker's wife.

6. *botcher*] a mender of old clothes, a patcher up (hence the pun on 'Shred').

16. *lattice-windows*] criss-cross patterned windows. Lattice-work windows (usually painted red) were a common mark of an inn.

2 *Woman.* Come, I'll go and help, for my husband is there too. But we
shall be both beaten by them.
1 *Woman.* I care not, for I will not suffer him to be drunk, and I and
my children starve. I had better be dead.   *Exeunt.*   20

SCENE 3

Enter a Lady *and her* Maid.

Lady. O I am sick!
Maid. You are breeding a child, madam.
Lady. I have not one minute's time of health.   *Exeunt.*

SCENE 4

Enter Two Ladies.

1 Lady. Why weep you, madam?
2 Lady. Have I not cause to weep when my husband hath played all
his estate away at dice and cards, even to the clothes on his back?
1 Lady. I have as much cause to weep then as you, for though my
husband hath not lost his estate at play, yet he hath spent it   5
amongst his whores, and is not content to keep whores abroad but
in my house, under my roof, and they must rule as chief mistresses.
2 Lady. But my husband hath not only lost his own estate, but also my
portion, and hath forced me with threats to yield up my jointure
so that I must beg for my living for anything I know as yet.   10
1 Lady. If all married women were as unhappy as I, marriage were a
curse.
2 Lady. No doubt of it.   *Exeunt.*

SCENE 5

Enter a Lady *almost distracted, running about the stage with
her* Maid *following her.*

Lady. O! My child is dead, my child is dead. What shall I do, what
what shall I do?

Scene 5, 0SD] *This ed.; Enter a Lady, as almost distracted, running about the Stage,
and her Maid follows her. F.*   1. dead, . . . dead.] *This ed.;* dead, . . . dead, *F.*

---

9. *portion*] dowry, marriage gift.
jointure] part of the husband's estate designated in the marriage settlement as due
to his widow on his death.
0SD *distracted*] insane.

Maid. You must have patience, madam.
Lady. Who can have patience to lose their only child? Who can? Oh,
    I shall run mad, for I have no patience.   5
                    Runs off the stage. Exit Maid *after her.*

SCENE 6

    Enter a Citizen's Wife *as if going into a tavern where a bush is
        hung out. She meets some* Gentlemen *there.*

Citizen's Wife. Pray gentlemen, is my husband, Mr Negligent, here?
1 Gentleman. He was, but he is gone some quarter of an hour since.
Citizen's Wife. Could he go, gentlemen?
2 Gentleman. Yes, with a supporter.
Citizen's Wife. Out upon him! Must he be supported? Upon my credit,   5
    gentlemen, he will undo himself and me too with his drinking and
    carelessness; leaving his shop and all his commodities at sixes and
    sevens – and his 'prentices and journeymen are as careless and idle
    as he. Besides, they cozen him of his wares. But was it a he or she-
    supporter my husband was supported by?   10
1 Gentleman. A she-supporter, for it was one of the maidservants
    which belong to this tavern.
Citizen's Wife. Out upon him, knave! Must he have a she-supporter,
    in the devil's name? But I'll go and seek them both out with a
    vengeance.   15
2 Gentleman. Pray, let us entreat your stay to drink a cup of wine with
    us.
Citizen's Wife. I will take your kind offer, for wine may chance to abate
    choleric vapours and pacify the spleen.

---

4. Who can?] *This ed.*; who can! *F.*

oSD *as if going into] This ed.; as into F.*   oSD *out. She] This ed.; out, and F.*

---

oSD *bush*] a branch or bunch of ivy hung up as a vintner's sign; hence, the sign-
board of a tavern. Cf. Epilogue to *AYLI* and Jonson, *New Inn* 1.2.28.
3. *go*] walk.
8. *journeymen*] employed craftsmen.
9. *cozen*] cheat.
19. *choleric*] giving rise to anger; choler means yellow bile, one of the four so-called
humours believed in early physiology to be responsible for shaping people's different
physical and mental characteristics. The other three humours were black bile, blood,
and phlegm, associated respectively with melancholy, sanguine, and phlegmatic temperaments.
    vapours] harmful exhalations believed to be developed within the body's organs.
    spleen] bodily organ which was viewed as the seat of the emotions and passions; by
extension, a term for fiery temper or malice.

1 Gentleman. That it will, for wine and good company are the only   20
    abaters of vapours.
2 Gentleman. It doth not abate vapours so much as cure melancholy.
Citizen's Wife. In truth, I find a cup of wine doth comfort me
    sometimes.
1 Gentleman. It will cheer the heart.   25
2 Gentleman. Yes, and enlighten the understanding.
Citizen's Wife. Indeed, and my understanding requires enlightening.
                                                           Exeunt.

SCENE 7

> *Enter a* Lady *groaning in labour, with a* Company of Women.

Lady. O my back! My back will break! O! O! O!
1 Woman. Is the midwife sent for?
2 Woman. Yes, but she is with another lady.
Lady. O my back! O! O! O Juno, give me some ease!   *Exeunt.*

SCENE 8

> *Enter* Two Ancient Ladies.

1 Lady. I have brought my son into the world with great pains, bred
    him with tender care, much pains, and great cost, and must he now
    be hanged for killing a man in a quarrel? When he should be a
    comfort and staff of my age, is he to be my age's affliction?
2 Lady. I confess it is a great affliction, but I have had as great, having   5
    had but two daughters and them fair ones though I say it, and
    might have matched them well. But one of them was got with child
    to my great disgrace, the other run away with my butler, not worth
    the droppings of his taps.
1 Lady. Who would desire children, since they come to such   10
    misfortunes?   *Exeunt.*

SCENE 9

> *Enter* Two Women.

1 Woman. Is the midwife come, for my lady is in a strong labour?

Scene 7, 0SD] *This ed.; Enter . . . big with Child, groaning as in labour, and a Company
of Women with her. F.*
Scene 9, 0SD] *This ed.; Enter one Woman meeting another. F.*

---

   4. *Juno*] wife of Jupiter and goddess of childbirth.

   8. *butler*] servant in charge of the wine cellar.

2 *Woman.* No, she cannot come, for she hath been with a lady that
hath been in strong labour these three days of a dead child and 'tis
thought she cannot be delivered.

Enter another Woman.

3 *Woman.* Come away, the midwife is come.   5
1 *Woman.* Is the lady delivered she was withal?
3 *Woman.* Yes, of life, for she could not be delivered and so she died.
2 *Woman.* Pray, tell not our lady so, for the very fright of not being
able to bring forth a child will kill her.   *Exeunt.*

SCENE 10

Enter a Gentleman *who meets a fair* Young Lady.

Gentleman. Madam, my lord desires you to command whatsoever you
please and it shall be obeyed.
Lady. I dare not command, but I humbly entreat, I may live quiet and
free from his amours.
Gentleman. He says he cannot live and not love you.   5
Lady. But he may live and not lie with me.
Gentleman. He cannot be happy unless he enjoy you.
Lady. And I must be unhappy if he should.
Gentleman. He commanded me to tell you that he will part from his
lady for your sake.   10
Lady. Heaven forbid I should part man and wife.
Gentleman. Lady, he will be divorced for your sake.
Lady. Heaven forbid I should be the cause of a divorce between a noble
pair.
Gentleman. You had best consent, for otherwise he will have you   15
against your will.
Lady. I will send his lordship an answer tomorrow. Pray him to give
me so much time.
Gentleman. I shall, lady.   *Exit* Gentleman.

Lady *alone.*

Lady. I must prevent my own ruin and the sweet virtuous lady's by   20
going into a nunnery, wherefore I'll put myself into one tonight.
There will I live and serve the gods on high
And leave this wicked world and vanity.   *Exit.*

One *enters and speaks the epilogue.*

[*Epilogue*]. Marriage is a curse we find,
Especially to womenkind: 25

19SD *alone*] *This ed.; Sola* F.   23SD *Exit*] *This ed.; Exeunt* F.

From the cobbler's wife we see
To ladies, they unhappy be.

Lady Happy. [*To the Princess*] Pray, servant, how do you like this play?

Princess. My sweet mistress, I cannot in conscience approve of it, for
    though some few be unhappy in marriage, yet there are many more   30
    that are so happy as they would not change their condition.

Lady Happy. Oh, servant, I fear you will become an apostate.

Princess. Not to you, sweet mistress.   *Exeunt.*

               Enter the Gentlemen.

1 Gentleman. There is no hopes of dissolving this convent of pleasure.

2 Gentleman. Faith, not as I can perceive.   35

3 Gentleman. We may be sure this convent will never be dissolved by
    reason it is ennobled with the company of great princesses and glo-
    rified with a great fame, but the fear is that all the rich heirs will
    make convents and all the young beauties associate themselves in
    such convents.   40

1 Gentleman. You speak reason; wherefore, let us endeavour to get
    wives before they are incloistered.   *Exeunt.*

28SD] *Rowsell; to the Prin. F.*

32. *apostate*] one who forsakes his or her religious faith. Lady Happy is playing on
the established conceit of her community as a quasi-religious order.

33SD *Gentlemen*] presumably the gentlemen who appeared in 1.1. Although this
short coda featuring the gentlemen might be regarded as a fresh scene, we have opted
to retain F's original inclusion of it as part of 3.10 since this offers an important insight
into the way in which Cavendish appears to imagine – and expects her readers to
imagine – different orders of dramatic action. The Act 3 playlet, as an overt and formally presented play-within-a-play, with its rapid succession of short scenes in widely
varying locations, is allotted explicit scene divisions. Elsewhere, however, Cavendish
appears to have a more fluid sense of the possibilities for scene-shifting offered by a
drama staged in the imaginations of author and readers. See below 4.1.159SD and
4.1.194SD.

ACT 4

Enter LADY HAPPY *dressed as a shepherdess, walking in*
a melancholy way and speaking to herself.

Lady Happy. My name is Happy and so was my condition before I saw
this princess. But now I am like to be the most unhappy maid alive.
But why may not I love a woman with the same affection I could
a man?
No, no, nature is nature and still will be   5
The same she was from all eternity.

Enter the PRINCESS *in masculine shepherd's clothes.*

Princess. My dearest mistress, do you shun my company? Is your
servant become an offence to your sight?
Lady Happy. No, servant! Your presence is more acceptable to me than
the presence of our goddess, nature, for which she (I fear) will   10
punish me for loving you more than I ought to love you.
Princess. Can lovers love too much?
Lady Happy. Yes, if they love not well.
Princess. Can any love be more virtuous, innocent, and harmless than
ours?   15
Lady Happy. I hope not.
Princess. Then let us please ourselves as harmless lovers use to do.
Lady Happy. How can harmless lovers please themselves?
Princess. Why, very well: as to discourse, embrace, and kiss – so mingle
souls together.   20
Lady Happy. But innocent lovers do not use to kiss.
Princess. Not any act more frequent amongst us womenkind. Nay, it
were a sin in friendship should we not kiss. Then let us not prove
ourselves reprobates.
They embrace and kiss and hold each other in their arms.
Princess. These my embraces, though of female kind,   25
May be as fervent as a masculine mind.

A pastoral scene is revealed and the PRINCESS *and* LADY HAPPY

0SD] *This ed.; Enter Lady* Happy *drest as a Shepherdess; She walks very Melancholy,*
then speaks as to her self. F.

26SD] For Cavendish's use of the phrase '*The Scene is open'd*' in the original SD,
see above, 3.1.24SD. '*Enter others dressed as shepherds and shepherdesses*' is added to

*go in. The scene then changes to a green or plain where sheep
are feeding with a maypole in the middle. The* PRINCESS *and*
LADY HAPPY *are seated, dressed as a shepherd and shepherdess.
Enter others dressed as shepherds and shepherdesses.*

1 Shepherd. [*To Lady Happy*] Fair shepherdess, do not my suit deny,
Oh grant my suit, let me not for love die.
Pity my flocks, oh save their shepherd's life;
Grant you my suit, be you their shepherd's wife.   30
Lady Happy. How can I grant to everyone's request?
Each shepherd's suit lets me not be at rest;
For which I wish the winds might blow them far,
That no love-suit might enter to my ear.

Enter MADAM MEDIATOR *dressed as a shepherdess with
another* Shepherd.

2 Shepherd. [*To Madam Mediator*] Good dame, unto your daughter
speak for me.   35
Persuade her I your son-in-law may be.
I'll serve your swine, your cows bring home to milk,
Attend your sheep, whose wool's as soft as silk.
I'll plough your grounds, corn I'll in winter sow,
Then reap your harvest and your grass I'll mow,   40
Gather your fruits in autumn from the tree:
All this and more I'll do if you speak for me.
Madam Mediator. My daughter vows a single life
And swears she ne'er will be a wife
But live a maid, and flocks will keep,   45
And her chief company shall be sheep.
Princess. [*To Lady Happy*] My shepherdess, your wit flies high,
Up to the sky,

26SD] *This ed.; The Scene is open'd, the* Princess *and* L. Happy *go in. A Pastoral
within the Scene. The Scene is changed into a Green, or Plain, where Sheep are feeding,
and a May-Pole in the middle.* L. Happy *as a Shepherdess, and the* Princess, *as a
Shepherd are sitting there. Enter another Shepherd, and Wooes the Lady* Happy. F;
The . . . Lady Happy go in. A Pastoral with the Scene. The . . . Happy. Rowsell; *The
Scene is open'd and . . .* HAPPY. Shaver.   27SP/SD.] *This ed.; Shepherd.* F.   34SD]
This ed.; Enter Madam Mediator in a Shepherdess dress, and another Shepherd. F.
35SP/SD] *This ed.; Sheph.* F.   43SP] *This ed.; Shepherdess.* F.   47SP/SD.] *This ed.; F
has only Prin. as SP but precedes the line with the SD, The* Princess *as a Shepherd,
speaks to the Lady* Happy.

---

the original SD in this edition to provide for the dancing and '*rural sports*' which take
place at 136SD. See Introduction, p. 42.
    47–127.] an instance of Cavendish's tendency to embed reflections on natural phi-
losophy within works of other genres, as, for example, in *Poems and Fancies* and her
story 'The She Anchoret' (see Introduction, pp. 35, 37). See also above, 1.2.41 and
below, 211–16.

And views the gates of heaven
Which are the planets seven;   50
Sees how fixed stars are placed
And how the meteors waste;
What makes the snow so white,
And how the sun makes light;
What makes the biting cold   55
On everything take hold;
And hail a mixed degree
'Twixt snow and ice you see.
From whence the winds do blow,
What thunder is you know,   60
And what makes lightning flow
Like liquid streams you show.
From sky you come to th' Earth
And view each creature's birth;
Sink to the centre deep   65
Where all dead bodies sleep,
And there observe to know
What makes the minerals grow;
How vegetables sprout,
And how the plants come out.   70
Take notice of all seed
And what the earth doth breed;
Then view the springs below
And mark how waters flow;

49–50. *And . . . seven*] See e.g. 'Of the Motion of the Planets', in Cavendish, *Philosophical and Physical Opinions*, p. 24; 'Of the Planets', in Cavendish, *Philosophical and Physical Opinions*, second edition (London, 1663), p. 241. There were seven planets in the Ptolemaic universe: the Moon, Mercury, Venus, the Sun, Mars, Jupiter, and Saturn.

51. *fixed stars*] The stars were considered to be 'fixed' because their number was seen as finite, because their relative positions were thought not to vary, and because they were imagined as lying on the surface of a sphere – hence fixed in their distance from the Earth; see J.C. Eade, *The Forgotten Sky: A Guide to Astrology in English Literature* (Oxford: Clarendon Press, 1984), pp. 21–2.

55–8. *What . . . see*] See e.g. 'Of Congealation and Freezing', in Cavendish, *Observations Upon Experimental Philosophy*, pp. 104–22.

60–2. *What . . . show*] See e.g. 'Of Thunder', in Cavendish, *The Worlds Olio* (London, 1655), p. 66; 'Of thunder and lightning', in Cavendish, *Philosophical and Physical Opinions* (1655), pp. 92–3.

65–72. *Sink . . . breed*] See e.g. 'What Atomes make Vegetables, Minerals, and Animals', in Cavendish, *Poems and Fancies*, pp. 12–13; 'The Sun peirceth not deep into the Earth', in Cavendish, *Worlds Olio*, p. 171; 'Of the Seeds of Vegetables', in Cavendish, *Observations Upon Experimental Philosophy*, pp. 40–6.

What makes the tides to rise   75
Up proudly to the skies,
And shrinking back descend
As fearing to offend.
Also your wit doth view
The vapour and the dew;   80
In summer's heat, that wet
Doth seem like the earth's sweat;
In winter time, that dew
Like paint's white to the view:
Cold makes that thick, white, dry,   85
As cerusse it doth lie
On th' earth's black face, so fair
As painted ladies are;
But when a heat is felt,
That frosty paint doth melt.   90
Thus heaven and earth you view,
And see what's old, what's new;
How bodies transmigrate,
Lives are predestinate.
Thus doth your wit reveal   95
What nature would conceal.
Lady Happy. My shepherd,
All those that live do know it,
That you are born a poet.
Your wit doth search mankind   100

79–80. *Also . . . dew*] See e.g. 'Of Vapour', in Cavendish, *Poems and Fancies*, p. 24;
'*Of several sorts of Vapour*', in Cavendish, *Worlds Olio*, p. 165. See also below, 213–16.
81–90. *In . . . melt*] See e.g. 'A Dialogue *between* Earth, *and* Cold', in Cavendish,
Poems and Fancies, p. 63; '*The Difference of Heat and Cold in the Spring and Autumn*',
in Cavendish, *Worlds Olio*, p. 184. The metaphor of 'the earth's sweat' is used in '*Of
the* Sun *and the* Earth', in Cavendish, *Poems and Fancies*, p. 157.
86. *cerusse*] white lead, used largely as paint, especially as a cosmetic for the skin.
87–8. *earth's . . . are*] play on words involving the dual senses of 'black' as dark-
complexioned or ugly, and 'fair' as light-complexioned or beautiful.
93. *transmigrate*] Cavendish's essay '*Of Transmigrations*', in *Philosophical and
Physical Opinions* (1655), p. 47, states that 'all bodies are in the way of transmigrations' and gives the transformation of food into blood as an example.
94. *predestinate*] See e.g. '*The Predestination of Nature*' in Cavendish, *Worlds Olio*,
p. 176, which claims that 'there is a Predestination in Nature, that whatever she gives
Life to, she gives Death to; she hath also predestinated such Effects from such Causes'.
Cavendish, a life-long practising Anglican (see Katie Whitaker, *Mad Madge: Margaret
Cavendish, Duchess of Newcastle, Royalist, Writer and Romantic* (London: Chatto and
Windus, 2003), pp. 35, 160, 322), is not endorsing the influential post-Reformation
notion of human beings' predestination either to be damned or saved according to
Calvinist theology.

In body and in mind;
The appetites you measure
And weigh each several pleasure;
Do figure every passion
And every humour's fashion;   105
See how the fancy's wrought,
And what makes every thought;
Fathom conceptions low
From whence opinions flow;
Observe the memory's length   110
And understanding's strength.
Your wit doth reason find,
The centre of the mind
Wherein the rational soul
Doth govern and control.   115
There doth she sit in state,
Predestinate by fate,
And by the gods' decree
That sovereign she should be.
And thus your wit can tell   120
How souls in bodies dwell;
As that the mind dwells in the brain,
And in the mind the soul doth reign,
And in the soul the life doth last,
For with the body it doth not waste;   125
Nor shall wit like the body die,
But live in the world's memory.

Princess. May I live in your favour and be possessed with your love
  and person is the height of my ambitions.
Lady Happy. I can neither deny you my love nor person.   130
Princess. In amorous pastoral verse we did not woo

---

120. your wit] *This ed.*; your Wit F; you it *Rowsell.*

---

104. *Do ... passion*] See e.g. '*Of different passions*' in Cavendish, *Philosophical
and Physical Opinions* (1655), p. 107; '*Of Appetite and Passion*', in Cavendish, *Worlds
Olio*, pp. 144–5. Venet, 'Margaret Cavendish's Drama: An Aesthetic of Fragmentation',
in Line Cottegnies and Nancy Weitz (eds), *Authorial Conquests: Essays on Genre in
the Writings of Margaret Cavendish* (London: Associated University Presses, 2003), pp.
224, 228 n. 25, characterises this speech as an ' "Anatomy" ... based on a treatise of
the passions' recalling Robert Burton's famous *Anatomy of Melancholy* (London,
1621).
108. *low*] deep, profound.
114. *rational soul*] see above, 1.2.41.
122–5. *As ... waste*] See e.g. '*Of the Rational Soul of Man*', in Cavendish, *Observations Upon Experimental Philosophy*, pp. 301–2; '*Soule, and Body*', in Cavendish,
Poems and Fancies, p. 135.

As other pastoral lovers use to do.
Lady Happy. Which doth express we shall more constant be,
  And in a married life better agree.
Princess. We shall agree, for we true love inherit,   135
  Join as one body and soul or heavenly spirit.
      Rural sports such as country dances about the maypole begin.
Lady Happy. [*To the Princess*] Let me tell you, servant, that our custom
  is to dance about this maypole, and that pair which dances best is
  crowned king and queen of all the shepherds and shepherdesses
  this year, which sport if it please you we will begin.   140
Princess. Nothing, sweetest mistress, that pleases you can displease me.

      They dance. After the dancing the PRINCESS *and* LADY HAPPY
          are crowned with a garland of flowers.

1 Shepherd. You've won the prize and justly; so we all
  Acknowledge it with joy, and offer here
  Our hatchments up, our sheep-hooks as your due,
  And scrips of cordwain, and oaten pipe.   145
  So all our pastoral ornaments we lay
  Here at your feet, with homage to obey
  All your commands, and all these things we bring
  In honour of our dancing queen and king.
  For dancing heretofore has got more riches   150
  Than we can find in all our shepherds' breeches;
  Witness rich Holmby: long then may you live!

136SD] *This ed.; Here come Rural Sports, as Country Dances about the Map-Pole:
that Pair which Dances best is Crowned King and Queen of the Shepherds that year;
which happens to the* Princess, *and the Lady* Happy. F, *except* Ch *which has MS correction of 'Map-Pole' to 'May-Pole', an amendment followed by Rowsell and Shaver.*
137SP/SD.] *This ed.; L. Happy to the Princ. F*; Lady Happy (to the Princess) *Rowsell.=*
141SD] *This ed.; They Dance; . . . Flowers: a Shepherd speaks. F.*   142SP] *This ed.;
not in F.*   145. cordwain] *This ed.; Corduant F.*

141SD] recalls the dancing and presentation of flowers at the sheep-shearing feast
in *WT* 4.4. As at 4.1.153SD and 5.2.0SD a printed slip which reads 'Written by my
Lord Duke' has been pasted in after the SD in the majority of copies of *F* collated, see
Introduction, pp. 36, 45.
    144. *hatchments*] coats of arms.
    145. *scrips of cordwain*] small bags – carried by shepherds, pilgrims, or beggars –
made out of Spanish leather, originally manufactured at Cordova.
    oaten pipe] musical instrument conventionally associated with shepherds in pastoral
poetry.
    152. *rich Holmby*] Sir Christopher Hatton (1540–91), appointed lord chancellor in
1587, and renowned for his skill as a dancer. He took part in a splendid masque at the
Inner Temple in 1561 and later attracted the attention of Elizabeth I when he appeared
in a masque at court. As a result of her favour towards him, he was able to build a

And for your dancing what we have we give.
　　　A cup of wassail and syllabubs are carried round.
2 *Shepherd.* [*Speaking or singing*] The jolly wassail now do bring
　　　With apples drowned in stronger ale,   155
　　　And fresher syllabubs, and sing;
　　　Then each to tell their lovesick tale,
　　　So home by couples and thus draw
　　　Ourselves by holy Hymen's law.   *Exeunt.*

　　The pastoral scene vanishes. Enter the PRINCESS *alone. She*
　　walks round once or twice, musing, and then looks at herself.

Princess. What! Have I on a petticoat? O Mars! Thou god of war,   160
pardon my sloth, but yet remember thou art a lover and so am I.
But you will say my kingdom wants me not only to rule and govern
it but to defend it. But what is a kingdom in comparison of a beautiful mistress? Base thoughts fly off! For I will not go did not only
a kingdom, but the world, want me.   *Exit.*   165

　　Enter LADY HAPPY *alone and melancholy. She muses briefly*
　　　　　　　then speaks.

153SD] *This ed.*; *A Wassel is carried about and Syllibubs. Another Shepherd speaks,*
or Sings this that follows. F; *A Wassel . . . Syllabubs.* Rowsell.   154 SP/SD] *This ed.*;
no SP/SD in F.   159SD] *This ed.*; *The Scene Vanishes. Enter the* Princess *Sola, and*
walks a turn or two in a Musing posture, then views her Self, and speaks. F.   165SD]
This ed.; *Exeunt.* F.   165SD] *This ed.*; *Enter the Lady* Happy *Sola, and Melancholy,*
and after a short Musing speaks.

---

fine house on his family's lands at Holmby (now Holdenby). Julie Crawford, 'Convents
and Pleasures: Margaret Cavendish and the Drama of Property', *RO*, 32 (2003),
177–223 (187), indicates that the house at Holmby was the site of a 1634 masque also
'held "in honour of our dancing Queen and King" '.
　　153SD *wassail*] liquor in which healths were drunk, especially spiced ale used in
Twelfth Night or Christmas Eve celebrations. Crawford, 'Convents and Pleasures',
213 n. 46, shows how 'wassail and syllabubs' symbolise 'Cavendish high life and
resistance'.
　　syllabub] dish made of milk or cream, curdled by adding wine, cider, or another acid,
and often sweetened and flavoured.
　　159. *Hymen*] Greek and Roman god of marriage who appears in Jonson's court
masque, *Hymenaei* (1606). The combination of masque and pastoral here, along with
the ritualised marital pairing-off under Hymen's aegis, recalls the closing stages of *AYLI*
in which Hymen descends to the play's pastoral setting to preside over the formal disposition of couples; see *AYLI* 5.4.106–44. See also below, 5.3.7.
　　159SD] Here, and at 4.1.194SD, the omission of formal, numbered scene-breaks
reflects the degree to which Cavendish envisages her stage in Act 4 as having the meta-
morphic properties available in court masques and retains the somewhat dream-like
tendency to elide the characters and their multiple roles in this section of the play.
　　160–5. *What. . . . me*] Venet, 'Margaret Cavendish's Drama', p. 224, notes the link

Lady Happy. O nature, o you gods above,
Suffer me not to fall in love!
Oh, strike me dead here in this place
Rather than fall into disgrace.

Enter MADAM MEDIATOR.

Madam Mediator. What, Lady Happy, solitary, alone, and musing like   170
a disconsolate lover!
Lady Happy. No, I was meditating of holy things.
Madam Mediator. Holy things! What holy things?
Lady Happy. Why, such holy things as the gods are.
Madam Mediator. By my truth, whether your contemplation be of gods   175
or of men, you are become lean and pale since I was in the convent
last!

Enter the PRINCESS.

Princess. Come, my sweet mistress, shall we go to our sports and
recreations?
Madam Mediator. Beshrew me, your highness hath sported too much   180
I fear.
Princess. Why, Madam Mediator, say you so?
Madam Mediator. Because the Lady Happy looks not well – she is
become pale and lean.
Princess. Madam Mediator, your eyes are become dim with time, for   185
my sweet mistress appears with greater splendour than the god of
light.
Madam Mediator. For all you are a great princess, give me leave to tell
you:
I am not so old, nor yet so blind,   190
But that I see you are too kind.
Princess. Well, Madam Mediator, when we return from our recreations
I will ask your pardon for saying your eyes are dim, conditionally
you will ask pardon for saying my mistress looks not well.
                                                                                Exeunt.

194. pardon] F; my pardon *Shaver.*   194SD] *This ed.; The* Scene *is opened, and there
is presented a Rock as in the Sea, whereupon sits the Princess and the Lady* Happy;
the Princess *as' the Sea-God* Neptune, *the Lady* Happy *as a Sea-Goddess: the rest of
the Ladies sit somewhat lower, drest like Water-Nymphs; the* Princess *begins to speak
a Speech in Verse, and after her the Lady* Happy *makes her Speech. F; The ... as the
Sea-God ... Speech. Rowsell; The ... Sea; ... as the Sea-God ... Speech. Shaver.*

with Sir Philip Sidney's pastoral prose romance, *Arcadia*, in which Prince Pyrocles
'finally discloses his true identity after long concealment in female dress'.
   180. *Beshrew me*] the devil take me.
   sported] taken your pleasure.
   193. *conditionally*] on condition that.

The scene changes to reveal the PRINCESS *and* LADY HAPPY
sitting on a rock as if in the sea. The PRINCESS *is dressed as*
Neptune and LADY HAPPY *as a sea-goddess. The rest of the*
Ladies *sit a little lower down dressed as water-nymphs.*

Princess. I am the king of all the seas,   195
All watery creatures do me please,
Obey my power and command,
And bring me presents from the land.
The waters open their floodgates,
Where ships do pass, sent by the Fates;   200
Which Fates do yearly, as May-dew,
Send me a tribute from Peru.
From other nations besides,
Brought by their servants, winds, and tides,
Ships fraught and men to me they bring;   205
My watery kingdom lays them in.
Thus from the earth a tribute I
Receive, which shows my power thereby.
Besides, my kindgom's richer far
Than all the earth and every star.   210
Lady Happy. I feed the sun which gives them light
And makes them shine in darkest night.
Moist vapour from my breast I give
Which he sucks forth and makes him live,
Or else his fire would soon go out,   215
Grow dark, or burn the world throughout.
Princess. What earthly creature's like to me,
That hath such power and majesty?
My palaces are rocks of stone,
And built by nature's hand alone;   220
No base, dissembling, cozening art

194SD *The scene . . . nymphs*] redolent of marine settings and characters deployed
in a number of Stuart court masques. See e.g. Jonson's court entertainments *The Masque*
of Blackness (1605); *Neptune's Triumph for the Return of Albion* (1624); *Love's*
Triumph Through Callipolis (1631); Samuel Daniel, *Tethys' Festival* (1610). Tanya
Wood, 'The Fall and Rise of Absolutism: Margaret Cavendish's Manipulation of
Masque Conventions in "The Claspe: *Fantasmes* Masque" and *The Blazing World*', *In-*
Between: Essays and Studies: Literary Criticism, 9 (2000): 287–99 (294–5), discusses
Cavendish's depiction of masque-like scenes in a marine setting in *Blazing-World*.
    200. *Fates*] three classical goddesses representing the powers of destiny.
    203. *nations*] pronounced as having three syllables.
    205. *fraught*] laden.
    211–14. *I feed . . . live*] See e.g. 'A Complaint *of* Water, Earth, *and* Aire, *against the*
Sun', in *Poems and Fancies*, p. 61. See also above, ll. 79–80.
    221. *cozening*] See above, 3.6.9.

Do I employ in any part.
In all my kingdom large and wide,
Nature directs and doth provide
Me all provisions which I need,   225
And cooks my meat on which I feed.
Lady Happy. My cabinets are oyster-shells,
In which I keep my orient pearls.
To open them I use the tide,
As keys to locks which opens wide   230
The oyster-shells; then out I take
Those orient pearls and crowns do make,
And modest coral I do wear
Which blushes when it touches air.
On silver waves I sit and sing,   235
And then the fish lie listening:
Then sitting on a rocky stone,
I comb my hair with fish's bone;
The whilst Apollo with his beams
Doth dry my hair from watery streams.   240
His light doth glaze the water's face,
Make the large sea my looking-glass;
So when I swim on waters high,
I see myself as I glide by.
But when the sun begins to burn,   245
I back into my waters turn,
And dive unto the bottom low:
Then on my head the waters flow
In curlèd waves and circles round;
And thus with waters am I crowned.   250
Princess. Besides, within the waters deep,
In hollow rocks my court I keep.
Of ambergris my bed is made,
Whereon my softer limbs are laid.
There take I rest, and whilst I sleep,   255
The sea doth guard and safe me keep
From danger; and when I awake
A present of a ship doth make.

224–58] *F; not in Rowsell.*

228. *orient pearls*] pearls from the Indian seas, hence brilliant or precious pearls.
239. *Apollo*] Greek and Roman god of the sun, patron of music and poetry.
253. *ambergris*] wax-like substance of a marbled, ashy colour, found floating in tropical seas; fragrant and used in perfumery.

No prince on earth hath more resort,
Nor keeps more servants in his court.   260
Of mermaids you are waited on,
And mermen do attend upon
My person; some are counsellors
Which order all my great affairs;
Within my watery kingdom wide,   265
They help to rule and so to guide
The commonwealth, and are by me
Preferred unto an high degree.
Some judges are and magistrates,
Decide each cause and end debates;   270
Others, commanders in the war,
And some to governments prefer;
Others are Neptune's priests which pray
And preach when is a holy day:
And thus with method order I   275
And govern all with majesty.
I am sole monarch of the sea
And all therein belongs to me.
Sea-Nymphs. *[Singing] We watery nymphs rejoice and sing*
          About God Neptune our sea's king;   280
          In sea-green habits for to move
          His godhead for to fall in love.

          That with his trident he doth stay
          Rough foaming billows which obey:
          And when in triumph he doth stride   285
          His managed dolphin for to ride,

---

261. mermaids you are] *This ed.*; Mare-maids you're *F.*   279SP/SD.] *This ed.*; *no SP
in F but the song is preceded by the stage direction 'A Sea-Nymph Sings this following
SONG.' Stanzas are numbered in F.*

259–78. *No . . . me*] reflects Cavendish's recurrent concern to explore the structures
of a well-ordered (usually monarchical) state. See, e.g, *Blazing World*, pp. 101, 121–2;
'*An Oration to prevent Civil Warr*' and '*An Oration concerning Disorders, Rebellion,
and Change of Governments*', in *Orations*, pp. 11–12, 283–7; 'The Animall Parliament', in *Poems and Fancies*, pp. 199–211; *Worlds Olio*, pp. 47–57, 205–12, 217–19.
See also Margaret Cavendish, *Political Writings*, ed. Susan James (Cambridge University Press, 2003), pp. ix, xxiv–xxviii. William Cavendish also considers such questions
in his short book of 'advice' sent to King Charles II in 1660 (see Bodleian Library,
Oxford, MS Clarendon 109).
   269. *magistrates*] officers with executive power within the state.
   283. *trident*] three-pronged fish spear, conventionally an attribute of Neptune.
   286. *managed*] trained. William Cavendish was a dedicated proponent of the formal
training or 'manage' of horses, a subject about which he published a lavish treatise in

All his sea-people to his wish,
From whale to herring subject fish,
With acclamations do attend him,
And pray more riches still to send him.   *Exeunt.*   290

The scene vanishes.

---

290. *pray*] *This ed.; pray's* F.

French in 1658 which reappeared in English as *A New Method and Extraordinary Invention to Dress Horses* (London, 1667).

ACT 5

Enter the PRINCESS *and* LADY HAPPY. *The* PRINCESS *is dressed in a man's dancing outfit. They whisper for a while, then* LADY HAPPY *takes a ribbon from her arm and gives it to the* PRINCESS *who gives her another in return and kisses her hand. They exit briefly and then soon enter again with all the company to dance. Music plays and, after they have danced for a short time, enter* MADAM MEDIATOR *wringing her hands and spreading her arms.*

Madam Mediator. [*Crying out passionately*] Oh, ladies, ladies, you're all betrayed, undone, undone! For there is a man disguised in the convent. Search and you'll find it.

They all skip from each other as if afraid. Only the PRINCESS *and* LADY HAPPY *stand still together.*

Princess. You may make the search, Madam Mediator; but you will quit me, I am sure.   5

Madam Mediator. By my faith, but I will not, for you are most to be suspected!

Princess. But you say the man is disguised like a woman – and I am accoutred like a man.

Madam Mediator. Fiddle faddle! That is nothing to the purpose.   10

Enter an Ambassador *to the* PRINCE. *He kneels and the* PRINCE *bids him rise.*

0SD] *This ed.*; *Enter the* Princess *and the* Lady Happy; *The* Princess *is in a Man's Apparel as going to Dance; they Whisper sometime; then the* Lady Happy *takes a Ribbon from her arm, and gives it to the* Princess, *who gives her another instead of that, and kisses her hand. They go in and come presently out again with all the Company to Dance, the Musick plays; And after they have Danced a little while, in comes Madam* Mediator *wringing her hands, and spreading her arms; and full of Passion cries out.* F; *Enter . . . Music . . . out.* Rowsell.   1SP/SD] *This ed.; no SP in* F *which conveys how the line should be said in the stage direction which precedes it.*   2. undone! For] *This ed.*; undone; for F.   3SD] *This ed.*; *They all skip from each other, as afraid of each other; only the* Princess *and the* Lady Happy *stand still together.* F.   7. suspected!] *This ed.*; suspected. F.   8. woman –] *This ed.*; Woman, F.   10. Fiddle faddle!] *This ed.*; Fidle, fadle, F.; Fiddle, Faddle, Rowsell.   10SD Ambassador . . . PRINCE. *He kneels and the* PRINCE] *This ed.*; Embassador . . . Prince; *the Embassador kneels, the* Prince F.

Prince. What came you here for?

Ambassador. May it please your highness, the lords of your council
sent me to inform your highness that your subjects are so discon-
tented at your absence that, if your highness do not return into
your kingdom soon, they'll enter this kingdom by reason they hear   15
you are here and some report as if your highness were restrained
as prisoner.

Prince. So I am, but not by the state, but by this fair lady who must be
your sovereigness.

> *The* Ambassador *kneels and kisses* LADY HAPPY'S *hand.*

Prince. But since I am discovered, go from me to the councillors of this   20
state and inform them of my being here, as also the reason, and
that I ask their leave I may marry this lady. Otherwise, tell them I
will have her by force of arms.   *Exit* Ambassador.

Madam Mediator. O the Lord! I hope you will not bring an army to
take away all the women will you?   25

Prince. No, Madam Mediator, we will leave you behind us.   *Exeunt.*

SCENE 2

> *Enter* MADAM MEDIATOR, *to* ADVISER *and* COURTLY,
> *lamenting and crying with a handkerchief in her hand.*

Madam Mediator. Oh, gentlemen, that I never had been born! We're
all undone and lost!

Adviser. Why, what's the matter?

Madam Mediator. Matter? Nay, I doubt there's too much matter.

Adviser. How?   5

Madam Mediator. How? Never such a mistake! Why, we have taken a
man for a woman.

Adviser. Why, a man is for a woman.

Madam Mediator. Fiddle faddle! I know that as well as you can tell
me, but there was a young man dressed in woman's apparel and   10

---

16. here] *This ed.*; here; *F.*

0.SD] *This ed.*; *Enter Madam* Mediator *lamenting . . . hand. F.*   1SP] *This ed.*; *not in*
F.

11SP. PRINCE] This is the first time Cavendish refers to him as 'the Prince' despite
having explicitly disclosed his true sex in the previous scene; see 4.1.160. All
Cavendish's original speech headings are abbreviated 'Princ.' or 'Prin.' so she is able to
use this form to denote both 'Princess' and 'Prince'. However, for clarity's sake, I have
chosen to adopt the speech-heading 'Prince' as opposed to 'Princess' from this point.

entered our convent and the gods know what he hath done. He is
mighty handsome and that's a great temptation to virtue, but I
hope all is well. But this wicked world will lay aspersion upon anything or nothing and therefore I doubt all my sweet young birds
are undone, the gods comfort them.   15
Courtly. But could you never discover it nor have no hint he was a man?
Madam Mediator. No, truly, only once I saw him kiss the Lady Happy
and you know women's kisses are unnatural, and methought they
kissed with more alacrity than women use, a kind of titillation and
more vigorous.   20
Adviser. Why did you not then examine it?
Madam Mediator. Why, they would have said I was but an old jealous
fool and laughed at me, but experience is a great matter. If the gods
had not been merciful to me he might have fallen upon me.
Courtly. Why, what if he had?   25
Madam Mediator. Nay, if he had I care not, for I defy the flesh as much
as I renounce the devil and the pomp of this wicked world. But, if
I could but have saved my young sweet virgins, I would willingly
have sacrificed my body for them; for we are not born for ourselves but for others.   30
Adviser. 'Tis piously said – truly, lovingly, and kindly.
Madam Mediator. Nay, I have read *The Practice of Piety*, but further,
they say he is a foreign prince and they say they're very hot.
Courtly. Why, you are Madam Mediator, you must mediate and make
a friendship.   35
Madam Mediator. 'Ods body! What do you talk of mediation: I doubt
they are too good friends. Well, this will be news for court,
town, and country, in private letters, in the *Gazette*, and in
abominable ballads before it be long, and jeered to death by the

---

23. great] *F*; greater *Rowsell*.

---

14. *birds*] perhaps another echo of *The Bird in a Cage*.

26–7. *I defy . . . world*] echoes the terms of the request made by the priest to the
godfathers and godmothers in the service of baptism from the *Book of Common Prayer*
(1662): 'Dost thou . . . renounce the devil and all his works, the vain pomp and glory
of the world . . . and the carnal desires of the flesh . . . ?'

32. The Practice of Piety] *The Practise of Piety: Directing a Christian how to walke
that he may please God*, written by Lewis Bayly, Bishop of Bangor (d. 1631), ran to
numerous editions, but there is bibliographical confusion as to the date of the first; see
Pollard and Redgrave, who record the 1612 'second' edition as the earliest extant
example.

33. *hot*] ardent, passionate.

36. *'Ods body!*] exclamation, i.e. God's body!

38. *Gazette*] *The London Gazette*, a journal issued twice a week under the authority of the Secretary of State.

39. *ballads*] popular songs often scurrilously attacking individuals or institutions.

pretending wits. But, good gentlemen, keep this as a secret and let   40
not me be the author, for you will hear abundantly of it before it
be long.

Adviser. But, Madam Mediator, this is no secret: it is known all the
town over and the state is preparing to entertain the prince.

Madam Mediator. Lord! To see how ill news will fly so soon abroad.   45

Courtly. Ill news indeed for us wooers.

Adviser. We only wooed in imagination but not in reality.

Madam Mediator. But you all had hopes.

Adviser. We had so, but she only has the fruition: for, it is said, the
prince and she are agreed to marry, and the state is so willing as   50
they account it an honour and hope shall reap much advantage by
the match.

Madam Mediator. Yes, yes, but there is an old and true saying, 'there's
much between the cup and the lip'.   *Exeunt.*

SCENE 3

> *Enter the* PRINCE *and* LADY HAPPY *as bridegroom and bride,*
> *hand in hand, under a canopy carried over their heads by* Men.
> *The* Magistrates *march in front followed by oboes and then the*
> Bridal Guests, *as if coming from the church where the couple*
> *has been married. The whole company bids them joy and they*
> *thank them.*

Madam Mediator. Although your highness will not stay to feast with
your guests, pray dance before you go.

Prince. We will both dance and feast before we go. Come, madam, let
us dance to please Madam Mediator.
                             The PRINCE *and* LADY HAPPY *dance.*

Prince. Now, noble friends, dance you, and the princess and I will rest   5
ourselves.
                 After the dancing has finished, LADY HAPPY
                                 speaks to LADY VIRTUE.

53–4. 'there's . . . lip'.] *This ed.; in italics with no quotation marks* F.

oSD] *This ed.; Enter the* Prince *as Bridegroom, and the* Lady Happy *as Bride, hand in hand under a Canopy born over their heads by* Men; *the* Magistrates *march before, then the* Hoboys; *and then the* Bridal-Guests, *as coming from the Church, where they were Married. All the Company bids them joy, they thank them.* F; *Enter . . . Bridal Guests . . . them. Shaver.* 4SD LADY HAPPY] *This ed.;* Princess F. 6SD] *This ed.; After they have Danced, the* Lady Happy, *as now* Princess, *speaks to the* Lady Vertue. F.

53–4. 'there's . . . lip'] proverbial (Dent T191)

Lady Happy. Lady Virtue, I perceive you keep Mimic still. [*To the Prince*] Sir, this is the mimic I told you of. [*To Mimic*] Mimic, will you leave your lady and go with me?

Mimic. I am a married man and have married my lady's maid, Nan,   10
and she will keep me at home do what I can, but you've now a mimic of your own, for the prince has imitated a woman.

Lady Happy. What, you rogue, do you call me a fool?

Mimic. Not I, please your highness, unless all women be fools.

Prince. Is your wife a fool?   15

Mimic. Man and wife, 'tis said, makes but one fool.

                    He kneels to the PRINCE.

Mimic. I have an humble petition to your highness.

Prince. Rise, what petition is that?

Mimic. That your highness would be pleased to divide the convent in two equal parts, one for fools and th' other for married men as   20
mad men.

Prince. I'll divide it for virgins and widows.

Mimic. That will prove a convent of pleasure indeed, but they will never agree, especially if there be some disguised prince amongst them. But you had better bestow it on old decrepit and bedrid matrons   25
and then it may be called the convent of charity if it cannot possibly be named the convent of chastity.

Prince. Well, to show my charity, and to keep your wife's chastity, I'll bestow my bounty in a present, on the condition you speak the epilogue. Come, noble friends, let us feast before we part.   30

                    Exeunt all but MIMIC.

Mimic. An epilogue, says he, the devil an epilogue have I: let me study. I have it, I have it. No, faith, I have it not. I lie, I have it. I say, I

7SP] *This ed.; L. Happy speaks to L. Vertue* F.   7–8SD] *This ed.; L. Happy to the Princ.* F; Lady Happy (to the Prince). *Rowsell.*   8SD] *This ed.; L. Happy to Mimick.* F; Lady Happy (to Mimick). *Rowsell.*   10. lady's maid, Nan,] *This ed.; Ladies Maid Nan* F.   30SD] *This ed.; Exeunt. Mimick Solus.* F.   31.] *This ed.; F includes the SD, 'He questions and answers Himself.'*   32. I have it, I have it. No,] *This ed.;* I have it, I have it; No F.   32. I lie, I have it.] *This ed.;* I lie, I have it, F; I like I have it, *Rowsell.*

---

7. Mimic] (1) a jester; (2) one with an aptitude for mimicry or imitation. As a licensed fool employed by a noble mistress and given to wordplay, often as a means of attempting to ensnare the characters of more elevated rank, Mimic is in the tradition of Feste in *TwN* and Touchstone in *AYLI*. His marriage to Nan echoes the pairing of Touchstone with the country wench, Audrey, in *AYLI* 3.3, 5.4.

31–9.] preceded in F by the redundant SD 'He questions and answers Himself', which serves to underline the speech's status as an apparent parody of dramatic soliloquies.

32–5. I have it . . . never had it.] Cf. Macbeth's soliloquy which begins, 'Is this a dagger, which I see before me . . . ?', *Mac.* 2.1.33–41 (esp. 35, 'I have thee not, and yet I see thee still').

have it not. Fie Mimic, will you lie? Yes, Mimic, I will lie, if it be
my pleasure. But, I say, it is gone. What is gone? The epilogue.
When had you it? I never had it. Then you did not lose it. That is   35
all one, but I must speak it although I never had it. How can you
speak it and never had it? Ay, marry, that's the question, but words
are nothing and then an epilogue is nothing and so I may speak
nothing; then nothing be my speech.

He speaks the epilogue

Noble spectators, by this candlelight,   40
I know not what to say, but bid goodnight:
I dare not beg applause, our poetess then
Will be enraged and kill me with her pen;
For she is careless and is void of fear:
If you dislike her play she doth not care.   45
But I shall weep, my inward grief shall show
Through floods of tears that through my eyes will flow.
And so, poor Mimic, he for sorrow die.
And then through pity you may chance to cry:
But, if you please, you may a cordial give,   50
Made up with praise, and so he long may live.   *Exit.*

---

47. that through my eyes] *This ed.; that your my Eyes* F, *with MS correction of 'your'
to 'through' (except* H2 *and PFL); that my Eyes Rowsell.*   51SD] *This ed.; no final
SD in* F *which concludes with the word* 'FINIS'.

---

37. *that's the question*] Cf. the opening of Hamlet's 'To be, or not to be' soliloquy,
Ham. 3.1.58.
37–9. *but . . . speech*] Cf. *Ham.* 4.5.7; *Lear* 1.1.81–2.

APPENDIX A: PRESS VARIANTS

Key: = = long s. ~ = same as previous state.

Copies collated

1. Melbourne, State Library of Victoria, *SF 822.35, bound with 1647 Folio
2. Oxford, Bodleian Library, Bod. H.1.9 Art Selden
3. Oxford, Bodleian Library, Bod. Mal. 25
4. Cambridge, University Library, SSS.21.16 (2)
5. Cambridge, University Library, Brett Smith 50
6. Washington DC, Folger Shakespeare Library, B1616
7. Washington DC, Library of Congress, PR2420 Fabyan Collection, bound with 1647 Folio
8. Washington DC, Library of Congress, PR2420 Copy 2, bound with 1647 Folio
9. Princeton, New Jersey, Firestone Library, Robert H. Taylor collection, bound with 1647 Folio
10. Harry Ransome Centre, University of Austin, Texas, PFORZ 52
11. Harry Ransome Centre, University of Austin, Texas, STARK +6450
12. Tomlinson-Haynes private collection
13. Christchurch, New Zealand, University of Canterbury Library, Bib. 504401, Conway Rose, bound with 1647 Folio
14. Christchurch, New Zealand, University of Canterbury Library, Bib. 504401, Copy 2, Booth Estate, bound with 1647 Folio
15. Wellington, New Zealand, Alexander Turnbull Library, qREng BEAU Come 1647 (Acc. 292726), copy-text
16. London, British Library, C.102.k.7 (STC 1616), viewed on microfilm

Notes

3. The title page to *The Wild-Goose Chase* is inscribed 'Edward Proger / his Booke / Catherine Proger'. This was probably the Royalist Edward Proger (Prodger, 1621–1713) who, as a reward for his loyalty to King Charles II during his exile, was made Keeper of the Middle Park and was commanded by Charles to build a lodge in North Park at Hampton Court, the building which became known as Bushy House (http://www.npl.co.uk/about/bushyhousehistory; viewed 22 March 2004).

4. On p. 1 of the text of *The Wild-Goose Chase*, the name 'Rich: Matthew' is written above the first line of dialogue. The name appears on other plays in the volume.
8. The title page of the 1647 Folio is inscribed 'Florence Baber Her Booke'. Florence Baber may have been related to Sir John Baber, physician to Charles II (*DNB*).
9. The title page of the 1647 Folio is inscribed 'D. Winde'. The name appears in a different character on p. 55 of *The Wild-Goose Chase*, where above the running-title is written, 'Dorothy Winde hers'.

Press variants

a2v	State 1	State 2
28	*Peale*	*Pearl*

State 1: 4
State 2: All other copies

a1r	State 1	State 2
10	bare;	bare,

State 1: 9
State 2: All other copies

a1v	State 1	State 2
Title of Jephson's poem	*WILD-CHASE*	*WILD-GOOSE* ['*GOOSE*' = cancel slip]

State 1: 1, 4, 6, 11, 12, 14, 16
State 2: All other copies

4	*grave?)*	*grave?*
6	prayse?	prayse?)
15	down	down,
16	wont	won't
16	goe	go
18	giv'n	giv'n,

State 1: 1, 3, 5, 16
State 2: All other copies

a2v	State 1	State 2
5	Noe	No
5	intranc't	intranc'd
signature	a	a 2

State 1: 1, 3, 5, 16
State 2: All other copies

B1r	State 1	State 2
3	hard;	hard,

State 1: All other copies
State 2: 12.

C1r	State 1	State 2
6	brawnfall'n:	brawnfall'n.

State 1: 12
State 2: All other copies

F1v	State 1	State 2
34SD	in right margin	in right margin
	opp. l.33	opp. l.34

State 1: 5
State 2: All other copies

F2r	State 1	State 2
36	again,	again;
37	rack,	rack;
39	escaped	=cap'd
43	Now	Now?

State 1: 5
State 2: All other copies

I1r	State 1	State 2	State 3
2	Fortune	Fortune;	~
5	courts him,	courts him;	~
6	too:	too,	~
9	thosand	~	thousand
11	Lil.	~	Lel.
11	Forture	~	Fortune
13	Pinac,	Pinac;	~
18	Lil.	~	Lel.
20	perfection	~	perfection.
21	for tis	for 'tis	~
43	wonder.	wonder!	~
51	Lil.	~	Lel.

State 1: 1, 6, 16
State 2: 2, 3, 5, 12, 14
State 3: 4, 7, 8, 9, 10, 11, 13, 15

I1v	State 1	State 2	State 3	State 4
9	=tale	~	~	Stale
27	quit	~	~	quiet
42SD	Ex	Ex.	Exit.	~

State 1: 16
State 2: 1, 3, 6
State 3: 5, 14
State 4: 2, 4, 7, 8, 9, 10, 11, 12, 13, 15

I2r	State 1	State 2
10	triffles.	triffles?

State 1: 1, 3, 5, 6, 14, 16,
State 2: All other copies

I2v	State 1	State 2
12SD	*Lever- / duce*	*Lever- / duce,*
32	affection.	affection :
34	in,	in;
39	follow,	follow :

State 1: 1, 6, 16
State 2: All other copies

K2r	State 1	State 2
22	remedy	remedy;

State 1: 3, 8, 13, 14
State 2: All other copies

K2v	State 1	State 2
17.1	*Priest, R. Baxt. Attendants.*	*Priest, Attendants.*

State 1: 4
State 2: All other copies

L1r	State 1	State 2
4	service,	service.
5	Srike	Strike
14	shew	shews
18	Hatern	Patern
36	women	woman

State 1: 1, 3, 4, 5, 6, 12, 14
State 2: All other copies

L2v	State 1	State 2
6	manner :	manners :
7	Curtsy	Curt'sy
31	counsel	counseld
39	the	thee
41	vez'd	vex'd
46	turned 'n' in 'and'	and
49	thou not deserve	thou deserve

State 1: 1, 3, 4, 5, 6, 12, 14
State 2: All other copies

M1r	State 1	State 2
41	Gentlewoman	Gentlewomen

State 1: 2, 3, 6
State 2: All other copies

N1v	State 1	State 2
	mispaginated 49	paginated 46

State 1: 4, 12
State 2: All other copies

Notes

K2v

17.1. This variant supplies further evidence of prompt-book origin for the copy-text of *F1*. Richard Baxter played minor parts in plays presented by the King's Men in the late 1620s and 1630s. His name appears in a stage direction to Fletcher's *The Mad Lover* and in marginal annotations to Philip Massinger's *Believe as You List* (Nungezer, p. 32).

N2r

The catchword is 'For', but the first line of dialogue on sig. N2v is 'What'.

THE BIRD IN A CAGE

Copies collated

1. London, British Library, C.12.f.15
2. London, British Library, 644.c.42
3. London, British Library, Ashley 1700
4. Cambridge, University Library, Syn.7.63.379
5. Cambridge, King's College, C.6.3 (STC 22436)
6. Boston, Public Library, G.3976.43
7. Harvard University, Houghton Library, 14433.30.25* (STC 22436)
8. Washington DC, Folger Shakespeare Library, B cs231 (STC 22436).
9. Washington DC, Library of Congress, PR 3144.B51633
10. Oxford, Bodleian Library, Bod. 4° S 34 (10) Art
11. Oxford, Bodleian Library, Bod. Mal. 163 (3)
12. Oxford, Bodleian Library, Bod. Mal. 253 (3)
13. Oxford, St. John's College, HB4/3a.5.23 (8) (STC 22436)
14. Oxford, Worcester College, Plays 3.38 (STC 22436)
15. Oxford, All Souls' College, PP.14.15
16. Pasadena, Huntington Library, HM 69453
17. Pasadena, Huntington Library, HM 69454

Notes

2. B2, B3, I3, K1, K2, missing [all inserted in 3]; C3, D2, F3, H1, I4, now in Texas but xerox provided; F2, H2, I1,I2, missing entirely.

12, 14, and 15. The errata sheet (K4r) has not been bound in but in 12 the errata have been inked in so seems to have been available to the seventeenth-century owner (seventeenth-century binding).
17. From the Bridgewater Library.

Press variants

B1r	State 1	State 2
2SD	*Enter . . . Orpiano, passing.*	*Enter . . . Orpiano.*
7	therc	there

State 1: 1, 3, 4, 6, 15, 16, 17
State 2: All other copies

B2v	State 1	State 2
31	more	not

State 1: 1, 4, 6, 15, 16
State 2: All other copies

B4v	State 1	State 2	State 3
2–6	I take it: I can see greatne=e big with an Impo=tume, yet towring in the Ayre like a Fawlcon: I can heare a man =weare I am thy Eternall Slave, and will =erve thee: whè if opportunity were offer'd, for price of a Plu=h Cloak, . . .	Five, the =mall birds dare not peepe for him, I take it: I can see greatne=e big with an Impo=tume, yet towring in the Ayre like a Fawlcon: I can heare a man =weare I am thy Eternall Slave, and will serve thee: whè if opportunity were offer'd, for price of a Plus=h Cloak,	Five, I take it: I can see greatne= e big with an Impo=tume, yet towring in the Ayre like a Fawlcon, the=mall Birds dare not peepe for him: I can heare a man sweare I am thy Eternall Slave, and will serve thee: when if opportunity were offer'd, for price of a Plu=h Cloake, . .

State 1: 1, 3, 4, 6, 15, 16, 17
State 2: 7, 8, 9, 10, 11, 12, 14
State 3: 2, 5, 13

12–13	ha lo=t my	~	ha not lo=t my

State 1 and 2: 1, 3, 4, 6, 7, 8, 9, 10, 11, 12, 14, 15, 16, 17
State 3: 2, 5, 13

16   Ile . . . anything /   Ile . . . =omewhat.   ~
        Duke. You'l . . .
        =omewhat.
State 1 and 2: 1, 3, 4, 6, 15, 16, 17
State 3: All other copies

34SH '*ul*' upside down in *Fulvio*.   *Fulvio*.   ~
State 1 and 2: 3, 4, 6, 15, 16, 17
State 3: 2, 5, 7, 8, 9, 10, 11, 12, 13, 14
[1 is missing owing to a torn corner]

C1r	State 1	State 2	State 3
18	wit	wit	wit,
30	prohibite	prohibite,	prohibite,
32	Circle	Circle	Ci cle
36	eate a dinner	eate a dinner	eate dinner

State 1: 1, 2, 3, 4, 5, 6, 7, 10, 11, 15
State 2: 16, 17
State 3: 8, 9, 12, 13, 14

C2r	State 1	State 2
18	guarded,	guarded
25	nough,	nough
34	*Mor.* .	period up near top of line

State 1: 2, 3, 4, 5, 6, 10, 15, 16
State 2: All other copies

C2v	State 1	State 2
2	Knights,	Knights

State 1: 1, 2, 3, 4, 5, 6, 7, 10, 11, 15, 16, 17
State 2: All other copies

C3r	State 1	State 2
12	pre=ume't,	pre=ume't

State 1: 1, 2, 3, 4, 5, 6, 7, 10, 11, 15, 16, 17
State 2: All other copies

C3v	State 1	State 2
24	Diuell,	Diuell
27	are	are,
31	invi=ible,	invi=ible
35	*Roll.*	o damaged or dropped
39	Infernall . . . Rules	1st line on C4v
39 catchword	Are	Infer –

State 1: 2, 3, 4, 5, 6, 10, 15, 16
State 2: All other copies

C4r	State 1	State 2	State 3	State 4
1	line 39 on C3v	Infernall . . .	~	~
5–6	you would be / Invi=ible, my fine Knave.	Rules you would be / Invi=ible, fine my Knave.	you my would / be Invi=ible, fine Knave.	~
16	expectation	~	~	expecta ion
33	Knave, =o	Knave, & =o	~	~
34–5	=ome . . . been con- / verted at all . . . it. / 1. I . . . Sir.	=õe . . . be cõverted / 1. I will . . . Sir.	~	~

State 1: 2, 3, 4, 5, 6, 10, 11, 15, 16
State 2: 17
State 3: 1, 7, 9, 12, 13, 14
State 4: 8

C4v	State 1	State 2
5	Knave,	Knave

State 1: 1, 2, 3, 4, 5, 6, 7, 10, 11, 15, 16, 17
State 2: 8, 9, 12, 13, 14

D1r	State 1	State 2
22	keepe	keepes
26	oppertunity	opportunity
30	Signiour.	Signiour?
31	hopes.	hopes?

State 1: 1, 2, 3, 4, 5, 6, 10, 12, 13, 15, 16
State 2: 7, 8, 9, 11, 14, 17

D2v	State 1	State 2
2	vs.	vs?
22SD	*Enter Bonamico.*	*Enter Bonamico, di=gui=ed.*
30SD	*Enter Servant.*	*Enter Servant to Bon: di=gui=ed.*
32	pray.	pray ?

State 1: 1, 2, 3, 4, 5, 6, 10, 12, 13, 15, 16
State 2: All other copies

D3r	State 1	State 2
13SD	*Enter Bonanico [sic] and Seruant.*	*Enter Bonamico and Seruant in other di=gui=es.*
15	him	him,
16	acquainted	acquainted,
19	this.	this ?
24	faith	faith,
32	preuented	preuented,

State 1: 1, 2, 3, 4, 5, 6, 10, 12, 13, 15, 16
State 2: All other copies

D4v	State 1	State 2
3	Di=ciple.	Di=ciples.
5	t'o -	to o-
8	invi=ible.	invi=ible ?
24	are	=hall be
28	omitted	*Exit.*

State 1: 1, 2, 3, 4, 5, 6, 10, 12, 12, 15, 16
State 2: All other copies

E1v	State 1	State 2
34	many	mony
35	a=pire my	a=pire to my

State 1: 1, 5, 6
State 2: All other copies

E2r	State 1	State 2
1	Theyr	There
6	relea=t	relea=t?
33	*Flori=h.*	Inner margin blank.

State 1: 1, 5, 6
State 2: All other copies

E3r	State 1	State 2
10	turned 'n' in 'valiant'	valiant

State 1: 5, 6
State 2: All other copies

E3v	State 1	State 2	State 3
7	Gentleman, do'=t heare him,	~	Gentleman? do'=t heare him?
25	(have it. appears at 23	(have it.	~
35	clothes.	~	clothes?

State 1: 5, 6
State 2: 1
State 3: 2, 3, 4, 7, 8, 9, 10, 11, 12, 13, 14, 15, 16, 17

E4r	State 1	State 2	State 3
6	*Thornes*	Thornes	~
9	sport,	sport;	~
34	Diamonds,	~	Diamonds

State 1: 5, 6
State 2: 1
State 3: 2, 3, 4, 7, 8, 9, 10, 11, 12, 13, 14, 15, 16, 17

G1r	State 1	State 2	State 3
7SH	omitted	*Bo.*	~
8	scurvily	*sc*urvily	~
8	becomes	~	ecomes

State 1: 1, 2, 3, 4, 5, 6, 7, 10, 11, 16
State 2: 9, 12, 13, 14, 15, 17
State 3: 8

G4v	State 1	State 2	State 3
19	play	p ly	ply

State 1: 1
State 2: 3, 4, 6, 10, 16
State 3: 2, 5, 7, 8, 9, 11, 12, 13, 14, 15, 17

THE CONVENT OF PLEASURE

Copies collated

1. Cambridge, Corpus Christi College, M.5.3
2. Cambridge, Christ's College, o.2.31
3. Cambridge, Gonville and Caius College, A.16.3
4. Cambridge, King's College, J.6.2.
5. Cambridge, St John's College, Dd.3.14
6. Cambridge, University Library, P*.3.15
7. Cambridge, University Library, Brett-Smith.a.10
8. Cambridge, University Library, Brett-Smith.a.11
9. Chicago, Newberry Library, Y 135. N 43
10. London, British Library, G.19053.(2)
11. London, British Library, C.102. k. 18
12. London, British Library, 79.1.15
13. Oxford, Bodleian Library, Bod. Vet. A3 c. 113
14. Oxford, Bodleian Library, Bod. Harding D 559
15. Pasadena, Huntington Library, Huntington 120140
16. Pasadena, Huntington Library, Huntington 120158
17. Princeton, New Jersey, Firestone Library, 3873.98.1668q
18. Washington, Folger Library, DC N867
19. Washington, Library of Congress, DC PR3605 N2 A68 1668

Press variants

B1r	State 1	State 2
19	happine=s	hapine=s

State 1: 3, 4, 6, 8, 11, 16, 17, 19
State 2: All other copies

K2v	State 1	State 2
17		Written by my Lord Duke
		[printed slip]

State 1: 13, 16, 17
State 2: All other copies

L1r	State 1	State 2
7		Written by my Lord Duke
		[printed slip]

State 1: 11, 13, 16, 17
State 2: All other copies

M1v	State 1	State 2
16	Holy day	Holy-day

State 1: 2, 3, 4, 5, 6, 8, 15, 16
State 2: All other copies

N1r	State 1	State 2
15		Written by my Lord Duke
		[printed slip]

State 1: 11, 13, 16, 17
State 2: All other copies

APPENDIX B: COMMENDATORY VERSES TO
THE WILD-GOOSE CHASE (1652)

On the best, last, and only remaining comedy of Master Fletcher.

I'm un-o'erclouded too; clear from the mist!
The blind and late heaven's eye's great oculist,
Obscurèd with the false fires of his scheme,
Not half those souls are lightened by this theme.
Unhappy murmurers that still repine 5
(After th' eclipse our sun doth brighter shine),
Recant your false grief and your true joys know,
Your bliss is endless, as you feared your woe!
What fort'nate flood is this, what storm of wit?
O who would live and not o'erwhelmed in it? 10
No more a fatal deluge shall be hurled,
This inundation hath saved the world.
Once more the mighty Fletcher doth arise,
Robed in a vest studded with stars and eyes
Of all his former glories; his last worth 15
Embroidered with what yet light e'er brought forth.
See, in this glad farewell he doth appear

---

0. Master] Dyce; Mr F1.   3. scheme] Dyce; Sceme F1.

0. last] Lovelace may mean that *The Wild-Goose Chase* was the last play of Fletcher's to be printed. It was not the last work written by Fletcher; Cyrus Hoy believes that *The Fair Maid of the Inn* was 'the last play on which Fletcher worked; that his share . . . was never brought to completion; that it was finished by the trio of Webster, Massinger and Ford' (Textual Introduction, Bowers, *DW*, 10.555).
'These verses (with several errors) are found also in *Lucasta, Posthume Poems of Richard Lovelace, esq.* 1659' (Dyce).
1. un-o'erclouded] the oppression of Puritan hostility to playhouses and theatrical concerns is figured as a mist, which the publication of this Folio helps dissipate.
2. heaven's . . . oculist] the sun.
3. scheme] astrological position.
5–6.] These lines conflate the political dissatisfaction of Royalist supporters at the death of Charles I with the dissatisfaction of would-be theatregoers, who will be cheered by the reappearance of Fletcher ('our sun') in print (see l. 24n, below).
12. This inundation] i.e. the very handsome Folio edition of *The Wild-Goose Chase* which these verses accompany, with biblical resonances of flood and revival. For metrical reasons 'inundation' is pronounced with five syllables.
14. vest] gown.

320

Stuck with the constellations of his sphere!
Fearing we, numbed, feared no flagration,
Hath curled all his fires in this one one,   20
Which, as they guard his hallowèd chaste urn,
The dull approaching heretics do burn.
    Fletcher at his adieu carouses thus
To the luxurious ingenious:
As Cleopatra did of old outvie   25
Th' unnumbered dishes of her Anthony,
When (he at th' empty board a wonderer),
Smiling, she calls for pearl and vinegar;
First pledges him in's breath, then at one draught
Swallows three kingdoms off to his best thought.   30
Hear, o ye valiant writers and subscribe!
His force set by, y' are conquered by this bribe;
Though you hold out yourselves, he doth commit
In this, a sacred treason on your wit;
Although in poems desperately stout,   35
Give up; this overture must buy you out.
    Thus with some prodigal usurer it doth fare
That keeps his gold still veiled, his steel-breast bare,
That doth exclude his coffers all but's eye,

---

19. we, numbed,] *Dyce*; we num'd *F1*.   20. one one] *Dyce*; one ONE *F1*.   25. As]
Dyce; A *F1*.   37. usurer it] *Dyce*; Us'rer 't *F1*.

19. *Fearing . . . flagration*] 'i.e. fearing that we, benumbed, feared, etc.' (Dyce).
    21. *chaste urn*] a classical conceit by which the corpus of Fletcher's work is hal-
lowed as ashes contained within a funerary urn.
    22. *heretics*] i.e. London city fathers, Puritans, and those hostile to the playhouses.
    24. *luxurious ingenious*] those who seek to satisfy their desire for theatrical enter-
tainment. The official closure of public theatres did not prevent actors giving what
Lawrence Wallis refers to as 'surreptitious performances'. He notes that 'on the three
occasions when the authorities halted the performance of a play specifically named in
the account of the occurrence, the piece is a Beaumont and Fletcher one' (Lawrence B.
Wallis, *Fletcher, Beaumont and Company: Entertainers to the Jacobean Gentry* (Morn-
ingside Heights, New York: King's Crown Press, 1947), pp. 10–11).
    25. *Cleopatra*] An allusion to the competition in extravagance between Cleopatra
and Mark Antony, when the Egyptian Queen, possessing the two finest pearls then
known, fashioned as earrings, dissolved one of them in vinegar and drank it off; Pliny,
Natural History, trans. H. Rackham (London: William Heinemann, 1940), Vol. 3, Book
IX, lviii, 119–21.
    30. *three kingdoms*] the territories of Egypt, Italy, and Africa ruled over by the tri-
umvirate of Antony, Octavius, and Lepidus between 42 and 36 BC.
    31. *subscribe*] a rallying call to other dramatists.
    37–42. Possibly an evocation of the miserly Volpone's attempt to seduce Celia in 3.2
of Jonson's *Volpone*.

And his eye's idol, the winged deity;   40
That cannot lock his mines with half the art
As some rich beauty doth his wretched heart:
Wild at his real poverty, and so wise
To win her, turns himself into a prize;
First startles her with th' emerald *Mad Lover*,   45
The ruby Arcas; lest she should recover
Her dazzled thought, a diamond he throws
Splendid in all the bright Aspatia's woes;
Then, to sum up the abstract of his store
He flings a rope of pearl of forty more.   50
Ah see, the staggering virtue faints! Which he
Beholding, darts his wealth's epitome,
And now, to consummate her wishèd fall
Shows this one carbuncle that darkens all.

                                    Richard Lovelace   55

On Master Fletcher's excellent play, *The Wild-Goose Chase*.

Methinks I see thy angered ashes rise,
Fletcher; I feel them smarting in my eyes.
Methinks thou sayst, 'What would this rhymer have?
He raises me, yet gives my fame a grave!'
Methinks (like that old moralist's complaint,   5
'What ill of mine has gained this ill man's praise?')
I hear thee say, 'Sure, this play has some taint,

0. Master] *Dyce*; Mr. *F1*.

45–8. Mad Lover ... Aspatia] Fletcher's dramas and their characters are figured as
jewels; *The Mad Lover* was performed in 1617; Arcas is the hero of Fletcher's *The
Loyal Subject* (performed in 1618); Aspatia is the heroine of Beaumont and Fletcher's
The Maid's Tragedy (performed 1610).
  50. *forty more*] forty other plays in the Beaumont and Fletcher canon.
  54. *carbuncle*] bright red precious stone, also applied to a mythical gem said to emit
light in the dark (*OED* 1). *The Wild-Goose Chase* is imaged as a jewel whose splendour bedims the other plays in the Beaumont and Fletcher canon.
  55. *Richard Lovelace*] (1618–57/8) a Royalist and poet, writer of *Lucasta; Epodes,
Odes, Sonnets, Songs etc*, composed while imprisoned for supporting Charles I.
Lovelace contributed a commendatory verse to the 1647 Beaumont and Fletcher First
Folio publication of *Comedies and Tragedies* (see Glover and Waller, Vol. 1, pp.
xxiv–xxv).

  5. *old moralist*] unknown. Lines 1–8 of this poem draw on a Latin proverb, 'Turpe
est laudari ab illaudatis' – It is discreditable to be praised by the undeserving (see W.
Gurney Benham, *Benham's Book of Quotations, Proverbs and Household Words*,
revised edn (London and Melbourne: Ward, Lock and Co., 1929), p. 673a.).

That this ill poet gives his withered bays!'
Perhaps this good philosopher's life began
To make the ill man good: as in a man   10
To love the good's a step to being so,
Love to thy muse may be to me so too.
Then I shall know how to commend thy muse
When her own self the praises shall infuse;
Till then I must sit down, confess the wonder,   15
'Bove which I cannot go, and won't go under.
But where's the praise, you'll say, to Fletcher's wit?
I would 'a' given, but had no offering fit.
Then let these lines be thought to Fletcher's muse
Not an encomium, but an excuse.   20

Norreys Jephson.

An Epigram
Upon the long lost and fortunately recovered *Wild-Goose Chase*, and
as seasonably bestowed on Master John Lowin and Master Joseph
Taylor, for their best advantage.

In this late dearth of wit, when Jose and Jack
Were hunger-bit for want of fowl and sack,
His nobleness found out this happy means
To mend their diet with these *Wild-Goose* scenes;
By which he hath revivèd in a day   5
Two poets and two actors with one play.

W.E.

0.2 *Master John*] Dyce; Mr. JOHN F1.   0.2 *Master Jospeh*] Dyce; Mr. JOSEPH F1.

8. *bays*] A wreath of bay leaves was traditionally awarded to poets of merit.
21. *Norreys Jephson*] unidentified.

1. *Jose and Jack*] Joseph Taylor and John Lowin (see Dramatis Personae, l. 9n and
l. 14n).
2. *sack*] a general name for a class of white wine formerly imported from Spain and
the Canaries (*OED* 1a).
3. *His nobleness*] John Fletcher.
6. *Two poets*] 'Although the actors' dedication makes it clear that the play is by
Fletcher alone, W.E. is misled by the ascription of it to Beaumont and Fletcher on the
title-page' (Lister).
7. W.E.] Bentley conjectures that this was William Eccleston, who prepared numerous cast-lists while a member of the King's Company (*JCS*, 2.430-1).

To the incomparable Master Fletcher, upon his excellent play, *The Wild-Goose Chase.*

Sole soul of dramas! Thou who only art
Whole in the whole, and whole in every part;
Thy fury every scene with spirit warms,
And that same spirit every line informs;
No commas lie entranced, and rise up sense   5
Three, four lines off, such is thy influence;
Thy words are all alive, and thou ne'er writ
Things to come to themselves, nor types of wit;
All lives, and is fulfilled: and for thy plot,
Whene'er we read, we have and have it not,   10
And glad to be deceived, finding thy drift
T' excel our guess at every turn and shift;
Some new meanders still do put us out,
Yet find that nearest what we thought about;
Through all intrigues we are securely led,   15
And all the way we pass, we've hold o' th' thread,
Which a long while we feel not, till thy close,
Winding the bottom up, the bottom shows.

                              H[enry] Harington

On Master Fletcher's *Wild-Goose Chase* recovered.

This sprightly posthume, whom our pious fear

0. Master] *Dyce*; Mr. *F1.*   16. we've] *Dyce*; w' ave *F1.*

0. Master] *Dyce*; Mr. *F1.*

---

3. *fury*] inspired rush of creativity.

8. *types of wit*] symbols prefiguring meanings which are revealed later; in theology, a biblical 'type' is an Old Testament person, thing or event foreshadowing a person, thing or event in the New Testament. In contrast to his plots, Fletcher's verbal wit is depicted as easily intelligible.

14. *find . . . about*] find that what eventuates is what we thought least likely to happen.

17. *close*] ending.

18. *bottom*] the core on which the weaver's skein of yarn was wound. 'Caxton, in his translation of Virgil's *Aeneid*, had Ariadne give Theseus a "botome of threde" to help him find his way through the labyrinth' (*MND*, ed. Peter Holland (Oxford University Press, 1995), 1.2.16n).

19. *H. Harington*] Henry Harington contributed a commendatory verse to the First Folio of Beaumont and Fletcher's *Comedies and Tragedies* (see Glover and Waller, 1.lii–liii). 'According to some M.S. notes, by Lawes the musician, in a copy of Beaumont's *Poems*, 1640, Harington was the author of two pieces in that collection, – the one entitled *A Charm*, the other *Love's Freedom*' (Dyce).

1. *posthume*] work appearing after the death of its originator.

Bewailed as if it an abortive were,
(And out of sense of that, no gen'rous breast
But a forsaken lover's grief expressed)
Hath forced his way through the pangs of fate,   5
And in his infancy's at man's estate.
Thus that famed flood that's plunged into a grave
For many leagues, at length exalts his wave,
Leaps from his sepulchre, and proudly slides
Through's banks in deeper, more expanded tides,   10
Till to his wat'ry centre he hath got
By wriggling twines, subtle as Fletcher's plot.
That 'tis a sacred birth from hence we know,
It doth by burial more glorious grow:
For saints by persecution thrive; and none   15
Is martyred, but's oppressed into a throne.
There reign he to time's end! While we from this
Do calculate his apotheosis.

                                        James Ramsey

---

2. *abortive*] imperfect result of an endeavour; for the loss of the manuscript of *The Wild-Goose Chase* and its omission from the Folio of 1647 see 'The Texts', pp. 42–3.

7. *famed flood*] 'the river Alpheus who, pursuing the nymph Arethusa, followed her under the sea from Arcadia to Sicily and there combined with her in one sacred fountain' (Lister).

16. *oppressed*] pun on 'press'.

19. *James Ramsey*] unidentified.

INDEX

In addition to listing important items from the Introduction, this index includes words, phrases, and topics which receive some discussion in the commentary; those which are simply glossed or paraphrased do not appear unless they are of unusual interest or particular relevance to the book's themes. Characters' names are included only if they are expanded upon in commentary other than that on cast-lists.

An asterisk before a word indicates that the note contains information about meaning, usage, or date which supplements that given in the OED.

References to *The Wild-Goose Chase*, *The Bird in a Cage*, and *The Convent of Pleasure* are distinguished by prefatory W/, B/, and C/ respectively, e.g. W/4.3.25. References to poems in Appendix B are given by page and line number and are distinguished by prefatory App/, e.g. App/321.19.

Acrisius, 29; B/1.1.275–6, 3.3.49
affable, W/2.1.25
Altomaro, B/2.1.338
Amadis de Gaul, 12–13;
    W/1.1.110–11, 4.3.56
Amazons, W/5.2.51
Amsterdam, B/4.1.166
anchorite, B/3.3.14, 5.1.156
Anna of Denmark, Queen, 1, 3, 13, 14
antic, W/3.1.449
apostate, C/3.10.32
Arabian woodcock, B/4.1.141–2
arras, B/4.2.28–9
aurum palpabile, B/1.1.245

baffelled, W/5.2.32
barley-break, B/5.1.412
Bay of Matrimony, W/5.2.18
Beaumont, Francis, 6, 8, 12, 15, 42
bed, W/4.3.51SD
Bedlam, B/2.1.433
Beeston, Christopher, 23
Behn, Aphra, 11, 19, 52 n53
    Rover, The, 53 n75

Bethlem Gabor, B/4.1.141–2
bilbo lord, W/3.1.416
bills, B/2.1.5
bird-pots, W/3.1.442
birds, B/4.1.104SD; C/5.2.14
Blackfriars theatre, 14, 22, 45
black santis, W/4.3.50
blatant beast, W/4.3.43
'Book of Sports', 4, 32
bottom, App/324.18
bouncing bum, W/5.4.32
boy actors, 2, 28, 29; B/
    Dedication o
Brackley, Elizabeth, Lady, *see*
    Cavendish Sisters
brave, B/3.4.17SD
Brutus B/3.3.4
burn my book, W/5.6.87
bush, C/3.6.0SD
buzzard, B/2.1.450

calves, one of her, B/2.1.441
Capitol, B/3.2.61–2
capon, B/1.1.189
capon-worshippers, W/1.2.30

carpe diem, B/4.2.258
Cartwright, William
    Lady Errant, The, 38
    Royal Slave, The, 8
    Siege, The, or Love's Convert, 8
castle of comfort, B/3.4.106
cavalier, B/2.1.48, 4.1.118
Cavendish, Charles, Sir, 33
Cavendish, Jane, Lady, see
    Cavendish Sisters
Cavendish, Margaret, Duchess of
    Newcastle, 26, 57–8 n121
    Bell in Campo, 8
    Bridals, The, 35
    'Contract, The,' 41
    Convent of Pleasure, The, 1, 2, 4,
        5, 7, 8, 9, 10, 11, 15, 22,
        26, 29, 32–42, 45, 48–9
    Description of a New World
        Called the Blazing-World,
        The, 39
    Female Academy, The, 6, 34
    Orations of Divers Sorts, 6, 36
    Poems and Fancies, 33
    Sociable Companions, The, 34
    World's Olio, 37
    Youth's Glory and Death's
        Banquet, 34
Cavendish Sisters, 3, 9, 10, 22
    Concealed Fancies, The, 9, 22
    Pastorall, A, 9, 22, 42
Cavendish, William, Duke of
    Newcastle, 3, 7, 9, 22, 33,
        34, 45, 57–8 n121;
        C/4.1.259–78, 286
    Country Captain, The, 22
cerusse, C/4.1.86
Chapman, George, 12
Charles I, King, 1, 4, 5, 9, 19, 31;
    W/Dedication 19–20;
    App/320.5–6
Charles II, King, 1, 33
charmed, B/3.2.23
chivalric romance, 12–13, 32;
    B/1.1.368–9, 3.2.53;
    W/1.1.110–11

choleric, C/3.6.19
chopping-knives, W/5.2.44,
    4.2.80SD
chronicle, B/5.1.76
circle, B/1.1.294
civil laws, C/2.4.14
Cleopatra, App/321.25
close as a cockle, W/1.3.123
closet drama, 2, 9; B/4.2.28–9
closure of public theatres, 1, 7, 8;
    W/Dedication 4, 27
cobbler, W/1.3.126, 129
Cockpit theatre, 23, 24, 25, 29, 43,
    46
colours, W/3.1.434, 4.1.146
compliment, B/1.1.26
confessor, C/2.1.58
conjured, B/1.1.292, 2.1.94
contract, W/2.1.82
convent theatricals, 38
Cooke, William, 22, 43
copy, W/2.2.141
court fool, B/1.1.30–1, 4.1.40,
    47SD, 5.1.30
cranes, B/2.1.447
credit, B/5.1.38
creditors, B/3.4.6
crinkles i' th' hams, B/2.1.49
cross-dressing, 20, 23, 24, 28–9;
    B/Dedication 0, 3.3.49;
    W/5.4.58
crows, B/3.4.7
crucify my arms, B/2.1.207
cuckoldry, B/2.1.445–6; W/1.3.49,
    146, 2.1.108, 5.4.30–1

damsel, W/4.3.136
Danae, 25, 26, 28, 29, 30, 31, 32,
    38; B/1.1.275–6,
    2.1.462–3, 4.2.2
dancing, 14; C/4.1.141SD, 152
Davenant, William, 6, 11
Democritus, B/2.1.440
Descartes, René, 33
Destinies, B/2.1.61, 3.4.39, 110
devotees, C/2.3.7

devotion, C/1.2.69–70
die, W/4.3.35–6
dog-days, B/1.1.212
dogs and monkeys, B/1.1.154
Donzel del Phebo and Rosicleer,
    B/3.2.53
dor, W/4.1.15
double-hatched, B/3.4.48
drolleries, W/1.2.21
dry pudding, W/4.2.83
duke of Venice, B/4.1.144–5
dulcis odor lucri e re qualibet,
    B/3.2.72–3
Dunkirks, B/4.1.168

earnest, B/1.1.355, 3.4.115,
    4.2.186, 5.1.30
earth's black face, C/4.1.87–8
earth's sweat, C/4.1.81–90
Egerton, Alice, Lady, 3
Etherege, George, 19, 46
    Sir Fopling Flutter, or The Man
        of Mode, 53 n75
execution, W/4.2.29
exile, 1, 10, 33, 41

Factor, W/5.2.71SD
fall, W/4.1.140
Fane, Rachel, Lady, 3
Fanshawe, Richard, 10
    Faithfull Shepherd, The, 10
Farquhar, George, 46–7
fast and loose, W/2.3.78, 3.1.70, 72
favour, W/1.2.79
feathers, B/4.1.118
female same-sex relations, 39;
    C/3.1.20–3
femme forte tradition, 4, 8
Field, Nathan, 12, 13
figary, B/3.2.48, 3.3.24
fixed stars, C/4.1.51
Fletcher, John
    Faithful Shepherdess, The, 5, 6,
        19
    Island Princess, The, 47
    Knight of Malta, The, 13

Philaster, or Love Lies a-Bleeding,
    7
Rule a Wife and Have a Wife, 6
Scornful Lady, The, 13
Sea Voyage, The, 38
Wild-Goose Chase, The, 1, 4, 6,
    8, 9, 11–21, 30, 32, 34,
    42, 42–3, 45–7
Woman Hater, The, 6, 12, 13
Woman's Prize, The, or The
    Tamer Tamed, 6, 15, 47
Women Pleased, 7, 25
football, B/4.1.53
Ford, John, 23
    Broken Heart, The, 24
    Love's Sacrifice, 24
    'Tis Pity She's a Whore, 24
'Fortune, my Foe' (song),
    W/3.1.445
free-born maids, W/4.1.78
French, W/4.1.131
French teeth, B/2.1.376
full state, W/5.3.26
Furies, W/4.2.73

game, B/4.2.270
Ganymede, B/4.2.146
Gazette, C/5.2.38
gentlemen, C/3.10.33SD
ghost-walking, B/3.2.92
glade, W/5.4.31
Gondomar, B/4.1.154
Goodwife Bias, W/1.3.194
Goody, C/3.2.4
grate, B/3.4.4, 117; C/2.1.53, 2.4.30
great duke, B/3.2.68
Guarini, Giovanni Battista
    pastor fido, Il, 10
gymnosophist, B/3.2.85

Habington, William, 21
hair-cloth, C/1.2.46
hangings, B/3.3.46, 4.2.41
Harington, Henry, App/324.19
Hastings, Henry, fifth Earl of
    Huntingdon, 12

Hatton, Sir Christopher, C/4.1.152
Hay, Lucy, Countess of Carlisle, 3
Henrietta Maria, Queen, 1, 2, 3, 4,
    5, 9, 10–11, 21, 23, 24,
    25, 27, 31, 33, 38, 39, 40,
    41, 48, 56 n109;
    B/Dedication 1, 4.2.62;
    W/Dramatis Personae 9
Herbert, Henry, Sir, 46
Hercules, B/3.1.7
Hobbes, Thomas, 33
hobby-horse, B/5.1.53
homoeroticism, B/4.2.136–8
honesty, W/5.2.49
horse-race, 21; B/2.1.511
household theatricals, 2, 9
Howell, James
    Nuptials of Peleus and Thetis,
        The, 10
humorist, B.3.2.59
humorous fluxes, W/1.1.62
humours, C/3.6.19
Hymen, C/4.1.159

ignorance, B/Dedication 19
Inns of Court, 21, 25; B/Dedication
    0, 1.1.223
interlude, B/Dedication 14, 3.3.40
Italian liberty, W/1.2.86
i' th' suds, W/2.3.40

James VI and I, King, 1, 4, 18, 19,
    45
Johnanapes, B/2.1.237
jointure, C/3.4.9
Jones, Inigo, 3, 20, 41
Jonson, Ben, 3, 5, 7, 9, 12, 28, 33,
    41
    Epicene, 28
    King's Entertainment at Welbeck,
        The, 9, 42
    Love's Welcome at Bolsover, 9
    Masque of Blackness, 3
    Masque of Queens, 10
    Volpone, 17
Jordan, Thomas, 11

Jumping Joan, W/4.1.142
Jupiter, 6, 25–7, 30, 31, 32, 38;
    B/1.1.275–6, 2.1.462–3,
    3.1.8, 4.2.24; C/2.4.3

kennel, B/2.1.47
Killigrew, Thomas, 19
    Thomaso, or The Wanderer, 53
        n75
King's Men, 5, 45

ladies-in-waiting, 23; B/1.1.111
lard, W/3.1.126
lattice-windows, C/3.2.16
lavoltas, W/5.2.9
leak-barks, W/2.1.98
lessoned, W/2.2.96
letters, B/5.1.127SD
Lovelace, Richard, 8; App/322.55
Lowin, John, 45; W/Dedication 4,
    36, Dramatis Personae 14;
    App/323.1
Lucretia, W/1.1.116
lulled, W/2.3.86
luxurious ingenious, App/321.24
luxury, C/1.2.63, 126

managed, C/4.1.286
Marmion, Shakerly, 5
marriage, 35–7
marriage negotiations, 20;
    B/1.1.139–40
masque, 2, 3, 5, 7, 10, 14, 15,
    22–3, 41; B/4.1.104SD;
    C/4.1.159SD, 194SD;
    W/2.2.89, 5.2.8
Massinger, Philip, 12, 13, 22
May games, 4; W/3.1.9, 3.1.277
melancholy, B/2.1.437
mettle, C/3.2.4; W/1.3.227
mewed, W/1.1.60–1
Milton, John
    Maske Presented at Ludlow
        Castle (Comus), 3
Mimic, C/5.3.7
Mirabell, W/1.1.129, 5.6.10

mistress, C/3.1.9
Molina, Tirsode, 13
money enough, B/1.1.224, 2.1.42–3
Montagu, Walter, Sir, 3
  Shepherds' Paradise, The, 3, 5,
    10, 20, 23, 24, 29, 39–40,
    56 n109; B/Dedication 0;
    C/1.2.113; W/Dramatis
    Personae 9
morris, B/5.1.52; W/3.1.81
Moseley, Humphrey, 8, 42
motion, W/Dedication 18
mountebank, B/1.1.328, 2.1.0SD,
    2.1.14–15
mushroom, B/2.1.484
music, B/3.3.20, 4.2.30, 5.1.397
musicians, W/2.1.60SD
musk-cat, B/2.1.440
musk-melons, W/1.3.109

natural philosophy, 35, 37;
    C/4.1.47–127
nature, C/1.2.43, 2.1.71–2
Neoplatonism, 39, 41;
    B/5.1.101–5
nest, B/3.2.51
Neville, Henry, 7
New Prison, B/Dedication 14, 1.1.1,
    174, 4.2.25
nightingale, B/4.2.199

oaten pipe, C/4.1.145
opera, 11
outfacing, W/3.1.9

pageantry, B/4.2.174
pair of gulls, B/4.1.196
Paracelsus, B/2.1.17
parts, B/3.3.37, W/1.3.29–30
passion, C/4.1.104
pastoral, 2, 3, 4, 5, 7, 9, 41;
    B/3.3.32–3
Pegasus, B/Dedication 21
pensioner, B/2.1.135
Pepys, Samuel, 46
petition, C/2.1.85

phantasmas, B/3.4.64
Philips, Katherine, 39
philosophers' stone, W/1.3.195
pickteeth, W/1.2.26
planets seven, C/4.1.49–50
play, B/4.2.169
play the chemist, B/2.1.464
play the cook, B/4.2.37
play titles, B/4.2.26, 5.1.221
plot, B/4.2.3
plush, B/5.1.26–7
portcullis, W/1.1.101
Porter, Endymion, 21
predestinate, C/4.1.94
Primum Mobile, W/Dedication 17
prince of Florence, B/4.2.285
prodigal son, C/2.4.60–1
proud, W/4.2.39
Prynne, William, 2, 26, 27, 29, 48,
    56 n109; B/Dedication
    (passim)
  Histriomastix 2, 3, 4, 23, 24, 25,
    27, 28, 43; B/Dedication 0,
    4–5, 15, 3.3.44–5
  Unloveliness of Love-locks, The,
    27; B/Dedication 9, 10,
    1.1.23
puissant pike, W/3.1.129
puppets, B/2.1.511
puritans, 1, 2, 23, 42; B/Dedication
    0, 18, 25–6, 4.1.166;
    App/320.1, 321.22

querelle des femmes, 6, 7, 36
Quicksilver, W/3.1.101
quit, C/1.2.27, 2.1.8, 3.1.3

Racan, Honorat de Bueil, Sieur
    de,
  Artenice, 3, 23, 29, 56 n109
rack, B/1.1.28
rail, B/4.1.165
rational creature, C/1.2.41
rational soul, C/4.1.114
rib, W/4.1.101–2
rich Holmby, C/4.1.152

right Italian, W/5.2.151
Roman Catholicism, 21–2, 37;
   B/Dedication 34
Rowley, William, 12
rural sports, 4–5, 31–2;
   C/4.1.26SD, 136SD

Saint-Germain, W/2.2.125
salary, B/1.1.288–90
salon culture, 4, 20
Saturn's (cold as), B/4.2.89–90
satyr, B/4.1.39
scene is opened, C/3.1.24SD,
   4.1.26SD
scrips of cordwain, C/4.1.145
servant, B/1.1.125; C/3.1.9, 16
service, W/1.3.162
services, C/2.4.70–1
Shakespeare, William, 6, 7, 12, 35
   All's Well That Ends Well, 13
   Antony and Cleopatra, 17
   As You Like It, 42
   Cymbeline, 7
   Love's Labour's Lost, 14, 34–5
   Much Ado About Nothing, 14
   Romeo and Juliet, 30
   Taming of the Shrew, The, 6, 14,
      15
   Winter's Tale, The, 42
   and John Fletcher,
      All Is True (Henry VIII), 12
      Don Quixote, 12
      Two Noble Kinsmen, The,
        12
she-cannibals, W/2.1.72
shift, C/2.2.54, 2.4.54–5, 69;
   W/1.2.36, 3.1.463
Shirley, James, 33
   Bewties, The, 23, 48
   Bird in a Cage, The, 1, 2, 4, 5, 6,
      7, 15, 21–32, 38, 42,
      43–5, 47–8
   Contention of Ajax and Ulysses
      for the Armour of Achilles,
      The, 22
   Coronation, The, 6

Cupid and Death, 10
Gamester, The, 19, 43
Hyde Park, 27
Lady of Pleasure, The, 19, 27,
   38
Love in a Maze, 56 n114
Triumph of Peace, The, 25
Sibyl, B/5.1.78
Sidney, Sir Philip,
   Lady of May, The, 42
siege of Bergen, B/4.1.160
silk-damask, C/2.2.14
small shot, W/3.1.129
special warrant, W/4.1.21
Speght, Rachel, 18
Spinola, B/4.1.155
spleen, C/3.6.19
sport, B/2.1.492, 4.1.18, 54
soliciting, B/1.1.62
state, W/2.1.2
stateswoman, W/4.1.122
*stir, W/1.1.1
stock, W/1.3.164–5
suburbs, W/2.3.103
surquedry, W/3.1.103, 4.2.59
Swetnam, Joseph, 18

tall, W/5.4.3
Taylor, Joseph, 5, 45; W/Dramatis
   Personae 9,
   App/323.1
Thebes, B/3.3.12
thunder, B/4.1.60–2
top and topgallant, W/3.1.350
Townshend, Aurelian, 3
traffic, B/2.1.112, 152
tragicomedy, 5, 6, 7
transmigrate, C/4.1.93
travel, 12; W/1.1.18–19
Triumph over Time and Women,
   The, W/3.1.107
trunk-hosed, W/5.4.58
turtle, B/4.2.199, 5.1.201–3

*underground, W/5.6.40
un-o'erclouded, App/320.1

vacation, B/1.1.223
vapour, C/4.1.79–80, 213–16
vapours, C/3.6.19
vengeance squibber, W/2.1.45
Venice, W/1.2.7, 5.4.3, 31
Vespasian, B/3.2.70
virgin zone, B/3.4.108

warlike age, W/1.1.101
wassail, C/4.1.153SD
weighty, W/1.2.69
Werburgh Street theatre, 22

White, Robert
    Cupid's Banishment, 50 n10
wild-goose chase, 21; W/title page
with a fading, B/4.1.65
women actors, Introduction, *passim*;
    B/Dedication 0, 3.3.44–5,
    4.2.17–18
women's education, 17–18, 32–3;
    W/1.3.25–6
worry, W/5.2.153

Yehochanan, B/3.2.66

Lightning Source UK Ltd.
Milton Keynes UK
UKOW02f0226031014

239500UK00002B/28/P